CORPORATE TURNAROUND

How Managers Turn Losers Into Winners!

CORPORATE TURNAROUND

How Managers Turn Losers Into Winners!

BY DONALD B. BIBEAULT

BeardBooks
Washington, DC

Library of Congress Cataloging-in-Publication Data

Bibeault, Donald B.
Corporate turnaround : how managers turn losers into winners! / Donald B. Bibeault.
p. cm.
Originally published: New York : McGraw-Hill, [1981] c1982.
Includes bibliographical references and index.
ISBN 1-893122-02-6
1. Corporate turnarounds—Management. 2. Organizational change. 3. Business failures. 4. Business planning. 5. Industrial planning. I. Title
HD58.8.B5 1998
658.4'063—dc21 98-54764
CIP

Printed in the United States of America

To my friend and colleague, Dr. Otto Butz, president of Golden Gate University, who leads an institution dedicated to fostering a rare combination of theory and practice in service to business.

CONTENTS

LIST OF TABLES

PREFACE

Everybody thinks about the upside potential of business, but what about troubled firms? Until now, nothing definitive has been written about the art of turning around losing operations. This arcane skill has been viewed as a sort of "black magic," practiced by a few highly talented (and richly rewarded) practitioners. These action-oriented survival specialists lack the time or inclination to write about their field. Conversely, academics have no feel for the real nuts-and-bolts, crisis-oriented leadership skills necessary to turn a troubled company around.

This book is for managers who now face or will face crisis situations in the companies they manage. This book is also for all those who are charged or will be charged with preventing decline in currently healthy enterprises. This means that business executives, academics, and advanced students can gain insights into the management practices that lead to the decline of business organizations, as well as practices that make it possible to sustain organizational vitality, or turn businesses around when they are headed for failure.

I pursue this subject because of my own keen interest, but also because of the fact that very little has been written about it. The lack of published material is due to three factors. One, it is a very difficult subject and very broad in scope. Two, people who are capable of managing turnarounds are usually very busy people. They are fast-paced, aggressive individuals who seldom have the time to speak about, let alone to write about, turnarounds. Third, many of them cultivate a lone gunslinger image: the image of a man in a white hat, coming into a tough Western town to clean it up. Robert Wilson, formerly chairman and president of Memorex, has called turning around Memorex a *Mission Impossible* assignment.

What I have attempted to do in this book is to take the mystery out of turnaround management. To do this, I followed a four-pronged approach. First, I drew upon my own experience of working on turnaround activities for a number of years. Second, I interviewed sixteen of the top turnaround artists in the country. Third, eighty-one corporate presidents answered an extensive questionnaire outlining the major reasons for decline and renewal. Fourth, an exhaustive search of the literature came up with about 400 references, periodicals, books, and scholarly works. Put together, this is an extensive amount of information that was blended into the framework that is the core of this book.

The book is divided into four parts. Part 1 examines why businesses decline. Part 2 offers a general discussion of turnaround management, including an analysis of the stages in a turnaround cycle, and the key factors in turnaround success and failure. Part 3 focuses on the decisive role of leadership in the turnaround, with special attention to the personality characteristics of turnaround leaders. It also elaborates on the crucial steps entailed in taking charge of a company. Part 4 expands in great detail on the management tasks and practices required to achieve the objectives of each stage in the turnaround cycle.

It is my hope that the information in this book has been blended into a form that is structurally sound, makes common sense, and is readable. A turnaround is a very difficult kind of task; often basic business tenets are reversed in the struggle to survive. It is my belief that business organizations are not programmed by nature (as is speculated about civilizations) to have their beginnings, flourish, decline, and disappear. Many do live out that predicted destiny. Perhaps in Lord Keynes's long run that will prove true of them all. In the short run, however, in the given here and now, such fatalism is belied by our instincts as well as a record. There's no denying that survival is beset by continuous external and internal challenges. Yet, every challenge is also an opportunity—provided it is reacted to by an appropriate response. And the instrument of that response is management, the life-giving, acting, dynamic force of the organization.

Donald B. Bibeault

ACKNOWLEDGMENTS

In undertaking this book, I incurred an indebtedness to many people. I owe gratitude to the eighty-one company presidents who responded to my questionnaire about their turnaround experiences. My thanks go to the seventeen business leaders, named below, with firsthand knowledge of turnaround management, who took long hours out of their busy schedule to share their experiences and insights with me. Three of these leaders should be singled out, however, because of the unique influence they have exerted on my effort. A critical role in helping me interpret my materials and keeping my exposition attuned to practical realities was played by Frank Grisanti, president, Grisanti and Galef in Los Angeles. I also received valuable perspectives and suggestions from Ransom Cook, retired chairman and president of Wells Fargo Bank. And last, but not least, of these three, I want to thank Dr. Otto Butz, president of Golden Gate University, who served as my principal adviser and worked with me in laying out the plan for the doctoral dissertation that formed the basis of this book.

The other business leaders that were especially helpful are: Jack A. Byers, vice president, Wells Fargo Bank; Robert C. Brown, president, R. C. Brown and Company; Jeffrey Chanin, former executive vice president, Daylin Corporation; Robert Di Giorgio, chairman, Di Giorgio Corporation; Gary Friedman, former vice chairman and co-founder, Itel Corporation; Ross Gwinner, former president, Capital Film Laboratories; Richard B. Madden, chairman, Potlach Corporation; Glenn F. Penisten, president, American Microsystems, Inc.; Robert Sackman, president, Rodal Corporation; Chauncey F. Schmidt, president, Bank of California; Thaddeus N. Taube, former chairman, Koracorp Industries; John S. Thompson, senior vice president, Crocker National Bank; Robert C. Wilson, former chairman and president, Memorex Corporation; and Roy Woodman, president, International Video Corporation.

Final notes of appreciation are due Mark C. Hungerford, president of PLM, Inc., for giving me the time and support to complete the book and Jane Parker, who spent hundreds of hours actually typing the manuscript.

INTRODUCTION

A turnaround is a very difficult kind of task. It's all got to be done fast. It means, without a wealth of experience, without incredible insights, without the kind of personality that permits you to make bold decisive moves quickly, without the ability to change your mind and reverse your feelings when you have made a mistake, you are not going to succeed. Timing is of key importance because, when a company is bleeding millions of dollars per month, you can't afford the luxury of fact-finding junkets. You have to be able to make decisions based upon your experience.[1]

Frank Grisanti, President,
Grisanti and Galef

At some time during their history, most companies are likely to face a turnaround situation. Whether they then recover their vitality, continue to stagnate, or disappear altogether depends on whether their management can effect the turnaround successfully. For a firm to sustain itself, there are certain preconditions. It must be economically viable. At least at its core, it must have a sound economic raison d'être. It must have the human, physical, and financial resources that can be deployed to meet a challenge or take advantage of an opportunity. And, most importantly, it must have a management that is sensitive to internal as well as external challenges. Whatever the company, sooner or later such challenges are encountered. Its management is not always equal to the test, and for this reason few companies survive intact for centuries, and I know of only one which has prospered over a millennium. Stora Kopparbergs Bergslags AB of Sweden traces its origins to the Middle Ages, to a lode of copper that legend says was discovered by a goat around the year 1000. Over the years, the firm branched out to include the manufacture of paper, power, and steel—and in time these came to dwarf the mine in importance.[2]

A turnaround situation is an abnormal period in any company's history. It requires management approaches unique and distinctly different from those of stable or growth management. In turnaround situations, many of the old and proven management tenets, applicable to more stable situations, lose their validity. Basic principles still hold, but their implementation can take on an entirely new, and sometimes contradictory, appearance. Growth considerations no longer exercise their magic appeal; even the bottom line takes a back seat to cash flow objectives. It's no longer a matter of doing things by the book. Sometimes even chief executive directives go unheeded, as when Chairman William Anderson of National Cash Register (NCR) ordered division heads to submit plans for reorganizing and reducing their staffs. No one complied. "Everyone knew we were fat, but claimed it must be another division," says Anderson. "Turning around NCR was like turning around a supertanker. They keep steaming ahead for twenty minutes after engines have been thrust in reverse."[3]

Businesses always have problems; they vary only in number and complexity. Some involve growth, others liquidation. In a turnaround situation, a firm suffers from excessive liquidation problems. A turnaround leader must solve these problems and provide a stable platform for renewed growth. In the process, he may uncover additional liquidation problems, previously undetected, festering beneath the surface. He must find a cure. Its potency determines the success or failure of his turnaround effort.

Debate continues within business circles as to whether performing a turnaround is a more difficult management task than managing a noncrisis company. Yet both sides agree that the turnaround man is a hero. He is the lone gunslinger with a white hat riding into the Western town to clean it up. The well-known turnaround artists help perpetuate their hero image. Robert C. Wilson compares the job of rebuilding Memorex Corporation, which was in serious financial trouble when he became president six years ago, to a "Mission Impossible" assignment.

A turnaround is a decidedly more difficult situation than that of a stable dead-center company. Trying to make substantial improvements in a troubled company cannot but be a more trying test for management than running a stable operation. It is also quite different. It is relatively simple to take over a smoothly operating company and fine-tune it for volume and profitability. It is another matter altogether to assume responsibility for a company that has been declining for so long that its customers, creditors, and employees are in an uproar. The problems of customer and creditor pressure, employee resistance, the risks of change, and people's impatience all become acute. These problems must be combated in the first effort. A second chance is a rarity. By contrast, managing a stable operation is relatively easy. As investment advisor Robert Brown says, "If a business is big enough and strong enough, it will run itself. All you need is a guy that will just oversee it and not make any major mistakes."[4]

Compared with a sustained high-growth situation, however, it is the turnaround that seems easier. Roy Woodman, president of International

Video Corporation, who has twenty years of turnaround experience, feels this way.

> The tough job is hanging on to high share of market and consistently improving your profitability in that market in the face of competition over the long term. But if you are down, hell, there is only one way to go and that is up. And every change you make looks good. When a company is down, you can be right 40 percent of the time—or 20 percent—it does not matter. The times you are wrong don't impact on you to the same degree because things are already bad and you probably haven't made them much worse. But the times you are right can make some substantial improvements. Improvement is the name of the game. The job gets tougher way down the road.[5]

Certainly, in the decision process, a turnaround allows a hard-nosed, objective executive only a limited number of available options. This situation can make a manager look good. When things are really bad, it's easy to show improvement—at least for a while. Other aspects of a turnaround are more difficult. As turnaround consultant Frank Grisanti points out, the turnaround involves a number of negative forces, a general lack of resources, and exceptional time pressures.

> You have to perform the surgery and reposture the platform with all kinds of negative forces working against you in an environment of shortages: shortages of money, shortages of products, shortage of cooperation, shortages of everything. That is an environment that most people really don't understand. They've never been there before. You can't expect them to understand. It is very rare to pull a guy out of a General Electric environment or an ITT environment, where he has the umbrella that comes with being in a large corporation with all kinds of resources. You take a guy out of that environment and throw him into something that is on the verge of bankruptcy and he wouldn't do a proper job.[6]

For all these reasons, successful turnaround performance requires technical management knowledge and human energy of a higher order. It calls for a penetrating viability analysis and a ruthless adherence to objectives. And it demands a great deal of self-confidence and a large dose of hard work. As in most other undertakings, there are no formulas, because a turnaround comes down to the human equation. Rather than Adam Smith's invisible hand, the key to successful turnarounds is the visible hand of management. It is the purpose of this book to enumerate, define, rank, and examine examples of those management practices that contribute to the decline of business corporations and those that can bring about their renewal.

REFERENCES

[1]Interview with Frank A. Grisanti, president, Grisanti and Galef, Los Angeles, Calif., February and April 1978.

[2]Eric Morgenthaler, "Swedish Firm Tries Not to Let History Impede Its Progress," *Wall Street Journal*, Oct. 10, 1978, p. 1.

[3]Linda Grant Martin, "When the Boss Declared Martial Law at NCR," *Fortune*, September 1976, p. 104.

[4]Interview with Robert C. Brown, president, R.C. Brown & Co., San Francisco, Calif., February 1978.

[5]Interview with Roy Woodman, president, International Video Corp., Sunnyvale, Calif., February 1978.

[6]Grisanti, interview, February and April 1978.

PART ONE
THE REASONS FOR CORPORATE DECLINE

When the group or civilization declines, it is through no mystic limitation of a corporate life, but through the failure of its political or intellectual leaders to meet the challenge of change.

Will and Ariel Durant, *The Lessons of History*

1
FAILURE AND DECLINE IN PERSPECTIVE

Business is like riding a bicycle. Either you keep moving or you fall down.

John David Wright

THE PERSPECTIVE

To many Americans, business failure is anathema, something that happens to someone else but hopefully never touches their own lives. Yet I recall very few instances where the phenomenal success of an entrepreneur or manager did not follow on the heels of earlier failure. It is almost axiomatic that the lessons learned in failure temper the personal character and abilities of us all. Few among us would advocate studying failure in order to succeed. Studying failure to avoid failure does make a lot of sense, however. Those of us entrusted with the management of sound, ongoing businesses have a particular responsibility to learn from the past mistakes of others.

The most dramatic examples of business failure often come to us in startling media headlines. One such example is the final demise of W. T. Grant and Company, the once vast retail chain, that shrank from 1100 stores to 359, and from 75,000 employees to 30,000. Without warning, W. T. Grant and Co. was forced to liquidate. The ensuing bankruptcy proceeding was the largest in the history of retailing—with the company's debt totaling more than $800 million.

Often collapse follows years and decades of outstanding success. A case in point is the sudden collapse of GEICO (Government Employees Insurance Company) in 1975. Just how could this unique company go so suddenly and spectacularly from the heights of success to the brink of insolvency? Of several words appropriate to describe GEICO's collapse—"shocking" and "incredible" are two—the most fitting is perhaps "sad," for GEICO was no ordinary company. GEICO grew in less than forty years from nothing to the country's fifth-largest auto insurer. Along the way it pulled off the rare feat of delivering a large payoff both to its stockholders and its customers. That era ended early in 1976 when GEICO, lurching to the brink amid a series of announcements about its financial condition, revealed that it had in 1975, on $603 million of earned premiums, lost a staggering $126 million.

Itel Corporation went from record expectations at the beginning of 1979 to a huge second-quarter loss of $60 million. Even more startling was its truly staggering $170 million third-quarter loss. As I write this book, the combination of these large losses casts a black cloud over Itel's former high-flying days.

The assumption that failure or sudden collapse is news to the public, but not to management, is not borne out by the facts. United Merchants knew it had problems but did not anticipate its sudden slide into bankruptcy. One Monday morning in July 1977, Bankers Trust informed United Merchants & Manufacturers (UMM) that it had seized the company's $5 million bank balance for itself and other creditors. With considerable understatement, UMM's chairman, Martin Schwab, said: "We expected to be able to work out a plan to pay our creditors."

The violations of basic business principles and the consistent pattern of mistakes give credence to hindsight in the case of business failure and decline. If I didn't believe there was a pattern to decline and to turnaround activities, I would never have undertaken this book. Spectacular business failures that suddenly hit the headlines were years in the brewing. The warning signs and symptoms of decline should have been apparent to a concerned, sensitive management.

DEFINITIONS OF FAILURE AND DECLINE

Business failure can be defined from at least four standpoints: social, economic, legal, and managerial.

Social Impact

Differences of opinion on the social impact of decline and failure cannot mask the human suffering that such a phenomenon usually brings. Most, but not all, concerned individuals view the unsuccessful business as a negative economic event, both to the principals of the unfortunate economic entity and to society in general. In addition to the obvious, and usually quantifiable, costs to employees, creditors, and owners of the debtor, there usually are serious second-order effects borne by the community at large. The larger the bankrupt's interface with others, the more profound the effect. Suppliers suffer reduced demand, customers are often inconvenienced, even if alternative goods or services are available, and the public in general often is forced to shoulder a portion of overall bankruptcy costs because of increased tax burdens.

Not everyone agrees that the longer-range social impact of corporate failure is negative. Many economists advocate the cleansing effect business failure has on competition and innovation. Turnaround consultant Frank Grisanti points out:

> Some companies never have a reason to exist in the first place. In a lot of markets there is room for two or three companies and no more. Usually the last guy in beyond that point barely makes a living in good times and is extremely vulnerable in bad times, and for good reason, because he shouldn't exist in the first place. Any good turnaround man will spot that situation right away and avoid it like the plague.[1]

The competitive environment is often favorably cited for its weeding out of inefficient and poorly managed entities in order to perpetuate a healthy, vibrant economy.

Whatever your philosophical bent, liquidation of a multimillion-dollar enterprise is still a poignant business drama, even played out where the public most often views it—at the level of the lawyers, the accountants, and the creditors' committees. A company's decline and fall takes on a different, more human perspective when it is perceived at floor-level, so to speak, where men and women are fighting for their livelihood as well as the survival of the organization.

Economic Failure

From an economic standpoint, failure represents a situation where the realized rate of return on invested capital is significantly and continually lower than prevailing rates on similar investments. It should be noted that a company can be an economic failure for years and yet, in the absence of legally enforceable debt, be able to meet its current obligations and thus not be a legal failure. Economic failure is rather subjective, and there are very few data available on industry or company incidence of economic failure. The decline of whole industry sectors is the best evaluation of economic failure, but, as I point out in Chapter 5, in any sick industry there are one or more cases of outstanding corporate success. The difference between the best performer, the average performer, and the worst performer in both sick and healthy industries is enormous.

Legal Failure

Legal failure statistics are compiled by Dun & Bradstreet, but they do not include discontinuances or data on strategic liquidations under voluntary circumstances. An entrepreneur may discontinue operations for a variety of reasons, such as loss of capital, inadequate profits, ill health, or retirement, but if his creditors are paid in full, the entrepreneur is not tallied as a failure by Dun & Bradstreet. Although failures comprise only a small percentage of total discontinuances, they represent the most severe impact upon the economy and pinpoint the most vulnerable industries and locations in a specific time period. Every year several hundred thousand firms are started, almost an equal number are discontinued, and even more transfer ownership or control. Dun & Bradstreet usually classifies about 4 percent of discontinuances as failures.

Managerial Failure

Decline is business failure from a managerial standpoint. A business can be a failure from a managerial standpoint before it is an economic failure and certainly long before it is declared a legal failure. As John Barriger, president of the Missouri-Kansas-Texas Railroad says, "Penn Central was a managerial bankruptcy before it was a financial one." Management usually receives pressure when profitability plateaus or declines, and several back-to-back years mean real trouble. If decline leads to large write-offs and to losses at the bottom line, there usually is intense pressure for a change in management. Losses of the magnitude that threaten the life of the enterprise inevitably lead to management change (see Chapter 14).

Decline, in this study, means several years of deteriorating profits. In four out of five cases decline includes one or more years of unprofitable operations, large nonoperating write-offs, or both. Since statistics on decline were not otherwise available, I compiled them independently as part of the research for this book. Care was used in screening out unusual external industry conditions or one-time write-offs that can occur in successful businesses.

FAILURE AND DECLINE STATISTICS

The most detailed statistics on failure are tabulated by Dun & Bradstreet (D & B). These statistics go back to 1920 and give us some insight into the economic dimensions of failure. Although, according to D & B, the failure rate per 10,000 has remained rather constant during the last few years, the average liability per failure has increased dramatically. Generally, larger firms seek Chapter 11 protection under the Federal Bankruptcy Act. The $4 billion of liabilities in failed firms each year is not an insignificant economic loss. There are no commensurate statistics on the losses incurred by discontinued firms.

Decline statistics are more difficult to obtain. All the failed firms suffered decline, but many firms were declining but had not yet failed.

Declining firms that have not yet failed and those that are subsequently saved by turnaround efforts seldom show up in the failure statistics. Those firms that file for Chapter 11 protection or reorganization and subsequently resume healthy operations are considered in turnaround management. Only about one-third of these firms continued in operation two years after their chapter proceedings closed.

In order to get around the paucity of data on decline and turnaround, I examined the corporate records of the 4,000 listed companies of the New York Stock Exchange (NYSE), the American Stock Exchange, and the NASDAQ/Over-the-Counter (NASDAQ/OTC) Exchange to identify companies that declined to the point of sustaining losses in net income or had severe earnings decline (80 percent or more). About 1,100 of these companies were found for the period 1967–1976. Of these, about 370 had turnarounds during the same period. The distribution of these statistics by exchange is shown in Table 9-1. The statistics are surprising in a number of ways, although they are subject to a number of qualitative interpretations. One unexpected result is the high incidence of losses among American Stock Exchange companies (47 percent) as compared with the incidence of losses among NYSE and NASDAQ/OTC companies. Surprisingly, the NASDAQ/OTC Exchange had the lowest loss rate (16 percent), while the New York Exchange had a moderate loss rate (22 percent). Less than one-third of the companies that sustained losses had accomplished a turnaround. Further observation indicates that about 25 percent sustained one-time losses, thus leaving about 45 percent of the cases either to accomplish a future turnaround or to finally wind up as stagnant, dead-center companies or legal failures.

Of the approximately 370 companies that had accomplished a turnaround, 320 were sent an extensive questionnaire (fifty questions) on their experiences during the decline and turnaround cycle. About 50 firms were eliminated from the 370 for various reasons, such as being investment trusts or real estate investment trusts, or being located outside of the United States. Eighty-one firms returned the questionnaire in a useful form. These data were analyzed by computer and are presented in tabular form throughout this book. Table 1-1 summarizes the corporate economic structure of the United States and how it relates to the concerns of this book. I might point out that the 4,000 listed companies have 70 percent of the corporate assets and 90 percent of the net profits of American industry.

TRAJECTORIES OF FAILURE

Another more qualitative perspective on decline and failure is provided by reviewing the various trajectories that companies follow on their way to failure. For purposes of perspective, I am going to quote liberally from the observations of John Argenti in his book *Corporate Collapse*.[2] Argenti utilized his own experience, available data, and his discussions with a number of experts on failure to construct a model of the three types of corporate failure. Type 1 companies are small companies that never rise above a poor level of performance. They usually have a very short life span. In 1976 more than half (55 percent) of all business failures occurred in firms of less than five years life span. In 1950 nearly 70 percent of all failed firms fell into this category. The number of Type 1 companies is even larger, because it includes discontinued as well as failed companies. They are, however, of minor economic consequence and of lesser managerial interest for purposes of this book.

TABLE 1-1
A Perspective on This Study Related to the U.S. Corporate Economy
(Numbers are approximate)

Number of persons in the labor force	100,000,000
Number of economic units (business, professionals, etc.)	13,000,000
Number of business establishments	4,100,000
Number of corporations filing with U.S. Treasury	2,000,000
Number of public companies	11,000
Number of listed companies	4,000
Percent median income of listed companies vs. U.S. Total	90
Number of listed companies with losses 1967–76	1,094
Number of listed companies with turnarounds 1967–76	369
Number of turnaround companies responding to questionnaire	81
Number of additional companies covered in in-depth interviews	16

Sources: (1) Approximate figures from Economic Indicators, U.S. Department of Commerce. (2) *New York Stock Exchange 1977 Fact Book*, p. 35.

Type 2 companies definitely get off the ground and usually do so in a spectacular manner, often shooting upward to fantastic heights before crashing down again, as did Investors Overseas Service, Ltd. (IOS), National Student Marketing, Equity Funding, Stirling Homes, and Itel Corporation. While the proprietor of a Type 1 company is not generally characterized by a remarkable personality, the proprietor of a Type 2 firm often is. Type 1 proprietors are usually engineers, technicians, marketing men, welders, and other mortals. Type 2 proprietors are supersalesmen, leaders of men, flamboyant, loquacious, restless, and bubbling with ideas. As Argenti says:

> The scale of their ambition is almost pathological. They never accept advice, they know all. In a frantic attempt to keep turnover and profits rising at the rate that the proprietor, his backers, his public, his employees have come to expect he now reaches into the absurd. Bernie Cornfeld's IOS controlled so many shares that within a matter of years he would rule the world. Billie Sol Estes had invented so much ammonia that the tanks required to hold it would have blotted out the American countryside—someone was bound to notice that the tanks weren't there! Beyond the clouds lie the stars. Beyond the stars lies the Great Absurd.[3]

As Argenti conjecturers, Type 2 failures are fairly rare, perhaps less than ten per year in the United States. They attract attention far beyond their social or economic significance because of the squeals of delight from the press on their way up—and again on the way down.

This book's main interest is the mature, professionally managed Type 3 company. Often Type 3 companies are sluggish and have lost touch with their markets or the needs of their customers. The larger of them can be called institutions and have lost their old competitive edge. As Robert Townsend says in *Up the Organization:* "Big successful institutions aren't successful because of the way they operate, but in spite of it. They didn't get to the top doing things the way they do them now."[4]

Type 3 companies usually have a number of management and control defects that will be discussed in Chapters 5 and 6. Usually the first decline takes place when a number of internal and external events of a detrimental nature occur simultaneously. While such events would be a setback even to a healthy company, they cause severe decline in susceptible companies. The staying power of a Type 3 company lies in its balance sheet, which is now utilized as a buffer to ward off collapse. Often debt financing is used to increase leverage in a futile attempt to regain its old position.

A plateau of performance mediocrity is reached where the financial position is deteriorating because the company is trying to hold on to all its activities, including its losing ones. When a company has lost its competitive edge and at the same time is in the process of becoming highly leveraged, it is "waterlogged." To get off this deteriorating plateau a company has three alternatives. It can do nothing and wait until a wave in the shape of a business hazard comes along to sink it like a foundering vessel. It can initiate stringent profit improvement programs. This usually takes a change of management and a change in the "culture" of a company. It can sell off its losing operations and pay back part of its debt to decrease leverage. Doing this, however, would reduce the physical size of the company, and such a move is alien to most managers, who have been nurtured on growth.

If a company successfully undertook one of the last two above mentioned alternatives, it might effect a turnaround. In most cases of failure the company does nothing and continues to be vulnerable. It can continue on this plateau as long as its balance sheet can act as a buffer and as long as its creditors are willing to let it borrow. There is usually a lenghty period of plateau, after the first collapse and before the final plunge, when there is a golden opportunity for rescue either by correction of internal problems or by merger with a stronger company.

Sound strategic alternatives are often rejected by companies, particularly those afflicted with one-man rule. A take-over by a larger or stronger company is often fought on the basis that current management can effect a solution. The other way out, liquidation, is usually rejected, particularly in companies that up to that point have only had a severe drop in profits, but not necessarily a loss. Too often management holds on to an obsolete strategy or fights a constantly escalating war with inadequate and diminishing resources.

Companies that fail do not undertake well-executed profit improvement programs, do not sell off losing activities, and do not allow a stronger company to take them over. Their stubbornness in not following one of these paths is usually because of one-man rule. Companies that fail invariably try to boost themselves off the plateau with an ambitious scheme that eats up their last available credit. They either launch a new project (new product, diversification, acqusitions, merger with a smaller company) or a campaign to expand sales from existing facilities. Usually leverage is so high and spare cash resources so small at this point that any project big enough to get the company moving will be too big for the available resources. These projects also fail because the companies invariably underestimate costs and overestimate revenues. Sales campaigns usually fail if the company has lost touch with its customers, its market, and its technology.

Mature companies, then, generally go through three stages on their way to failure: initial collapse, a plateau, and final collapse. The length of the plateau stage is directly related to the strength of the balance sheet built up over the years and the timing, size, and type of project that is attempted to get off the plateau.

REFERENCES

[1]Interview with Frank A. Grisanti, president, Grisanti and Galef, Los Angeles, Calif., March 1978.

[2]John Argenti, *Corporate Collapse: The Causes and Symptoms* (New York: Wiley, 1976).

[3]Ibid., p. 159.

[4]Robert Townsend, *Up the Organization* (Greenwich, Conn.: Fawcett, 1971), p.ix.

2
PREDICTABLE ORGANIZATIONAL CRISIS

Like people and plants, organizations have a life cycle. They have a green and supple youth, a time of flourishing strength and a gnarled old age. . . . An organization may go from youth to old age in two or three decades, or it may last for centuries.[1]

John W. Gardner

THE SEEDS OF FUTURE CRISIS

It might be observed that many business organizations die early, or nearly so, while a few like Lloyd's of London and Du Pont seem to go on forever. Management's response to a predictable series of organizational and people crises is often the decisive factor in determining whether a firm dies early or goes on seemingly forever. These problems become particularly severe as a company goes from one development stage to the next. Organizations that get into trouble do not cope with the serious internal challenges created by change. They fail to recognize the significant crises that occur in the organizational life cycle.

Why does an organization fail to recognize these problems? In John Gardner's words: "Most ailing organizations have developed a functional blindess to their own defects. They are not suffering because they cannot solve their problems but because they cannot see their problems."[2] When an organization does recognize an organizational or people problem it may have difficulty confronting it. Such problems do not readily reduce themselves to finite terms. Businessmen learn the dimensions and character of financial crisis in an organization largely because these problems are reducible to familiar finite terms. But understanding the nonfinancial situation is more difficult because it is seldom finite and because it is often a matter of subjective judgment.

The seeds of future financial crisis are sown by failure to cope with current people and organizational problems. The future of an organization is therefore less determined by outside forces than by the organization's history. The growth of the organization must match its external needs in the marketplace, and the growth of the people in the organization must match the needs of the organization itself. Management, in its haste to grow, often overlooks critical organizational issues. Nevertheless, at certain times it is inevitable that one of these issues will acquire exceptional importance. At these times, the organization must recognize, confront, and cope with these concerns—or it may suffer crippling, perhaps fatal, damage if outside external conditions turn negative. In general internal problems relate to the people who lead the organization and to the organization itself.

STAGES OF CORPORATE DEVELOPMENT

An organization has three stages of development. Drucker[3] speaks of the small, the fair-sized, and the big business stages; Thain[4] refers to Stage I, Stage II, and Stage III companies, while Lippitt and Schmidt[5] call the stages birth, youth, and maturity. There is general agreement that the transition from one stage to another poses serious organizational problems. Each of the three stages can be subdivided into two phases. The phase boundaries pose less serious organizational problems than the stage boundaries, but they do pose serious managerial problems. As Greiner says:

> As a company progresses through developmental phases, each evolutionary period creates its own revolution. For instance, centralized practices eventually lead to demands for decentralization. Moreover, the nature of management's solution to each revolutionary period determines whether a company will move forward into its next stage of evolutionary growth.[6]

The survey research for this book indicates that almost 40 percent of the companies surveyed were in a transition period during the decline phase of their turnaround. In addition, the current organizational structure of these companies varies considerably from the structure of the company when the decline phase began. This is shown in Appendix Table A. The turnaround companies showed a substantial swing away from the centralized, functional structure and a substantial swing toward the decentralized, product-division structure by the end of the turnaround period. These results indicate that turnaround companies tend to be structured in a more centralized and less product-divisional manner than Fortune 500 companies.

The Entrepreneurship

Management development problems also pose serious threats to the company and make it susceptible to decline as it passes from one phase to another. The company's founders are usually technically or entrepreneurially oriented and disdain management activities; their physical and mental energies are absorbed entirely in making and selling a new product. This energy and creativity can be successful initially, even when long-term viability is doubtful. The founders are usually adept at survival techniques, thus delaying the ultimate day of reckoning. This problem is pointed out by turnaround expert Frank Grisanti:

> Survival techniques are used by a guy whose product seems to have some acceptance in the marketplace, but who doesn't look at how big that market really is. All he knows is that he got some orders and there was a response to his product and, therefore, he thinks he has got a business. He never really examined it, whether it was a one-shot opportunity or whether it was really a business. So many one-shot opportunities in the hands of creative kinds of people who are fast on their feet begin to emerge and look like business, but they really aren't. And the minute that creative guy who is fast on his feet slows down a little bit, the whole thing caves in.[7]

Creative activities are essential before a company can get off the ground. Once it does, however, new management skills are needed to take the company to its next stage. Sometimes these skills are there, but in more cases they're not. As Robert Sackman, president of Rodal Corporation, says: "Very rarely do you find a situation where the founders are capable of carrying a company through all of the stages of growth."

Greiner points out that the dominant management characteristic in getting a company off the ground is creativity. But soon the creative founders find themselves burdened with unwanted management responsibilities. As Glenn Penisten, president of American Microsystems, indicates:

> There are a lot of young companies that grew up being managed by entrepreneurs. You end up reaching a critical mass where the management experience to get beyond that critical mass is just not there. Once they get into trouble, the solutions used are too entrepreneurial. . . . There are critical-mass problems and opportunities reached which one type of management can handle and another kind can't. You must bring in a professional manager who could never start a company successfully. Most entrepreneurial managers can't manage beyond the critical mass.[8]

At this point a crisis of leadership occurs, which is the onset of the first revolution. The problems were often caused by the top man himself. As Frank Grisanti states:

> The biggest problem is the top man himself. Well balanced businessmen don't build companies. Entrepreneurs who are out-of-balance super-

> salesmen or highly creative individuals build companies. The imbalance tends to make them lean over and the need for balance becomes more and more important. Entrepreneurs, therefore, have to be backed up by nonentrepreneurial businessmen.[9]

Quite obviously, a strong manager is needed who has the necessary knowledge and skill to introduce new business techniques. But this is easier said than done. The founders often hate to step aside, even though they are probably not temperamentally suited to be managers. So here is the first critical step in the developmental process—to locate and install a strong business manager who is acceptable to the founders and who can pull the organization together. The crisis of leadership is solved by strong direction from a seasoned businessman.

The Fair-Sized Company

The companies that survive the first phase by installing a capable business manager usually embark on a period of sustained growth under able and directive leadership. As in each stage of development, organizational solutions create problems for the future. Companies that survive the first critical phase are then faced with the crisis of autonomy.

Although the new directive techniques channel employee energy more efficiently into growth, they eventually become inappropriate for controlling a larger, more diverse and more complex organization. Lower-level employees find themselves restricted by a cumbersome and centralized hierarchy. They have come to possess more direct knowledge about markets and machinery than the leaders at the top; consequently, they feel torn between following procedures and taking initiative on their own. The companies that decline usually maintain a centralized functional organization structure. Companies that survive and grow do so through the successful application of a decentralized organization structure. The solution to the crisis of autonomy is, therefore, delegation of authority.

Operations are broken up into profit centers that grow to be highly diversified. Eventually, however, a serious problem arises as top executives sense that they are losing control over a highly diversified field operation. Richard Madden, chairman of Potlatch Corporation, points out that when companies expand and integrate in various directions, managers sometimes lose an overall picture of the business that the company is actually in.

When management does not understand the business it is really involved in, a crisis of control occurs. This is usually solved by the introduction of formal systems for achieving greater coordination. Formal planning procedures are established and intensely reviewed.

The Institution

Eventually the company, if successful, reaches a red-tape crisis. It is now a flabby institution. Glenn Penisten points out an example of this red tape and how it is perceived differently by the chairman of the board of a major company.

> I can remember talking to a chairman of an institution. I said to him, "You know, we have problems. We have become such an institution that it's getting difficult for the P&L manager to act—we're becoming more reactive. We are becoming more reactive because simple things like getting capital approved takes too long." He said, "There's no problem there. We make our decisions within a day." That's true. The board and capital-review committee of the board met once a month and made their decisions, but the groups were going to be sure that they were prepared to meet all the requirements of the board, so it took them a month after they got it. . . . By the time you got down to the guy in the department who needed the assets to be competitive in the market, you were four to five months away from getting a decision. The chairman of the board thought that capital decisions were made in that company in one day. That's an institution? It's like looking at things in a two-way mirror: one's a mirror and the other is a glass you can look through.[10]

If the company this size is to avoid decline, it must deal with the looking-glass problem. Communication must change from a red-tape system to one of interpersonal collaboration. When companies don't approach this problem correctly, they get all the disadvantages of a small company and none of the advantages of a larger company.

Through recognition of an organization's present stage in the evolutionary process and knowledge of the likely future problems it may encounter, a great deal can be done to attenuate organizational problems. In general, corporate development is poorly planned, and managers encounter many problems in making the transition between stages. Many of these problems result from an inadequate understanding of the different problems and functions of management that are related to the different stages of development of an organization.

The manager who is good at setting short-range objectives and taking necessary risks at the birth of an organization may be much less useful in shaping long-range plans and laying the groundwork for growth at a period in which a youthful organization is seeking stability. The manager who can act directly and decisively in a crisis of survival may prove to be less than adroit in guiding the search for uniqueness. The managerial capabilities required at various times in an organization's life cycle vary considerably.

Although there is no evidence of any limit to the size of organizations, there are many basic limits to the rate of growth, evolution, and transition between stages of development. All organizations face growth problems, and continued inability of management to understand organizational and management development problems can result in a company's becoming frozen at a particular stage of evolution, and can ultimately lead to failure. One thing is clear: Periods of transition and evolution impose greater risks of decline than do periods of stability and evolution.

REFERENCES

[1]John W. Gardner, "How to Prevent Organizational Dry Rot", *Harper's Magazine*, October 1965, p. 20.

[2]Ibid., p. 24.

[3]Peter F. Drucker, "Managing the Small, the Fair Sized, the Big Business," *Management: Tasks, Responsibilities, Practices* (New York: Harper & Row, 1974), pp. 644–663.

[4]Donald H. Thain, "Stages of Corporate Development," *Business Quarterly Review*, Winter 1969, pp. 33–45.

[5]Gordon L. Lippitt and Warren H. Schmidt, "Crisis in Developing Organizations," *Harvard Business Review*, November-December 1967, pp. 48–58.

[6]Larry E. Greiner, "Evolution and Revolution as Organizations Grow," *Harvard Business Review*, July-August 1972, pp. 37–46.

[7]Interview with Frank A. Grisanti, president, Grisanti and Galef, Los Angeles, Calif., March 1978.

[8]Interview with Glenn E. Penisten, president, American Microsystems, Santa Clara, Calif., Febraury 1978.

[9]"They Do Repair Jobs on Small Companies," *Business Week*, Feb. 17, 1973, p. 78.

[10]Penisten, interview, February 1978.

3
IS DECLINE EXTERNALLY OR INTERNALLY CAUSED?

It is never sensible to push any analogy too far, but the collapse of a company is in some ways similar to the sinking of a ship. If a ship is in good condition and the captain is competent, it is almost impossible for it to be sunk by a wave or a succession of waves. Even if there is a storm, the competent captain will have heard the weather forecast and taken whatever measures are needed. Only a freak storm for which quite inadequate notice has been given will sink the ship.[1]

John Argenti

Placing the blame for failure and decline in proper perspective is an age-old debate akin to the chicken-and-the-egg debate. Businesses decline for both uncontrollable external reasons and for controllable internal reasons. In most cases, however, business problems are internally generated. As Jeffrey Chanin, formerly executive vice president of Daylin Corporation, indicates:

> I think that ultimately the reasons for decline are largely internal. I've probably been involved in 200 turnaround situations, from the grocery store on the corner to companies substantially larger than Daylin. My own view, both as an outside lawyer and as an insider, is that in most situations where the management is openminded enough to pay heed to the signals, it will be able to head off at least a good portion of the outside factors which created the crisis.[2]

Management is not always able to deal with outside forces, even when they can see them gathering. Sometimes political, economic, or stock price considerations prevent decisive action. These are *constraints:* those external conditions that prevent reaction even when management senses action is required and has made the correct decision. In a majority of cases, management can work around external changes but has more difficulty with external constraints. External changes pose problems for good managers, even when decimating external constraints are not present. Their very nature makes life more difficult for management. Glenn Penisten feels this way:

> External factors are the ones that you cannot control yourself. You are reacting toward them, or you know that something is happening out there and you need to do something about it, but you're guessing. You can't get a good data-handle on those external factors and break them down. You nearly always seem to be in a reactive mode with regard to external factors.[3]

Management's responsibility goes beyond protecting the company from the adverse consequences of external challenges. It includes getting a company into a posture, both from a marketing and financial point of view, where it can resist normal business hazards and other more serious external challenges. After all, that is what management is there for in the first place. A manager who blames external forces for a company's decline, suggests John Argenti, is like a ship's captain who has not heard the weather forecast. As he says:

> What does he expect—a world in which taxes and laws are not changed? This is like the captain of a ship which is grossly overloaded blaming a two-foot wave for the sinking—and, in one case, he is right; it was a two-foot wave that sank it! But what about all the other ships near by which are still afloat?[4]

There is a spectrum of external events at one end of which are normal hazards and at the other end of which are events or combinations of events such as sheer bad luck, against which no firm could protect itself. While fully recognizing that bad luck can cause failure, we should also recognize that it is a very rare cause indeed in large companies. (Dun & Bradstreet estimates that sheer bad luck accounts for only 1.1 percent of business failure.) As for the normal business hazards, they can never be valid excuses for failure.

Sudden changes in the external environment happen more frequently than sheer bad luck these days. They are beyond management's control in the short run. Ransom Cook, formerly president of Wells Fargo Bank, believes that outside forces can wreak havoc upon an overconcentrated or marginal business. As Mr. Cook says:

> If a company was only involved in defense production, and defense budgets were cut in a major way, there is nothing management can do except avoid being so heavily concentrated in the defense business in the first place. A situation can come up where unions may force a company out of business because it was marginal in the first place. . . . When

> a company gets into trouble, the first thing necessary to do is find out whether it is a turnaround situation that is internally correctable or has to be externally corrected, by either political or economic changes.[5]

At this point in the decline-cause spectrum both external and internal reasons can cause decline. We are at the point where problems are no longer purely external. Instead, there is an interaction of both kinds of causes. As Robert Di Giorgio, chairman of Di Giorgio Corporation, states it:

> The problem does not arise from external conditions, but a change of external conditions causes imbalance. The problems come from an internal problem, but the triggering mechanism that suddenly makes things that formerly worked no longer work is a change in external things—a condition of tight money, a condition of high interest rates, a condition of faltering industry sales, or any combination of those things. It works on your internal problems so that you can no longer live with them, so you have at this point to either fall by the wayside or correct the internal problems.[6]

A summary view of decline causes from a survey of chief executive officers is shown in Table 3-1. External factors do cause decline, but only in about 9 percent of the cases are they the sole cause. In another 20 percent of the cases, decline is caused by both external and internal causes. About 70 percent of the time decline is internally caused,

TABLE 3-1
The Principal Reasons for Corporate Decline

	Percent
Sheer bad luck (Dun & Bradstreet 1977)	1
External factors beyond management's control	8
Real balance of external and internal factors	24
Internal problems triggered by external factors	15
Internally generated problems within management's control	52
TOTAL	100

Source: Donald B. Bibeault, Survey of Eighty-One Turnaround Company Chief Executives, April 1978.

although in some cases internal weaknesses are triggered by outside forces.

There is nothing particularly new and novel about what I am saying in this chapter. Indeed, Machiavelli summarized the central question of the chapter centuries ago in this way:

> So these princes of ours who had been for many years entrenched in their states have no cause to complain of fortune because they have lost them; the fault lies rather in their own ineptitude, for, as in tranquil times they had given no thought to the possibility of change (a common failing of men, who rarely think of storms to come while the sun yet shines), adversity caught them unprepared.[7]

REFERENCES

[1] John Argenti, *Corporate Collapse: The Cause and Symptoms* (New York: Wiley, 1976), p. 122.

[2] Interview with Jeffrey Chanin, executive vice president, Daylin Corp., Los Angeles, Calif., March 1978.

[3] Interview with Glenn E. Penisten, president, American Microsystems, Santa Clara, Calif., February 1978.

[4] Argenti, *Corporate Collapse*, p. 134.

[5] Interview with Ransom Cook, chairman and president (retired), Wells Fargo Bank, San Francisco, Calif., February 1978.

[6] Interview with Robert Di Giorgio, chairman, Di Giorgio Corp., San Francisco, Calif., February 1978.

[7] Niccolo Machiavelli, *The Prince*, translated by Thomas G. Begin (Franklin Center, Pennsylvania: Franklin Library, 1978), p. 135.

4
EXTERNAL REASONS FOR DECLINE

Organizations are born in a climate of excitement and hope; they must survive in a world of test and challenge.[1]

John W. Gardner

THE IMPACT OF CHANGE

In today's unstable planning climate, unions can shut down industries overnight; government regulations can force capital expenditures for pollution control, noise abatement, safety and health improvements; consumer organizations can suddenly place artificial pressures on pricing or quality; energy and raw material shortages can interfere with production or create great variance in costs; Congress can increase business incentives (investment credit, solar power, tax credits, etc.) and just as quickly take them away. Experiences of the mobile home industry in 1974 illustrate how quickly disaster can occur. In May, sales were good; industry expansion and new equipment orders were normal. Sixty days later sales had plummeted to less than 10 percent of the May figures. The speed of that change is not typical, but it does stress how short-term projections can err and how necessary it is to be able to take immediate steps for survival.

The external changes I am discussing here are not the many minor changes of everyday business life but the relatively few trends and events that strike at the core of a company's business. A company does not operate in isolation; it acts upon and reacts to a very complex environment which is continually changing, constantly moving. Some of these changes, such as population trends in peacetime, take place slowly and predictably. Others occur with such shocking suddenness and severity that no one can foretell how they will change the shape of the world—as indeed was the case in 1973, when the Arab producers quadrupled the price of oil. Not to foresee such events or not to calculate their consequences, not to take note of such trends and their implications for one's business, is a sure and certain way to failure.

External factors can be divided into two types: external changes and external constraints. The difference between the two lies in their degree of severity. External constraints block management action and, as such, are more difficult to deal with than most external changes. We have all heard that the pace of change is now so rapid that most companies cannot respond adequately. Most chief executive officers disagree and see change as a challenge that management can generally meet. What increasingly alarms them are government constraints.

We can divide external factors into five categories: economic change, competitive change, government constraints, social change, and technological change. I have listed these factors in their order of importance as perceived by the chief executive officers whom I interviewed. They ranked the external causes of decline as: economic change, competitive change, government constraints, social change, and, lastly, technological change. (Exact figures are in Appendix Table B.)

ECONOMIC CHANGE

You can get away with a great deal when times are good, but a business slump turns many minor worries into major problems. A boom covers many sins, and a bust uncovers many weaknesses. Economic problems come in many forms, including slackening overall demand, devaluation of currencies, international monetary crises, interest rate hikes, and credit squeezes. At the time of writing, inflation is by far the most severe economic problem. Common sense would suggest that when economic activity levels off or declines, the number of company failures will increase, and vice versa. And so it is. Edward Altman examined this association more closely and learned what other factors outside the firm itself affect failures.[2] He developed a number of equations in order to examine the influence on failure rates of such things as money market conditions and investor expectations. It is generally believed, for example, that a credit squeeze is one of the most potent causes of collapse.

Altman went further, using techniques of multiple regression to develop an equation for predicting the change in the number of failed businesses given changes in various economic indicators. After much analysis he was able to come up with the following reliable equation linking failure rates with GNP, the stock market index, and the money supply:

$$FR = 1.54 - 0.222GNP_1 - 1.90SP_1 + 0.495MS_1 + e$$

where FR is the change in the failure rate (Dun & Bradstreet again) from one quarter of the year to the next; GNP_1 is the change in GNP in billions of dollars between those quarters; SP_1 is the change in the Standard and

Poor Index of Common Stock Prices; MS, is the change in the money supply in billions of dollars; and *e* is an error term. Altman's work is certainly worthwhile, although it is not too useful for our purposes because we are concerned primarily with the larger companies that comprise about 2 percent of the Dun & Bradstreet statistics. Altman's primary point is that if you are looking for a way to predict failure, it is not enough to look at the firm itself. There are powerful external forces acting from outside the firm.

Although economic change does cause decline and failure, it is important to keep its role in proper perspective. According to my study, external factors cause 10 percent of decline and are partially responsible for 22 percent. If we simply give half credit for partial effects, external factors appear to be responsible for 21 percent of the total decline. Economic factors by themselves are the chief cause of only 9 percent of all decline.

These results are backed up by practical experience and further in-depth analysis by other researchers. Of the 4,000 listed companies, my research indicates that about 55 percent that suffered failure or decline were "threshold" or fair-sized companies in the $30 to $300 million annual revenue range. These 600 companies compare closely with roughly 500 threshold companies that were identified as having suffered decline in a study undertaken by Donald K. Clifford of McKinsey and Company.[3]

What Clifford discovered was that during the same economic cycle good performers outperformed the laggards by astonishing rates. The good performers' earnings per share grew at 33 percent annually, while the poor performers' earnings per share declined 23 percent annually. Clifford found that the well-managed company in the $30 to $300 million size range outperforms even the better giant corporations in bad times as well as good. They do so through disciplined control over the economics of the business, intensive development of the right market niches and products, and, most important, a leadership style that sustains entrepreneurial drive and commitment among its key managers. Good management can offset poor economic conditions.

COMPETITIVE CHANGE

Most companies operate in a world of constantly shifting competition. The emergence of foreign, low-cost producers, the merger of two competitors, the announcement of a competitor's new range of products, the appearance of an entirely new company in your industry are changes that can have a profound impact upon your company. If you don't keep your ear close to the ground, try to calculate and quantify the consequences of such changes, and take appropriate action, then your company is certain to lose some of its competitive edge. Customers seek improved products and services, and competition forces the company to provide them. Turnaround executives believe that competitive change accounts for about one-quarter of externally caused decline. On an overall basis competitive change accounts for 6 percent (26 × 21 percent) of total decline in the companies evaluated.

Competitive change often takes the form of price competition where other firms lower prices to introduce their products to new markets. Many firms suffer lowered selling prices during their downturn phase in order to ward off a competitor's attempt to introduce lower-priced, substitute materials. Sometimes management is caught flat-footed by the sudden appearance of competitors. This quick entry usually is due to new technology or unknown foreign companies. National Cash Register (NCR) is a case in point. That firm had been a leader in the cash register market for eighty-five years, but found itself faced with a host of new competitors in the early seventies. At the time, NCR was still producing mechanical data-capturing equipment, while its competitors were well under way manufacturing lower-cost electronic equipment.

Foreign price competition has existed for many years and has had a particularly devastating effect on industries such as shoes, consumer electronics, and steel. While there are domestic success stories in each of these industries, failure rates have been high.

Competition can cause decline, but usually this happens to companies that are not monitoring the outside environment. Competition is a positive force, as Robert Di Giorgio points out:

> I think that the important thing is to try to be a leader instead of a follower by not letting the company sit around and wait until the competitor develops a whole new line or products that do the same as yours, only better and in a different way. Companies that get in trouble are not foresighted enough to feel the need for change. Every change is an opportunity.[4]

Robert Sackman says, "I think if you have been caught by competition, you haven't been doing your homework."

GOVERNMENT CONSTRAINTS

Government constraints are very revelant to business problems whether at the local level, where politicians may affect one's production resources, or at the national or international level, where they can affect one's raw materials, markets, and finance. Politicians are playing a growing role in business all over the world. New quotas and duties and taxes and levies and legislation of all sorts pour out of government agencies like confetti. Even more insidious (because they are not written down and published) are the changes in political attitudes toward business in general and certain industries in particular.

The government impinges on corporate life by taxation, involvement in employee records, welfare legislation, pollution control, and product safety and consumer welfare legislation. Increasing regulation of business demands the use of outside service organizations such as consultants, auditors, lawyers, tax advisers, advertising agencies, and public relations firms. Moreover, the internal workings of the corporation must be geared to work with these outside agencies. Some executives, like Glenn Penisten of American Microsystems, feel that government is a major problem: "I suspect that all of those other external problems are contributed to in one way or another by government policies. Economic problems and government problems are one and the same."[5]

A list of recent government constraints on business would have to include the following well-known cases: delaying merger for six years while the government argues with itself (Penn Central); subsidizing the nation's exports out of one's profits (Rolls-Royce); delaying the construction of an oil pipeline across Alaska while environmentalists argue; prohibiting an oil-rig construction site in Scotland; barring the closing of a factory in Sweden; forbidding firms from raising prices (U.K., 1974). These are just a few examples of the massive constraints that government can place on business.

Whether one holds the view that these constraints have now become excessive or that, on the contrary, capitalism must be further controlled is irrelevant. We have to deal with the world as it is. Certainly one can point to specific examples of government causing corporate failure, but when it comes right down to it, government is not yet the main culprit. My survey indicates that government causes 16 percent of the external failure, which amounts to a little less than 4 percent of total failure and decline. Perhaps we must strike a philosophical posture while we try to change the political system. Rules in business change, as Robert Sackman says: "I don't care if it is government or anybody else, if you are not prepared or flexible enough to make necessary adjustments to change, then that is another cause of trouble. Government can always be coped with."[6]

SOCIAL CHANGE

A fairly long time span is required to accommodate many of the changes in society. The first signs of changes in work attitudes, for example, were evident more than a decade ago, but many companies have still not really understood how profound the movement toward "participation" and "job satisfaction" is. Not to understand this and respond to it is to risk losing touch with one's employees and perhaps precipitating strikes. Indeed, it appears that strikes are caused by social change that companies have not accommodated themselves to.

A greater number of companies have lost touch with their market or their customers because they did not see, or did not react to, such social trends as changes in life-styles, in composition by age or color of a given population, and in attitudes toward pollution and consumer decline. The answer is not so black-and-white, though, because social change affects some industries much more than others. As Robert Di Giorgio says: "If you are in the entertainment business or a style-oriented business, then you have to be more adept at monitoring social change."[7]

Most of the corporate chief executive officers (CEOs) agreed with my opinion that social change is moving at a rate that should allow reasonably astute management to keep up with it in most industries. My survey results indicate that social change was perceived to cause 9 percent of external decline or about 2 percent of overall decline.

TECHNOLOGICAL CHANGE

Technological progess in the past decade has created so many new materials, processes, and manufacturing techniques that the possible combinations of products and the means of getting them stagger the imagination. Consumers can choose from a host of options in materials, quality, price, service features, dependability, style, color, and shape. Never before have they had such freedom of choice. But the need to create and satisfy product demands has put manufacturing organizations in the contradictory position of being both contributors to change, and its victims.

Most executives agree that companies that are victims of technological change are only victims of their own lack of foresight. The conversion of AT&T from an 80 percent electromechanical industry five years ago to an 80 percent electronic one today caused AT&T many problems. But AT&T management was deliberately behind and had fought off innovative competitors. When the government regulatory bodies got out of the way, competition forced them to change. NCR in the late 1960s is another example. They had huge amounts of capital tied up in producing mechanical equipment and were simply unprepared for the second phase of the electronic revolution that hit the cash register industry in the early seventies.

It is often said that changes in technology are the most influential today. While this must be true in some industries, I personally believe it to be a very weak generalization. My survey indicates that about 7 percent of external decline, or a little more than 1 percent of total decline, is due to technological change. It is also worth reminding ourselves that no well-managed firm should be caught out to lunch by a change in technology even in these days of rapid change. As Robert Sackman, who has seen a lot of technological warfare, says: "I don't believe I've ever seen a technological change that completely wiped out any company's products. It has hindered them; it has changed their strategy; and it's lowered their profit, but it has not destroyed them as a profit-making enterprise."[8]

In summary, I do not believe that the rate of change has accelerated so fast in recent times as to make life excessively difficult for the well-managed company. I have no doubt, however, that it has made life more difficult for the poorly managed company.

REFERENCES

[1] John W. Gardner, "How to Prevent Organizational Dry Rot," *Harper's Magazine*, October 1965, p. 20.

[2] Edward I. Altman, *Corporate Bankruptcy in America* (Lexington, Mass.: Heath-Lexington, 1971), Chapter 3.

[3] Donald K. Clifford, Jr., "Thriving in a Recession," *Harvard Business Review*, July–August 1977, pp. 57, 59.

[4] Interview with Robert Di Giorgio, chairman, Di Giorgio Corp., San Francisco, Calif., February 1978.

[5] Interview with Glenn F. Penisten, president, American Microsystems, Santa Clara, Calif., February 1978.

[6] Inverview with Robert Sackman, president, Rodal Corp., Palo Alto, California, February 1978.

[7] Di Giorgio, interview, February 1978.

[8] Sackman, interview, February 1978.

5
INTERNAL REASONS FOR DECLINE

If I had to blame one specific element for business failure, it would be lack of discipline on somebody's part.[1]

Frank A. Grisanti

THE MANAGEMENT FACTOR

My opinion, based upon surveys and discussions with over 100 turnaround leaders, is that in seven out of ten cases decline is internally generated. In another 20 percent of the cases, internal reasons are partially responsible for decline. In broad terms, decline is therefore caused by internal factors about eight out of ten times. In this chapter these internal factors are brought into sharper focus. There is no great mystery about the principal reason for internal problems. As Robert Brown says: "Obviously, the primary cause for decline is bad management. The main reason why corporations get into trouble is failure to recognize the signs when things are starting to rot at the core."[2] John Argenti agrees: "The prime cause of failure is bad management. Good managers will seldom make the same fatal mistakes as poor managers; but, if they do make them, their managerial ability will protect the company from the worst consequences."[3]

Management problems also had a preeminent place in my survey of corporate turnaround leaders. The executives indicated that in those cases where decline was internally caused, management was the principal reason for decline 85 percent of the time. According to Herbert N. Woodward, consultant for small businesses, failure is due, not to bad luck, but to recurring patterns of nonconstructive conduct by management.

It should be noted that, as much as businessmen rail against internal constraints, such as unions, they appear to be of minor importance as an ultimate cause of decline or failure. Fraud and bad luck deserve no more than a passing mention.

One company chief executive gave a very candid scenario of the problems besetting his company prior to his arrival.

> What got us into trouble? Sure, I can talk about that because we analyzed our past. The problem was really at the top, not "hands-on" management. We were totally marketing-oriented and nothing else. The budget was never dragged out of the files. We tried to be all things to all people using a scatter-gun approach to branching. A belief in size and numbers, while the profits are going straight down the tubes. No attention to margins. We had the highest occupancy cost in the country. Earnings started to plunge, and then the whole organization seemed to say "what the hell." It was floundering with no direction.[4]

It is insufficient simply to say the major reason for decline is bad management. The problem of bad management can be better understood by answering three key questions:

1. Why does "bad" management exist?
2. What are the visible symptoms of bad management?
3. What are the most common errors that bad management commits or omits that cause corporate decline and failure?

Why Bad Management Exists

Incompetence. As much as we would like to believe otherwise, bad management exists for many of the same reasons other human problems exist. According to Robert Di Giorgio, it's that old common denominator—people.

> Unless you are in a very esoteric or highly specialized business, your problem is generally a people problem, not a product problem. If your product costs too much, it's generally because of people. If your product is not the quality of your competitors', that's usually because of people. Seventy-five percent of most problems are people.[5]

It does not follow that because a person has been elevated to a position of high executive responsibility he can do the job. As Glenn Penisten of American Microsystems says:

> It all boils down to human frailties. Some people have the natural abilities to manage and some don't. In lots of situations somebody incompetent will be promoted into top management. If the business factors are all lining up reasonably well, it probably doesn't matter. In rough

economic times or in an unusually competitive situation, management is not capable of dealing with the adverse factors.[6]

Narrow Vision. Often companies promote a man into the top position because he has had some success in a narrow functional area. This narrow outlook can be dangerous because the president's job requires breadth of vision. The widening of one's horizons can be a frustrating, harrowing, and even dangerous experience for the unprepared individual and the company alike. An example of this narrow vision occurred in a company (to remain unnamed) that elevated a vice president to company president as a reward for outstanding success in sales. The new president was in reality a glorified salesman whose success was largely due to his ability to get along well with key house accounts and maintain a steady volume of sales to them. But he knew little about the other aspects of the business such as finance, accounting, production and inventory control, shipping, and engineering.

When he assumed the duties of president, he made some attempts to broaden his knowledge of the company. But he was under pressure to make a showing as a successful president, and it was easier to do the things he knew and liked best. So he concentrated on selling. He became a part-time selling president. He delegated the responsibilities for finance, engineering, and production to others, but major decisions had to wait until he returned from a sales trip. In this managerial vacuum, the factory and home office became a battleground in a power struggle between his vice presidents. During this period costs began to climb alarmingly.

Up until this time the president spent a portion of his time in the office, but his efforts even then were confined to marketing decisions. Faced with increasing costs and dwindling profits, he reverted even more to his earlier work habits; he decided to concentrate on personal selling. Now he was almost totally unavailable for his true role as president. Things got worse. They improved only when the selling president was finally replaced.

Displacement Activity. Many a businessman is so busy doing the things he likes to do that he has no time for the things he should do. This form of displacement activity can reach dangerous proportions in a troubled company. One company chief executive with whom I'm familiar spent the better part of two years at a drafting board in the engineering department while his company's financial position severely deteriorated. He rationalized his behavior by indicating that no one else in the company could design a new rolling mill except him. In fact, the technical part of the work could have been done by moderately experienced engineers.

Because he was controlling stockholder, no one questioned his behavior or his failure to come to grips with the realities of a very troubled company.

It amounts to an appalling lack of objectives and discipline. The board of directors does not discipline top management; top management does not discipline middle management; and so on down the line. The lack of discipline is an important reason for business failure. In the final analysis discipline means people looking at things when they should look at them, recognizing what they should see when they do see it, and doing something about it once the impact of what it all means is seen.

The Visible Symptoms of Bad Management

All of the above reasons for the existence of bad management—and there are many more—are difficult for an outsider to detect. Experience and research confirm that the principal symptoms of bad management are: (1) one-man rule, (2) lack of management depth, (3) management succession problems, (4) inbred bureaucratic management, (5) a weak financial executive, (6) an unbalanced top management team, and, finally, (7) a nonparticipative board. These symptoms, presented in order of importance from my survey of chief executives, are shown in Appendix Table C.

Management Errors

Most turnaround leaders agree patterns of decline are attributable to internal factors. If management of a company is poorly handled, it will make two types of errors: errors of omission and errors of commission. Errors of omission fall into two main categories: (1) the company fails to respond properly to changes in its external environment, and (2) it is lax in developing or utilizing control information. The errors of omission will result if the company fails to develop and communicate a unified and directed strategy to which all members of the organization can relate. The lack of strategy will eventually lead to errors of commission that put the company in grave danger. The company will generally overexpand while becoming noncompetitive. As the company declines, it will compound its errors by borrowing and becoming excessively leveraged. At this point, even normal business hazards become constant threats.

ONE-MAN RULE

Emerson's metaphor, "An institution is the lengthened shadow of one man," typifies American business success. Joel E. Ross and Michael J.

Kami say: "The rise of each of many of today's largest corporations is due to the individual genius of one determined entrepreneur. The Mellons, the Carnegies, the Rockefellers—robber barons of the turn of the century—were extraordinarily successful without practicing consultative or participative management."[7]

A lesser-known case illustrates the singular impact one man can make. Ernest Dale calls Ernest Tenner Weir of National Steel the "Iconoclast of Management." Weir started with a small tin plate mill. His tenure—some twenty-seven years as chief executive—was turbulent and authoritarian. During the Great Depression, National Steel was the only steel company to make a profit. It is said, U.S. Steel offered Weir the presidency at $1 million annually. Weir refused—he liked to run his own show.[8]

Walt Disney, Thomas Watson of IBM, Harold Geneen of ITT all illustrate the point. On the other hand, consider these giant corporations whose past crises can be traced partially to a one-man rule: Ling-Temco-Vought (James Ling), Investors Overseas (Bernard Cornfeld), 20th Century-Fox (Darryl Zanuck), and Singer Corporation (Donald Kircher).

These are particularly tragic cases where a company that once succeeded under one-man rule plummeted because of the total dominance of that one man. Singer Corporation, as led by Donald Kircher, is an example. Kircher believed in one-man rule. "If the chief executive is not a dominant personality, he ought to get the hell out," Kircher says. But a chief executive can become too insulated in his own point of view. Subordinates were silenced by the strength of Kircher's arguments. In this way, Kircher robbed himself of counsel he sometimes sorely needed.[9]

When Is a Company Ripe for One-Man Rule?

The success or failure of one-man rule depends on the size and organizational complexity of the company, problems of the industry, and the new "human" requirements of organizations in the 1970s. As pointed out in Chapter 2 on predictable organizational crisis, management needs vary as the organization grows. One-man rule is necessary at the entrepreneurial stage but later causes problems. As Glenn Penisten points out: "An entrepreneur has the personality of a creative individual. Very seldom does that personality type bring in disciplined management—a structure which listens to other people, has a board that sets policies. More often that entrepreneur nurtures a submissive management."[10]

The entire airline industry, recently in deep trouble, was the product of rugged individualists and entrepreneurs. But, again in the late sixties and seventies, changing priorities changed the fortunes of the airlines. The old pilots had the ability to fly and manage by the seats of their pants. But the sixties brought new complexities, new problems, and a demand for more precise management. The mistakes with jumbo jets, lack of planning for physical handling facilities, gradual neglect of customer service, employee rudeness and inefficiency all combined to make new management and new techniques necessary.

One-Man Band

The difference between one-man rule and a one-man band is substantial. A one-man band is necessarily acceptable for a small company; the fact that it is small means that it may have only two directors—the proprietor and his wife, for example. The chief executive, unavoidably, has to make all the decisions himself. That is a one-man band. *One-man rule* is intended to describe chief executives who make decisions in spite of their colleagues' hostility or reticence; they allow no discussion, will hear no advice. These men are autocrats—Henry Ford, Jim Ling, Donald Kircher, Bernie Cornfeld, Darryl Zanuck and many others. Not all autocrats are overambitious supersalesmen, so set upon hypersuccessful performance that they cease to believe in the existence of failure. Some are relatively retiring people who impose their will by their superior knowledge.

One-man rule is not always bad and is sometimes needed. Thaddeus Taube points out:

> One-man rule is a two-edged sword. There's a lot of inbred lethargy in group management. Very strong one-man leadership can sometimes steer a business entity in the wrong direction. Yet, it takes very strong leadership to steer a company in any direction. A company must tread a very fine line between imparting a great deal of authority and strength to a leader while hoping he will be responsive to advice from business associates.[11]

Although the strong, capable leader has served his purpose in the past and may do so in the future, it is the rare company that can prosper in the long run with one-man rule. In the extraordinarily complex organizations of the 1970s and 1980s, it is essential to have management depth and permit managers to participate in decision making. This corporate attribute is necessary for two reasons: first, one man simply cannot handle the complexity of running the organization single-handedly; second, it is essential that the company provide for management succession.

LACK OF MANAGEMENT DEPTH

One-man rule and the lack of management depth go hand in hand. Often an autocratic ruler will not tolerate strong people around him. The lack of management depth abets the autocrat in continuing to play an exaggerated role in the company. It is no coincidence that year after year the President's Panel of *Dun's Review* identifies management depth as one of the prime characteristics of the "Ten Best Managed Companies." Yet Michael Kami says "in the 'not very well managed companies' a common characteristic is lack of management depth." He attributes this lack either to one-man rule or to rapid growth. In both cases, however, Kami says, "It is safe to say that their recent downhill slide is partly due to bench strength being absent or silent."[12]

MANAGEMENT CHANGE PROBLEMS

One of the consequences of one-man rule and the lack of management depth is that management change becomes a disorderly process, amplifying the natural functional conflicts that exist in every organization. According to Anthony Glueck, the most frequently perceived strategic disadvantages for a large firm are changes or problems in top management. The disadvantages do not appear equally frequently in all phases of the business cycle. Changes or problems in top management appear most frequently during the economic extremes of the cycle (depression and prosperity).

Marlene's is a successful apparel company that has grown during both good years and bad. Chairman Charles Meltzer is a "one-man-business" leader of whom everyone reports, "Charlie is the kind of guy who can eat three corned beef sandwiches simultaneously." While Marlene's has been spared the other problems that accompany one-man rule, it does have a potential succession problem. Pan American had succession problems after its founder, Juan Trippe, left. He did not anticipate the managerial needs of the company, and management development was almost totally ignored.

It is imperative that upon succession, the top man assert his position so that there is no question about who is in charge. The way you take charge should be a deliberate and well-planned tactical program (see Chapter 15). If the new management were to give way to existing organization, it would soon face the problems encountered by Frank Pace of General Dynamics. When Pace took over in 1957, he found himself virtually a prisoner of his own managers. His head office staff numbered 200, in a company of 106,000, made up of nine virtually autonomous divisions. Most of the divisions had been independent enterprises—each with its own tough presidents, and separate legal and financial staffs. Pace decided to leave them more or less alone. The only way to success, he said, "is to operate on a decentralized basis." But General Dynamics lost $425 million between 1960 and 1962.

The plain fact is that top management changes, if not smoothly handled, can throw an organization off-balance, rendering it vulnerable to decline. Management changes at other levels can have a serious negative impact as well. The critical importance of management change in crisis companies is underscored by the fact that a new chief executive officer was appointed in 74 percent of the cases to effect a turnaround.

INBRED BUREAUCRATIC MANAGEMENT

Organizations can decay because their people structure becomes too rigid. As organizations mature and management becomes entrenched, they tend to become rigid and unresponsive to change, even senile—not alert enough to see competitive changes. John W. Gardner, former chairman of Common Cause, correlates the aging process of organizations to the amortization of the American frontier settlements. The vitality which originally marked the American frontier settlement eventually succumbed to tradition. Similarly, once management is entrenched, it loses its capacity to meet challenges from unexpected directions.

Evidence of organizational senility can be found in the low survival rate of ideas. Survival is minimal in aged and highly political structures. Trying out new ideas means taking chances, and each has a degree or risk associated with it. Senile organizations are so controlled that they don't take chances. Because some internal forces demand change while others resist it, all organizations are in tension and conflict. As the rate of change accelerates, these tensions and conflicts reach a point where useless friction and bickering consume the energies that should be devoted to productive purposes.

Frederick R. Kappel, then president of AT&T and guest lecturer at Columbia University, articulated six danger signs of inbred management:

1. People cling to old ways of working even though they have been confronted by a new situation.
2. They fail to define new goals with meaning and challenge.
3. Action is taken without studied reflection.
4. Institutionalized contentment: Business becomes secure and stable, not venturesome.
5. Old "wisdom" is passed on to new people. Older managers tend to adhere too rigidly to old ideas, to antiquated approaches and methods. Note, they mold the minds of young managers.
6. Low tolerance for criticism acts to stifle independent thinking.[13]

The system does not promote self-criticism. It admonishes, "Don't rock the boat." Danger signals are ignored or carefully sugarcoated so as not to upset anyone at any level. These danger signals are greatly relevant to most business enterprises, and particularly to Kappel's own Bell System. One can only conclude that there is a vast difference between the theories expounded and actions taken by members of top management.

Roy Woodman, turnaround executive and president of International Video Corporation, has a pet theory for preventing inbred management: "One thing to look for in a large company is people hanging onto one job too long. Move before the rot sets in. Give people a challenge—keep them moving into new jobs. Get the guy who is ready to take a chance. Give him as much help as you can but don't tell him how to do it. Create the right climate for performance and he'll surprise you."[14]

THE UNBALANCED TOP MANAGEMENT TEAM

A parallel but easier to observe defect is the presence of an unbalanced top management team. The phenomenon of imbalance is plainly visible in many engineering companies, where both the chief executive and the board members are engineers. This arrangement suits the autocrat, for none of his subordinates will challenge him on engineering decisions, though all his subordinates are engineers. He is thus not challenged at all! If the management does not contain a wide spectrum of skills, then the chance of a new threat appearing unnoticed is severely increased. Many observers attribute Chrysler Corporation's troubles in the last ten years to dominance by the engineering department. Balance in the top management group is a function of the size and complexity of the business. According to Richard Madden:

> If you said huge companies like Mobil had nothing but chemical engineers and Potlach had nothing but mechanical engineers, sure that is a problem. I am not so sure that you can rely on that as an indicator of management defects in smaller companies. You have to look at your situation. You want a balanced view. If you have an absolutely superior technological product, the engineer—who isn't the best salesman in the world and perhaps doesn't wear the right color tie—will make sales to business people because the product is superior.[15]

WEAK FINANCE FUNCTION

A special case of imbalance in the top team—particularly at board level—is a weak finance function. This may appear throughout the company as a general phenomenon, resulting in inadequate financial and accounting controls. But even when these systems are perfectly adequate, their message may not be heard at board level because the finance function is not strongly represented there. A strong finance man organizes his function and articulates it from the top. Jeffrey Chanin of Daylin Corporation says: "Not having a strong finance man can cause trouble. You've got to have a good strong person who doesn't take any bull from the troops, who is capable of administering believable data to management. Believable doesn't mean a lot of data; when you are in trouble, believable means reliable. Otherwise, who's going to hold council with the president?"[16]

Robert Brown brings out the importance of the strong finance man when he says, "I think it is self evident that every time the business cycle goes down, the premium hiring is for financial planning and control people. The chief financial officer is the key man to hire."[17]

To be "good," the chief financial officer must have technical skills, be creative, and have the courage and ethics to stand up to the chief executive officer. Robert Sackman indicates:

> You've got to have a good man in there who also has enough authority to operate on his own. That type of financial man would make an analysis of the business and say, "Look, Mr. President, this is how the money in this corporation is actually being made, and here is the way it really comes in, and here are the danger points." I think that is the flexible and creative role of the finance officer—and a man like that is hard to find. In the end, it comes down to both the president knowing that he needs such a man and the man himself having the independence and courage to make such presentations to him.[18]

One great danger during a decline is management resorting to "creative accounting" to cover up reality. While this is more a symptom of decline than a cause, a strong financial officer will prevent this type of activity. He ought to have an attitude like Robert Di Giorgio: "'Creative accounting' is just a polite word for being a crook. I'm not interested in creative accounting. The purpose of accounting is to tell yourself and your owners how your business is doing—frankly and simply. I believe in complete disclosure. I want the facts. You shouldn't color the facts to suit your own fantasies."[19]

NONPARTICIPATIVE BOARD OF DIRECTORS

In my experience, the board of directors of most companies functions in a ritualistic manner rather than as an active representative of the shareholders. Robert Townsend says, "I've spent years on various boards. I've never heard one suggestion from a board meeting director that produced any result at all."

The Securities and Exchange Commission has scored corporate directors for lax scrutiny of management acts. There have been all types of suggestions for changing this outdated system. J. Wilson Newman, retired chairman of Dun & Bradstreet and currently a director of Lockheed Aircraft Corporation and other companies, asserts, "Traditionally, boards of directors and their company managements have striven for hand-in-glove cooperation. But such a system offers too much potential for laxity." Frank Grisanti feels the key problem is that very few companies define the responsibility and authority retained by the board versus that which is delegated to management: "Where does counseling end and meddling begin?"

So what is the role of the board in preventing decline? I believe when it comes to preventing decline, the current reformers are asking too much of boards as they are currently structured. Certain committees, such as the audit committee, do perform a valuable function if made up of knowledgeable outsiders. Unless board membership becomes a professional activity, we cannot expect that board members will be capable of knowing the business satisfactorily to make concrete contributions. Even when a board member is experienced and capable, the current structure does not allow him to be of much assistance. As Robert Sackman of Rodal indicates:

> It's difficult for a board member to interject himself to a sufficient degree to catch problems in the bud. The only time I could do it as a board member was when I had a job that extended beyond board membership. That is, I came in once a week and I was able to talk to all of the managers and the president. As a board member you are usually handling the crisis when it occurs, not before.[20]

My survey results indicate that as far as decline is concerned, a nonparticipative board is one of the lesser problems. The board of directors does not cause decline; that is obviously caused by management, usually senior management. The board does have a role in preventing decline, however. This role centers on two areas: first, the selection of the chief executive officer and his team and, second, the careful appraisal of company information in order to pick up the early-warning signals of decline. To perform both these tasks, the board should be composed of independent, outside directors, possessed of experience and competence in fields applicable to the corporate business at hand. In addition, these directors should have at least two to four days per month to devote to corporate matters and be adequately compensated for their efforts.

Robert Brown says of a board in a problem company:

> The Boise Cascade board was like any other board. They really didn't understand the internal operating problems inside the business. They

> were up there listening to all the grand plans of management. It all sounds good and looks good on paper; feasibility studies that are shown will always be the solutions to the problems. The real guts of the problems were insolvable. They were businesses where the economics had changed considerably; and they were overly committed, relative to their balance sheet. The only way they could get out of the problem was to have someone come in here and bring in a sledgehammer and break it up.[21]

Myles Mace, author of *Directors: Myth and Reality,* indicates that the board of a problem company is lax and ill-equipped to judge a president. Individual directors are scarcely able to separate plausible explanation for mismanagement. To the extent that boards of directors have failed to take timely action in firing incompetent chief executives, they have failed to prevent business decline. Observations made by myself and other turnaround leaders indicate that boards of directors are frequently not at fault. But change is needed and is coming to the board. Management problems are the core of decline problems. A company's future depends on the past, current, and future management performance. Whereas the comparative performance of companies, both from a financial and a market standpoint, can be quantified, management can not.

REFERENCES

[1] Interview with Frank A. Grisanti, president, Gristanti and Galef, Los Angeles, Calif., February 1978.

[2] Interview with Robert C. Brown, president, R. C. Brown & Co., San Francisco, Calif., February 1978.

[3] John Argenti, *Corporate Collapse: The Cause and Symptoms* (New York: Wiley, 1976), p. 122.

[4] Name withheld due to sensitivity of material, interview, February 1978.

[5] Interview with Robert Di Giorgio, chairman, Di Giorgio Corp., San Francisco, Calif., February 1978.

[6] Interview with Glenn E. Penisten, president, American Microsystems, Santa Clara, Calif., February 1978.

[7] Joel E. Ross and Michael J. Kami, *Corporate Management in Crisis: May the Mighty Fall* (Englewood Cliffs, N.J.: Prentice-Hall, 1973), p. 168.

[8] Ernest Dale, *The Great Organizers* (New York: McGraw-Hill, 1960), p. 113.

[9] "How the Directors Kept Singer Stitched Together," *Fortune,* December 1975, pp. 100, 102, 103, 190.

[10] Penisten, interview, February 1978.

[11] Interview with Thaddeus N. Taube, chairman, Koracorp Industries, San Francisco, Calif., February 1978.

[12] Ross and Kami, *Corporate Management in Crisis*, p. 173.

[13] Frederick R. Kappel, "Vitality in Business Enterprise," McKinsey Foundation for Management Research Lectures series, Graduate School of Business, Columbia University, 1964.

[14] Interview with Roy Woodman, president, International Video Corp., Sunnyvale, Calif., February 1978.

[15] Interview with Richard Madden, chairman, Potlach Corp., San Francisco, Calif., February 1978.

[16] Interview with Jeffrey Chanin, former executive vice president, Daylin Corp., Los Angeles, Calif., February 1978.

[17] Brown, interview, February 1978.

[18] Interview with Robert Sackman, president, Rodal Corp., Palo Alto, Calif., February 1978.

[19] Di Giorgio, interview, February 1978.

[20] Sackman, interview, February 1978.

[21] Brown, interview, February 1978.

6

THE MOST COMMON ERRORS OF BAD MANAGEMENT

Without a strategy the organization is like a ship without a rudder, going around in circles. It's like a tramp; it has no place to go. And incidentally, such platitudes as "make a profit" or "increase market share" do not provide the unified direction we are seeking.[1]

Joel E. Ross and Michael J. Kami

As Chapter 5 illustrates, when management is weak, it is prone to commit errors that lead to decline. The vital errors of omission are: (1) failure to respond adequately to marketplace changes and (2) inadequate control over operations. The errors of commission are: (1) overexpansion and (2) excessive leverage. Lack of response to change in the marketplace and inadequate controls result when management fails to develop a strategy to which the organization can relate.

FAILURE TO KEEP PACE WITH CHANGES IN THE MARKETPLACE

Earlier, I concluded that change, even the accelerating rate of change, does not threaten a well-managed company. In less well managed companies failure to keep pace with change causes about one-quarter of the internal management mistakes. Failure to react properly to change is an outgrowth of the company's historical self-image. Before William Anderson applied shock therapy to NCR operations, a mentality of inertia, based upon a history of corporate success, prevailed. The company's top managers looked backward instead of forward. Myopia and overreach climaxed with the premature launching of the Century series computer, which eventually drained NCR of $150 million.[2]

Roy Woodman of International Video Corporation remembers how myopia about change in the marketplace can lead to inconsistent decisions based on low expectations. His first turnaround assignment was an autonomous beer business which had been losing $1 million a year for three successive years. The root of the problem, Woodman says, is that the senior management assumed that no one in the industry could ever move their share of the market more than 1 percent per year. Believing that "You were beat from the time you started because your goal was just too low," Woodman was able to turn the division around in one year, once he was able to change this basic assumption.[3]

Deceptive reasoning shapes a firm's response to external change more than any other factor. Management's capacity to adapt to the magnitude of the change also influences its failure rate. Companies, like individuals, demonstrate resistance to change. Some have produced goods long after the market for them disappeared. But consumer demand patterns shift, and product life cycles get shorter. Competitors' new products make existing stocks of merchandise obsolete. To keep pace, a company must develop a market intelligence network with internal mechanisms responsive to change.

Companies also get locked into set response patterns. Some sales-oriented companies are so dominated by sales mentality, they are oblivious to other aspects of the company. One such company doggedly pursued sales when its factory was hopelessly obsolete. Modernized production would have increased sales potential and reduced selling prices, while simultaneously increasing profits substantially. In actuality, the more the company sold, the less money it earned.

Production-oriented companies fare no better. They think more profits come from producing goods a little cheaper or a little faster. They suffer from the same kind of nearsightedness and neglect as that of the sales department of their business. Once a company begins moving in a certain direction, momentum builds, accelerating movement in that direction. Thus, when profits are derived largely from technological skills, management strongly supports enlargement of those skills and downgrades other efforts.

Many executives are ill-equipped to make sweeping changes because their years of business experience have locked them into certain work-response patterns. Management consciously applies blinders. Then they adjust peripheral details, leaving fundamental problems unresolved. Since these executives collectively are the company, it's no wonder that so many companies are changing the wrong things. The human preference for the status quo is near universal, but executives cannot let themselves be lulled into believing that changes are final rather than continuous (see Appendix Table D).

LACK OF OPERATING CONTROLS

Jeffrey Chanin, former executive vice president of Daylin Corporation, says an almost universal feature of troubled companies is the absence of a basic control system. "I don't know if the crisis creates the poor financial management, or if the poor financial management creates the crisis. Actually, both contribute."[4]

The survey results indicate that about 30 percent of decline mistakes can be attributed to lack of control, caused by lack of information or failure to make use of existing information. These findings do not contradict Chanin's universality pronouncement because, in an otherwise well run company, weak controls will not by themselves cause decline. In a poorly managed company weak controls are usually just one symptom along with others.

Control information goes beyond financial accounting statements and delves into the heart of any business. Good controls are geared to the knowledge of the business and, where that knowledge is weak (as in overdiversified businesses), controls, by definition, tend to be inadequate. Control information of any type—operational, qualitative, economic, cost accounting, product margin analysis, etc.—should begin with objectives defined by the chief executive of the company. As Glenn Penisten indicates: "The lack of control information does get people in trouble, but I wouldn't lay that at the controller's feet. I lay that right on the president's desk."[5]

A lot of control information is not the solution. If all that information is compiled by people lacking a sensitivity to business, then that information will be ignored. Frank Grisanti explains: "Accountants are trained to treat everybody in a technical fashion. Accountants, for the most part, have very little understanding of what the numbers that they are preparing truly mean."[6]

For that reason and many more, control information responsibility cannot be left to the accountants. It's the domain of management. Top management has got to decide what eight to ten factors they need to run the business. They shouldn't rely on fallout from the accounting system.

Types of Control Information

To do a proper control job, additional information is needed. Five key types of control information are needed. In order of their importance in affecting decline, areas requiring information control are: (1) budgetary control problems, (2) product costing problems, (3) responsibility accounting problems, (4) asset accounting problems, and (5) cash flow forecasting problems. Survey results are shown in Appendix Table E.

Briefly reviewing each type of control is worthwhile.

Budgetary Control. Well-managed companies draw up an annual budget showing sales, revenues, interest payments, wages, rents, overheads, materials, etc. The budget is usually done monthly or in thirteen four-week periods. As the year progresses, the accounting department publishes "actual" figures for managers to compare with "budget." In this way, variances can be identified and corrective action can be taken continuously. In poorly managed companies this system is not used, or is defective, or is entirely absent, and the managers may not have the slightest idea whether the company is doing well or badly. Budgetary control is of particular relevance for holding companies that do not wish to lose control of subsidiaries to which they have delegated wide autonomy.

Product Costing. Many companies do not know production costs for each product; they do not know the effect an increase in sales would have on profits, nor the profit each subsidiary company is making. Unfortunately there are several different costs for each activity—marginal, opportunity, and variable, for example. Very few managers really understand this. Nevertheless, it appears that in companies that fail, either no costing figures are produced, or they are manifestly inadequate, misleading, or inaccurate.

Responsibility Accounting. Responsibility accounting ties cost, revenue, gross profit, or profit-and-loss responsibility to the appropriate manager at every level of the organization. Well-managed companies have flexible systems that build results from the lowest organizational activity to the top. Poorly run companies either totally lack this type of "cut", or merely pay lip service to it. To be effective, responsibility accounting must master the real organization, not the formal or legal one. Poorly run companies have inadequate and, often, outdated shells in comparison to a good responsibility accounting system.

Asset Accounting (Valuation). This is an extremely difficult thing to do, partly because accounting rules are necessarily loose and open to different interpretations, partly because inflation makes "value" so flexible. It appears that incorrect valuation of assets is associated with failure (Itel overvalued the residual value of its computer systems; Rolls-Royce treated R&D as an asset; Penn Central overvalued its property). While failing companies often exaggerate asset values, this is a symptom of failure, not a cause.

Cash Flow Forecasts. These are similar to budgets but show cash flows, bank balances, loans due to mature, profits, tax payments, etc. Again, in some companies these are absent and in others they exist but are not updated. When this is the case, a cash crisis can arrive unheralded.

Don't Ignore Controls

Correcting the key control system weaknesses should go a long way toward giving a company an early-warning capability that will enable it to spot decline problems in their early states. In addition to the formal quantitative approach that relies on past data, a number of qualitative signals are available to a sensitive management. These are outlined in more detail in Chapter 7, "Early-Warning Signals of Decline."

Even companies that have developed good formal controls can get into trouble by ignoring them. In some ways, control information is a passive restraint system. It has to be used at all times to provide protection. Lynn Townsend of Chrysler Corporation believed in tight controls, instituted them, and turned the company around. But then he relaxed on the facts and trusted his "feel" and intuition. Chrysler's downhill slide started all over again after just a year of casualness.[7]

Tight cost and overall controls are among the most important managerial tools. A moment of inattention to this fundamental can erase years of work and progress. Many executives blame management's consciously applied blinders on a lack of good control systems. I've seen this myself in an unnamed private steel company, where margin information indicated an overall deterioration of cost discipline and an imbalance in product lines. Yet management refused to believe a once-profitable line needed the termination button. Management argued about minor cost accounting discrepancies, though they barely impinged on the picture. In addition, they stubbornly refused to believe that inflationary costs were grinding their teeth on the revenue gains.

Robert Brown points out that even when adequate controls are available they are often ignored: "This guy knows that he has got a tremendous amount of debt. He has problems at the bank. But he continues to acquire anyway; he continues to diversify in areas where he has no operating skill . . . he keeps looking for the light that will shine on the business and bring it back to health."[8]

OVEREXPANSION

As Robert Townsend says, "Almost everybody subscribes to the myth that a company has to keep growing. 'If you stand still, you die,' they say."[9] But there's no need to extend last year's graphs, Townsend states. Many companies ignored Townsend's admonition and later found themselves in deep trouble. My experience and research also found that this is true. Overexpansion is the number one mistake management made in declining companies. Overexpansion can be strategic—getting into the wrong businesses—and operational—internal growth problems. Both of these types of problems arise from the misconception that the only road to success is through growth. The growth syndrome has pervaded the American business establishment since World War II. It stirs our competitive spirit, spurs us on to greater effort, and lauds us with material rewards. Growth by itself is a delusion. An enlarging company is not an inherent virtue. By itself, growth is vanity. Misdirected growth, egged on with no recipe and no competent chef, is likely to smolder. Robert Townsend notes George Santayana's truism that fanaticism is redoubling your efforts when you have forgotten your aim. He says, "If your company plateaus, take the time to look around. Get your bearings. You may discover new direction."[10]

Overdiversification

Most problems stem from strategic moves into unfamiliar territory. These are usually problems of overdiversification. Although there are many legitimate reasons for diversifying, frustration, though compelling, is not one of them. Thaddeus Taube, chairman of Koracorp Industries, explains: "Companies will stray from areas they know well when they are frustrated in not being able to expand within their own area of expertise as rapidly as desired. Some are convinced that their area of business has intermediate-term viability problems."[11]

The Pressure to Diversify. Business feels pressured to diversify in order to reduce risk. Peter Drucker indicates the opposite is true.

> The belief that the business that "diversifies" into many areas will do better than the business that concentrates in one area is myth. Complexity is a competitive disadvantage. Complex businesses have repeatedly evidenced their vulnerability to small but highly concentrated single-market or single-technology business. If anything goes wrong, there is a premium on knowing your business.[12]

The business of diversification is, at best, a risky affair. What might seem a good buy today can turn out, for the most unexpected reasons, to be tomorrow's disaster. The more canny "conglomerators" carefully study each acquisition rather than plunging precipitously into every rosy deal. They seek profitable enterprises with a substantial market share, even if a premium price has to be paid. And they are concerned with the buying of real assets, rather than diversification for its own sake.

Diversification for its own sake was apparently the strategy at USM Corporation. When the company's monopoly on shoe-manufacturing equipment was stampeded, USM managers bought companies of dubious value. Most are now written off the books. Under Nicolas Salgo, Bangor Punta paid sky-high prices for an agglomeration of enterprises later sold at a loss.

Overlooking Business Fundamentals. Conglomerates failed because they overlooked management fundamentals. James Ling is an example. Like several other conglomerates who soared and soared, LTV depended less on sound operational management and legitimate growth than it did upon a variety of accounting and financial manipulations. The growing house of cards unjustifiably raised LTV's stock price. Indeed, in the late 1960s the bloom was off the rose. LTV went to the money market once too often and found itself with a debt of $700 million—but what's worse, there was little prospect that earnings could pay the interest on this staggering sum.

William Miller of Textron concluded that the philosophy behind LTV is "Business fundamentals be damned. Jazz up the stock—on with the races!" This attitude delivered hundreds of unlikely combinations in the acquisition binge of the 1960s. Among these were steel, airline, meat packing, and sporting goods companies. Car rental companies acquired by LTV, an electronics and aerospace business, were part of the binge. The strategic blunder of LTV was to adopt "growth at any price" as a philosophy of life. This lack of strategy violates the fundamentals of management. Yet even companies that are not trying to jazz up the stock fall victim to the syndrome. As Frank Grisanti points out:

> A spectrum of companies are managed by the growth-for-growth's-sake principal. They begin with good intentions and a credible plan. They aim for a homogeneous package; with a good return on investment; based upon business fundamentals. Later, frustrated, they rationalize their acquisitions. They build a box thay can't get out of. Hundreds of companies nurtured in a clean, orderly fashion are now conglomerate messes. They wanted to grow faster than opportunity would permit. They got locked into bad deals. They didn't gear up to and then couldn't manage them.[13]

The Singer Corp. is a good example of a company that failed to meet its goal to become homogeneous. The sequels to some of the Singer chairman's acquisitions demonstrate that rhetoric is neither a justification for acquisition nor an assurance of success. Because Singer had always made a bundle on their wooden cabinets, Chairman Donald Kircher expanded into a faintly related business—he bought an Italian refrigerator and washing machine manufacturing plant. Today, the furniture business isn't doing well either, and the mail-order company—which cost Singer more than $25 million—was given away.[14]

As a result of accounting manipulations and ill-conceived diversification moves, the conglomerates of the 1960s fell on hard times. Ransom Cook attributes their decline to a fundamental management flaw. The rules of general and financial management may be the same, but technical and marketing know-how is different. Once a conglomerate buys a company, the original entrepreneur eventually goes out of the picture. New but seasoned management is a must. Unfortunately, it is rare to see new conglomerates capable of attracting the requisite industry know-how.[15]

A company, no matter how cleverly capitalized, is no stronger than its underlying business. Bookkeeping is no substitute for the feel of real cash flow. That's the indicator of a well-managed business. If a company lacks experience of a particular kind, but management insists on rapid growth, it is vulnerable to decline.

Sales Mania

The mania for growth is expressed by a craze to increase sales. A company encountering problems sees growth of sales as the solution. Senior management and directors are all too willing to accept optimistic projections: sell more. Standard methods of accounting can be misconstrued to imply that higher profits automatically follow from higher sales. There is an unawareness that in reality there is no such thing as fixed overhead. Managers, trapped by the concept of marginal-income accounting, bring out additional products. Inadequate product-cost analysis blinds managers to losses thereby incurred.

In fact, shrinking the number of products or product lines is usually the surest route to higher profit and return on investment. Gearing operations to the income statement, rather than the balance sheet, is all too common. Ignoring cash flow and the productivity of capital employed can be fatal. Managers often seek new funds rather than making better use of what they have.

A surprising number of managers, while attempting to build a bigger empire, seek to increase volume and share of the market despite margins and profits. This is to be discouraged. Ambitious and challenging targets should be set in terms of turnover and market share. In the wrong context or in the hands of the wrong managers, seeking increased volume and share of the market can result in a "fool's mate."

GEICO abandoned its original quality business practices to pursue growth. During the four years that David Kreeger was chief executive officer, beginning early 1970, GEICO was digging hard for growth. When competition turned fierce, the company slackened its eligibility stan-

TABLE 6-1
Reasons for Decline Caused by Overexpansion Problems

	Number one rank		*Total weighted ranks*	
	No.	*Percent*	*No.*	*Percent*
Exceeded management resources	36	70	62	52
Exceeded financial resources	10	20	46	48
Exceeded physical resources	4	8	11	8
Other	1	2	2	2
TOTAL	51	100	121	100

Source: Donald B. Bibeault, Survey of eighty-one turnaround company chief executives, April 1978.

dards. GEICO opened its gates to blue-collar workers and teenagers. GEICO soon lost $191 million.[16]

I have indicated that overexpansion can be external or internal. Fundamentally the underlying reason why growth strategies go bad is that the growth created exceeds the tangible resources of the business. If growth doesn't exceed resources, you have simple expansion. Companies have three resources at hand: human, capital, and physical. To exceed any of the three is a prelude to decline. By far the most important reason for decline is the exceeding of human resources (management). Pertinent survey results are illustrated in Table 6-1.

Overexpansion correlates with management saturation. As Thaddeus Taube indicates: "I would say that in a very broad sense companies that get into expansion problems almost always venture into areas that are foreign to the expertise of their management."[17]

Control of Diversity

If top management doesn't understand the business, the company will simply go through day-to-day motions. Top management allocates resources for expansion and must establish a rationale for profit. Though proper controls can counteract complexity to a point, controls are ultimately insufficient tools. Peter Drucker says, "Complexity after a point is indecipherable. When top management must depend totally on abstractions, formal reports, and quantitative data, business has become unmanageable. A business is manageable only if top management judges abstract data against concrete reality."[18]

Businesses large and small need management balance. Top management requires a growth-oriented entrepreneur, a tough control executive, and a good operations executive. Management balance brings balance to the business. If you are on a high-growth path, take Frank Grisanti's advice: "The life cycle of a business is no different than the life cycle of a person. After a growth spurt you must pause to evaluate. When you are obsessed with rapid growth, and fail to pause to reorient, you will eventually collapse of your own weight."[19]

EXCESSIVE LEVERAGE

Overexpansion causes financial problems. The basics of this come down to some fundamental arithmetic that companies often ignore.

When a company expands, it has to inject cash into the business at approximately the rate at which the entire company is expanding. If a company has a capital employed of $1 million and is expanding at 20 percent per annum, then (as a crude oversimplification) it needs $200,000 in cash to finance inventories, debtors, advance payments, capital expenditure, and so on. Now, if that company makes a fairly respectable 20 percent return on capital employed, half will go to taxes and one-quarter to dividends, leaving one-quarter to finance planned expansion. When a company expands at a faster rate than the internally generated cash flow, the company must borrow.

No Margin for Error

Often unhealthy companies underestimate the size and time loss associated with financial loans. Rapid Data's founder and president, E. A. Clive Raymond, blamed his immediate problems on capitalization that was too dry to sustain rapid growth, caused by a fund-raising-by-crisis style, that is, raising money as it was needed.[20] Smaller companies can afford fewer mistakes. So they go down the drain at a faster rate of speed. Larger companies can absorb more mistakes with greater ease. Still, they are not immune to the problems of overexpansion. LTV's staggering debt load accelerated its decline. Massey-Ferguson Ltd. fell victim to overexpansion and at the worst time. Massey-Ferguson pegged its rapid growth on aggressive expansion in the Third World. It shouldn't have. Interest charges in 1977 were $198.5 million compared to $48 million in 1973. Massey-Ferguson's entire industrial and contruction machinery operation generated losses of $50 million in 1977 alone.[21] By 1980, continued losses had put Massey-Ferguson on the knife's edge, teetering toward potential financial reorganization.

Overexpansion beyond a company's financial resources leads to excessive leverage. It is fundamental that loans carry a fixed interest rate. The rate does not depend upon how well or badly the company is doing. Equity dividends do. Also, loans are usually ranked before equity in a bankruptcy proceeding. Loans are normally a much cheaper source of capital than equity. The lender's interest and capital are both less at risk than the shareholder's dividend and equity. So the well-managed company funds its business with loans rather than equity. There is a prudent limit, different for each business, beyond which the risks of high leveraging outrun the advantages. The optimum point is determined by a number of factors, including the legally binding terms of any deeds relating to debentures. Another determinant is the stability of the company's earnings.

High leverage is a warning signal that no one should ignore. Let us also remember that providing your bankers have not lost confidence in you, they are only too pleased to let you leverage your company to the rooftops. Poorly managed companies tend to leverage their equity beyond the prudent level. If there is a negative turn in the cycle, or if one of the pieces of a company cannot service its debt, a chain of events leading to demise is started.

The Coup de Grace

An alert management can arrest this chain of events. An incompetent manager often delivers a coup de grace to an overleveraged company by starting a *big project*. A big project could be a merger, diversification program, expansion program, the launching of a major new product or introduction of a new service, a research program, bulk purchase of materials, etc.—any undertaking or obligation that is large compared with the resources of the company.

There is wide agreement that big project costs and times are frequently underestimated or revenues overestimated. This miscalculation often leads to disaster. Companies that make nominal mistakes do not go bust. Companies run by one-man rulers are much more likely than other companies to adopt grandiose schemes. Boise Cascade is a classic case of overexpansion and overleveraging. Robert Brown summarizes:

> Boise Cascade, a timber company, entered the paper business and did extremely well for a time. They attracted top flight people: Harvard Business School grads. . . . Then they diversified. That decision led them into a lot of areas in which they had no skill. They ran out of money trying to finance all the real estate installment sales. They bought the old American Foreign Power as a cash source. That plan failed. As a result, Boise was completely cash dry. To turn Boise around, the board fired the president, the financial vice president and a lot of the operating V.P.s. Then they brought in one big strong guy who sat up on top of it and just started whacking off the pieces and started solving the problems.[22]

REFERENCES

[1]Joel E. Ross and Michael J. Kami, *Corporate Management in Crisis: Why the Mighty Fall* (Englewood Cliffs, N.J.: Prentice-Hall, 1973), p. 132.

[2]Linda Grant Martin, "What Happened at NCR after the Boss Declared Martial Law," *Fortune*, September 1975, p. 102.

[3]Interview with Roy Woodman, president, International Video Corp., Sunnyvale, Calif., February 1978.

[4]Interview with Jeffrey Chanin, former executive vice president, Daylin Corp., Los Angeles, Calif., February 1978.

[5]Interview with Glenn E. Penisten, president, American Microsystems, Santa Clara, Calif., February 1978.

[6]Interview with Frank A. Grisanti, president, Grisanti and Galef, Los Angeles, Calif., February 1978.

[7]Ross and Kami, *Corporate Management in Crisis*, p. 93.

[8]Interview with Robert C. Brown, president, R. C. Brown & Co., San Francisco, Calif., February 1978.

[9]Robert Townsend, *Up the organization: How to Stop the Organization from Stifling People and Strangling Profits* (Greenwich, Conn.: Fawcett Publications, 1970), p. 196.

[10]Ibid, p. 197.

[11]Interview with Thaddeus N. Taube, chairman, Koracorp Industries, San Francisco, Calif., February 1978.

[12]Peter F. Drucker, *Management: Tasks, Responsibilities, Practices* (New York: Harper & Row, 1974), p. 680.

[13]Grisanti, interview, February 1978.

[14]"How the Directors Kept Singer Stitched Together," *Fortune*, December 1975, p. 103.

[15]Interview with Ransom Cook, chairman and president (retired), Wells Fargo Bank, San Francisco, Calif., February 1978.

[16]Carol J. Loomis, "An Accident Report on GEICO," *Fortune*, June 1976, p. 127.

[17]Taube, interview, February 1978.

[18]Drucker, *Management*, p. 681.

[19]Grisanti, interview, February 1978.

[20]"The Miscalculations at Rapid Data," *Business Week*, Feb. 9, 1974, p. 26.

[21]"Untimely Expansions Hurt Massey-Ferguson," *Business Week*, Mar. 6, 1978, p. 34.

[22] Brown, interview, February 1978.

7
EARLY-WARNING SIGNALS OF DECLINE

Most ailing organizations have developed a functional blindness to their own defects. They are not suffering because they cannot solve their problems but because they cannot see their problems.[1]

John W. Gardner

FUNCTIONAL BLINDERS

Despite John Gardner's statement, it is genuinely difficult to discern and diagnose company problems before they threaten the progress or even the very existance of an enterprise. For the most part, business warning signals don't jump up and demand to be heeded; they have to be sought out. That can be a tough job. Problems are rarely clear enough to be acted upon when they are first discovered. Early problem signals are, almost by definition, weak signals. Often these weak surface manifestations are, at best, symptoms, rather than causes, and often the least revealing ones. Depending on which side of the "looking glass" we are on, symptoms may be picked up early or not really seen until the last desperate days of a failing enterprise. If you are on the outside looking in, your task of discerning trouble is all the more difficult. In the last few months before collapse, the number and severity of the symptoms rapidly increase. Even at this late stage, however, top management is often protesting loudly that all is well, that the embarrassment is temporary or nonexistent.

A great number of warning signals have been presented to me over the years in my discussions with executives. Everybody has his pet signal. There is, however, a relatively high convergence of opinion on signals if we properly sift out the various roles the signals play. Certain signals are good for certain applications. Executives generally agree that early-warning signals of decline are ignored or not acted upon. As I mentioned earlier, a stagnating or declining company needs to be shocked into constructive action. People almost always wait until there is a crisis of some kind before they take constructive action. The principal problem is human nature (management). My survey results indicate that in eight out of ten cases early-warning signals were ignored (see Appendix Table F).

TYPES OF WARNING SIGNALS

There are three basic categories of signals. The first is mathematical forecasting methods used to red-flag potential bankruptcies. Mathematical forecasting methods deal in financial measurements for the overall firm, although they can be applied to larger divisions within a firm. These methods are fairly reliable in predicting bankruptcy. They are also predictors of decline because today many companies are kept alive by artificial means. Government aid (in the form of direct grants or life-supporting contracts), for example, keeps many companies afloat during tough years.

Todd Shipyards is a case in point. The firm experienced a financial crisis in 1974, when profit losses amounted to $43 million on sales of only $146 million. As a result, working capital almost ran out. But Uncle Sam stepped in: Todd got a bank loan that was 90 percent guaranteed by the federal government to replenish its diminishing working capital.

The second category of signals—adverse trend signals—is more subjective and less mathematically precise; it applies equally well to a total company or separate divisions of a multidivision company. Adverse trend signals cover a variety of functions, but are principally market-oriented. There are no absolute good or bad values for these measures, since they can vary from industry to industry and even among companies within an industry. It is the relative trend of these factors and their comparison to industry numbers that is significant.

The third category of signals is even more subjective and a great deal more behavioral. These signals center on observation and communication within an organization. Seasoned turnaround executives attest to the value of this kind of signal in multidivision companies. I call these signals adverse behavioral signals.

MATHEMATICAL FORECASTING SIGNALS

These methods are advanced developments of earlier methods using financial ratios. The problem with the earlier methods is that they usually centered on traditional one-variable-at-a-time, or univariate, approaches. Although some authors (e.g., Beaver[2]) claimed that certain measures were quite accurate, there was no satisfactory discrimination between bankrupt and nonbankrupt firms.

The Z-Score Method

Two more recent developments in the last few years have been adequately tested to be of some practical value. The first centers on the *Z score,* or bankruptcy rating.[3] Developed by Edward I. Altman of the Graduate school of Business of New York University, the Z score is designed to forecast failure in the short term—that is, up to two years.

There are two formulas: one for manufacturing companies, which uses five ratios of management ability and financial strength to arrive at a Z score; the other for railroads, which uses seven ratios. Altman's study indicates that companies with a Z score lower than 1.81 have a high probability of failure within two years. Any company with a Z score higher than 3.00, on the other hand, has a low probability of bankruptcy. An exclusive study done for *Dun's Review* in 1975 (see Appendix Tables H and I) shows the fourteen weakest and fourteen strongest U.S. manufacturing companies ranked according to the Z score.

How well do these formulas actually work in predicting corporate failure? Examining the financial statements of companies that had already gone bankrupt, Altman's formula forecast failure up to two years ahead in better than eight out of ten cases. The accuracy of the model falls off consistently the farther ahead the forecast is made, to the point at which—at the fifth year—it is accurate in only one out of three cases (see Appendix Table G).

From the standpoint of spotting trouble, Altman's Z score appears to have a very high batting average. We have only to examine our list of "worst performers" from 1975—i.e., Memorex, Sanders Associates, Todd Shipyards, and Mohawk Data Sciences—and apply the score.

Note, however, that this opinion differs markedly from the conclusions drawn by Schendel, Patton, and Riggs in their study of turnaround companies.[4] I must conclude, however, that Schendel et al. did not use the total Z-score screen used by *Dun's Review. Dun's* identified known troubled companies. Schendel's observation of ratio change patterns might be a case of viewing the trees but failing to see the forest.

Once derived, Altman's formula is relatively easy to work with. To identify this indicator, Altman compared statistics for thirty-three firms (with assets between $0.7 and $25.9 million) which had filed bankruptcy petitions with thirty-three firms (paired sample on stratified random basis) which were "nonbankrupt." Five ratios turned out to be really important for bankruptcy prediction. The equation for manufacturing companies that gave the best results was this one:

$$Z = 1.2X_1 + 1.4X_2 + 3.3X_3 + 0.6X_4 + 1.0X_5$$

The five ratios are as follows.

X_1 Is Working Capital/Total Assets. To calculate $0.012X_1$ then, you simply take the difference between current assets and current liabilities, divide by the total book value of the company, and multiply by 0.012. That is the first term in the equation. It is worth noting that Altman did test two other liquidity ratios (the "current" ratio and the "quick" ratio), but working capital/total assets proved best.

X_2 Is Retained Earnings/Total Assets. Retained earnings is the sum of profits that the company has retained over its lifetime. The shorter the life, the less fat it will have accumulated and, probably, the lower this ratio. It may seem unfair that the equation will give a young company a weaker Z score; but, as we have seen, most bankruptcies are of young companies.

X_3 Is Earnings before Interest and Taxes/Total Assets. It is simply our old friend "return on capital employed," which is a measure of the pretax profits earned on all capital employed regardless of whether it is ordinary, preferred, a loan, or whatever.

X_4 Is Market Value of Equity/Book Value of Total Debt. Here, for the first time, we have a nonaccounting measure—the stock market capitalization. All the other ratios in Altman's equation are based on book values. Thus a company with 10 million ordinary shares standing at $5 and 1 million preferred shares at $4 will have a market value of $54 million. To compute here you combine long-term and current debts.

X_5 Is Sales/Total Assets. This is that very common ratio of capital to turnover, used by managers for years past.

So there is the equation. You work out the five ratios for your company, multiply each by its own constant, tally them, and arrive at Z. If Z is less than 1.8, you are almost certain to go bust; if it is more than 3.0, you almost certainly will not.[5] Notice that the equation demands that all ratios be used together and that the weighting given to each be maintained by the right constant.

Gambler's Ruin Prediction of Bankruptcy

The second method that has found its way into practical use is the Gambler's Ruin Prediction of Bankruptcy. This formula is designed to predict five years in advance failure for both manufacturing and retailing companies. It was advanced by management consultant Jarrod Wilcox of the Boston Consulting Group when he was an assistant professor at MIT's Sloan School of Business. With this method, investors compute the probability of bankruptcy by using calculations of a corporation's estimated "liquidation" value and the rate of change in this liquidation value.

The result depends on the company's previous ability to fund dividends and capital expenditures and hold on to or increase its financial resources. The formula produces a percentage result similar to a weather forecast probability percentage. It estimates the company's chance to stay afloat, providing its present management policies and the nature of its business stay the same. As any blackjack gambler could tell you, in a high stakes game the underlying principle is that the odds are against a player with a small pile of chips. He may be out of the game before he can win.

To compute it, the investor first calculates a company's liquidation value. All current liabilities and long-term debt are subtracted from its assets (valuing cash and marketable securities at market; valuing inventories, accounts receivable, and prepaid expenses at 70 percent of the balance sheet figures; and valuing the remaining assets at 50 percent of the balance sheet figures). Then the investor determines how much the liquidation value changed from the previous year by subtracting from earnings, after special items, all dividends and 50 percent of the year's capital expenditures and depreciation; then subtracting 30 percent of the increase in inventories and accounts receivable since last year.

According to the formula, clothing maker Botany Industries could have liquidated and realized cash five years before it filed bankruptcy papers in 1962. But one year later its liquidation value had dropped to zero. And in 1969 further reverses had brought the liquidation value down to a negative number. Considerably weakened, Botany might still have come through in a good year; unfortunately, 1970 was one of the worst for almost every company. "When a company's 'liquidation' value drops to negative," says Wilcox, "it needs to see a big upswing immediately to pull through at all."[6] Also testing against companies that had already gone bankrupt, Wilcox's formula predicted bankruptcy five years beforehand in 76 percent of the cases. When applied to companies one year prior to bankruptcy filing, its rate of success was 96 percent.

Remember, these formulas depend on data from companies' own financial statements. So the formulas may not be able to predict bankruptcy in cases where the financial statements incorporate gross misstatements. "I completely failed in predicting failure on Westec," Wilcox admits, "because the numbers were misstated."[7]

Auditors' "Going Concern" Opinions

It probably comes as no surprise, but those people who depend on auditors' opinions to point out impending doom and decline are living in a fool's paradise. In a joint article written by Edward Altman and Thomas

P. McGough, CPA auditors' flesh-and-blood methods were compared to the more antiseptic quantitative approaches originally worked out by Altman. The Z-score method won hands down.[8]

In all fairness, I have to point out that the bankruptcy model and the auditors' report have different, but analogous, functions. The model was developed to predict bankruptcy. The auditor does not attempt any such prediction. An unqualified opinion is not a guarantee that a company will continue as a going concern, and a qualified opinion—made because of going-concern problems—is not a prediction of liquidation. An opinion expressing doubts concerning a company's ability to continue as a going concern is based on the uncertainty of the fairness of presentation of the financial statements. It would be possible for financial statements based upon historical cost to be fairly presented when a company were facing bankruptcy if the carrying value of the assets of that company represented the realizable value of those assets. In any case, the Z-score method was consistently twice as accurate as auditors' opinions in predicting going-concern problems.

ADVERSE TREND SIGNALS

Mathematical approaches are based upon published information that in turn is dependent upon the proper statement of financial results by management. Interim statements, in particular, are prone to misstatement. Another major handicap of mathematical approaches is that they depend on relatively old information. This time lag may pose no great problem for outsiders, but it is not sufficient for internal management. Internal management can circumvent some of these problems by using internal data, but the quantitative approaches cannot pinpoint the dynamic reality of ongoing problems at an early stage. Other early-warning signals are definitely needed.

Declining Margins

Both my in-depth interviews and the survey questionnaire addressed the problem of adverse trend signals from a practical sense. There is a fair degree of agreement about the adverse trend signals in a declining company. Robert Brown's view was representative: "The first tip-off on the overall company is when growth of sales is not translated into profits. Declining margins are the first key. The second key is price incompatibility in the market, with loss of market share. The minute you see both, that's a company that is headed for trouble."[9]

There could, however, be a planned decline in margins, depending on product sales, mix factors, or other known variables. But trouble is

TABLE 7-1
Adverse Trend Signals Ranked By Importance

	Ranked first		*Weighted rank*	
Early-warning signal	*Number*	*Percent*	*Number*	*Percent*
Declining margins	22	32	40	25
Declining market share	16	25	29	18
Debt increasing rapidly	12	19	33	21
Working capital declining	5	8	25	16
Management turnover	4	6	16	10
Other (specified)	6	9	17	10
TOTAL	65	100	160	100

Source: Donald B. Bibeault, survey of eighty-one turnaround company chief executives, April 1978.

brewing when a company has deteriorating margins that don't meet plan. Volume can fall off, but you can still hold your profits with good cost control. In my survey of executive opinions, declining margins came out as the strongest adverse trend signal. Summary results are shown in Table 7-1.

Frank Grisanti has strong reservations about the effectiveness of margins in smaller, growing companies. He says margins start deterioriating in a company long before the record tells it. He blames accounting treatment for this. "Accounting treatment can hide deteriorating margins for a long, long time. It all depends on how the accountants capitalize cost. A truer early-warning signal system is the proliferation of products. If . . . a company has an infinite variation of the same model, . . . or is all things to all people, you know you have a breeding ground for trouble. . . . You know your inventory is loaded with crap, even though the balance sheet doesn't show it. You could have inventory turning four times, looking perfectly good. . . . but still have 80 percent of that inventory gathering dust. Although the balance sheet looks good, the seeds are there and some day trouble will sprout."[10]

Declining Market Share

The second most important early-warning signal that came up was declining market share. John Harris, of Booz Allen & Hamilton in New York, says: "Declining market share must be carefully observed. Has market share been falling or staying flat? That's the critical sign, because it monitors the foundation of the business."[11]

Rapidly Increasing Debt

It's almost axiomatic that rapidly increasing debt is a tip-off. Robert Brown says: "On an internal basis, when you begin to see a company stretching the limits of its cash flow, when it must have certain levels of performance to stay liquid, it's in trouble. It has no room for error, and generally you could just look at a guy's balance sheet and tell that right off."[12] Debt has to be looked at on both an absolute and a relative basis. As credit rises, banks require shorter-term loans; the firm has clearly reached its comfortable debt level. This factor is tied in with declining working capital. As we saw previously in Altman's Z-score method, a declining working capital/total assets ratio is a warning signal.

Other Financial Red Flags

Lenders often look at other financial red flags in order to be tipped off to impending trouble. These signals cannot be classified as early-warning signals, however. K. D. Martin, vice president of the Bank of America, has developed a list of red flags.[13] They are shown in Appendix Table J.

Another tip-off is the rapid turnover of people. Generally, the problem is turnover in the middle ranks. John Thompson and Frank Grisanti agree that one of the earliest warning signals is a rapid turnover in middle ranks and subsequent labor unrest.

In my opinion, the earliest warning signal of decline is the rate of reinvestment. Track investment schedule on plant, equipment, and maintenance. A "constant dollar" decline is a bad sign. A bad trend doesn't occur overnight; a real problem will span years as a trend.

ADVERSE BEHAVIORAL SIGNALS

The most important adverse behavioral signal is poor communications. While most of the adverse trend signals can be measured, poor communication can not. Its only gauge is the feel of the people involved. The communication problem is an early-warning signal most appropriate for monitoring divisions of a multidivision company. It is less effective as an early-warning signal for the overall company; many troubled companies voice optimistic ballyhoo until the day they close their doors. Bad communication as a warning may not come early at the divisional level; it can crop up just before the manure hits the fan.

A Good Early-Warning Signal

Good communication, not its opposite, is the best early-warning signal. Jeffrey Chanin, formerly of Daylin Corporation, says the key to good communication in a corporation is a three-way information system between division, operating, and staff people. The operating people are the backbone of the system. They answer the phones and, thereby, have the opportunity to spot trouble first. A sign of poor communication is no response to telephone calls. Good communication means operating people are:

> . . . up here or on the phone telling you what is going on. . . . Good communication stops during a crisis situation if operating people perceive that (a) the messenger who is delivering bad news will be harmed, which happens in many companies, or (b) even more common, that they're not going to be listened to. Fearing they will incur the disfavor of their superiors for neither saying nor doing anything, they try to do it themselves. Corporate is left in the dark, and I blame that on corporate.[14]

Top management must rely on feel and on the operating people—not on abstract reports alone. Robert Brown says:

> When operating people quit telling you problems you have a big coverup. You know the operating people are trying to solve the problems themselves. That's when you're dead. Even if the business has good controls it's difficult for the guy on top to understand what tertiary management is doing.[15]

Good communication doesn't just happen. It has to be cultivated, informally organized. According to Jeffrey Chanin:

> You don't create heroes out of operating people unless you make it more important for them to tell you bad news than good news. Some one at corporate level must be open to this kind of discussion. If an operating person senses something is not going well and he wants to talk to somebody off the record, then the second or third level person in the company must have an open-door policy. He acts as a sounding board so operating people can get it off their chests. Likewise, a chief financial officer should have . . . direct lines of communication to the division controllers. The controllers see the numbers first. If they don't like what they see, they have a direct information wire to the financial officer. If the officer gets on the line, he'll get current adverse information.[16]

Robert Sackman feels that good communication is a key management responsibility:

> I think that a close contact with your key managers and their feeling of confidence in talking to you, their ability to speak to you frankly, is

> important. In fact, I always used to say, "Yes, I like to hear the nice things, but first I want to know all the things that are bad in your estimation. Don't spare me, and let me know what you're doing about it."[17]

If the experts are correct, nonfinancial symptoms of decline not only characterize failing companies but nonfailing companies as well. This conclusion is based on confirmatory evidence from case studies.

Is Low Morale a Signal?

Admittedly, nonfinancial symptoms are seen less in companies that are highly successful. Low morale is symptomatic of a company that is neither successful nor failing. Surprisingly, low morale can exist in a relatively successful company; even more surprising is that in a company close to failure, morale can be high. These arguments apply to nearly all the nonfinancial symptoms discussed here, but I believe that, in spite of this, they do have some confirmatory value in predicting failure.

Particularly in small companies, a visit to the top managers is useful. A visitor can see obvious symptoms of decline, such as dingy offices, poor maintenance, and a general air of financial stringency. As Roy Woodman says:

> When a small company is experiencing low morale, if your eyes are open and your other senses alert, you can smell problems as you walk through the door. If you can't make a joke, can't talk to the girl at the switchboard, something is wrong. And then you become aware that the place is a little dirty and that people aren't pleasant. But if the reverse is true, i.e. someone smiles and says "hi" when you go by things are probably not too bad. It is another story in bigger companies. A bad division of a big company probably still has money to spend to make things look good for PR. The office climate is probably still disguising what might be a bad morale problem. A good turnaround person develops a "sixth sense" about these situations.[18]

Problems are rarely clear enough to be acted upon when they are first discovered. The surface manifestations are, at best, symptoms, and often the least revealing ones. Good problem definition, to be effective, must be directed toward the underlying problem, not a superficial symptom. For example, management may see excessive paperwork as a disease when actually it is symptomatic of an insecure organization. The real problem may be a loss of communication or control. One creative way of getting a feel for your company is to call your company and pretend you are a customer asking for help. You'll run into some real horror shows. Then try calling yourself up and see what indignities you have built into your own defenses.

As a company gets close to the point of failure, a lot of other signals surface, but these are final warning signals. Customers will note a decline in quality or service, price cuts, and the firm's tightening credit policies. Suppliers will notice that the firm is running down stocks of components or materials, or reducing the size of orders, or taking longer to pay. Employees will observe a greater resistance to pay increases, cuts in overtime, and generally less generous treatment; delays in capital expenditure authorizations; rising inventory; outdated product; declining market share; a growing volume of customer complaints; and an increasing desperation among top and, middle management.

All these people will see that something unusual is happening. Though they will marvel and wonder at it, they will keep their peace. For, while they each hold a part of the jigsaw, none of them, except the chief executive, can see the whole puzzle. The one possible exception is the outside directors, who, having had an excellent boardroom luncheon, are sound asleep. All the signs are there. The trouble is, so few people recognize them for what they are.

REFERENCES

[1]John W. Gardner, "How to Prevent Organizational Dry Rot," *Harper's Magazine*, October 1965, p. 24.

[2]W. Beaver, "Financial Ratios as Predictors of Failures," Supplement to *The Journal of Accounting Research*, January 1967, pp. 71–111.

[3]Edward I. Altman, "Financial Ratios, Discriminant Analysis and the Prediction of Corporate Bankruptcy," *Journal of Finance*, September 1968. The model is explained in more detail in Edward I. Altman, *Corporate Bankruptcy in America* (Lexington, Mass.: Heath Lexington, 1971), Chapter 3.

[4]Dan Schendel, Richard Patton, and James Riggs, *Corporate Turnaround Strategies* (West Lafayette, Indiana: Krannert Graduate School of Industrial Administration, Purdue University, Paper No. 486, March 1975), p. 30.

[5]Altman, *Corporate Bankruptcy in America*, Chapter 3.

[6]Jarrod Wilcox, *Review of Corporate Bankruptcy in America*, by Edward I. Altman, in *Journal of Accountancy*, February 1973, pp. 92–93.

[7]*Ibid.*, p. 64.

[8]Edward I. Altman and Thomas P. McGough, "Evaluation of a Firm as a Going Concern," *The Journal of Accounting*, December 1974, p. 53.

[9]Interview with Robert C. Brown, president, R. C. Brown and Co., San Francisco, Calif., February 1978.

[10]Interview with Frank A. Grisanti, president, Grisanti and Galef, Los Angeles, Calif., February 1978.

[11]John Harris, "Major Reason Companies Get into Trouble," *Boardroom's Business Secrets*, New York Boardroom Reports, Inc., 1977, p. 4.

[12]Brown, interview, February 1978.

[13]K. D. Martin, "Problem Loan Signals and Follow Up," *Journal of Commercial Bank Lending*, September 1973, pp. 38–44.

[14]Interview with Jeffrey Chanin, former executive vice president, Daylin Corp., Los Angeles, Calif., Febuary 1978.

[15]Brown, interview, February 1978.

[16]Chanin, personal interview.

[17]Interview with Robert Sackman, president, Rodal Corp., Palo Alto, Calif., February 1978.

[18]Interview with Roy Woodman, president, International Video Corp., Sunnyvale, Calif., February 1978.

8
THE MOMENT OF TRUTH FOR MANAGEMENT

It was the worst of times. After eighty-five years of uninterrupted success, NCR had arrived at its moment of truth . . . it was being said both privately and publicly that NCR was on its last legs.[1]

William S. Anderson,
Chairman, NCR Corporation

A crisis point is indeed the moment of truth for many companies. A central question is why some companies face this moment of truth and respond successfully to its challenges while others are doomed to reorganization and eventual bankruptcy. Excuses of uncontrollable external factors cannot be accepted in a high percentage of cases. A changing economy, increasing competitive pressures, changing consumer tastes, government legislation, and a host of other external challenges are part of doing business and running a company. Most problems are caused by top management, but top management often will not admit its errors.

There is a school of thought (almost completely inhabited by managements who have been removed from power) that some turnaround efforts can rob a company of its brightest opportunities. A turnaround can be hard to see, and the old management usually protests mightily that they were on the verge of a rosy future. As Richard Madden, chairman of Potlatch Corporation, points out, some of these protests have limited validity:

> The old chief executive officer, if he had had proper financial support, may have been very close to major breakthroughs in five new technologies, and he might have just been on the verge of making a $100 million business over the next decade into a $30 billion business that was making 20 percent profit after tax. But he did not have the financial backing to do so? So the new man comes in. What does he do? Very simple: He looks and says, "I am sorry, the bank will give so much money. I have five projects; I can only do one of them, so close the other four down. I am a turnaround manager. I'm a great hero." Was that a turnaround situation?[2]

I feel that it was a legitimate turnaround because, at a certain point, the old president had so endangered the company's existence that the risk of death was too great to justify the future potential of the projects. The causes of decline are set into motion long before their outward manifestation. Corporations can be declining when the performance record shows they are going up. As Frank Grisanti says:

> You can have an increase in sales and an increase in earnings while your guts are rotting. Sales are going up because you bought them with low prices. You have no real gross margins. The profits are there because you capitalize the losses and create false gross margins. The quality of earnings is very hard to discern from statements, but eventually the balance sheet can no longer hide reality, and it all catches up.[3]

THE OSTRICH APPROACH

In many cases I've seen, prior management went about their business blissfully unaware of the gathering storm until it was too late. A stagnating or declining company seems to first need a deepened threat or shock to spur it to action. Steadily poor performace, so long as it does not develop a crisis, seems to be tolerated. This seems to occur most frequently in privately held companies where there is no public, or its representatives, to answer to. The principal reason for this blindness centers on the top man's ego. An entrepreneur who developed a market often cannot bring himself to withdraw from it.

Often the old management is so close to the problem and so enmeshed in detail that their overall vision is clouded. In this case they overlook the real problems, as well as opportunities that could have brought success. Even when trouble is brewing, many a businessman is so busy doing the things he likes to do that he has no time for the things he should do. Calling on the trade when internal difficulties need to be straightened out is a direct route to oblivion.

When a company is not doing well, its executives may refuse to admit it and may put forth impressive arguments to justify their poor showing. A clever executive may even make it appear that he alone can turn the tide of events and may convince everyone, including himself, that if it weren't for him, things would be much worse. Dodging the truth can go on for some time. Consider the Penn Central Railroad, whose complex accounting information was digested, consolidated, and disguised to such an extent that even sophisticated investors couldn't determine the seriousness of the company's financial crisis. Such delaying tactics forestall any attempt to face the facts.

Convincing management and the board to take action when there is a general realization that a problem exists can be hard. John Byers, who spent many years in the problem loans department of Wells Fargo Bank, has had to live with many of these frustrations: "It's amazing how difficult it is to convince either management or its board that something has to be done. It's very rare that a company will pick up on its own initiative and recognize the facts. It all ends when the bank account is zero, when the trade is 50 percent on COD, and when their last trip to the investment banking house lasted fifteen minutes.[4]

FIGHTING REALITY

The crisis that brings a firm to its moment of truth can take different forms, depending on the size of the firm. In smaller firms there is, in general, no crisis until severe losses threaten the firm. This usually exhibits itself as a liquidity crisis. Management usually is unwilling to acknowledge the problem until they run out of money. The first time this happens to a firm, financial institutions are willing to support the company as a practical matter. The second time they balk, and the third time they say "No way."

In medium-size and larger companies, the "day of reckoning" can be delayed by using the balance sheet as a buffer. Inventory can bury excess costs, and accounts receivable can cover bad debts, which will later be called notes receivable. At some point in time, after the operating cash flow becomes negative, the balance sheet can no longer absorb it, and even larger companies run into a liquidity crisis. In larger companies the "moment of truth" is not always clearly defined. Arcata National, a thriving redwood business, avoided a liquidity crisis and gave the new management plenty of time to plan a comeback. In very large companies, made up of a series of large divisions, turnarounds can be even fuzzier. Sometimes, the companies can delay crisis by eating off the stockholders' net worth. They can start liquidating assets or underwriting the losses that they are burying, but soon they run out of net worth, and then they are in big trouble. In the largest firms, whose borrowing capacity is less limited, the firm finally reaches its moment of truth.

The fact that the balance sheet can no longer act as a buffer to absorb poor performance pushes the management of a company toward reality. They can no longer get credit from their suppliers and can't borrow any more from their banks. They've already got their machinery and fixed assets in hock. They've plain run out of credit! Now they are in a total liquidating crisis, and it's unnecessary, because the signals were there a year or two years prior. It was happening all along, but no one was really looking.

One of the closest brushes with bankruptcy of a major company was Pan American Airlines in 1974. In October 1974, the huge international airline had only enough cash to last three weeks. There was no assurance that its banks, led by Citibank, would lend it enough money to get through the normal winter traffic slump, let alone the indeterminate period of soaring fuel prices and worldwide recession that lay ahead. Chairman William T. Seawell and his top officers met with a special bankruptcy law firm away from Pan Am's offices. No one there wanted to believe that the company was going under, but they thought they had best be prepared for the worst. It was a gathering that no one present is apt to forget. The banks did come to Pan Am's aid, and it was able to stave off disaster.

For Pan American, Saturday, October 19, 1974, was definitely its moment of truth, because it was what could have been only months away from piecemeal sale on the courthouse steps.

REALITY ARRIVES

Eventually, a company that is sliding downhill has to admit to the seriousness of the situation. The time is then at hand when the leaders begin seeking answers to their problems and can no longer be satisfied with excuses. This is the critical time, for what they do and how they do it will determine whether they survive. Most managers are not prepared to face the many negative forces at work when the company reaches its crisis point. As Frank Grisanti describes it:

> Now you've got a very difficult environment. You've got trade creditors on your back, you are failing to deliver to your customers, the employees are all upset because they know that you are in trouble. And they are starting to abandon ship. The structure is starting to fall apart. There is an environment of pressure and shortage that most people don't want to cope with. When they get dumped into the crisis pressure cooker, they don't know what the hell to do.[5]

For many companies, the consequences have been acutely traumatic. Board meetings become angry battlegrounds where Draconian resolutions are proposed. Financial institutions that only yesterday were pressing additional funds on the company mutter darkly about getting guarantees on everything, or perhaps even calling their existing loans. On Wall Street, the price of the company's stock plummets. Options are often driven "underwater"—unfairly penalizing other executives who may have made superb contributions in unaffected areas of the company. And everywhere morale sags, while the company gropes for a way out of the crisis.

The process of self-extrication is inevitably painful, but it seldom needs to be as agonizing as many companies make it. Admittedly, calm in the midst of crisis is easier to preach than to practice. Yet often a company's losses—financial, strategic, and psychological—can be substantially reduced if management takes a systematic and rational approach to the problem. The blame for decline can be laid on management's desk in all but a few cases. But if decline is the agony of defeat for management, then management can also claim credit for the thrill of victory. The achievement of a successful turnaround is mostly a victory of management performance. It is also a testament to the foresight of directors, the courage of employees, and the loyalty of customers and creditors.

REFERENCES

[1]William S. Anderson, "The Turnaround at NCR Corporation," address at Beta Gamma Sigma Dinner, Wright State University, Apr. 19, 1976, p. 5.

[2]Interview with Richard Madden, chairman, Potlatch Corp., San Francisco, Calif., February 1978.

[3]Interview with Frank A. Grisanti, president, Grisanti & Galef, Los Angeles, Calif., February 1978.

[4]Interview with John Byers, vice president, Wells Fargo Bank, San Francisco, Calif., May 1978.

[5]Grisanti, interview, February 1978.

PART TWO

THE BASICS OF CORPORATE TURNAROUND MANAGEMENT

It must be remembered that there is nothing more difficult to plan, more doubtful of success, nor more dangerous to manage than the creation of a new system. For the initiator has the enmity of all who would profit by the preservation of the old institutions and merely lukewarm defenders in those who would gain by the new ones. The hesitation of the latter arises in part from the fear of their adversaries, who have the laws on their side, and in part from the general skepticism of mankind which does not really believe in an innovation until experience proves its value.

Niccolò Machiavelli, *The Prince*

9
THE CORPORATE TURNAROUND PERSPECTIVE

In early 1974, when I arrived at Memorex, there was no question but that the company was in a crisis situation. The Chinese character for the word "crisis" has two meanings. One of them indicates danger—the other one indicates opportunity. The press had adequately pointed out many of the dangers. However, the opportunities were also substantial.[1]

Robert C. Wilson,
President and
Chairman (retired),
Memorex Corporation

THE PERSPECTIVE

By a corporate turnaround I mean a substantial and sustained positive change in the performance of a business. In most cases a turnaround follows several years of declining profitability. In its most severe form, this decline usually culminates in substantial losses that threaten the financial viability of the enterprise. In its mildest form, declining performance may not threaten the financial viability of the firm, but it has serious negative impacts on market competitiveness, customer confidence, and employee morale. Why and how some firms break out of stagnating or declining performance and others do not is the primary subject of this book.

In this chapter and the chapters to follow, I will be describing the turnaround from many perspectives. These will include quantitative descriptions, types of turnarounds, stages in a turnaround, key factors, and so on. I must state emphatically that this part of the book is not exclusively the "how to" part, if indeed the how to can ever be explained. In Parts 3 and 4, I will define various approaches to implement turnaround management.

In its simplest form, we can view the scenario of decline and renewal as a thumbnail qualitative sketch. It looks like this. The extended absence of properly timed, fresh management input causes the firm a slow but sure, inevitable decline—first in gross margins, then in new orders, backlog, sales, and, finally, return on investment. The firm will then fail to invest (as a stopgap measure to avoid pressing cash problems) and continue toward bottom line losses and ultimate oblivion. However, when sleepy or complacent management is replaced by new and eager management, this trend is reversed dramatically. Losses are stopped, employee morale is rebuilt, customer confidence is regained, and the company returns to robust and healthy growth. It sounds so easy, but in reality it is not easy at all. At least two-thirds of the companies that find themselves in trouble fail to take the right actions in time and impair or eliminate their future forever. As with cancer, the earlier the recognition, the higher the probability of survival. Early recognition is critical because, without it, a company may survive but never flourish again. It takes concerned and sensitive management to see the early-warning signs because on the outside a company can appear healthy.

Change is a hallmark in turnaround situations. There is usually a rapid turnover of leadership and people. Sometimes product lines or whole divisions disappear from the corporate landscape. People often resist the changes. Attitudes toward change depend on whether individuals think the new system will be an advantage or disadvantage to them. In a demoralized company, change can bring either additional fear or welcomed relief. Acceptance of change is critical in a turnaround. When this acceptance ceases in any company, hardening of the arteries starts to set in.

A QUANTITATIVE VIEW OF TURNAROUNDS

In the highly qualitative and intuitive world of the corporate turnaround, quantitative data plays a useful role in describing the relative influences and forces at work. Data alone, however, is insufficient to develop a deeper understanding of underlying causes. When supported by the opinion of practitioners, our relative perspective is enhanced. Throughout this book, opinions are provided in order to reveal a qualitative perspective in addition to quantitative data.

As I mentioned in Chapter 1, I examined the financial statements of all 4,000 "listed" companies to determine those that declined and turned around during the last ten years. This was a highly subjective task and a rather exhausting one. Its purpose was to gain insight into the magnitude of decline and turnaround among the listed companies and also to identify turnaround companies by name. These companies were mailed an extensive questionnaire, which about 25 percent returned. The distribution of decline and turnaround by stock exchange is shown again in Table 9-1.

Some 320 companies of the 4,000 Standard and Poor's companies were determined to have gone through a turnaround in the last ten years. The determinations were based upon a company-by-company review of financial data and other records. Each company had to have at least three years of sustained, but not necessarily monotonic, decline in net income. About 80 percent of the companies suffered one or more years of losses. The upturn recovery phase was normally four years or longer.

Eighty-one chief executives returned a detailed questionnaire on their turnaround experiences. Quantitative data obtained included the length of the turnaround cycle. For the eighty-one firms that returned the questionnaire, the average duration of the decline phase was 3.7 years, and the average duration of the upturn recovery phase was 4.1 years. The turnaround cycle thus averaged 7.8 years. Larger companies take longer to turnaround in the opinion of nearly every one of the corporate leaders interviewed.

Bloodbaths

In reviewing the data, some striking numbers emerge. One is the often mind-boggling size of the write-offs that some of the corporate giants take. Singer Corporation wrote off over $400 million in 1977. Monte Edison, a large Italian utility, had losses of nearly $600 million, while British National Steel topped that mark. Chrysler's losses of over $1 billion in 1979 set a modern day record. General Dynamics's losses of $420 million between 1960 and 1962 were large when you consider the value of the dollar then. Relative losses can stagger the imagination, as when GEICO lost two-thirds of its $150 million net worth in one bad year. Lev-

TABLE 9-1
Losses and Turnaround among Listed Stocks by Stock Exchange

	New York Stock Exchange	*American Stock Exchange*	*NASDAQ/ over the counter*	*Total "listed" stocks*
Total stocks listed	1,560	1,120	1,410	4,090
Stocks with at least one loss year 1967–76	340	526	228	1,094
Percentage loss to total listed	22	47	16	27
Turnarounds after loss	105	104	92	301
Percentage turnaround to losses	31	20	40	28
Turnaround without loss	40	17	11	68
Total turnarounds	145	121	103	369
Percentage not turnaround	13	38	10	19

Source: Unpublished statistical study by Donald B. Bibeault, 1977, utilizing Standard & Poor's and Moody's data on the 4,000 listed companies on the U.S. exchanges.

itt's loss of $54 million on sales of $120 million is appalling. It must be understood that many of these write-offs had been building for years and that their actual economic occurrence was not in the write-off year. Some of the write-offs are undisguised strategies to make the incoming turnaround manager look good in the future.

Turnaround Versus Nonturnaround

By comparing turnaround firms against matched pairs of nonturnaround firms in the same industry for a number of financial measures, Dan E. Schendel and G. R. Patton were able to show significant differences in financial performance. Turnaround firms were characterized by both the down phase and the up phase of the turnaround cycle. For example, the average rate of decline in normal income (relative to GNP) during the decline phase was a negative 15 percent, while income grew at a positive

TABLE 9-2
Turnaround Companies versus Nonturnaround Companies: Average Percent Rates of Change of Selected Variables

Variable	*Turnaround*		*Nonturn around*
	Down	*Up*	
Income	−15.0	15.4	−4.0
Sales	0.9	25.1	8.8
Invested capital	6.5	19.0	11.3
Invested capital/sales	7.6*	−1.5	2.7*
Equipment/sales	8.2*	−1.9	3.2*
Plant and equipment age	−0.9*	1.1	−1.1*
Sales/employee	1.8*	7.3	2.5*
Cost of goods/sales	1.6	−7.9	6.7
Profit margin	−11.3	22.1	−4.4
Cash flow	−5.0	38.5	4.1
Working capital	5.6*	15.1	5.1*
Inventory turnover	−5.1*	6.5	−3.4*
Value added	4.2*	−0.7	0.6*

*All pairs of variables are significantly different at the 0.05 level or better with the exception of the seven starred pairs.

Source: Dan E. Schendel and G. R. Patton, "Corporate Stagnation and Turnaround," *Journal of Economics and Business*, 28 (Spring-Summer 1976): 237.

TABLE 9-3
Incidence of Turnaround Types

Type	*Percent*
Management process turnaround	68
Economic (business cycle) turnaround	16
Competitive environment turnaround	5
Product breakthrough turnaround	4
Government-related turnaround	4
Other	3
TOTAL	100

Source: Donald B. Bibeault, survey of eighty-one turnaround company chief executives, April 1978.

15.4 percent during the upturn phase. The quantitative results of the Schendel and Patton study are shown in Table 9-2.

We will see later that cash flow and profit margin differences play critical roles in the turnaround story. During the downturn phase, cash flows were decreasing at an average 5 percent rate, but staged a dramatic turnaround to increase at a positive 38.5 percent rate during the upturn phase. Profit margins were tumbling at a negative 11.3 percent rate during the downturn phase, but increased dramatically to a positive 22.1 percent during the upturn phase. Of additional interest is the fact that the turnaround firms outperformed the nonturnaround firms during their upturn phase in most important categories. Most striking is the fact that turnaround firms increased sales at a rate almost three times greater than nonturnaround firms. While the nonturnaround firms did not suffer obvious decline, they also did not achieve notable results.

Types of Turnarounds

One of the reasons that there can be no turnaround formulas is that there are many different types of turnarounds and differing circumstances within each type. The principal types of turnarounds are: the management process turnaround, the economic or business cycle turnaround, the competitive environment turnaround, the product breakthrough turnaround, and, finally, the government-related turnaround. By far the most important type of turnaround is the management process turnaround. It accounts for more than two-thirds of the turnarounds reported in my survey, and most of the in-depth interviewees believed it was the only "real" kind of turnaround. Table 9-3 shows the relative incidence of turnaround types as determined by my survey.

THE MANAGEMENT PROCESS TURNAROUND

A management process turnaround means that the principal factors that were changed to accomplish the turnaround were management processes. Since the principal reason for decline was management problems, the principal reason for turnaround must be the correction of management weaknesses that caused decline. At a certain point this reasoning departs somewhat from my survey evidence, but not by much. I previously indicated that eight out of ten declines were internally caused, and, of these, slightly less than nine out of ten were due to management. Combining these percentages leads to about seven out of ten total declines caused by management, which compares closely with independent results on the type of correction or turnaround effected. The key to tying these two concepts together is the fact that they were independently derived.

A management process turnaround, to be successful, must include something much more fundamental than correcting management deficiencies. Fundamentally, the whole culture of the company must change.

Sleepy Management

No one factor predominates among the management process changes. What does emerge from our scenario of decline is that a sleepy management, unwilling to adapt to change and loosely running the enterprise, is replaced by new management that introduces tighter controls and a tougher management style. The tougher style does not turn people off—rather, they see it as a necessary precondition to straightening out the mess they're in. The fundamental importance of changing culture in a company must be stressed further because it brings up a very important issue.

The Turnaround Myth

Some people have called the turnaround phenomenon a "myth." One of my interviewees felt very strongly that most turnarounds were "patchup-and-sellout jobs." He had seen many divisions of larger companies handled in this manner. He said, "Let the buyer beware." He was right, of course. This situation does happen on numerous occasions. What is going on is simple. Some quick surgery makes the bottom line look all right, but the fundamentals have not been changed. The "bad culture" is being passed on to the buyer. If he is aware of it and adjusts his buying price accordingly, then he's got a shot at getting his return on investment. Otherwise, he is buying a pack of trouble. Making a poor performer change is not easy. "It's hard to turn a dog into a cat."

As hard as this type of acquisition turnaround is, some companies feel confident enough of their management processes actually to specialize in it. A case in point is Trafalgar House, Ltd., which has grown from a tiny, entrepreneurial investment company to a billion dollar conglomerate by succeeding where others have failed. From London's posh Ritz Hotel to the Queen Elizabeth II, Trafalgar has made a practice of buying some of the grand old names of England that have fallen on hard times. Trafalgar has succeeded in turning around these ailing institutions through a combination of stronger management, new marketing ideas, and money.

Another example of well-run companies taking over ailing divisions of other companies is White Consolidated's acquisition of Westinghouse Corporation's Consumer Products Division in 1975. Under Westinghouse, the operation had lost $24 million on sales of $375 million in 1974. White has been able to turn the division around and make it a substantial contributor to profits. This was accomplished by substantial overhead reductions and increased labor productivity. White increased production by 20 percent, while decreasing the work force by 15 percent.

These examples point out that turnarounds are anything but a myth and that management is as much the key to turnaround success as it is the key to decline. A small number of executives, such as Robert Wilson of Memorex, Thomas Wilcox of Crocker National, Frank Grisanti of "you name it," and others, have a national reputation for achieving turnaround results. There are others who are "riding the circuit" and many other solid executives who will face a turnaround situation during their careers. A few well-known executives are staking a great deal on their abilities to change troubled companies. One of these, Roy Ash of Addressograph-Multigraph (now A-M International), believes that good managerial skills are transferable. "At a sufficiently high level of abstraction," he says, "all businesses are the same."

What Roy Ash says may be true, but most turnarounds require a great deal of "roll-up-your-sleeves"-type effort and can seem considerably different when the bullets are flying. Richard Madden of Potlatch says, "One must very carefully appraise each set of circumstances on its own merit. It is dangerous to make broad generalizations. I have done four turnaround situations. Not one of them was like any other and each had very different requirements that lent themselves to different solutions and they required different kinds of people too."[2]

THE ECONOMIC (OR BUSINESS CYCLE) TURNAROUND

The second major type of turnaround is the economic (or business cycle) turnaround. This type of turnaround affects cyclical industries, such as real estate, a great deal. Other industries associated with cyclical primary industries appear to have their up-and-down periods amplified. Although about one out of six upturns is caused by economic improvement, only about half as many downturns are due to poor economic situations. I can only surmise that a number of managements "luck out" and are saved by an economic upswing. While both decline and upswing can be attributed to economic shifts, companies that perform poorly cannot blame the economy or their industry from a fundamental standpoint. On the other hand, an economic turnaround is not just a joyride up the economic roller coaster. Keeping things together during the downturn can be tough, very tough. Jeffrey Chanin feels this way: "I consider an economic cycle turnaround a real turnaround. The art of dealing with that kind of a turnaround is keeping the business alive long enough for the economy to run around and back again. And that can take as much talent as the redirection of a company's product line and all the rest—just keeping everything together. It's extremely difficult—as a matter of fact."[3]

Economic improvement, however, can be a big boost in an otherwise dismal scene. The well-managed company can outperform its competitors in bad times as well as good. It can do so through disciplined control over the economics of the business, intensive development of the right market niches and products, and, most importantly, a leadership style that sustains entrepreneurial drive and commitment among its key managers. Good management processes, rather than economics or industry trends, are the key.

THE COMPETITIVE ENVIRONMENT TURNAROUND

Turnaround executives had some specific ideas on how the turn in economic and competitive factors assisted them. Of the total, 58 percent felt that increased industry volume was most helpful, while 17 percent felt that competitive price increases were the main improvement in competitive turnarounds. Although economic and competitive factors definitely affect company performance, Donald Clifford discovered that during the same economic cycle good performers astonishingly outperformed the laggards. Clifford says:

> A second hypothesis I sought to test was that the top performers owed their success to being at the right place at the right time, that is, to being clustered in industries like energy, which has gained rather than suffered from inflation and material shortage. Wrong again. With the exception of textiles, each of the 31 industries I studied contained at least one threshold company with strong earnings and a five-year sales

growth rate in excess of 20%. And every industry but two—water transportation and petroleum—also contained companies growing at less than 10% compounded sales, and those were mediocre at best.[4]

THE PRODUCT BREAKTHROUGH TURNAROUND

Although product breakthrough turnarounds only account for about 4 percent of the turnarounds surveyed, they can cause such an astonishing reversal in a company's fortune that they are worth pointing out. Product breakthroughs can take two major forms: breakthroughs in consumer tastes and technical or scientific breakthroughs. In both cases, timing is critical and reliance on a product can make or break you. In the case of Twentieth Century-Fox Film Corporation, one major consumer breakthrough turned it around and set it on a diversification course. In 1977 Fox brought out *Jaws*, and *Star Wars* followed in 1978, reversing Fox's performance—and changing it from a laggard to a winner. Fox's $48 million cash offer for Aspen Skiing Corporation was funded by these earnings.

Sometimes companies pin their hopes for a turnaround on the acceptance of a technically advanced product that has a lead in the marketplace. Jeffrey Chanin thinks that technological breakthroughs are limited and marketing breakthroughs are often more effective. But some companies give it a try anyway. France's Aerospatiale Corporation bet on a sleek new helicopter to help get it out of the staggering $160 million loss it suffered in 1977 as a result of its adventure with the Concorde and to a lesser extent with the Airbus.

THE GOVERNMENT-RELATED TURNAROUND

Government-related turnarounds account for only a small fraction of total turnarounds. Usually these are related to a major change in government procurement policies, i.e., the dissolution of contracts; a major shift in regulation, such as environmental controls; or direct government assistance for bridge financing as in the case of Lockheed Corporation and Chrysler Corporation.

As I've pointed out, there are many types of turnarounds. In fact, turnarounds, like beauty, are often dependent on the eye of the beholder.

There are no magic formulas in this book, although there are a lot of experiences and insights contained in the parts to follow. What I can't supply is the key ingredient to turnaround success—the human understanding and energy that must be applied to a company in trouble. Causing those things to happen that are necessary to work in a crisis situation takes the human touch. Some people have it and some people don't, and for the most part, people don't have it. The real business leader is a rare individual.

REFERENCES

[1]Robert C. Wilson, "Memorex Today," address before the Peninsula Stock and Bond Club, June 3, 1976.

[2]Interview with Richard B. Madden, chairman, Potlatch Corporation, San Francisco, Calif., February 1978.

[3]Interview with Jeffrey Chanin, former executive vice president, Daylin Corp., Los Angeles, Calif., February 1978.

[4]Donald K. Clifford, Jr., "Thriving in a Recession," *Harvard Business Review*, July–August 1977, p. 59.

10
STAGES IN THE TURNAROUND CYCLE

The stages you go through vary, depending upon the situation. There are those instances in which you evolve through a number of stages very, very rapidly or even skip some desired stages. This depends upon how critical the problem is. Terminal, if something isn't done radically and immediately, then you better damn well do it radically even if it isn't the preferred way to do it.[1]

Glenn Penisten, President,
American Microsystems

In this chapter I am going to describe a general sequence of events that a company goes through in pulling out of a decline and finally returning to healthy growth. I believe the stages are discrete and well-defined. Because a turnaround can take many different forms, however, stages in a turnaround may not appear to be discrete, either to an insider or to a more casual outside observer. Turnaround activity commences at various stages in a company's decline. The more serious cases, for example, those companies that are working out of Chapter 11 protection under the Bankruptcy Act, usually go through all the stages I am describing. Other companies, which may have spotted decline signals earlier, appear to skip over some of the stages or at least move very rapidly through one stage into another. Sometimes serious situations require that very little time be spent diagnosing problems; action is of the essence, due to financial pressure. In other cases, e.g., that of a moribund, but stable, company, deliberate diagnosis and planning may be possible. Much to the surprise of quick-action practitioners, I have seen cases where "McKinsey-like" studies were undertaken before any substantial action began.

A company can be involved in tasks and activities that apply to more than one stage at a time. The blending of activities and the overlapping of stages in a specific situation must be left to the hands-on judgment of the person leading the turnaround. This chapter's main purpose is to outline the sequence of events with enough clarity and insight to allow practicing executives to understand where they are in the cycle. Its secondary purpose is to describe each stage in such detail as to allow a person to get a feel for what goes on. This chapter is not written to provide specific "nuts-and-bolts" techniques. The nuts and bolts will follow in Parts 3 and 4 of this book.

THE STAGES OF A TURNAROUND

Based upon my experience and that of other turnaround leaders, the discrete stages of a turnaround are the following:

1. The management change stage
2. The evaluation stage
3. The emergency stage
4. The stabilization stage
5. The return-to-normal-growth stage

One of the best summaries of the turnaround stages was given to me by Robert Brown:

> The first stage is to take the "Big Bath." The new manager comes in and takes everything that he can find—including the kitchen sink—and writes it off. He usually over-reserves so that he has some spread coming up on the outside. You're not thinking about anything but survival. He gets back tax money from Uncle Sam, as much as he can. The "Big Bad Bath" clears the way for the banks, the creditors, and the suppliers. You've laid yourself upon the table and told everybody how bad it is. From this point on, it can only get better. And you've left yourself a cushion to make it better within the first year. The second cycle is the identification of the reallocation of resources. Generally, what you do is cut all the losers out and try to put all the emphasis on the winners. Capital expenditure-wise, management resource-wise, everything else goes to the winners. Get profitable, show profit, show progress. After you have done that, and you've pretty much got out of trouble, you try to recapitalize. This is the third stage. And you do that along conservative lines—trying to get your short-term bank borrowings and all your money funded out in the long end of the market. Get it as long as you can so that you've got more "breathability" in your balance sheet, so you have some money to work with and you have financial capacity to do something. Then it branches off into two areas, both of which are development-oriented. The last stage is either to go into the acquisition game or to innovate—make new products, design new things, enter new markets, and hopefully you are back on the growth curve.[2]

The length of time necessary to perform each stage can vary dramatically. It takes anywhere from two weeks to six months to make value judgments about a business. A small company takes two weeks; a billion dollar company takes six months. If you are going to liquidate parts of the business, it takes ninety days from the time you decide to liquidate until you actually clean out the warehouse. If you are selling off segments of the business, it's a six-month process from the time you decide to sell. The period of stabilization takes six months to a year. The return to growth phase takes at least another year. Altogether, we are talking about anywhere from one to three years, with a $20 million company taking one year and a company the size of Memorex taking three years.

THE MANAGEMENT CHANGE STAGE

The Moment of Truth

Before a company can cure its problems, it must realize that it has major problems and make the decision to do something about them. This is what I call reaching the moment of truth. At the point where a company reaches its moment of truth and decides to make fundamental changes, it has gone from absolute decline to potential turnaround. It may continue in a downslide after this point, but basically there is now a new element in the corporate mix that has, at least potentially, begun a turnaround process.

Reaching the moment of truth is not an easy task or always well-defined, but at some point the people in power decide to act. As Robert Sackman says:

> There has to come a point somewhere along the line where the board and the president make the decision that the company is in serious enough trouble to require Trojan measures to get it out. Before you do that, it's like any other decision—to divorce or do something else—you really worry and stew but you're not doing anything. Then suddenly somebody makes the decision that you are going to do whatever is necessary to get this company back on its feet. Somebody is authorized to either take the steps or prepare the plan necessary for those steps to take place. Now you can do things which are no longer in the ordinary course of business planning.[3]

Existing Management

Now the question is whether current management can make the necessary corrections to cope with the problems confronting the company. In more than seven out of ten cases, management has to be replaced because they either cannot cope with the problem or they themselves (or at least the CEO) are the problem. Those managements that do hold on do so because the problems are recognized as external, they recognize problems early enough, or, in rare cases, they take bold action. Existing management is a problem because it lacks credibility and it cannot cope with the job at hand. It lacks credibility because it was the cause of the problem. It did not recognize the problems early enough, and it didn't want to do anything about them. It cannot cope with the difficult step of firing lots and lots of people, an action which is almost inevitable in a serious turnaround. It doesn't matter whether you use an ax or scalpel, the cutting back of unprofitable operations is very difficult for existing management for emotional reasons.

Top management change does not always mean changing the top man. Sometimes the chief operating officer is changed, but the CEO remains. In other cases, particularly where the top man has a strong ownership position, top management change means simply a change of heart, a new thrust, or an ability to make the tough decisions to save the business. The changes in direction are rare, however, because most turnaround leaders believe that the problem lies with the top man himself, particularly in smaller companies. The problem is different in larger companies, as Frank Grisanti points out:

> In a larger company, the CEO is thinking long term and really away from it all. He's not close to work on the bottom line, insofar as operations are concerned. The chief operating officer gets it out on the bottom line and, in most cases, is the culprit. He usually has some pretty competent people who are frustrated by him and his style of operation. Those people leave and are easily replaced by the weaker people who will tolerate his style. The longer it goes on, the weaker the organization becomes.[4]

Even when the major problem in the company is the top man, the board of directors is reluctant to move. Mace found the board ill-equipped to replace a poor performer. To terminate a poor performer briskly was virtually impossible. After all, the board could only base its evaluation of performance on data usually provided by the president. The capacity of individual members to separate plausible management explanations from mismanagement was extremely limited.

The New Leader

When the board does decide to act to make a change, it does not always go to the outside to find a new leader. An insider has both advantages and disadvantages. If he is familiar with the operation and has run a division that has performed well, he may be superior to a rank outsider. The directors of NCR chose William Anderson on the strength of his superior record in NCR's international operations. He had demonstrated a remarkable ability to get things done under difficult circumstances. Larger companies often have that kind of management depth, but smaller companies do not. Western Auto is an example of a medium-size company which chose an insider to lead its turnaround.

The problem with choosing an insider is that the person may have been a party to past mistakes the company made. Insiders may be tainted, as Thaddeus Taube indicates:

> The management reputation of insiders, a function of confidence plus credibility, has been tainted. The insider has been a party to those elements that caused the decline and now must draw upon those people involved to act instantly under his direction. The normal reaction is: "Well, what does he know; he is as much responsible for getting into the hole as we were."[5]

In really tough turnarounds, where survival is at stake, the board usually picks an outsider with few ties to the past. An outsider has the advantage of objectivity in evaluating the situation and, subsequently, is more capable of taking drastic measures. As Robert Brown points out:

> There is too much in-house fellowship, and you need a bloody bastard to go in and do it. Generally, companies that get into trouble in the first place are managed by "nice guys" and "good old boys," and it's the good old boy who generally gets into more trouble than the "mean old son-of-a-bitch." When directors recognize the company as a turnaround candidate, they usually get an outsider. Often half the board quits; who needs it—catching all this heat, all the bad publicity, and being part of the decision-making team. The other half will go out and bring in the Star. The Star is the guy who says, "Okay, here's what we're going to do."[6]

THE EVALUATION STAGE

The next stage is the evaluation stage, which focuses on the viability of the company and the preparation of a survival and/or turnaround plan. The viability analysis cannot be performed unless the new leader has taken charge of the company and shown that he means business. The organization must be yanked, symbolically at least, in the first few days. A new leader who acts like a bull in a china shop the first day is making a mistake. He should be aware of his ignorance of the company he has just joined. It is possible to take immediate action that smacks of toughness without upsetting the applecart.

Action must be the result of "appropriate" study because the approach needed to turn a business around is significantly different from managing a profitable company. Since speed is essential in any turnaround operation, it is vital that the executive have a proven framework for tackling the problem. Usually the new man is under time pressure to show results. But no matter what the time pressure, he should resist change which lacks evaluation. Evaluation under extreme pressure can be a quick study lasting just a few days. In view of time pressure, he should do two things before making any major changes: (1) gain a sufficient understanding of the situation to determine where to concentrate his efforts so as to get the greatest leverage in the shortest period of time; and (2) develop his plan of action. A good understanding of the business before taking action is critical for credibility and can allow a new leader to exercise more control. Every operation of the business has to be individually studied for viability. Until a leader does a viability analysis, unless there is a defined problem that he knows about, he shouldn't act.

Identifying Problems

Before a company can recover, it must recognize the nature and magnitude of its illness. As Robert Di Giorgio says, "You have to find out first—'What have I got? Anemia or cancer?' Then you can determine the cure." In turnaround situations, the magnitude of the illness is sometimes so great that action takes precedence over diagnosis. Some companies need emergency treatement until their condition is stabilized and more refined evaluations can take place.

The turnaround leader must quickly determine whether the company faces short- or intermediate-term survival questions, or less severe profitability performance problems. Less severe signs often are early-warning symptoms of a sick organization and require turnaround effort as much as survival cases. The difference is in the types of cures and the dispatch with which they are imposed. In many cases, the sick company is not treated until it's almost too late and Draconian measures are required. In cases of impending bankruptcy or severe cash flow problems, the probability of survival must be determined quickly. Frank Grisanti works on a lot of these cases, and he does not use swarms of analysts or charts and graphs. Grisanti often outlines a new plan of action on the blackboard. As he indicates:

> You must have the ability to quickly identify the viable segments of the business. You have to determine if there is a place in the market for you and your product or service, with an adequate gross margin that permits

> you to compete on a profitable basis. You have to have good guts and make judgments quickly. You are liable to liquidate good pieces of the business; and you may keep bad pieces. Those judgments are terribly important, but they are intuitive and based on experience. You don't have time to run any McKinsey-like studies.[7]

There is a common thread to both quick and slow studies, that is, a search for a viable company core and those problems that have real turnaround leverage. There's a danger in believing the conventional wisdom that there are many problems and that you've got to tackle all of them for your turnaround effort to succeed. There may be many problems, but adjustments in only one or two highly leveraged areas can make a dramatic shift. If the company has made serious mistakes for so long that it is in a bad way, you will have trouble getting management to focus calmly on the most important problems. Management often falls into a trap. It deals with the little problems it feels it can handle—simple areas, easily corrected—and they all lack turnaround leverage.

Solutions

With the major problems identified, the next step is deciding how to solve them. There are usually a readily apparent and limited number of options available. Don't be too critical of the solutions available. The worse the situation, the more likely that any strategy will work. You should not take courses of action that require extensive justification; stick to the critical problems that have turnaround leverage and are the cornerstones of an action plan. You should not try to cover every problem, or relate problems without pointing out solutions. It is more important to solve 80 percent of the problem with imperfect solutions than to go after the last 20 percent and take three times as long to produce results.

There is a temptation to jump in and start fire fighting without an action plan—I advise against it. During the initial weeks, there is normally a quiet period—often called the honeymoon—which is ideal for planning purposes. The board of directors often takes a hands-off approach and wants to see what you do without prodding. Generally, your subordinates will also be wary of coming to you with their problems until they have a chance to "read you" and determine how you react to them. Take advantage of this moratorium to develop your plans.

The Action Plan

Once the company's problems are understood and the appropriate amount of analysis is completed, a written action plan should be prepared. This is the game plan that will take the corporation from its current poor performance through at least one additional stage in the cycle. In serious situations the game plan is a cash flow plan because almost by definition serious situations are negative cash flow situations. Remember, a corporation can sustain itself if it has only one dollar more coming in than is going out. As Frank Grisanti describes it:

> Obviously, the first thing you have to do is stop the bleeding. That means that you lay out a cash flow and say, "Here are the businesses, these are the incomes, and these are the disbursements from those businesses. Here are the negative pieces. Now, how do we stop the negative cash flow and get it turned around to positive cash flow short term?" You do that before you do anything.[8]

Time is of the essence in a bleeding situation. No more than thirty days should be required to do this, even in large companies. In small companies, ten days to two weeks "max" is required. In contrast to the survival situation in some companies, others have less severe, but often more complex, malignancies. Further studies should be carried out if the company's financial status will allow it. A good case in point is Roy Ash's approach at Addressograph-Multigraph. Ash spent the first four months visiting A-M's widely scattered operations and asking a lot of questions. Ash stirred excitement and fear with his early discovery that no one in the corporation knew what products were profitable. Ash made A-M's executives "requestion everything." As one surviving manager said, "Roy opened up lots of closets that we hadn't gotten into yet."

Most turnarounds fall somewhere between the cash-impoverished survival situation and the cash-rich stagnation of Addressograph-Multigraph. In most cases a plan of action should not be deferred for more than ninety days after an executive takes over. The type of operating plan appropriate for the early stages of a turnaround is a great deal less formal than many of the massive planning studies prepared in large organizations that do not face operating difficulties.

Communicate the Plan

The action plan should be communicated in two directions: upward to the board for approval, and downward to the key management team. If the plan calls for less-than-Draconian measures, the board may have given prior authority to implement change. To get as much backing as possible, however, it's a good idea to communicate a cohesive plan, regardless. In addition, if lenders are in on the act, they should be informed of your intentions. Sideways communication is also important where outside parties, like banks, have an abiding interest.

The team management should be assembled at an outside location so that the plan can be reviewed without interruption. They must be involved in the act, and out of the meeting must come a consensus on action. This should include assignments, with deadlines, to subordinates. The basic strategy in communicating the plan in any direction is to get commitment from the parties concerned. Don't discuss the plan with anyone without real power in the situation or anyone without a stake in its implementation. Get commitment from those who are needed, and no more. Rely on those people and push the plan through the organization. Develop a plan and stick to it.

THE EMERGENCY STAGE

In the emergency stage a company does what is necessary to ensure survival. Emergency usually means surgery. If time and cash are available, surgery may be only mildly traumatic. In most cases, however, corporate surgery is as traumatic to the corporation as medical surgery is to the human body. In this stage the corporation moves beyond problem recognition and boldly into action. As Jeffrey Chanin indicates: "If you see the problem and you're satisfied with the solution, why wait around? Do it!" At this point in the turnaround the priority is to stop the bleeding. Unless you stop the overflow of cash, the business will die. Cash is king in this phase of the turnaround. Robert Wilson of Memorex sums up his feelings on the matter:

> To me, management liberation is spelled C-A-S-H. In early 1974, Memorex had barely enough cash to keep the doors open. Every aspect of cash management was pursued on an urgent basis, and every employee was encouraged to participate. Programs included such simple items as turning off lights as well as major efforts on such complex matters as lease-base management.[9]

Stop the Bleeding

The way to get your cash flow in order is similar to emergency room procedures. First you stop the bleeding with a tourniquet, then operate, to stop those internal actions that caused the bleeding. As Frank Grisanti puts it:

> The cash flow plan carries with it what I call purchase-order surgery and manpower. You first put a hold on the corporate structure. Stop anything from coming in. Put a freeze on the payment of all accounts payable until you can analyze where you stand. You have to control what

> goes into the pipeline in order to control what comes out. Automatically freeze all purchase orders and take control of purchasing.
>
> After you have put moratoriums on payments, perform surgery on payroll. Lop people off in a wholesale fashion, not arbitrarily, but by analyzing the segments of the business and relating income to outgo. You work fifteen, eighteen, twenty hours a day during that period, because in many cases you have to ask somebody for a payroll on Friday and you have to have a good check to clear that account. The computer is useless to me in a critical situation. A sharp pencil and a good mind is what I need at that point in time.[10]

A cash flow plan does not always mean drastic cuts. In well-financed companies that sense trouble brewing, other actions are taken, including borrowing to see the company through its rough period. Robert Di Giorgio, chairman of Di Giorgio Corporation, borrowed $28 million from eight banks to tide him over. "I didn't want to take time to worry about cash; I wanted to study the problem, not just keep the patient alive."

Companies that have moderately serious but not alarming cash flow problems also engage in surgery in order to trim the fat away and provide funds for more productive uses that keep the company competitive. A case in point is NCR, which had sales per employee only half as large as IBM when Robert Anderson took over as CEO. Over the next three years NCR dismissed over 10,000 workers in Dayton. As Anderson says about the cuts, "They knew NCR was too big, too complacent, and too blind for too long."

If at all possible, surgery should be done in one step. It's a very emotional time, with people getting laid off or fired, plants or departments closing, etc. When losses are stretched out, company morale sags ("When will the ax hit me?"). It's also generally best to cut a bit too much, rather than too little. Roy Woodman says, "If you have to make cuts, make them all; don't chuck ten people every week. Get it over with."

The best way to motivate big cuts is to make one big list of all the alternatives. The preparation of the list will involve so much analytical effort that the management team will become unified in the need to act and the direction to take. Roy Ash did this at Addressograph-Multigraph (sometimes referred to as Addressogrief-Multigrief). When he began swinging the axe, a sense of alarm swept through the company. Ash eased the psychic pain by guiding managers he had inherited into solving their own problems. He feels strongly that you guide others to joint analysis, rather than pronouncing policy from on high. Working through the organization is time-consuming, and it may take several weeks to explain the actions, digest the news, and allow it, finally, to sink in. In more critical situations the CEO must bypass his organization, centralize authority, and rule by executive fiat. He practically has to make the cuts himself.

If you are faced with improving near-term profit performance, the critical skill is determining where you can take action and achieve results fast. These actions might be taken in the absence of a well-formulated market or product strategy. Basically, you have to move in and break the business down into segments, make value judgments on those segments, and divest the company of those segments that aren't contributing to cash flow. Convert the losers to cash to reinforce your financial position.

Unloading a Loser

In a crisis situation, trying to unload a loser can be difficult. If you can't afford additional cash flow losses, liquidation may be the only alternative. Divestment is an orderly approach to getting rid of a loser, while liquidation is more an act of desperation. You can expect a substantial haircut from book value in a liquidation. A company should try to straighten out a loser by quick surgery and then attempt to sell it as a going concern.

Borderline situations are given only a few months to shape up. If they don't perform in the specified time, face up to liquidation. Grisanti says: "The question is, 'How do we get rid of it?' Set a target date that says, 'Okay, if I haven't sold it as a going concern by this date certain, than I should liquidate it. It's cheaper for me to start liquidating than to try to make it a going concern.'"

Expect losses when you are liquidating, because you are selling parts that are unsuccessful and you will have a hard time finding a buyer for them. Investors Diversified Services lost over $73 million in its real estate operations before Dyas P. Boothe, Jr., took over. Boothe slashed the payroll by 70 percent, unloaded losers, and got tough with defaulters. These actions raised almost $82 million in cash to pay off the banks. Boothe incurred very few additional losses below the written-down book values.

Out of the Wringer

When all these moves are accomplished, many companies come out of surgery smaller revenuewise, but no longer losing cash. Restoring profitability and stabilizing operations generally means shrinking back to those segments of business which have achieved, or can achieve, good gross margins. Levitt Corporation is a prime example of what shrinking looks like; the "new Levitt" came through its emergency phase a third of the size of old Levitt. The old Levitt's worst year included a loss of $51.3 million on sales of $190 million.

Some companies take another approach to the emergency stage by taking large write-downs before any actual divestments take place; they set up reserves (sometimes larger than necessary) to account for the anticipated losses when the losers are taken out. The new management tries to disassociate itself from past mistakes by doing a whopping housecleaning. As Robert Brown relates:

> Singer is a classic case about reserves. They identified every operating division losing money that didn't fit the master plan. The Big Bath was that they wrote all the bad stuff off and set up a huge $400 million reserve to clean it all out of there. You always want to look good on the upside. You always hope that you can prove that if you took a $100 million write-down, in essence only $50 million of it is realized. That makes you look better two to one. That's why the "star system" is so important—because there is only one guy who makes the decision "this is what we are going to do." He whops it all off, closes it all down, over-reserves it, and takes the bath.[11]

THE STABILIZATION STAGE

Eliminating losses is only part of the turnaround executive's job. That is only the first step, and often the easiest one. The second stage is achieving an acceptable return on the funds invested, or divesting the business as a going concern. Despite the effective implementation of head-count reduction, improved operational management, and the elimination of loss subsidiaries, the anticipated return from the funds invested may be unacceptable in the medium term, even though operating losses have been eliminated. As Jeffrey Chanin says: After you've cut out the cancers and identified plans for the renovation of the company, you still have a sick patient recovering from surgery and you're not sure yet how he's going to be affected in the long run. You've got to find out if your remaining corporations are capable of long-term survival—not just can they produce a decent cash flow right now, but are they worthy of being kept over the long haul?[12]

Looking beyond Today

During this period, the corporation begins to look beyond the day-to-day problems and the requirements of survival. It knows it can survive, but doubts it can perform again. Right between surgery and stabilization comes a kind of gray area, and good management teams usually start addressing that prior to or at the very early commencement of stabilization. Stabilization, by definition, implies a settling-down process that allows time to give the future more thought, since now nearly everyone believes there will be a future. How dark or how bright that future will be for the corporation is not yet known. Stabilization is a settling down after the trauma of the emergency stage.

During the surgery stage, corporate executives concentrated on cash flow and survival. During stabilization, the emphasis shifts to a three-pronged strategy: first, concentrating on profitability in addition to cash flow; second, running existing operations better; and third, reposturing the company to provide a sound platform for medium-term growth. Cost cutting and divestment can solve short-term cash flow problems, but only sustained profitability can make available the long-term cash required for healthy growth.

In addition to cutting costs by economizing measures rather than surgical cuts, the stabilization period allows a company to look at profit margins and profitability in more detail. The emphasis is on profit improvement rather than cost cutting. It is not enough to know the company's total cash flow situation or which division must be cut to save the company. Decisions now are a refinement process.

Protecting the Motherlode

Everything is examined in more detail, and thus puts strain on the longer-term systems requirements. At this point the company makes investments in running its current businesses better. Of particular concern is the main core business of the company that must be protected, cultivated, and purified. It is the core that will finance the turnaround and provide a platform for the future. As John Byers relates about a San Francisco company:

> The company had a heart as big as an elephant, but the appendages almost killed it. They had the obvious strategy of keeping that heart alive, and going back to what they did best. They performed quick surgery, went into the stabilization process, and devoted all their energies to the core. They did this by keeping the product and the quality as high as it had always been, by treasuring the normal purchasers of the line, people they had dealt with for years. They had different policies on their trade payables. They brought all the talent in the company in on and around that in order to keep it strong. They did everything they could to protect the core because it was their bread and butter.[13]

The process of purifying the retained operations to achieve higher profitability is begun. As Frank Grisanti states:

> The pieces of the business that you've kept, you begin to purify. Now, this is a refinement process, totally different from survival surgery. The

> people here are going to be here. Start to upgrade and create that environment of stability and strength. "We are now going up—no more down." That's stabilization.[14]

Glenn Penisten, president of American Microsystems, calls his stabilization period "the year of consistency," as opposed to his emergency phase, which he called "the year of corrections."

During the stabilization period, when things are settled down, the building of long-needed control systems is begun or refined. The lack of such control systems was one major reason the company had prior difficulties. I have to point out, however, that in critical situations a control system is not the key to the turnaround. It is executive action based upon a sharp pencil and a good mind. It doesn't do very much good to spend a lot of effort on systems during the surgery stage unless you know you'll be around and in what form you'll be. During stabilization a great deal more effort on these areas is expended and usually yields a high payoff. As Frank Grisanti puts it:

> We make sure that there are good cash, production, and planning-control procedures in place. We make sure there are routines in place that get out the red flags and permit management to be sensitive to those problems that repeat themselves. The key to good management is sensitivity and response. Any good management team must have in-place mechanisms that will cause them to be sensitive to things that are going on—good and bad—and that will permit them to respond quickly to take advantage of the good things and correct the bad things.[15]

Reposture the Company

If the need for achieving a turnaround has resulted from long-term changes in the market place of the company, then it will almost certainly be necessary to reposture the business. This involves a *planned* withdrawal from unprofitable products, services, market segments, and territories and the development or acquisition of alternative business—attractive from the standpoints of both profitability and future growth. The reposturing of the business may be relatively simple. For example, either the company should look for future growth in Europe, or it should concentrate on developing a higher-quality, higher-priced product range, or it should recognize that it has the ability to sell custom-made products profitably and devote more resources in this direction. It is equally possible that reposturing the business may require a modest degree of diversification, involving either a joint venture or an acquisition.

A detailed definition of the future is usually not possible during the stabilization period, but general direction and reposturing are definitely possible. This was the case at Whittaker Corporation. Joseph F. Alibrandi took over ailing Whittaker Corporation in 1971 and wielded a vigorous knife, slicing off and fusing 89 of the ill-managed and overleveraged 140 separate companies. After slashing Whittaker's monumental debt to create a more manageable fifty-one-unit conglomerate, Alibrandi still was not happy with what was left of his pared-down operation. As he reached his stabilization stage, he said, "If I were building a company from scratch, I wouldn't put these things together, but now the surgery is over."

When the Turnaround Fails

If efforts made during the stabilization period do not get a company into an acceptable return position, the turnaround executive may come to the conclusion that the business should be sold as a going concern to a company better placed to make an acceptable return from the funds invested. If this is the case, he must have the courage to present the facts to his board for approval. This must not be seen as a statement of failure. In the final analysis, the management of opportunity is more rewarding than the management of problems from the standpoint of shareholders, managers, and employees alike. Once approval for divestment is given, then the turnaround executive should expect to be actively involved in, and probably personally accountable for, identifying prospective purchasers and successfully negotiating the sale of the business. An example of such a strategy is the course taken by Overseas National Airways, which liquidated its jet fleet in 1968 for handsome profits after sustaining operating losses of $27 million over five years. In another case I recomended the shutdown and liquidation of a major private steel company to protect the sizable shareholder's equity built up over a ninety-year history.

At the other end of the spectrum of performance, a company with a successful turnaround may find itself the target of a takeover bid before it gets into a normal growth stage again. This happened to Green Giant Company, long one of the food processing industry's growth-and-profit laggards. Under Thomas E. Wyman, Green Giant hired more aggressive managers, tightened up operations, sparked a new product drive, and expanded the market for its prepared frozen foods. This successful turnaround strategy also got Wyman unwanted attention. When the Green Giant board accepted a Pillsbury tender offer, Wyman lost part of the precious autonomy he had sought at Green Giant. "It's ironic, because the more successful you are, the greater is the risk that you won't be able to keep your independence," Wyman says.

THE RETURN-TO-NORMAL-GROWTH STAGE

The emergency stage concentrates on retrenchment, the stabilization stage concentrates on controlled profit growth, and the final phase of a turnaround concentrates on development and revenue growth. This time around, margins are not sacrificed at the expense of revenue growth. If a management has learned its lessons, it will position itself in fast-growing, high-margin businesses. The emphasis is now on internal and external development. Internal development emphasizes new marketing thrusts, finding ways to broaden the base of the existing business, and finding ways to increase market penetration. Revenue growth again becomes a corporate priority. In order to facilitate revenue growth, new products are selectively added, additional markets developed, selling effectiveness increased, and customer service improved.

Creating a Sound Financial Platform

Producing sustained growth requires investment for future growth, and investment requires a strong balance sheet. From a financial standpoint the emphasis shifts to the balance sheet and return on investment. Jeffrey Chanin discussed this:

> The last stage is positioning the company for ten or fifteen years. You've got to look at your balance sheet. Is your capital structure messed up, now that you've done all these things? What do you have to do to the capital structure to get it in line again? Do you want it simple, do you want it complex, do you want to get rid of your debt? How do you build back the credibility of your company? What you do to your balance sheet is as important as what you do to your operations.[16]

Earlier I mentioned the plight of Thomas Wyman of Green Giant, which was taken over just as Wyman was reaching the return-to-growth stage. However, that takeover gave Wyman the financial muscle that he needed to pursue his aggressive growth plans. Even after the operating turnaround, Wyman was saddled with an anemic balance sheet. Pillsbury entered the picture with its financial clout just as Wyman's new-product program and his plans to expand Green Giant's meager restaurant operation were running into capital constraints. It is doubtful whether Wyman could have entered his return-to-growth stage as soon without Pillsbury's help.

In smaller companies the whole turnaround cycle can take place rather rapidly. A case in point is Sanitas Service Corporation, which underwent a dramatic retrenchment from its $100 million revenue size to just $18 million in revenues. Just two years before it began seeking new acquisitions, the company's financial situation was pitifully bad.

Liabilities were nine times current assets, bank loans were overdue, and the company had a negative net worth of nearly $10 million. The company came out of Chapter XI. Its $18 million in revenues was a far cry from its former status, but its president, Edward M. Moran, had settled the lawsuits, placated the SEC and IRS, fended off a Justice Department probe, and refinanced the company's huge debt. Moran felt that the company was then ready to resume orderly growth.

Larger companies often require a much longer turnaround period before expansion can take place. A case in point is McGraw-Edison Company, where Chairman Edward J. Williams spent six years selling off ailing businesses and inefficient plants, slashing thousands of jobs from the payroll, and recasting his management team. When he strolled to the altar at his daughter's wedding, Williams jokingly referred to it as his "last divestiture." Because he had so many internal problems to solve, Williams had put a long hiatus on acquisitions. By 1978, he felt that the company was in shape to go after both large and small opportunities outside the company.

Making acquisitions and pushing internal-growth programs can provide profitable growth only under strong leadership. In some cases, the turnaround leader may not be suited to manage this final phase of the turnaround. Commenting on the return-to-growth stage, Frank Grisanti says:

> It takes a creative imagination, optimism, and forward thinking, which isn't the negative constructive thinking that goes on in trying to stop the downslide. A guy who stops the downslide is always looking for bad things. You can't build a company thinking about bad things. You have to look for good things, you have to be optimistic; it's a fully different personality.[17]

Rebuilding momentum after a downslide can be a difficult chore and ultimately depends on transforming the negative culture of a once moribund company. This means the skills and attitudes of a company's people must be transformed to build a momentum for future growth.

WHEN IS THE COMPANY TURNED AROUND?

At some point in time, the turnaround leader feels that his company has been turned around. The feeling can change, but most turnaround leaders look for definitive signs that things have indeed changed. As Chauncey Schmidt indicates:

> In a turnaround, there are problems everywhere you go—it's rare that there is just one problem. Surprises keep popping up. In reality they are

> surprises only in the sense that a bad situation has finally surfaced. It always existed, just as America always existed before Columbus discovered it. At some point these bad surprises seem to stop or attenuate, and you begin to get good results. Then you get the feeling that the turn is beginning.[18]

Thaddeus Taube of Koracorp has a point of view that is shared by a lot of turnaround leaders:

> I think that the turnaround becomes a turnaround at that point in time when your financial partners begin to treat it as such. In most large businesses, the turnarounds are involved in partnerships of the company and its banks, and obviously the attitude of the banks in relation to the type of loan agreements and the type of stranglehold they have on the company is very direct measurement of when they have accepted the fact that a turnaround exists. When your financial partners begin to treat the company as a customer again, rather than the bank feeling like it's the customer, that's the point in which the turnaround has been effected.[19]

A good summary of feeling about a turnaround are provided in a speech made by Robert Wilson of Memorex:

> Probably the best way to convey the changing attitudes is through the expression of the reporters in the news media and investment service. In February, 1974, *Value Line* reviewed Memorex and asked the question, "Can This Company Survive?" In succeeding issues, its comments reflected the change at Memorex:
>
> NOVEMBER 1974 — "MEMOREX'S PROSPECTS FOR FINANCIAL SURVIVAL HAVE IMPROVED."
>
> AUGUST 1975 — "THE TURNAROUND CONTINUES."
>
> NOVEMBER 1975 — "MEMOREX IS BACK ALIVE AND KICKING."
>
> FEBRUARY 1976 — "MEMOREX IS SOLIDLY AFLOAT."
>
> MAY 1976 — "MEMOREX HAS BECOME A MONEY MACHINE."
>
> In 1974, Ray Hutchinson, the local business editor for CBS, was reported to have said, "The Arabs are going to buy IBM—and the Poles are going to buy Memorex." This year—well—let's let Ray speak for himself.[20]

Dramatic profit improvement, unless sustained for a period of time, does not mean that a company has turned around. The euphoria of quick results must be followed by the reality of successfully implementing turnaround strategies for two or three years. Besides generating profits, a company must rebuild its position in the marketplace, make the right strategic moves, and motivate its people to complete the turnaround cycle.

REFERENCES

[1]Interview with Glenn E. Penisten, president, American Microsystems, Santa Clara, Calif., February 1978.

[2]Interview with Robert C. Brown, president, R. C. Brown & Co,, San Francisco, Calif., February 1978.

[3]Interview with Robert Sackman, president, Rodal Corp., Palo Alto, Calif., February 1978.

[4]Interview with Frank A. Grisanti, president, Grisanti and Galef, Los Angeles, Calif., February 1978.

[5]Interview with Thaddeus N. Taube, chairman, Koracorp Industries, San Francisco, Calif., February 1978.

[6]Brown, interview, February 1978.

[7]Grisanti, interview, February 1978.

[8]Ibid.

[9]Robert C. Wilson, address before Arizona State University Business School, Mar. 13, 1975, p. 15.

[10]Grisanti, interview, February 1978.

[11]Brown, interview, February 1978.

[12]Interview with Jeffrey Chanin, former executive vice president, Daylin Corp., Los Angeles, Calif., February 1978.

[13]Interview with John Byers, vice president, Wells Fargo Bank, San Francisco, Calif., May 1978.

[14]Grisanti, interview, February 1978.

[15]Ibid

[16]Chanin, interview, February 1978.

[17]Grisanti, interview, February 1978.

[18]Interview with Chauncey Schmidt, chairman, Bank of California, San Francisco, Calif., February 1978.

[19]Taube, interview, February 1978.

[20]Robert C. Wilson, "Memorex Today," address before Peninsula Stock and Bond Club, June 3, 1976, p. 23.

11
THE KEY FACTORS IN TURNAROUND SUCCESS

There are three factors which affect all business, but which are more noticeable in a turnaround. There are people aspects; there are the business aspects of total competitiveness; and there are financial resources. When you start to look at these three factors, you can tell a lot about decline, turnaround, and sustained growth.[1]

Richard Madden, Chairman
Potatch Corporation

THE ELEMENTS

There are certain key elements that lead to turnaround success. In their absence, a turnaround effort is highly risky. It is tempting to say that turning a company around involves such a multiplicity of factors that their enumeration would fill a dictionary and it might be easier to list them in alphabetical order. Indeed, there are many factors, but certain ones stand out above the others and appear time and again in turnaround situations. In the most general sense there are key elements that apply to any business situation, whether it be a turnaround or not. My favorite summary of the key turnaround factors was presented by Bob Brown:

> You have to have four key elements to make the turnaround work. You've got to have the willingness. This means that the new man who is brought in to do the turnaround has to have absolute control. He has to report directly to the board, but he has to have the maximum flexibility that is given to any management. You cannot manage a turnaround by committee. It is strictly a star business, and you have to have a board that is willing to go along with that. The second thing is that he has to have something to work with. There has to be an economic reason for the business to be there. In other words, if you are making buggy whips, you can be the most efficient buggy-whip maker in the world; but, if there is no demand for buggies, you should recognize that, get out of the business, and get into something else. The third key element is the money and resources to turn around, to become a competitive entity. And the final ingredient is the motivation of people. You have to

> be able to attract and motivate top people in the key areas in which you are making the turnaround.[2]

In my survey of turnaround executives, improved management processes and motivation aspects received 71 percent of the first mentions as the key factor; competitive resource aspects (a viable core) received 17 percent; and financial resource aspects received 12 percent. (See Appendix Table L for a detailed breakdown of key factors in a turnaround.) All these factors are important and interact in creating a successful turnaround. In its simplest form the four principal keys to a turnaround are:

1. New competent management with full authority to make all the required changes
2. An economically and competitively viable core operation
3. "Bridge" capital from external and internal sources to finance the turnaround
4. A positive attitude and motivated people so that initial turnaround momentum is sustained

In the scenario that emerges most often the board of directors selects new competent management to initiate the turnaround effort. In successful cases the board realizes that this new management must have absolute control to make the required changes. In difficult situations, the new management stands a fighting chance only if it can quickly get to a positive cash flow position. This depends in the first instance on the ability of management to convince the creditors (banks, insurance companies, trade creditors, etc.) to provide bridge financing until management can dispose of losing operations and products. All this activity is for naught unless there exists a viable core operation to fall back upon. The viable core must be protected at all costs, because it is the base of the turnaround pivot; beyond the initial bridge financing, internal sources will be used to provide cash flow during the stabilization stage of the turnaround. In disposing of its losing operations, management should allow for a substantial paydown of the initial external bridge financing.

The key thing to realize in a turnaround situation, more than at any other time in the corporate life span, is that "cash is king." Beyond the emergency stage, the key to sustained success is positive attitude. When a new executive takes over a troubled company, he or she must immediately address the problems of attitude. The executive may simply act very tough in the early stages, but longer-range objectives must include the fostering of positive, opportunity-oriented attitudes. This positive attitude is the key to sustaining the early momentum initiated by the new management.

IMPROVING MANAGEMENT PROCESSES

As we saw earlier, seven out of ten turnarounds are management process turnarounds, and in about 90 percent of these there is change in management at the top. It's almost axiomatic that if management is the key cause of decline, then changing management will go a long way toward correcting the problem. But in real life, this change of management can be traumatic. Boards have to be careful in their choice. They have to look for the presence of needed strengths and the absence of certain weaknesses in the person they pick. And, as Leonard Laundergan, senior partner of Financial Consulting Associates, says, the key is to give the new person a clear charter to take the drastic actions that are necessary to accomplish the turnaround.

Management Style

Once new management moves in, it can make dramatic changes rather quickly. The management style that seems to work embodies at least the following:

1. Use of hands-on management style
2. Delegation of absolute authority to management by the board
3. Introduction of tight controls
4. Emphasis on good "people motivators"

The hands-on trait is not limited to the small company turnaround, as I could see at Memorex, when I met with Chairman Robert Wilson one morning over coffee in the company cafeteria. We watched his people coming in, and he knew about 300 people by name. I was astonished. As Frank Grisanti says about the necessity of hands-on management style for a turnaround:

> I may go into a situation. I'll be there a week. And I'll know more people than the CEO of that company. And yet, it is a very low profile. The reason for that is, in our work, in order to really find out what is going on, you have got to get into the bowels of the operation. I always go to see the action. I never have the action come to me. By doing that, you meet all the forces that you have to meet—people, or inventory, or

TABLE 11-1
Management Process Turnaround Key Factors

	Number one ranking		*Total weighted rank*	
	Number	*Percent*	*Number*	*Percent*
Instituting tight controls	17	23	41	21
Changing people's attitudes	9	12	38	20
Understanding business better	13	17	34	17
Absolute control to management	18	24	29	15
Visible leadership	9	12	26	13
Strong financial executive	3	4	13	7
More active board	5	7	11	6
Other	1	1	2	1
TOTAL	75	100	194	100

Source: Donald B. Bibeault, Survey of eighty-one turnaround company chief executives, April 1978.

> whatever. And that's why I'm sure that Bob (Wilson) knew so many people; because he got out there. He didn't meet those people by calling them into his office. He met them because he was out lifting rocks and moving rocks.[3]

My survey of the aspects of the management process that are essential to turnarounds yields some additional insights, as shown in Table 11-1. Control, both absolute and tight, gets the number one ranking. It is most important in the early stages when an executive is taking charge. So important is this to experienced turnaround experts that it becomes a hard and fast rule.

Management Control

Controls can take many forms, and I asked the turnaround leaders about their opinions on the key controls to turnaround purposes. The factors that emerged were the institution of tight budgetary controls, improved responsibility accounting, and product margin and cost controls. (Details from the survey are shown in Appendix Table M.) During the early surgery stage of a turnaround, tight controls over purchasing and head count are critically important. Management must control the cash flow pipeline. In the stabilization stage, budgetary performances and margin refinements should be brought in. One of the best examples of the effect of tight controls is afforded by Gary MacDougal at Mark Controls Corporation. His reliance on controls was particularly appropriate for the stodgy valves industry.

> MacDougal's plan was to find a company that needed hard-nosed professional management and tight financial controls and that had plenty of potential for expansion both internally and through acquisitions. In 1969 he zeroed in on tiny Mark Controls, then the 40th-largest of 600 manufacturers in the staid, barely profitable valve industry. At the time, Mark was just finishing up a year in which it had earned $300,000 on sales of $16.6 million. Today, Evanston (Ill.)-based Mark stands as the fifth-largest company in its industry. . . . The key to Mark's success so far has been tough financial controls and a methodical emphasis on profit margins.[4]

The two key elements that have to be built into any system of controls are sensitivity and response. Sensitivity means that the system and the people must be sensitive to those key factors that are the heart of any business. A control system will be sensitive if it is designed in the broadest sense by the people who are going to use it. It won't be successful if it doesn't measure a business in the same way (but in more detail) than a savvy operating manager would. Response is based on two key factors. One is that the executive must be able to take quantitative information and compare it to the concrete reality of what he knows about a business. In addition, the system itself is only passive; it requires a fresh dose of management effort. Richard S. Sloma compared management control of a firm to vitamins in the body: "A company needs a fresh dosage every day."

A VIABLE CORE BUSINESS

As I mentioned earlier in this chapter, next to the management and motivation, the competitive aspects of a business are most important in determining whether a company could be turned around. Of these competitive aspects, the most important is the existence of an economically viable core business to stabilize the company and finance the turnaround. As Frank Grisanti says:

> You've got to have a viable core. You've got to have a business that is worth perpetuating. Without a viable core a turnaround is a very difficult, if not impossible, task. Some turnarounds are accomplished by stripping out the old core business, but very few succeed in this way.[5]

The turnaround itself normally means shrinking back to those segments of the business that can provide positive cash flow and a platform to stabilize the company. A key factor in the turnaround is that the viable core of the business must be protected from the adverse conditions affecting the rest of the business. This often means different policies for the core operation, as compared with the other operations. Payables are paid on a different time schedule, customers are cultivated, creditors are treated differently, product development does not get cut as drastically, quality control is maintained, etc. The outward manifestations and the inward practices of a successful business must be maintained. As Robert Brown says:

> It's like any business; there are probably only two or three elements which are responsible for its success or failure. You have to identify those elements. If you were to look at Kodak, they could be losing money in fifty divisions and not worry; but, if you are losing money in the big one (80 percent of the profit margin), you're in deep trouble. Forget the rest of the little stuff; put a lot of your work on the one big guy and try to find out what you have to do. Once you've got him set up, then you start taking on the riffraff.[6]

Back to Basics

Time and again, in appraising turnaround success I hear the phrase "going back to basics," meaning that the company in question will be getting rid of or deemphasizing the acquisitions that it made earlier in order to return to its basic core business. There will be renewed effort to cultivate and stimulate the core toward increased profitability by capital investment programs and marketing approaches. A case in point is Western Auto, where a diversification program caused Western to lose sight of the traditional money-maker—automobile parts. As a result, sales flattened and profits tumbled. Profits were restored only after Western got back to basics.

Sometimes companies have to part with attractive operations in order to protect the core. This was the case at Avco Corporation during its crisis when Chairman Kerr began selling a series of smaller operations that ranged from a steel mill to a savings-and-loan association. He was forced to sell Avco Broadcasting, a healthy string of radio and television stations, to bring in a needed $93 million. This left Avco with two key core businesses and a positive cash flow, but some remaining weak spots.

Key to a Viable Core

In the broadest sense, where the basic viability of the core company is in doubt, there are five key requirements for a business to be worth turning around. These are:

1. *Positive cash flow.* Not profit, just cash after costs (but not after depreciation) of at least $1. Or the assurance that if there is negative cash flow, it can be covered for a prescribed period before turnaround (say, three to six months).

2. *Sales volume umbrella.* The likelihood there will be a large enough sales volume while the firm's troubles are defined and corrected.

3. *Competitive equipment.* Production process must be reasonably up to data compared with that of competitors.

4. *Competitive location.* Markets, raw materials, and workers must be accessible to plants at competitive costs.

5. *Awareness of changes* in the recent past or near future. New equipment, new products, loss of important personnel, imminent retirement of key people, anticipation of unfavorable government ruling—things that don't show up on financial statements but affect them significantly.

Sound Strategies

Supplementing the existence of a viable core, there are certain competitive strategies that separate winners from losers. Successful turnaround companies seem to follow two rules: they stay close to their market niches during stabilization, and they use their marketing ability opportunistically. Market strategies are born of necessity. Successful turnaround companies realize that if their product and market portfolio expands too rapidly, the business will get out of control. And if their niches are not soundly selected, they will cease to be competitive with their biggest rivals. So they use various tactics to solidify their positions.

First, they build on the strength of their core product lines and avoid excessive diversification, both geographic and technical, until they have the management processes and structure to cope with greater complexity. Second, they weed out market segments that their larger competitors consider too small, too risky, or just plain unappealing. Third, they steer clear of businesses in which the sheer market power of the big company puts them at a disadvantage. Examples are extractive and process industries where economic scale is a factor (unless a highly specialized niche can be found), and some mass consumer markets, such as detergents and razor blades—in which Lestoil and Wilkinson went futilely head-to-head with Procter & Gamble and Gillette, respectively.

During the late 1960s and early 1970s, the surge of market growth allowed companies to violate the market-niche rule. Some of the smaller growth companies of that era ran up enormous price/earnings multiples through aggressive diversification and paid little attention to the compatibility of the market segments they were selecting or to the level of complexity they were building. Some of them are just recovering from the shellacking they took during the recession. Others will not be heard from again.

In one out of six cases a turnaround is affected by competitive economics shifts in the marketplace. In those cases the shift had a favorable impact on industry volume and prices. More often competitive factors revolved around a viable core business and a high degree of commitment to concentrating on the winners. I am convinced that this that this commitment flows principally from a chief executive officer with the ability to create an organizational environment that focuses on creative, disciplined management.

ADEQUATE BRIDGE FINANCING

The third key area critical to a turnaround is adequate bridge financing. This depends upon both the external support available to the company or division and the internal ability to raise funds to finance the turnaround. If a large company or a sick division of an otherwise healthy company is involved, the financial resource aspects may not be as critical as they are in the case of a free-standing small company. Even large companies run into serious difficulties in obtaining credit if their record has been poor over a lengthy time period and no feasible survival plan has been proposed.

The Banker's Role

At some point the banks get in so deeply they they are nearly owners rather than creditors. At this juncture they are almost unable to pull the plug without endangering their reputation and the bank's balance sheet itself. Two earlier cases bear some mention. In the case of Pan American Airlines the banks were in a dangerous position by mid-October 1974. The company had only enough cash to last three weeks. There was no assurance that the banks, led by Citibank, would lend it the money to get through the normal winter traffic slump. Pan American offices laid out the preliminary plans for filing bankruptcy. But the company also formulated a survival plan that included raising cash by selling off everything that was losing money or was only marginally profitable, and everything that was not immediately needed. The plan was presented to the bank. Early in November 1974 the banks agreed to provide "bridge" credits, the money Pan Am needed to get from where it was to where it wanted to go under its survival plan.[7]

Another case was Lockheed's brush with bankruptcy in the early 1970s. Lockheed was almost broke, but the government and the banks had such a tremendous stake in keeping the company alive that they were prepared to accept any financial plan with a chance of turning Lockheed around.

Even in smaller companies, the key to a turnaround is lender and creditor support for bridge financing while the surgery is being performed. Money in this case is analogous to a blood transfusion, because cash is the lifeblood of the business. Lender support is the key to the turnaround. As Frank Grisanti indicates:

> When the business is in real trouble, the shareholders are no longer in control. They no longer own the business. The lenders; in other words, the bankers, or an insurance group, or trade creditors; really own the business, and you have to convince them that they own the business, and you have to get their cooperation in whatever form of reorganization takes place.[8]

To Help or Not to Help?

In sick divisions of otherwise healthy companies, the parent will foot the negative cash flow bill for only so long. Finally, the parent refuses to put good money after bad. Such a situation occurred at the Collins Division of Rockwell International, when Rockwell refused to put more money into an operation that was losing at the rate of $50 million per year. Instead, Rockwell sent in Robert Wilson to engineer the turnaround. As he recalls:

> No question about it, Collins at that time was headed toward a Chapter 11. When things continued to go from bad to worse at Collins, Rockwell called me in and asked, "Aren't you the one who recommended investing in Collins?" "That's right," I answered. "Well," he said, "you're the one to go down there and take over." I reported as president of Collins in November 1972. Rockwell would not put any more money in the till, so there was a need to do something drastic.[9]

In cases like this, the financial variable becomes key and transcends other considerations. In most classic turnaround situations, outside lenders, usually banks, are involved. They usually cooperate in several ways, as John Byers affirms:

> Time, outright debt forgiveness, those are the two extremes. It's easy to give time. It's very, very difficult to outright forgive debt. But it's done. And in between the two are no principal for three years, reduced rates

> of interest, all the things you see, for example, if you look at the REIT renegotiated packages.[10]

In some cases banks are not assertive enough in a troubled company situation, usually because of their fear of being sued. In the case of small companies, banks finally do act, usually bringing in an outside consultant. Leonard Laundergan relates the case of a firm with $1.2 million in sales and severe financial difficulties, including a debt of almost $1 million to one particular bank. Although the firm's president was not eager to listen to outsiders, the bank threatened to demand immediate payment of its loans unless the firm accepted the intervention of outside financial consultants. The consultants were brought in and in a few months they were able to stabilize the firm. This case demonstrates how creditor support is often obtained only when management credibility is restored.

The Creditor's Mistake

Creditors play a key role in seeing a company through not just the surgery stage with bridge capital but also the stabilization and return-to-growth stages. Many a turnaround has been stopped halfway up by overanxious creditors. As John Byers says:

> Yes, I think a lot of times the banks get too anxious to be paid off and they stop a turnaround. A lot of times the future is so uncertain that the bank agreement is, say, only a year long and at the end of that year, it is obvious a new agreement is going to have to be negotiated. Things look pretty good, so too tough a replacement agreement is negotiated. It puts too much of a burden on the company going into year two.[11]

Frank Grisanti concurs:

> What happens is that lenders, whether they be banks or insurance companies, don't recognize that the recovery of capital really ought to come out of the reinstated position of the company rather than the liquidation of the assets. Instead of leaving money in the company so that the company can grow, they take that money to reduce their debt position and then leave the company undercapitalized and short of working capital. So they create a hell of a struggle for any new management team. That is why I encourage any long-term guy to be very tough in his negotiations, not so much in personal income package, salary, but in insisting that, in the negotiation with the banks, they reconstruct the balance wheel so as to leave enough cash in the company to give him a little fighting chance to rebuild it.[12]

A well-planned turnaround may be able to get along without additional bank financing beyond the surgery stage if internal sources are properly cultivated. Frank Grisanti thinks so:

> Businesses that are in serious trouble, if they are any size at all, usually have enough resources within them so that, if you get all the factors working together, you don't need any more money. You don't need any money to finance the turnaround. You may need money to bridge the gap while you convert certain assets, because it takes time to convert fallow assets to cash.[13]

The initial internal cash sources come from divesting poor-performing subsidiaries that no longer fit the return-to-basics strategy of most turnaround companies. During the stabilization stage, a company can develop internal sources by managing for cash flow rather than profits alone, by working existing capital harder, and by slowing the growth rate in order to moderate the demand for new capital. This can take many forms, such as building balance sheet performance factors into personal objectives and management incentive plans, setting objectives for increasing suppliers' warehousing of raw materials, expanding use of lockboxes and new remittance procedures to cut receivables, installing and enforcing highly selective guidelines for extending payables, and requiring higher hurdle rates for new capital investment while replacement costs are taken into account.

Finally, may I suggest two other factors important to completing the turnaround: first, make absolutely sure that you have identified all the problems and cleaned them all out and, second, restructure the financial condition of the company so that you have adequate working capital to complete the turn.

IMPROVING MOTIVATION

Of extreme importance in ensuring the ongoing success of a turnaround effort is the motivation of the organization. Evaluating the problems and performing surgery on those problems can solve the problem of survival, clear up cash flows, and provide a measure of profitability. The turnaround is less than half-successful at that point in time. Unless the basic motivation of the people changes from a defeatist attitude to one of confidence, it is doubtful that the company can stabilize its base and return to growth. Motivation is the key to completing the turnaround cycle. As Robert Wilson of Memorex says, this is because the personality of a company is the sum total of its attitudes, and attitudes create the environment in which your company operates.[14] Even in this era of "scientific management" the attitudes of management play perhaps the most decisive role in the success or failure of a company.

The Power of Positive Thinking

In turnaround situations, the leadership must adopt a positive attitude and transmit this to the rest of the organization. As Michael Todd said, "I've never been poor, only broke. Being poor is a frame of mind. Being broke is only a temporary situation." You don't have people committed and enthusiastic until you have changed the culture in a company, and the cultural change has to start at the top and work its way down into the company. The threat of a company's demise and the trauma of the initial stages of a turnaround give management a golden opportunity to make major changes in the attitude of a company. Just going through a turnaround can help build spirit.

Roy Ash feels the really important change in Addressograph-Multigraph was the process of psychological transformation. One of Ash's big steps in reshaping company attitudes was to move its headquarters to Los Angeles. Cosmetic changes, like some Ash plans, are only the surface manifestation of the total culture change that has to take place in a company if the company is to complete its turnaround. That transformation is key to the turnaround but not easy to pull off.

Dealing with Uncertainty

The reader will recognize by now that the turnaround executive must cope effectively with the uncertainty, anxiety, and fear felt by the work force and management alike if he is to achieve a successful turnaround. The answers to uncertainty, anxiety, and fear include personal integrity, personal management standards, and, above all else, the ability to communicate. Whether he likes to accept it or not, the turnaround executive is communicating all the time he is with another person. It is important that he appear cheerful, assured, and poised at all times. If he appears despondent or out of his depth, the effect on morale may be shattering.

Changing the attitudes and the culture of a company is both an external and an internal effort. It's not just the people inside a company who matter, but all the constituencies involved in corporate well-being. As Robert Wilson says about the improvements in attitudes at Memorex:

> The attitude of everyone important to the future of Memorex improved substantially. Our *employees* appreciated the stability of employment, particularly in a recessionary period. They liked the cleaner facilities, improved benefits, and opportunities for promotion. They took pride in improved quality and began to develop new respect for a management

> that cleaned up old problems, eliminated nonperformers, and set up high standards. Our customers no longer questioned Memorex's viability. They were increasingly impressed with our quality, service, and customer orientation. They expressed their growing confidence in the most effective manner—by placing orders. Our vendors began to consider us a longterm growth company instead of a potential bad debt. Our bankers appreciated the substantial debt repayments. They are beginning to view Memorex as a profit opportunity instead of a potential loss. One of them even treated me as though I were a customer.[15]

Later, in the return-to-growth stage, management directs the organization toward development programs that are opportunistic in nature. This is a further refinement of the cultural change that is key to sustaining a turnaround. As Peter Drucker says, a firm will be more exciting and challenging if the firm's energies are directed toward new opportunities, rather than problems.

REFERENCES

[1]Interview with Richard Madden, chairman, Potlatch Corp., San Francisco, Calif., February 1978.

[2]Interview with Robert C. Brown, president, R. C. Brown & Co., San Francisco, Calif., February 1978.

[3]Interview with Frank A. Grisanti, president, Grisanti & Galef, Los Angeles, Calif., February 1978.

[4]"Financial Controls Help a Valve Maker Expand," *Business Week*, Aug. 1, 1977, pp. 47, 48.

[5]Grisanti, interview, February 1978.

[6]Brown, interview, February 1978.

[7]"Pan Am: In the Black—For Now," *Business Week*, Oct. 3, 1977, p. 52.

[8]Grisanti, interview, February 1978.

[9]Robert C. Wilson, address before Business School, Arizona State University, March 13, 1975, p. 15.

[10]Interview with John Byers, vice president, Wells Fargo Bank, San Francisco, California, February 1978.

[11]Ibid.

[12]Grisanti, interview, Feburary 1978.

[13]Ibid.

[14]Robert C. Wilson, "Memorex Today," address to Peninsula Stock and Bond Club, June 3, 1976, p. 14.

[15]Ibid. p. 5.

12
TURNAROUND FAILURES

Chrysler is not a company that you can judge by results of a single year. It has had turnarounds before, plenty of them, only to be followed by hair-raising reversals.[1]

Forbes Magazine, November 1976

MULTIPLE TURNAROUND ATTEMPTS

The skeptical and prophetic quote above about Chrysler Corporation points out one of the perennial roller coaster companies that always is in some sort of trouble or in the midst of a turnaround. The shareholders of Chrysler care little as to whether Lee Iacocca has finally put his finger on the core of Chrysler's long-standing problems. Chrysler management has cried wolf many times before. Chrysler, for over twenty years, has seemed to subscribe to M. H. Alderson's adage, "If at first you don't succeed, you are running about average."

Four times in the fifties, twice in the sixties, and three times in the seventies, Chrysler's earnings have tumbled dramatically. As I write this book, Lee Iacocca is struggling to right a company that is sinking deeper into the mire of financial insolvency, and the Congress of the United States has just voted a $3.5 billion aid package to come to Chrysler's rescue. Chrysler is in such grave circumstances that doubts are growing about Lee Iacocca's turnaround plan.

Classifying Failure

If we define the objective of a turnaround as the survival of a company, it's difficult to classify Chrysler as an outright turnaround failure. However, that's a very narrow definition. I agree with Robert Wilson of Memorex that a company has not really turned around unless it has achieved a solid basis of future growth, the final stage of a turnaround. On that more rigid basis, Chrysler should be deemed a turnaround failure on the evidence of its lackluster performance.

Chrysler has been on an overall downhill plunge in market share since 1968, a considerable time period. Chrysler's fundamental problems of lower margins, less integration, poor product mix, recession leveraged customer base, and late product entries have not been solved. In the Lynn Townsend era, there is a question as to whether they were ever attacked. Under John Riccardo negative events happened so fast that his plan was outflanked. Now that Chrysler has a plan to correct its fundamental problems, it does not have the money to do so. It now appears the lender of last resort, "Uncle Sam", will step in. Lawmakers, in an election year, fear having to accept the blame for a Chrysler bankruptcy.

As bad as Chrysler's problems are, they do not yet represent what many people refer to as turnaround failure. A turnaround failure, by definition, has to contain a substantial and recognized turnaround effort on the part of the company. It usually includes new management, with rather Draconian measures applied to turn the company around. The outside world is often aware that something out of the ordinary is afoot. If this effort fails to bring a company back to sustained health in a reasonable time frame (one to three years), I consider it a turnaround failure. Obvious turnaround failures are companies that file for Chapter 11 protection under the Bankruptcy Act, but are subsequently liquidated. Two-thirds of the companies that file Chapter 11 petitions are not in business two years later. I shall spend more time on Chapter 11 of the Bankruptcy Act in the second part of this chapter.

Stagnation

Another type of failure is stagnation. As Frank Grisanti says: "There are a few turnaround failures, but the only ones that people talk about as being failures are those that actually do fail . . . but, you know, the company that is on dead center and never really emerged into a strong, ongoing, profitable position is probably just as much a failure."[2] On the basis of market share, Chrysler was a dead-center company from 1963 to 1968. Since that time, it has been on a definite downhill slide.

There are plenty of examples of turnaround failures to examine. A few of the companies I discuss may now be on a sustained recovery, but, as I write this, their futures are clouded. Turnaround attempts are not like baseball. It doesn't necessarily take three strikes to be out. An example of this is the history of Arden-Mayfair, whose troubles go back to the mid-1960s. Arden-Mayfair has made five distinct turnaround attempts, including management changes, and all have failed. Each new management failed to stop the financial hemorrhaging that has taken place.

Most companies that fail a turnaround effort do so for three major reasons: first, ineffective management; second, insufficient financial resources; and third, a poor turnaround strategy.

INEFFECTIVE MANAGEMENT

The basic problem that has plagued Arden-Mayfair for many years is weak and decentralized management. The firm has seen its market share in southern California shrink from 10 percent in 1968 to less than 2 percent. Its problems go back to the mid-1960s when the Mayfair market chain merged with Arden Farms Co. Dairy executives from Arden, who lacked retailing experience, took over supermarket operations, and the company remained a loose association of small grocery chains, lacking the sophisticated inventory and distribution controls of its competitors.

The jury is still out on Arden-Mayfair, but the dairy division has lost considerable sales because other supermarkets have refused to carry Arden dairy products, owing to the the dairy's competitive connections. Arden-Mayfair's problems are basically management and operating deficiencies on top of a poor strategic concept. But until these basic deficiencies are corrected, Arden-Mayfair will totter along until a deep threat ends its corporate life or spurs it to action.

Usually management is ineffective in a turnaround for two reasons. Either the new manager cannot handle the pressures of the job, or the board tries to ride out the turnaround effort with the same management. In the former case, Frank Grisanti points out the most formidable problems an unequipped new manager faces:

> A traditional kind of professional manager is geared to grow something within a reasonably healthy environment, with adequate resources to get the job done. He is not used to negative forces working against him in an environment of shortages—shortages of money, shortages of products, shortages of cooperation, shortages of everything. That is an environment that most people really don't understand. They've never been there before.[3]

Old Management Problems

Old management is usually only effective when the problems are mainly external. When the board decides to ride with the same management, it is taking an illogical risk. Frank Grisanti asks, "How can someone who has been a mediocre manager suddenly become a crackerjack manager? Turnarounds require crackerjack managers." An example of a turnaround attempt that failed the first time is the Simmons Company (the largest U.S. bedding manufacturer). Simmons undertook some drastic moves to try to reverse a serious downtrend. Some, including the use of lower-quality materials and nonselective inventory reductions, proved counterproductive. Some of the other moves, such as giving the corporate staff more clout, streamlining marketing, trimming away many product lines, and cutting back a number of Simmons dealers, have had a positive effect. Even after trimming 600 white-collar and hourly employees from the corporate payroll, Simmons plants had low productivity. They ran only one shift, a lackadaisical pace by industry standards. The result of all this was that Simmons did not show solid evidence of genuine improvement. President Grant Simmons, a great-grandson of the founder, was asked to step down in June 1978. As one director said, "It's a pretty logical step. Grant Simmons was having trouble turning the company around." What Simmons had failed to do was to take charge personally and take even more Draconian steps to get the company moving again.

A similar situation existed at Sherwin-Williams Company, a billion-dollar paint manufacturer. Analysts who follow the company have been continually disappointed by management's prediction that each year would see a turnaround. The actual results—much worse than predicted—have raised serious doubts about the adequacy of Sherwin-Williams's financial controls. Although Sherwin-Williams operates in a mature, slow-growth industry, its competitors, such as Standard Brands Paint Co. and De Soto, Inc., a supplier to Sears, Roebuck & Co., posted record earnings while Sherwin-Williams floundered. The board of directors gave Walter O. Spencer years to turn Sherwin-Williams around before making him step down.

New Management Problems

Another company that has been plagued by bad management deficiencies is Genesco. First, young Frank Jarman seized control from his father, only to steer the company through the great apparel recession of 1974 to 75. In 1975, Frank made a case for Genesco's turnaround and indicated that analysts should concentrate their attention and judgment of potential to the new Genesco that emerged after 1975. The economy turned and Genesco didn't, largely because Frank Jarman had a devil of a time trying to integrate the myriad acquisitions his father had made. The strong-minded managers, accustomed to running their own shows, resisted the installation of financial controls necessary to keep track of operations in a multiline company. In early 1978, Frank Jarman lost his race against the clock and was replaced by John L. Hanigan. Hanigan has made the wholehearted housecleaning that both Frank and Maxey Jarman failed to come to grips with. He divested companies with a sales volume of over $200 million and losses of $20 million annually. As Hanigan says, "I found an organization that over the years had focused on gross sales. I had to change that focus."

Whether Hanigan will successfully complete Genesco's turnaround will depend on how well he can operate the remaining subsidiaries. A divestment program usually brings a huge write-down, which is followed by critical operating improvements. Whether these improvements can be sustained is the true test of sound management.

A classic case of failure to clean out a situation completely because of management inadequacies occurred at International Industries, where that old turnaround expert, Frank Grisanti, had to serve two separate terms as chief executive. Grisanti says: "I thought the company, with its food expertise, could change the pie chain from a cash-negative to a cash-positive position, but when that effort failed, it was a clear indication of deeper problems."

POOR TURNAROUND STRATEGY

The great Atlantic and Pacific Tea Company (A&P) has been in a slump since 1972. In 1974 A&P lost $157.1 million. Jonathan L. Scott, chairman of A&P for six years before his resignation in April 1980, shrugged off questions about A&P's viability with the usual "We're building for the future." But Robert D. Bolinder, who succeeded Scott as chairman of Albertsen's, points out, "A&P is a tough ship to turn around." A&P's fundamental problem is somewhat different from the other examples I have shown. A&P did bring in new management, and it was not burdened with scores of dissimilar acquisitions that have been the nemesis of other turnaround efforts, but fundamentally A&P has the wrong culture. Few of its employees still call it "grandma," but it has not shaken off the lethargy of the past. That lethargy is well represented among the ranks of its senior employees, most of whom have been retained through all the cutbacks A&P made.

Malaise

Scott did not cure the underlying malaise that pervades employee levels and store managers alike. He failed to change the poor culture at A&P so that a turnaround could be sustained. Scott shrank the supermarket chain, but the company had to abide by union seniority rules. As a result, older employees, often those who are the highest paid and least productive, have bumped younger ones, so that much of the force is now made up of long-term employees, set in the ways of the old pre-Scott A&P. Despite the fact that A&P has laid off 10 percent of its work force, its labor costs still run 12 percent of sales (the industry average is 10 percent). This can be deadly in a low-margin business.

A&P made a bold acquisition of National Tea's outlets in the Chicago area, only to see the A&P malaise cause sales to drop about 30 percent in the new outlets. Management eliminated unprofitable stores, only to see others take them over and double volume. It built new, larger stores, not always located for maximum market penetration. For a time even these poorly executed changes seemed to work, but then things appeared to go awry again.

Now that the company is back in the red and the initial buoyance in sales has fizzled, it is all too evident that the store-closing program failed as a remedy for A&P's difficulties. One reason it failed was that it was not accompanied by an adequate effort to overcome the managerial problems of the stores A&P retained. Scott spent a considerable amount of energy overhauling the organization—bringing in new people, building a sound real estate department, putting in tighter financial controls, improving the company's cash management, and installing information systems. But it remains to be seen whether these management improvements at the corporate level will translate into better performance where it counts—in the operation of A&P stores. A&P's future depends on increased sales and lower operating costs in the stores, and, in these nitty-gritty matters, the record so far has been grimly disappointing.

INSUFFICIENT FINANCIAL RESOURCES

Jeffrey Chanin summarizes his feelings about turnaround failures this way:

> I think my most significant experience with turnaround failures is that they didn't do a good enough job the first time. First, that means that you didn't solve the balance sheet problems. Second, you didn't cut deep enough the first time in any way. The third thing is to leave yourself cash-poor. Of all the things that I've seen, the worst is to leave yourself cash-poor. That may sound very difficult; how do you instill in the creditors a belief that they can do better by letting you manipulate the cash they leave you with.[4]

Support at Two Points

Creditor support is necessary at two critical times. The first is for bridge financing to finance the emergency stage. Usually a company of any size can self-finance through the stabilization part of the turnaround by making judicious divestments. The second time support is needed is beyond that, when the company wants to grow. This takes some convincing, and many a turnaround has failed for lack of creditor support at this point. Usually a company has shrunk in size, and a smaller entity cannot service the large debt previously accumulated. The lenders will have to reorganize the debt in order to sustain the turnaround. This can mean a combination of debt forgiveness, lowered interest rates, and conversion to equity participation. A lot of creditors balk at this stage and stall a turnaround from ever going full cycle.

American Motors Corporation has never been able to make a turnaround, because its lackluster operating performance has only exacerbated the company's need for capital to keep pace with its Big Three competitors. Few enterprises compare with the automobile business in the amounts of money it consumes in restyling and retooling. The resources American Motors can bring to the game have declined in recent years nearly to the vanishing point. AMC's general ability to generate cash in an industry that requires cash in huge amounts has been an insurmountable problem.

While some observers suggest that AMC should just drop out of building cars and concentrate on its profitable operations, the company is, in a sense, trapped. Its most profitable unit, AMC Jeep, shares tooling, engines, and other components with AMC autos. Without cars to share the tooling and other expenses, the cost of Jeep parts could soar. Management has decided its best option is to try to turn the car business around. But to do that, AMC requires the kind of capital it cannot generate internally and cannot raise externally through traditional sources. As I write this book, AMC has obtained assistance from Renault for capital and for filling out the economy end of its lackluster product line. In addition, it is now concentrating more effectively on the one or two areas (Jeeps and four-wheel-drive vehicles) where it has a competitive edge.

The problems faced by Massey-Ferguson, Ltd., stem largely from strategic decisions in the late 1960s to expand internationally, rather than scrap with Deere & Company and International Harvester Company for the North American market. By 1977, 70 percent of sales were outside North America—in Europe, Latin America, Africa, Asia, and Australia. That expansion was launched on borrowed money and, for a company of its size, Massey-Ferguson was operating on a shoestring. When the world farm equipment market shriveled in 1977, Massey-Ferguson was immediately in trouble. It has had large losses in each year since 1978 and at the date of this writing has not turned around yet.

GOVERNMENT INTERFERENCE

My litany of turnaround failures has to include the role of government in the success, and certainly the failure, of some turnarounds. An unusual dual example is that of the tangled affair of Chris-Craft Industries and Bangor-Punta over control of Piper Aircraft. During the long legal battle for control of Piper, both Chris-Craft and Bangor-Punta suffered serious operating declines. In a long-delayed court decision, Chris-Craft lost control of Piper to Bangor-Punta but made a sizable profit on its investment. Chris-Craft's main operating unit, its boat division, flowed red ink for years, while it went after Piper.

At the same time that Chris-Craft was looking for places to use its largess from the sale of its Piper stock, Bangor-Punta's own turnaround was being placed in jeopardy by the payoff to Chris-Craft. Piper proved to be a poor investment for Bangor; the legal tangles diverted incalculable amounts of management's attention and Piper had paltry earnings. It has taken years for Bangor to get its balance sheet restructured.

The effect of legal battles and government intervention can stall a turnaround. A classic case of government meddling is that of Rhone-Poulenc, S.A., a large French chemical and textile manufacturer that had its turnaround plans stalled before they could be implemented. Although the company had huge losses in 1975, 1976, and 1977, its managers' efforts to cut losses were constantly frustrated by the government. The company seemed determined to close down five fiber plants, eliminating 6,000 jobs, but Premier Raymond Barre shelved the plans. The only alternative was to struggle from one crisis to another, assisted by government financing. In frustration, President Fonauld Gillet told his shareholders, "We know the French are very sensitive to political logic and much less, unfortunately, to economic logic."

BAIL-OUT STRATEGIES SHORT OF CHAPTER 11

When a company becomes realistic after an unsuccessful turnaround effort, it has several alternatives short of filing for protection under the Bankruptcy Act. The alternative it chooses depends to a great extent on the state of its financial condition and the rate of its operating losses. A company can:

1. Cease operation and have an orderly liquidation of assets
2. Sell out as a going concern to an interested buyer who can better utilize the assets and expertise of the company
3. Seek a merger with a stronger company in the same industry

Cease Operations

I am familiar with several cases of companies whose balance sheets were sound which decided to liquidate rather than continue operations after making a turnaround attempt. Two examples come immediately to mind. In one of the classiest liquidations I've seen, Overseas National decided that its assets were more valuable to other airlines than as part of a going concern. It sold its fleet for $115 million for a gain of more than $23 million over book value and promptly shut down operations. In many cases managements have not been realistic and have run a company right into the ground. Holding out the hope that the external and internal forces that were giving the company problems would simply go away has proven disastrous to a number of companies.

Another case where realism prevailed is the case of Pacific States Steel Corporation of Union City, California. The company was beset by a combination of an ancient plant, featherbedding by its unions, and stiff foreign competition. Rather than forcing a showdown with its union that could have bled the company dry, Pacific States instead chose an orderly shutdown of operations. This strategy conserved net worth, which had been hurt by stiff operating losses. In addition, the company had certain fixed assets that were more valuable in liquid form than utilized in the steel industry.

Sell Out

The usual route that companies follow when a turnaround has not gotten them back on the right track is a sellout to a stronger company in the same industry. Usually companies in the same industry have the expertise and the market requirements to give the shareholders of the troubled company a higher price than other companies could offer. A classic case of this was Fibreboard's sale to Louisiana Pacific Corporation for roughly $50 million.

Merge

LTV Corporation has been lurching since the Jim Ling era. Its largest single unit, Jones & Laughlin Steel, has been beset by the classic problems of the steel industry. Obviously LTV could never have a viable turnaround without solving the J&L problem, which has been plaguing it for a number of years. Solving that problem, and, hence, LTV's turnaround problem, will be no mean trick. There are very few buyers for a sick steel company, certainly not other major steel companies, which have antitrust problems to contend with. LTV's solution was to combine the walking wounded and merge with the steel operations of Lykes Corporation. As one investment counselor reacted, "That's not a merger—

it's a suicide pact." It remains to be seen whether the merger can work, although 1980 results were encouraging.

LIFE IN THE TOILS OF THE BANKRUPTCY ACT

When turnaround efforts fail, a company in perilous condition files under the bankruptcy section on the reorganization section of Chapter 11 of the Bankruptcy Act. Filing under the bankruptcy section is tantamount to orderly liquidation because it offers little hope of a company ever resuming operations as a going concern. If the company is large enough, for example Penn Central, a viable portion of the company may emerge to operate again some day. Victor Palmieri revived the flagging real estate operations of Penn Central and made them a profitable entity.

The usual route to follow for a troubled company that has some possibility of future viability is to file under the reorganization section of Chapter 11. This protects the company against precipitous creditor action until the company can reorganize its operations and come up with an operating plan suitable to the courts. In essence, a company has a last try at a turnaround under some special legal protections. Most companies flunk this test. A study conducted by Dun and Bradstreet indicated that only 33 percent of the firms which had filed for Chapter XI (now a section of Chapter 11) relief between 1964 and 1968 were still in operation two years after their proceedings closed. Thirty-eight percent had either discontinued operations or were adjudicated bankrupts. The remaining 29 percent were either unaccounted for or merged or acquired.

Chapter 11 Trade-off

Chapter 11 is a last-ditch turnaround effort. There are numerous reasons, both logical and illogical, to seek Chapter 11 protection, but few managements properly assess the very real trade-offs that a company must make in that situation. Generally, I have not favored the Chapter 11 route, but if you need protection from your creditors, it is often the only way to go. Recent experience under the new Chapter 11 procedures has produced results more favorable for the stockholders than results obtained under the old Chapter XI procedures. In consumer-products situations, where you have lots of trade creditors who can't agree, it's usually the answer. In industrial or commercial products, where you have a limited number of highly sophisticated vendors, you usually can work out an arrangement and don't need Chapter 11. Another solid time for seeking protection is when creditor pressure is stifling the turnaround success. Such a situation occurred at Apeco Corporation when it filed for voluntary reorganization under the bankruptcy act. Apeco, which lost

$22 million on sales of $108 million in 1977, had spent six months negotiating with its banks for additional working capital. Although President Arthur S. Nicholas had launched a major corporate overhaul, slashing unprofitable divisions and cutting payroll nearly in half, the banks remained uncooperative. Interest payments of $2 million annually still ate most of whatever cash flow the company could generate. Nicholas preferred to file for bankruptcy, to take the creditor pressure off the company and give it time to rebuild.

Predicting Success

As I pointed out earlier, only one-third of the companies going into Chapter XI proceedings under the old code came out viable enough to be in operation two years afterward. Interestingly enough, Comerford has come up with a mathematical way of predicting who will succeed or fail before Chapter XI (not the new Chapter 11) is entered.[5] His mathematic model is 85 percent accurate. Table 12-1 below shows the success rate on a group of fifty-two companies. The formulation is derived from multivariate discriminant analysis and develops an equation not unlike Edward Altman's for predicting bankruptcy (See Chapter 7). In this case the Z value that discriminates winners and losers is zero. Thus, companies forecasted to fail have negative values of Z and companies forecasted to come through Chapter XI successfully have positive Z values. The greater the positive value, the greater the chance for success; and the greater the negative value, the less chance for success.

TABLE 12-1
Percentages of Model B Correct and Incorrect Classifications of Analysis Sample of United States Chapter XI Successes and Failures from 1963 to 1973*

	Computed Chapter XI group membership				
	Correct		*Incorrect*		
Actual group membership	*No.*	*%*	*No.*	*%*	*Total no.*
Failure	21	81	5	19	26
Success	23	88	3	12	26
TOTAL	44	85	8	15	52

Source: Robert Comerford, "Bankruptcy as a Business Strategy," p. 149.

*Note that Comerford conducted his study under the old Chapter 11 law, then known as Chapter XI.

The discriminant function which was derived by Comerford is:

$$Z = 1.44X_1 - 1.78X_2 + 6.06X_3 + .62X_4 - 2.56X_5 + .37X_6$$

where X_1 = Net Income/Total Assets
X_2 = Total Debt/Total Assets
X_3 = Quick Assets/Total Assets
X_4 = Current Assets/Current Liabilities
X_5 = Quick Assets/Current Liabilities
X_6 = Net Income/Stockholders' Equity

For example: $X_1 = -(0.1)$, $X_2 = 0.6$, $X_3 = 0.21$, $X_4 = 1.1$, $X_5 = 0.7$ and $X_6 = -(0.2)$. In this case $Z = -1.12$, and the company is forecasted to fail.

No Picnic

Life in the toils of Chapter 11 can be a downright nightmare. A case in point is the experience of Andrew Lozyniak, chief executive of Dynamics Corporation of America, which "successfully" went through Chapter XI (the name for Chapter 11 at that time) proceedings. Lozyniak felt that his twenty-eight-month battle with creditors, lawyers, accountants, suppliers, customers, and management consultants was definitely the worst period of his life. Lozyniak worked fifteen hours a day, practically seven days a week. He scarcely saw his family at all. One of his biggest fights was with the creditor committee over how to shrink his company enough to make it profitable. "They always want you to sell your winners," he complains. "That's a mistake; the winners are the ones that support the new debt you need to carry you." At one point, the committee wanted him to sell Waring, the company's largest division, which accounted for more than half of the revenues and even more of the cash flow. Lozyniak refused to sell because he was certain he could turn Waring around. Altogether, the bills for professional and court fees eventually exceeded $3 million before Dynamics Corporation came out of Chapter XI.

Dynamics Corporation's experience with Chapter XI points out one of its fundamental weaknesses—the dissimilar objectives of the creditors and the stockholders (as represented by the management). In most reorganization situations, the creditors are so deeply involved that they become, in effect, owners, but they still have different objectives from the management. Creditors often want the management to sell its winners or its only viable core operation in order to satisfy creditor claims. This action also has the effect of guaranteeing the demise of the business as a going concern.

REFERENCES

[1]"Another Chrysler Turnaround: But Is This One for Real?", *Forbes*, Nov. 15, 1976, p. 39.

[2]Interview with Frank A. Grisanti, president, Grisanti and Galef, Los Angeles, Calif., February 1978.

[3]Ibid.

[4]Interview with Jeffrey Chanin, former executive vice president, Daylin Corp., Los Angeles, Calif., February 1978.

[5]Robert A. Comerford, "Bankruptcy as a Business Strategy: A Multivariate Analysis of the Financial Characteristics of Firms Which Have Succeeded in Chapter XI Compared to Those Which Have Failed" (Ph.D. dissertation, University of Massachusetts, 1976), p. 29.

PART THREE
LEADERSHIP IN TURNAROUND

Every achievement of management is the achievement of a manager. Every failure is a failure of a manager. People manage rather than "forces" or "facts." The vision, dedication, and integrity of managers determines whether there is management or mismanagement.

Peter F. Drucker, *Management: Tasks, Responsibilities, Practices*

13
THE MANAGEMENT CHANGE STAGE

An effective general manager really doesn't need everybody's love; their respect will do just fine.[1]

Richard Sloma

This chapter begins the part of this book concerning the central role of management leadership in a turnaround situation. In Part 1, we have seen how management problems are the principal reason for corporate decline. In Part 2, I have shown that, given a viable core to work with and support from creditors, new management can make the difference between success and failure in a turnaround situation. Part 3 begins the more detailed presentation of the stages of a turnaround.

The corporation has reached its moment of truth and decided that something out of the ordinary is required to save the enterprise or get it back on the track. This period of self-doubt and hesitation can be costly if it is prolonged. In more than seven out of ten cases, management has to be replaced because they either cannot cope with the problem or they, themselves (or at least the CEO), are the problem. The board of directors has to make a decision on who will lead the turnaround.

THE MANAGEMENT CHANGE DECISION

Management change can mean either changing management or management changing its approach. The former case is more common, because few managements can change their stripes. A deep threat may spur them to a flurry of inadequate activity, but usually their timing is off, and they are looking at their company through rose-colored glasses. Sometimes the board decides to ride with current management, but usually there is a specific underlying reason for this. If the principal problems of a company are external, that is, beyond management control, a board may decide that change is inappropriate.

When Management Controls the Stock

In other instances, management may control through stockholdings or board membership ties. Rapid American's turnaround is a hybrid example of the continuity of management. Meshulem Ricklis put together a loosely run conglomerate that had initial success based upon accounting gimmickery. Ricklis receded from active management, not realizing that the long-run health of a company does not depend on good paper acquisitions, but rather on the ability to operate. Subsequent to his taking a low profile, Rapid American floundered. Ricklis, still possessing a strong ownership position, came back on the scene to take charge of the turnaround effort. He brought in some new, strong executives under him. He was forced to sell one of his larger winners, Playtex, to Esmark, Inc. His efforts have produced a turnaround that appears to have the ability to sustain itself.

Off the top of my head, I can recall two instances where the original management with a strong ownership position was forced out of a company when it was in trouble, only to return later after the company had been saved. The jury is still out on Farah, Inc., where its founder, William Farah, was forced out and a couple of years later staged a comeback. In the interim, while Farah was absent from company management, the company was able to get partially out of its difficulties. There's no doubt that he will win the popularity contest at Farah, but there is serious doubt as to whether he can complete the turnaround successfully in a company that he got into trouble.

Another case is that of Grubb & Ellis, a large San Francisco real estate firm that ran into trouble. In 1974, Harold A. Ellis, Jr., the founder, was deposed as head of the go-go firm and replaced by a turnaround specialist. The company returned to profitability a year later and began squirreling away money to pay off its debt to Wells Fargo Bank. Ellis is, if nothing else, tenacious and in early 1978 engineered his way back to the now-healthy company by enlisting the help of enough shareholders (he retained 18 percent) to take control.

The Timid Board of Directors

In public companies, the board of directors can move more effectively to deal with a problem at the top, but often it does not move briskly. A typical series of events in a large company involved the Singer Corporation. Although the directors eventually moved, in 1975, to change the top man in Singer, they did so rather reluctantly and with no great haste. As early as 1971, there were disturbing signs that should have been viewed with alarm by the board. In the late summer of 1974, some earlier diversification moves made by Donald Kircher, chairman of Singer, were starting to come apart at the seams. Kircher closed down part of Singer's Friden subsidiary, creating write-offs amounting to $30 million after taxes. The company's gamble against the dollar and foreign exchange cost $8.3 million. Altogether, Singer eventually reported a loss for 1974 of $10 million. It was the first year the company had run in the red since 1917, when it had to write off companies that were confiscated during the Russian Revolution. The Singer board hardly acted like a group of vigilantes; instead it then appointed committees that proceeded very cautiously.

The Singer case illustrates the general manner in which boards of directors operate when faced with poor management performance. This lack of decisive board action is partially understandable, considering the framework in which a board operates. As the president of a large eastern company said: "It's pretty easy for a smart management to snow a board of directors right up until the time that the profits start to cave in, and by that time, it's too damn late to do anything. The board really has very little access to inside information of a company." The board of directors gets snowed because it is only judging the outward manifestations of current success or failure. It is very difficult for issues of basic importance to a company's economic operation to be available to the board, unless the chief executive officer recognizes that the board members can give him help and is willing to throw the bad and good news on the table for them.

Most directors in this study owed their appointments to the CEO. Personal loyalties tend to go deep. Together with this kinship is a healthy dose of trust. Asking a president to resign is a traumatic experience under any circumstances. Loyalties, working relationships, and social relationships all get in the way of complete objectivity in appraising and concluding what is best for the company. Most outside directors try to avoid the high level of emotion that almost always attends a forced resignation. As indicated earlier, most outside directors resign to avoid the unpleasantness inevitably involved. And even some of those who chose not to resign, but to stay and participate in an eventual solution, tend to procrastinate and to defer the ultimate, but necessary, decision. They seem to keep hoping that things will somehow improve. This attitude was found particularly in outside directors who had professional, financial, or legal-service relationships with the company.

Existing Management

The perplexing situation of existing management is further pointed out by Ross Gwinner:

> It is extremely difficult to face your own mistakes and do the surgery that it takes to correct it. Because in order to do that surgery you have to

> break commitments to people that you hired in good times when everything was up. . . . "Come join us and everything will be super." You'll have to turn to them and say, "First, cut your budget back by 30 percent and then, secondly, cut your staff back and, thirdly, you're terminated." That's impossible for most people to do. That's because it's construed as being deceitful, a liar, etc. When you come in as an outsider, and you didn't have any part of creating the problem, you can objectively evaluate and make decisions which may not be popular.[2]

Too often current management will blame a series of losses on specifics: three years ago our sales manager was out ill for six weeks; two years ago the point on our product was defective and caused a lot of returns; last year our production of one product was held up for a month while a machine was being repaired; etc., etc. Management assumes no bad luck will occur this year, so there is really no problem. Realistic managements know that operations should be planned to show respectable profits at year-end despite a little hard luck. Unfortunately, some hard luck normally characterizes every year.

Taking drastic action, once it is required, is often more difficult in public companies, which are concerned more with gains in quarterly earnings than with fundamentals. Lenders, particularly banks, also have to be cautious in pushing for the removal of current management because of the Glass Steagall Act. Recently, in the W. T. Grant bankruptcy, bank creditors were sued by stockholders alleging that the company was being run for the benefit of banks rather than for the shareholders. In the Memorex case, however, the Bank of America, as primary lender, took a lead position in getting Robert Wilson to come in as the new CEO. In addition to a generous compensation package for Wilson himself, the bank restructured Memorex's debt. This whole package was designed to attract a proven performer to help save the bank's shaky position.

Gould, Inc., is a case where the directors chose to bring in a new CEO. A combination of problems had plagued the entire industry and the company for the prior five years. The company had gone through a major strike and had antiquated plant and equipment. The board of directors reached a point where they considered three options: selling the company outright, merging with another company, or finding new management. They chose to find new management and appointed William T. Vlvisaker as chief executive officer.

In the rare instance where a company is a regulated one, a government agency forces a change. A case in point is Citizens and Southern National Bank, where Richard Kattel was ousted in 1978 because of pressure over irregularities by Richard Hensel, the comptroller of the Currency's regional administrator.

Present management is most unlikely to accomplish a successful turnaround for two reasons: First, they got the company into its present difficulties. Basically, you can't make mediocre managers into crackerjack managers, and you need crackerjack managers in a turnaround situation. Second, present management is often emotionally inhibited and cannot apply the necessary remedies, such as laying off personnel (some of whom may be relatives or close friends) or closing down or disposing of a division or product line in which they have parental pride. Few turnaround leaders were willing to fault their predecessors, but almost to a man they felt that more decisive action is necessary in the face of impending difficulty and potential disaster.

QUANTITATIVE VIEWS OF MANAGEMENT CHANGE

Surprisingly, a vast majority of turnarounds are not performed by outsiders. Even when outsiders are brought in, less than half consider themselves turnaround specialists. Three out of four times a new CEO is appointed to make the turnaround. In about six out of ten of these cases the new man is an outsider. The results of the survey on this are shown in Table 13-1.

When we look at the total turnarounds, 56 percent were performed by insiders and only 44 percent by outsiders. This does not fit the general conception held by many people. Of course, about half the insiders were new people, so that the total number of new CEOs is high at 73 percent. The replacement of a CEO with an outsider always seems to get more headline attention in the media.

Change Affected by Reasons for Decline

Digging beneath the statistics shown in Table 13-1, I was able to gather some interesting insights. There are some significant interrelationships

TABLE 13-1
Matrix of New and Old CEOs for Turnaround Companies Compared to Insider/Outsider Status

New CEO?	*Insider**	*Outsider**	*Total companies**
Yes, New CEO	23 (39)	36 (41)	59 (73)
No, Same CEO	22 (100)	0 (0)	22 (27)
TOTAL COMPANIES	45 (56)	36 (44)	81 (100)

Source: Donald B. Bibeault, Survey of eighty-one turnaround company chief executives, April 1978.

*Percent in parentheses

TABLE 13-2
Comparison of Reason for Decline with Whether a New CEO Was Brought In

	New chief executive officer named?		
Reason for decline	***Yes****	***No****	***Total****
External factors only	1 (12)	7 (88)	8
Balance—external/internal	14 (70)	6 (30)	20
Internal triggered by external	9 (64)	5 (36)	14
Internal factors only	35 (90)	4 (10)	39
TOTAL	59 (73)	22 (27)	81

Source: Bibeault, Survey of eighty-one turnaround company chief executives, April, 1978.

*Percent in parentheses.

between whether a new CEO is brought in to do a turnaround and the reasons why a company got into trouble. These are shown in Table 13-2.

When a company is troubled by external factors, it sticks with its current CEO about 90 percent of the time. When a company is troubled by internal problems, it makes a change in 90 percent of the cases. When it is troubled by a mix of problems, it changes CEOs about 70 percent of the time. The survey findings make common sense and also conform to the in-depth interview results. One caveat must be pointed out, and that is that the survey is based on the perceptions of the CEOs themselves. A CEO who is able to ride through a decline may believe, and may have convinced others, that the problems were largely external.

A similar but revealing analysis is the comparison of whether the chief executive officer was an insider or an outsider and the reason for company decline. By definition, when there is not a change in CEOs, the CEO is an insider. Results of this comparison are shown in Table 13-3 below.

Insiders

Interestingly, in the one case where a turnaround was due to external causes and performed by a new CEO, that person was an insider. Insiders also predominate in situations that are a mix of external and internal factors. Only in the case of solely internal factors does the use of outsiders predominate. All that makes common sense when you think about it.

Insiders predominate in larger companies with substantial management depth. A case in point is NCR Corporation, where William Anderson was the extremely successful chairman of NCR's Japanese subsidiary. Anderson had already turned around NCR in Japan, transforming the subsidiary into a showcase. It was the largest, most profitable, and most innovative of NCR's forty-five foreign subsidiaries. Because of his track record, Anderson was such an obvious choice that no one else was really considered.

The advantage of the insider is that he knows where the bodies are buried, or how to find out where they're buried. If he can move with detachment and unchallenged authority, he will probably make fewer mistakes than the outsider. When the board is forced to go to the outside, it may have a difficult time spotting a turnaround leader, unless it can offer the challenge and rewards to attract an acknowledged star with a good track record.

Nonspecialists

Another aspect of the survey results is surprising. 81 percent of the turnarounds were led by chief executive officers who were not turnaround specialists, and only 19 percent were led by turnaround specialists. These results are based upon the opinions of the leaders themselves and are shown in Appendix Table O. A turnaround specialist connotation is a tag that some executives don't like to be stuck with. Even Robert Wilson of Memorex doesn't like the tag. He insists that despite his two turnaround triumphs, "I don't like to be considered a turnaround artist. That's the drudgery. I like building for the future."

TABLE 13-3
Comparison of Reason for Company Decline and Whether the Turnaround Was Performed by an "Insider" or an "Outsider"

	Chief executive officer		
Reason for decline	***Insider****	***Outsider****	***Total***
External factors only	8 (100)	0 (0)	8
Balance—external/internal	15 (75)	5 (25)	20
Internal triggered by external	10 (71)	4 (29)	14
Internal factors only	12 (31)	27 (69)	39
TOTAL	45 (56)	36 (44)	81

Source: Bibeault, Survey of eighty-one turnaround company chief executives, April 1978.

*Percent in parentheses

The needs of the organization for various types of management vary over time. Different types of problems require different solutions. What worked well in one turnaround may not work well in another, and vice versa. It is awfully hard to classify or pigeonhole people. A person may not change, but circumstances may show a side of him you never knew was there.

REFERENCES

[1]Richard S. Sloma, *No Nonsense Management* (New York: Macmillan, 1977), pp. 79, 80.

[2]Interview with Ross Gwinner, former president, Capitol Film Labs, Washington, D.C., August 1978.

14
TURNAROUND LEADER CHARACTERISTICS

Things get done in our society because of a man or a woman with conviction.[1]

Robert Townsend

A VARIETY OF STYLES

The arts and styles of leadership have always fascinated historians. For centuries, chroniclers as well as military men have mused on the generalship of Alexander. Herodotus and Thucydides observed the exercises of command on the battlegrounds of Greece and Asia Minor. From Socrates to Machiavelli, wise men have advised princes on the techniques of conquest. Whatever his style, the turnaround leader's individual personality leaves a vivid impression on company affairs. The mere projection of personal genius or desire does not render a turnaround strategy more effective, but, I know, without it the survival of a troubled company would be in doubt.

Architect of Strategy

We can identify three main aspects of leadership in a turnaround. First, the turnaround leader is the architect of the turnaround strategy. As architect he requires entrepreneurial skills, broad business experience, analytical ability, creativity, and self-awareness. In a few cases, in larger corporations these requirements are completed with a sensitivity to society's expectations regarding the businessman's broader social responsibilities. In most cases, social responsibility does not greatly influence corporate turnaround strategy.

Implementer of Strategy

Second, and most important, the turnaround leader is an implementer of strategy: he must supply organizational strategy; he must promote and defend it; he must integrate the conflicting interests which necessarily arise around it; he must see to it that the organization's essential needs are met; and he must be the judge of results. An implementer must be tough-minded and have objective orientation, self-confidence, decisiveness, good negotiating skills, good interviewing skills, high standards of evaluation, and, most importantly an impatience to get something done.

Personal Leader

Third, the turnaround leader is a personal leader, someone distinctive from all other persons in the organization. Within the range of choice permitted by his own knowledge and command of himself, he achieves a leadership style. This pattern of personal behavior reflects his individuality as much as his office; it does not follow inevitably from the organizational responsibilities he assumed. How the leader's personal style contributes to company performance, character, and tone is more important in a turnaround than at any other time in corporate life.

Men in turnaround positions are not required to have a personality of any given mold. The effort to relate personality traits to executive effectiveness is no longer pursued as naively as it once was. According to Kenneth Andrews: "Business leaders generally are likely to be characterized by drive, intellectual ability, initiative, creativeness, social ability, and flexibility. These qualities permit a fairly wide range of style so long as it is dynamic and energetic."[2]

Common Characteristics

What is important is that the personal traits inspire confidence in the ultimate survival and renewal of a troubled company. Not only must the turnaround leader be self-confident, he must project this fact. The difficulty of attributing a given executive style to turnaround leaders is compounded by their observed pattern of concentrating on objectives rather than methods. The turnaround leaders were inconsistent in the style of their approach but consistent in their pursuit of objectives. The leaders were inconsistent from two viewpoints: first, style varied among different turnaround leaders, and, second, individual leaders adopted different styles to suit the circumstances faced.

John Byers of Wells Fargo Bank, who has seen many turnaround leaders in action, has this to say about their common characteristics:

> The one thing that they do have in common is the ability to attract good people with a high feeling of loyalty to subordinates, who advocate the sixty- and eighty-hour week. I don't know how you define leadership, but without it you'll never get a turnaround. The only remaining char-

> acteristics a turnaround person needs are toughness and competitiveness. A highly competitive man enjoys a fight, enjoys dealing with bank creditors today, trade creditors tomorrow, and subordinated debt holders the next day. He should not have a vested interest in any decision that the company's made. A good turnaround guy can't waste energy defending past decisions.[3]

Successful turnaround leaders seem to sense which task merits the highest priority, are able to seize the initiative, and devote enormous energy to driving the organization and themselves to task completion. They consistently are dogged in their pursuit of objectives and the accomplishment of goals, while maintaining the flexibility to change intermediate goals as the situation develops. They are very determined people. Robert Wilson's first few days at Memorex is a case in point. Wilson took an apartment near the plant. There, unencumbered by family, he could devote virtually every waking hour to the job. To maintain absolute concentration, he abstained from all outside activities. For Memorex, he would do almost anything, anywhere, anytime.

SPOTTING THE TURNAROUND LEADER

It's extremely difficult to generalize about the characteristics of your "typical" turnaround leader. They can't be determined by looking for physical stereotypes. You have to see people in action to get some initial clues about them. Perhaps this little illustration can help.[4] In just about every staff meeting or production meeting or boardroom you will find the innovator and the "abominable no man"—and types who are somewhere in between. Here are some of them:

1. The bright-eyed zealot who feels that anything connected with growth and newness must be good, regardless of cost or net profit.
2. The man who waits for the boss to tip his hand so that he can agree. This kind of man is gutless.
3. The suave individual who makes progressive-sounding comments, uses the word "dynamic" often, and contrives largely to hold his job.
4. The tough-minded man who demands facts, a blueprint for action, and realistic controls, yet is impatient to get something done.
5. The man who is opposed to innovation of any kind if it involves courage and positive action. His usual reaction to new ideas is, "Come on, now, let's be realistic."

The Tough-Minded Manager

Obviously, type four is the man who best fits the bill of what I know as the turnaround man. Generally, but not always, the turnaround leader is thought of as a tough guy because he is dealing with a tough situation. Robert Sackman, president of Rodal Corporation, says:

> He must be willing to spread a little blood and guts around the organization. Many men break psychologically when it comes to firing a lot of people who have been in the corporation for fifteen years, and who have families, etc. This man must come in with the understanding that he is doing the greater good over the long pull. Not everybody is capable of really doing the shorter-term massacre.[5]

A capsule view of the typical turnaround man is offered by Robert Brown:

> They have learned how to identify sore spots. They aren't people-oriented; they're people users. They don't have a lot of friends, they are not social successes, they are just known as blood-and-guts guys. They are the George Pattons of the business world. Usually there is a lot of loner in them, too. They like to make decisions by themselves. They usually are very decisive—very, very decisive. This comes from a natural feel and lots of experience. I think there is less science to it and just a willingness to achieve results. They are very achievement-oriented people.[6]

Very few turnaround men describe themselves as "nice guys," although only about one-third subscribe to the term "tough guys." They usually agree that the classic nice guy could not succeed in a rough turnaround situation because turnaround men have to have tough skins. In one case, where a consultant was performing the turnaround, management of the company was understandably resentful. The rescuer in this situation was once assigned to an unairconditioned office facing the Gulf of Mexico during an August heat wave; another, in Maine, got an underheated office in February. And sometimes there's no office—just a small desk.

Action Orientation

Turnaround men move decisively but do so based on facts, not fantasy. An example of the thorough approach to things is the way Robert Wilson of Memorex operates. Wilson was known as one of the toughest, most exacting bosses at G.E. His management teams were consistently rated among the most prepared. Wilson demanded this. Since he knew all the answers, he demanded that those working for him know them too. He was both a perfectionist and a disciplinarian like his father. He demanded as much from his subordinates as he did from himself. But because he exuded confidence, he instilled in his subordinates the belief that they could accomplish almost anything.

One of the striking characteristics of turnaround leaders, whether in the military world or in business, is their desire to gain the initiative. Frank Grisanti refers to this desire as action orientation. "The characteristic that I like to see in a guy who has all the technical qualifications is a kind of hunger that enables him to motivate people, make them bust their tails for him. That's the kind of guy I need. He is hungry for achievement. He's a doer.[7]

Although he is a loner, the turnaround man likes to build a team, and he has the chemistry and charisma that link the team together. Vince Lombardi was a great turnaround man in football. Although he was tough and somewhat detached from his players, he had a warm and emotional relationship with them, and they really loved him. Although he is definitely not loved, the turnaround man does build an emotional bond to the organization. He maintains that bond, even though he has to get rid of a lot of people on occasion. A core of people usually remain intensely loyal to him and join him in making the company better.

REQUIRED SKILLS

There are four characteristics and skills that seem to appear time after time in my contacts with turnaround leaders. These are:

1. An entrepreneurial instinct coupled with professional management skills
2. Broad business experience
3. Expert negotiating skills
4. Expert interviewing skills

Entrepreneurial Instinct

Entrepreneurial instinct, coupled with strong professional management skills, is a rare combination among most business managers. Some managers have one of these characteristics, while others have the other characteristic. Few have both. Turnaround men need both characteristics to do an effective job. They need good professional management skills in order to evaluate and cope with the multifaceted problems facing a troubled company. They need entrepreneurial skills in devising, searching out, and seizing opportunities during every stage of the turnaround. According to Frank Grisanti:

> The guy who takes a company up the curve must have a lot of entrepreneurial instinct. A custodial manager doesn't need that. He has a lot of momentum. It's like a ship on the waves doing fifteen knots, really moving. It's easy for this guy to go forward. It's the opposite for a guy whose tugs just left him. He has a full, new head of steam coming, and he has to take it from ground zero up to fifteen knots. That takes a little different kind of a thrust. It takes more of an entrepreneurial drive—a go-go kind of thing. He has to deal with negative forces. It takes a gutsier guy.[8]

It appears to me that the turnaround man is a hybrid of both types and is flexible enough to know which type of instinct should command a given situation. In this sense the turnaround man must play both games at once.

Broad Business Experience

Most turnaround situations require broad business experience, usually operating experience. I differentiate here between hands-on operating experience of a broad nature and the broad experience consulting provides. Those people who work as successful turnaround consultants have had operating responsibility at other times in their careers. Very few, if any, had careers in pure staff activities. A turnaround man must be able to penetrate the paper-and-opinion screen that is often thrown up when he enters a new situation. He will probably face overly optimistic sales projections, the overestimation of the company's capacity to deliver finished products on schedule, and the assignment of inflated values to completed inventory that is actually out of fashion or to parts inventory that is out of balance. To cope with this the turnaround leader must bring some hardheaded and practical experience to the table. As Frank Grisanti says:

> We have to be darn realistic when we go into a situation. Most managers we find in such situations have an optimistic bias. We have to say, "Hey, maybe it's nice to say you ought to have more sales, but there is no way you are going to get more sales. The fact remains there are forty-seven people in this business, and the top three have 72 percent of the market. The other 28 percent of it is in the hands of this other great big group of people. You only have a half of one percent and you are struggling to increase share. There is only one way you can get it, and that is to lower prices, and that means lower margins. You're already in trouble,

so you shouldn't be in this business. There's no way you are going to increase sales profitably to meet your forecasts."[9]

An intimate knowledge of the industry of which the troubled company is a part, or the ability to acquire such knowledge quickly, is most helpful. It is true, as Roy Ash says, that at the highest level of abstraction all business problems are similar. This fact does not preclude the need for the specialized knowledge that is extremely helpful in evaluating specific company problems. A turnaround man has to have seen enough industries in depth to work at the operating level with a broader perspective in mind.

A case illustration may be helpful here. Robert McLaughlin was able to take Fibreboard Corporation partially through its turn by evaluating losing and winning parts of the business. Shortly after successfully selling off its troubled carton group, McLaughlin was let go. The board felt that McLaughlin was a "good-deals" man but could not take the company through its next stage, where better operating experience would be essential.

Negotiating Skills

One of the key abilities a turnaround leader needs is the ability to negotiate. This is important even before he steps into a turnaround situation. Usually he is faced with lender and board pressure. Before accepting a turnaround assignment, tough negotiations should be undertaken with both the lenders and the board. The lender negotiations can be critical to eventual success. Unless the lending parties are convinced that they are going to be much better off by being patient and providing support, the turnaround has a good chance of failing. Robert Wilson's negotiations prior to accepting the Memorex job are a classic example of how things should be handled. Wilson was considering the job, but there were some major stumbling blocks, particularly since the company owed the Bank of America $150 million. Wilson used George Bragg, a trusted colleague, to help develop his negotiating posture. What Memorex needed immediately was a restructuring of debt, and Bragg proceeded to work out a plan. In essence, it called for the Bank of America and thirteen other lenders to convert $40 million of their debt to equity and to accept 4 percent interest and a stretch-out repayment schedule on the rest. To cap it all, the Bank of America was to extend Memorex a new line of credit for $35 million. All during a turnaround effort, negotiating skills are tested. The turnaround man must conduct critical negotiations with involved parties, such as creditors, new suppliers, labor unions, and, finally, as a last resort, suitable merger partners or acquirers.

Interviewing Skills

To find out what is really going on, the turnaround leader has to have excellent interviewing skills. These are often necessary because the formal reporting systems in even the larger troubled companies are inadequate. Thomas Wilcox found this out when he first arrived at Crocker National Bank. The bank's management information system was so primitive that he could not even get answers to basic questions on costs, profitability, and management responsibilities. As Wilcox says wryly, "I don't think those who designed the information system ever anticipated the requirement that management could intercept the information flow."

MOTIVATING CHARACTERISTICS

Focus on Objectives

Motivation includes both the motivation of self and the motivation of others. In order to be effective, turnaround leaders have learned how to focus their energies strategically. John Thompson of Crocker Bank feels that the turnaround man is a much different breed of cat than a custodial executive. Just as he must be able to focus himself, he must be able to focus the organization:

> The turnaround man's job is to focus the organization on the right issues, provide the charisma, provide the leadership, and wedge everyone into an effective team that has a commonality of purpose. When he does this, he really becomes an energy force within the company. A good turnaround guy is able to transmit energy quite far down the organization.[10]

Table 14-1 shows the survey results of the motivational aspects of turnaround leadership.

Self-Confidence that Inspires

The second important trait of turnaround leaders is self-confidence. It comes from knowing where you are and the direction in which you are going. Self-confidence in their own abilities is key to turnaround leaders, and they like to call their own shots. They have to be self-reliant, and out of this self-reliance comes a high degree of self-confidence. As Thaddeus Taube says, "This self-confidence is needed because people are scared, and they want to see some reflection of strength coming from the top. A person who is imparting strength of that type cannot impart it unless he feels it."[11] Out of direction and self-confidence comes a positive

TABLE 14-1
Personal Characteristics of Turnaround Leaders

	Number one rank		*Total weighted rank*	
	Number	***Percent***	***Number***	***Percent***
Objective oriented	27	37	46	21
Self-confident	15	21	45	21
Maintains positive outlook	11	15	39	18
Inspires confidence in others	6	8	27	13
Innovative and creative	5	7	26	12
Highly visible and active	6	8	19	9
Has high ego needs	3	4	9	6
TOTAL	73	100	211	100

Source: Bibeault, Survey of eighty-one turnaround company chief executives, April 1978.

outlook, based on the fact that results can be achieved. This strength is transmitted throughout the organization. As Robert Brown says: "The board brings in the Star, and the Star is the guy who says, 'Okay, here is what we are going to do.'"

Innovative

Another important motivational characteristic of turnaround leaders is their approach to innovation. Innovation is often thought of as limited to new products. This is far too narrow a concept. Innovation may refer as well to new equipment, new policies and procedures, new people, new organizational structure, new distribution outlets, new plants, new layouts, new budgets and controls, new contracts, and even new records and forms. Companies have gone bankrupt owing to euphemistic day-dreams without any foundation of facts. But more companies have failed to grow, or failed altogether, because innovation was stifled. The turnaround leader has to know when to start and when to stop innovation. He has to know when to listen and when to command. This requires imagination. While the traditional entrepreneur has imagination, he doesn't usually have the experience or sophistication to operate a large-scale organization, and that's where he often gets into trouble.

The turnaround leaders that I surveyed strongly felt that they were no-nonsense executives. They led by example, and they were people-oriented. The caveat here is that in a tough turnaround, business needs come first, people come second. They also felt that they did not have strong ego needs, but I just can't agree with that. As Thaddeus Taube says:

> I think you are dealing with people that are on the egotistical side. Certainly they are entrepreneurially oriented, and an entrepreneur is almost always an egotist, because any start-up situation has more argument against doing it than for doing it. You have to understand that the problems that have to be overcome are often extreme, whether they be a start-up situation or a turnaround situation. [12]

An example of this self-confidence and ego was shown by Robert Wilson, chairman and president of Memorex Corporation. In one year, Wilson was able to turn the floundering Collins Radio around. In 1974, when Wilson assumed control of Memorex, which presented an even greater challenge, Tom Clausen, Bank of America president, asked Wilson, "Do you think you can walk on water twice?" Wilson replied, "Yes."

TURNAROUND LEADERS' STYLE

From many conversations with turnaround leaders and from my own observations, I have a strong impression that a turnaround leader's style differs from a custodial executive's in the degree of force and understanding he brings to five critical areas:

1. Leadership image
2. Performance standards and methods of evaluation
3. Decision-making techniques
4. Use of authority
5. Action orientation

Leadership Image

Turnarounds require a different breed of cat from a management standpoint than do more prosaic, stable business situations. That doesn't mean turnarounds require Clark Kent's better half. Rest assured that most turnarounds are accomplished by mortals, even rather ordinary mortals, who have certain strengths and, as in most mortals, weaknesses. I am not saying that turnarounds are easy, but they are just like most things in life, amenable to concerted human effort. No matter how awesome the task may seem, the turnaround job will yield to an organized approach. But that organized approach must be directed by a strong leader. As Robert Brown says:

> There is a tremendous difference between turnarounds and custodial management. You have to have the star system in a turnaround. That requires the big egotist, the guy who is willing to take the big risk. He needs a superabundance of confidence. He can take somebody else's mess and do the alchemy that's necessary. To do that he has to be insensitive to people. After the turnaround is achieved, the Star is gone, because he can't live with the board on a day-to-day, custodial basis. He's too controversial, argues too much, wants too much, demands too much—he's a pain in the butt.
>
> Good custodial managers are good "vanilla" managers. They stay in there; they do what has to be done. They run the business like it's supposed to be run; they watch the margins, supervise the marketing, take care. Custodial guys are clearly a different breed. If they make a major mistake or if they don't recognize the trends in the business, things will get rotten at the core, and then they will eventually lose the business to the Star again. The Star will be back.[13]

Turnarounds require intensive management. That means hands-on management and a great deal of hard work. As Robert Brown says: "You are always on call; it is an eighteen-hour day, seven days a week, and you work your buns off." Successful turnaround executives give every evidence of relishing hard work. With rare exceptions, they work harder than almost anyone else in the organization. It is not always clear whether hard work is the mainspring of their success or simply a reflection of their personal commitment and interest, but either way hard work appears to be a common denominator for success. Turnaround executives insist that distressed businesses require perhaps two or three times as much hands-on management effort as more stable companies. An example of this is Roy Ash's methods at Addressograph-Multigraph. Ash employs "immersion management." His aim is to reach the core of the problem. To accomplish this he probes deeply into operations through relentless questioning. Bureaucratic practices and long memos from management are employed as means only, never as a defense for a given end. And all policy suggestions must be accompanied by a penetrating financial analysis in order for Ash to accept the policy as viable.

Performance Standards

The turnaround executive, almost by necessity, requires high standards of performance and evaluation. Unlike custodial managers, he is intolerant of ineffective subordinates. Some managers who consider themselves excellent at developing subordinates take pride in attempting to get people to change their behavior radically. Many of these same managers are also quite reluctant to fire or replace an individual, always hoping that his or her performance will soon improve. Some offer mild hints and suggestions for improvement; others just ignore a bad situation in the apparent hope that the individual will be able to learn on his own. We commonly observe beliefs that "the best managers are those whose people are happy," that happiness comes from encouragement and praise, and that consistent demands for better performance are bad for morale. With this conventional wisdom often comes the simultaneous toleration of ineffective subordinates. Turnaround leaders do not tolerate ineffectiveness. They have the courage to "act on people." They clearly and substantively differentiate between outstanding and mediocre performers in their reward systems, and promptly terminate or move aside nonperformers and counterproductive politicians.

One rapidly growing chain retailer had a severe problem in one region, a problem that was dragging down the earnings of the whole corporation. After some abortive efforts to remedy the situation through normal organizational channels, the chief executive gave a free hand to one of the top corporate managers. The CEO told him he would receive half the profits from the region if he could turn it around within a year. The young executive accepted and succeeded, earning $400,000. By way of contrast, one poorly performing industrial goods company, with compensation levels 20 percent below those of the leaders in its industry, has been basing its salary levels on the number of people a manager supervises. The effect on cost control can readily be imagined!

Decision Making

Turnaround leaders tend to make bold, decisive moves quickly. They make fast decisions on new ideas and are quick to terminate losing or unpromising activities. People in sick companies see little justification for rushing, having already reached the point where they are spending a major portion of their time defending the status quo. The turnaround leader must change this situation. His accent is on action, on bold, decisive moves. He is willing to accept reasonable risk and even occasional failure and, with a minimum of cover-up, to ferret out mistakes early in the game. He focuses on one task of prime importance at a time. Among all the tasks facing him which could be accomplished, he defines and tackles the one that makes or breaks the situation in the short run. Such an explicit choice of operating task sets focus, strategy, and priorities. Everything in a turnaround situation is oriented inwardly to the immediate crisis at hand. The crisis usually dealt with and directly solved by the chief executive officer, who then sets it aside so that the next crisis can be attacked in the same manner.

Use of Authority

To offset the difficulties of a turnaround, particularly resource shortages, the turnaround manager is usually given a great deal more authority to steer the corporation off the shoals. As I pointed out earlier, absolute authority was a key factor in turnaround success. This authority is needed particularly to offset the shortage of cooperation a turnaround leader will have initially and to offset the tremendous time pressures he is usually working under. With adversity comes absolute power.

Action Orientation

The action orientation of most turnaround men I know leads to a basic restlessness. If the company can provide action past the turnaround period through growth and change, the turnaround leader will stay. In many cases he has a short "hitch." As Robert Brown says, "The history of a turnaround is usually a five-year hitch. Generally, after the fifth year, when the major part of the thing is accomplished, the guy is either bored with it, he gets into one big hell of a fight with the board, or he's lured off to someplace else."[14]

The turnaround leader usually charges in with a lot of enthusiasm, but that will burn out because he's more of a rocket than an ongoing general manager. At the onset he's going to step on a lot of toes, but if he doesn't step on a lot of toes, he probably hasn't done his job.

Some long-term turnaround leaders are more content to stay with their companies as long as there was a continued challenge. Robert Wilson of Memorex says he is lured by the idea of remaining with the corporation he successfully turned around, in order to build it up. But a far more magnetic appeal is additional fiery turnaround opportunities. He compares a turnaround man's attraction to a troubled company to a fire-horse's attraction to fire. "I'm like a firehorse. Where there's a fire, I want to go and put it out."

In summary, it is the mission of the business leader to instill in the organization a tone and quality which, though it may elude measurement, is not unimportant. It comes to the point where the influence of a turnaround leader takes effect through the person he is, rather than the roles he fills. The character of the turnaround leader must be decisive in creating organizational commitment of the depth and quality required by adverse circumstances and bold purposes.

REFERENCES

[1]Robert Townsend, *Up the Organization: How to Stop the Corporation from Stifling People and Strangling Profits* (Greenwich, Conn.: Fawcett Publication, 1970), p. 81.

[2]Kenneth Andrews, *The Concept of Corporate Strategy* (Homewood, Ill.: Dow Jones-Irwin, 1971, p. 236.

[3]Interview with John Byers, vice president, Wells Fargo Bank, San Francisco, Calif., February 1978.

[4]Joe D. Batten, *Tough-Minded Management* (New York, N.Y.: AMACOM, 1978) p. 23.

[5]Interview with Robert Sackman, president, Rodal Corp., Palo Alto, Calif., February 1978.

[6]Interview with Robert C. Brown, president, R. C. Brown & Co., San Francisco, Calif., February 1978.

[7]Interview with Frank A. Grisanti, president, Grisanti and Galef, Los Angeles, Calif., February 1978.

[8]Ibid.

[9]Ibid.

[10]Interview with John Thompson, senior vice president, Crocker National Bank, San Francisco, Calif., January 1978.

[11]Interview with Thaddeus Taube, former chairman, Koracorp Industries, San Francisco, Calif., February 1978.

[12]Ibid.

[13]Brown, interview, February 1978.

[14]Ibid.

15
TAKING CHARGE

For the actions of a new prince are much more closely scrutinized than those of an established one, and when they are seen to be intelligent and effective they may win over more men and create stronger bonds of obligation than have been felt to the old line.[1]

Niccolò Machiavelli

TAKE-CHARGE STRATEGIES

Taking charge of a company requires a deliberate and well-planned strategy of its own. To the experienced executive who has taken charge of many organizations during his career, taking charge of a troubled company may be a mere modification of his prior practices. On the other hand, a troubled company requires special techniques, responds to different approaches, and has special time pressures not found in smoothly running organizations. How an executive launches his stewardship during the first ninety days often spells the difference between success and failure. Generally, the toughest part of the turnaround is the first three months because, if you walk in and handle it wrong, everybody will get up and quit. If they quit, you may find yourself trying to learn a business you know nothing about and trying to bring people in to learn a business they know nothing about. This would compound the problem rather than help it.

Principal Purposes

With sales and profits down, you must take immediate steps to improve the near-term outlook and to develop a base for the long term. In this chapter, I will make suggestions for carrying out this job. These suggestions are heavily weighted with pragmatism and expediency. Such an action program has three principal purposes:

1. To give evidence of action and change and to make clear to your organization before much time elapses that you are in charge

2. To make some short-term improvements—either in cutting costs or increasing sales
3. To lay the groundwork both for an organized approach to the longer-term problems of the company and for a control system to tighten the company up

Managing a profitable company is one thing; turning around a business which has gone into loss is quite another. The key to success lies not in complicated systems of management control but in swift executive action which accomplishes a few simple things extremely well. It's a mistake to assume that because you've been given the title of chief executive officer, division vice president, or whatever, you have in fact taken charge of the organization. In a troubled company, your subordinates may not share your concern for the troubled state of the enterprise. A healthy percentage of them will breathe a sigh of relief if you display weak leadership characteristics and fail to act decisively.

Action Depends on Seriousness

Your actions during the initial period depend on the seriousness of the turnaround problem. It's my opinion that turnarounds fall into three categories of seriousness. The first, and most critical, is a company that is facing a liquidity crisis. This type of company is in a negative cashflow position and sometimes is facing Bankruptcy Act protection. I would consider companies already under Chapter 11 protection to be in this category. The second category of troubled companies includes those that are losing money but that still have an adequate balance sheet position. Such companies require minor surgery and heavy profit improvement work. The third category of troubled companies includes the dead-center companies, those that have stagnating sales and, usually, eroding market shares. These companies require profit improvement work and development programs.

There are certain take-charge actions common to all three situations that a company may be in. Slotting a company into one of these categories is something a turnaround leader has usually done even before he comes aboard. Other take-charge actions will differ with the seriousness of the problem. Obviously, the more serious the problem, the quicker and more decisive the action required. The less serious the problem, the more time there is available for evaluation. Most turnaround cases do not require the monolithic studies prepared in smoothly running companies.

Locus of Power. Taking charge of a company means bringing the organizational locus of power to your office. Turnarounds usually require a recentralization of power for the first few stages. The power may already be on your desk if an autocratic leader was your predecessor. In this case, however, you've got another kind of problem. The weak managers who usually surround an autocratic leader will be only too willing to surrender all their power, along with all of their problems, to you. Studiously avoid taking over their day-to-day problems. Your desire to take charge should center on important leverage issues in the turnaround, not on taking over subordinate activities.

The temptation to become involved with the work of a subordinate may occur when the subordinate fails to perform his job well. He is either not solving his problems or not exploiting his opportunities—in short, he is not doing his job. The solution is to replace that subordinate. If you don't, you'll end up doing his job.

Taking over power in stronger organizations poses a different set of problems. What occurs in most organizations when a new man is appointed is a period of uncertainty, characterized both by the desire to test the new leader and by the willingness to give him a chance to succeed. In a sense, the leader has a honeymoon period, but it's hardly like a marriage because the organization is watching the new leader closely and testing his mettle. Change is expected, and initially resistance to change will be minor. If the new leader fails to make changes appropriately during that period and fails to bring the force of his personality to bear, the organization's resistance to change will greatly increase at the end of the honeymoon period.

The Honeymoon

Every new turnaround leader has but one honeymoon period—so he's got to use it wisely. Resistance to change can be subtle, and he'll rarely encounter a vocal, visible demonstration of it; it's almost always expressed by a growing disregard for the spirit of existing rules and procedures, and by a concurrent adherence to the letter of those policies. Other symptoms include missed target dates, improper analysis, apathy, and erosion of morale.

Several factors determine the length of the honeymoon period. If the firm's previous performance was poor, then the organization will expect change. Some people will actually encourage change and even suggest specific changes. Generally, the poorer the previous performance, the shorter the honeymoon period. The tenure of one's predecessor is also a factor. The longer his tenure, the more satisfactory, presumably, was his performance, or else his tenure would have been shorter. Furthermore, the longer your predecessor held the office, the more the organization has been molded into a particular pattern. Conversely, the shorter his tenure, the less pervasive his influence. Generally, the shorter the tenure of your predecessor, the shorter the honeymoon period.

Finally, the size of the organization is an important factor in determining the honeymoon period. Organizations possess momentum; that is, they tend to continue on previous courses if change is not effected. The force of the organization's momentum is proportional to the number of individuals in the organization. Effective change requires effective communication, and the larger the organization, the longer it will take to communicate with a sufficient number of individuals to implement the change. Thus, the larger the firm is, the longer the honeymoon period is generally.

Remember, the honeymoon period doesn't last forever. Without being brash or impetuous, you should try to make key changes during this period when resistance in the organization is low. You should not let the honeymoon period lapse without making major changes, nor should you use the "bull-in-the-china-shop" approach and make early changes without a plan in mind.

Taking charge is no easy matter, and it had better be done correctly. There is no doubt that the power relationships in the company are in jeopardy during the period, and this could lead to resistance. On the other hand, the organization needs and sorely wants a leader. Experience indicates that existing management expects and wants immediate action from the new leader. Because of the company's situation, they expect that action to be tough. The honeymoon period provides an opportunity to seize the initiative because the organization is in a state of flux.

A positive and dynamic leader can make this situation work productively. His visible recognition of individual dignity, his publicized expectation of excellence, his observed selfless dedication to problem solving rather than manipulation of people, and his consistent adherence to achievement of results are critical to effective leadership. His people will follow loyally—if they're convinced that their own future power will be enhanced.

THE FIRST STEP – GETTING PEOPLE'S ATTENTION

On the first day, you must establish a tough self-discipline for yourself and your executive secretary. Emphasize businesslike, neat, orderly activity in every respect. The secretary should convey the impression of friendly efficiency to second- and third-echelon people. Your objective is to let everyone know you are in charge and to learn as much as you can, as soon as you can.

Shock the System

Now, what do you do? You have to get everyone's attention. You must perform an act—a series of acts—all of which meaningfully contribute to the turnaround situation and which may, by their very nature, be shocking. You must get everyone's attention, and the way you do that is by rationally shocking the system. You've got to make everyone in the organization, from the man who sweeps your floors to your immediate staff, understand that you mean business. Getting everyone's attention—shocking the system—is a dangerous task. As chief executive you have to be prepared to provide strong leadership and direction to the organization in order to keep its people from floundering.

Why do you shock the system? It's very simple: Losing money can become a way of life. As long as there is some godfather supplying the funds, no one really believes anything is amiss. The people on the line, and the people in operations don't understand what's going on. All they see is that the chief executive went to his board and got some more money., As Roy Woodman, president of International Video Corporation, says, "People get locked-in to certain performance patterns, and you have to shake them out of it."

Getting people's attention can take many forms. In smaller companies, it usually includes a initial shock meeting with the key staff and later, once some tentative decisions are made, a meeting with employees. In medium-size companies, a meeting or several meetings with management are usually conducted. In large companies, meetings are supplemented with written or visual media. A unique way of getting people's attention was used by William Anderson at NCR. Anderson responds quickly in any situtation, and he lost no time letting headquarters at Dayton know his intention of shaking the lethargy out of NCR. On video tape he declared with a solemn stare: "Complacency and apathy—these are NCR's greatest sins. Until we see a return to profitability, something akin to martial law will be in effect in Dayton." His audience was stunned. Once vice president said to himself, "Gentlemen, we have a leader."

In both tone and action the turnaround leader has to show that he is taking charge. His tone must be assertive and his action must be immediate. How he says things and how he does things are almost more important than what he says and what he does. Robert Brown, in jest, says:

> "Well, if he's got a reputation as a mean S.O.B., the first thing he needs to get people's attention is a slot in the parking lot with his name on it. That's sometimes enough.

More seriously, Brown continues:

> Most of the time, that's not enough. He must exude, "I'm running the show," and he must make every decision positively. He can't back off making hard decisions. The first thing he has to do is find a whipping boy. He has to have shock value in the organization. That's critical! Everyone has to be afraid of him, afraid for his job, and he doesn't even have to use the stick, but he must leave the impression that he's not afraid to use it.[2]

The Sacrificial Lamb

It seems that time and time again turnaround leaders employ the sacrificial-lamb concept in shocking the system, no matter what the state of the company situation is. This concept is part of the transition from setting the tone to taking immediate action. Usually someone at a visible level gets fired within days of the turnaround leader's arrival. That action is not necessarily an arbitrary one on the part of the turnaround leader, although it may appear to be. It seems that in a troubled company there always is a scapegoat who is already visible or who arises shortly after a takeover. Usually the visible scapegoat has been identified as part of a prior problem. A case in point is Donald Rumsfeld's abrupt firing of his research and development director on the eighth day of Rumsfeld's tenure as president of G. D. Searle & Co. Rumsfeld fired him just minutes after the R&D director stepped off a flight from London. Rumsfeld was using the same six-gun management style that made heads roll and knees tremble when he ran the Pentagon.

Roy Woodman of International Video Corporation prefers not to use this shock treatment. He prefers symbolic moves, but admits a sacrificial lamb always seems to appear in the first few days. Somebody steps out of line. Woodman tries to blend the positive, morale-building elements of his overall program with the possible necessity of firing someone: "If the turnaround leader is really clever, he moves them with a stick; after he shows success, he starts motivating with the carrot. 'You're a part of the team, you're a survivor, you're going to get some of the goodies. Here's your piece of the action.' That works extremely well."[3]

Various styles are used by turnaround leaders, depending on the situation at hand. Ransom Cook feels that precipitous action should be avoided and that it can cause costly errors. His approach is to move gradually, to indicate the way the company is going to run, and to deal swiftly and forcefully with the first person who violates the guidelines. He says, "You've got to be firm. Be good enough to get cooperation, but not so good that you're soft. You have to be more authoritarian than in normal business situations."[4]

IMMEDIATE ACTIONS

Now that you have people's attention, you take immediate action to back up your words. This calls for more than sacrificial lambs, and far less than a direct attack on the company's problems. A direct attack on company problems in the first few days should be made only in dire circumstances. Most turnaround situations dictate necessary actions, but usually you aren't ready to take on the core problems yet. Organizational change or the switching of key personnel, if implemented too quickly, might prove to be inadequate in the months to come. Those actions require a level of evaluation on the part of the turnaround leader.

Only when the corporation is in imminent danger of collapse or disintegration can an exception be made. In such a case, the problems and solutions literally scream out to even the casual observer. The options and alternatives are limited, so study takes a back seat. This was the situation when Robert Wilson arrived at Collins Radio in 1972. Wilson took immediate action to cut the losses. He completely reorganized Collins in ten days. As part of his groundwork for a $40 million cost-cutting program, he reduced salaried employment 25 percent and shut down half a dozen production facilities. He decentralized decision making and established fifteen profit centers. Collins had profits of $13 million the following year, after $64 million in losses the year before the reorganization. The company evolved into one of the most consistently profitable properties in the Rockwell stable.

Minimum immediate action should include:

1. Implementation of action programs that smack of toughness, which can be initiated without delay
2. The imposition of the turnaround executive's modus operandi at headquarters and the divisions
3. The delegation of authority to key lieutenants, but with retention of key decision authority by the CEO

Action Programs

Immediate action is necessary to set the pace for change, to show that the turnaround leader's words mean business, and to show that he is decisive. The first actions should smack of toughness and be initiated without delay. They need not be an occasion for agony because they are reversible decisions and do not get to the core problems of the company. Nevertheless, I have found that they are worthwhile in and of themselves and that they convey a feeling of decisiveness that lets people know who is in charge. It's equally important to establish your expectancy of similar behavior from subordinates. The tempo or pace of an organization is proportional both to the dispatch with which your subordinates treat the reversible decisions and to the speed with which irreversible decisions are brought to higher organizational levels with recommendations for action. Some immediate actions with which to start are:

1. Demand that all temporary help be terminated immediately and redeploy existing staff to fill gaps.
2. Require chief-executive approval before any action is taken on the recruitment of indirect personnel.
3. Require chief-executive approval for the recruitment of direct labor.
4. Require CEO approval of all capital expenditure requests above a defined minimum limit.
5. Have all redundant inventory identified and, if possible, disposed of at whatever price can be obtained.
6. Cut back sharply on the redecoration of offices and the replacement of office equipment.
7. Delay the replacement of company-supplied and -maintained cars whenever possible.
8. Require CEO approval of all foreign travel.
9. Check expense accounts to ensure that any entertaining of clients is not overly lavish.

The impact of a series of immediate actions such as those given above gets the message across that the decks are being cleared for action. The objective is to make the most effective use of the human and material resources already employed in the business. Admittedly, the impact of these actions is likely to be more important in terms of their effect on employee attitudes than on profitability and cash flow, but some tangible improvement will almost certainly result. Certainly, the turnaround executive will want to reduce the list of actions requiring his approval as soon as he is confident that his values and standards have been adopted by his management team.

Headquarters Modus Operandi

Next, turn your attention to the day-to-day operations at headquarters and impose your own routine. Providing leadership on a day-to-day basis can commence the first week you are on the job. Essentially this requires getting a handle on the operation and the way it works. Don't go along completely with the established routine of the headquarters, regardless of your experience with the operation. At least to begin with, I would impose my own modus operandi—principally in two areas—weekly operations meetings and delegated authority.

Weekly Meetings. A number of top executives find that weekly operations meetings of reasonable length (an hour or so) are an ideal vehicle for getting across their philosophy on operations, determining the current status of sales and profits, and uncovering current problems. You should hold such meetings regularly on Monday mornings. In the beginning you need repetitive exposure to progress on backlogs, pricing moves, inventories, and personnel matters. From the standpoint of travel Monday morning cuts into the week least, so department heads will find few excuses not to be there. The meetings should be get-tough, no-holds-barred reviews of every facet of operations. Distant locations should be tied in by telephone. Penetrating questions and assignment of specific tasks should come out of the meetings. Take extra time to keep everybody on target, to eliminate backtracking, and to prevent "procedural drift"—the tendency to get a little off course from required directions.

Authority Delegation

A clear-cut table of organization must be established at the very beginning. People in troubled companies usually suffer from confusion of roles—titles that don't match functions and authority chains that are unspecified or unclear. Let everybody see who does what to whom. Since your ultimate aim is to change the culture of the company, start early and at the top. The culture change must start with you, then expand to your key lietenants, and from there filter down into the organization. Glenn Penisten of American Microsystems started his culture change on day one:

> The first thing I did the day I walked into this company was change the offices around. We had officers scattered all over our grounds, and the next day they were all lined up right out here. I took them in the conference area and said, "We're all going to get damn sick and tired of each other because what you don't know how to do is live together, and we're going to learn to live together." We spent twelve to fifteen hours in that conference room, together, for thirty days before going back to a normal routine. They learned to work together.[5]

Give broad freedom to key people to run their own shows, once their roles have been defined by the table of organization. Introduce the idea of sole responsibility—no management by committee. Key people should be doing their own jobs, attacking problems, and taking risks—with assurances that the new boss will back them up for taking initiative. In every business there are key decisions in which the chief executive officer must be directly involved. Troubled companies invariable have pricing problems, and a CEO must set pricing guidelines right away. For example, one CEO in a rubber company ignored this tenet, only to wake up after a month or two and find that the field organization had over-committed the company on distributor-price protection in a rising market. Pricing authority was immediately taken away from the field organization.

Resentment can easily crop up if authority on such concerns as pricing and personnel is pulled back from seasoned executives. To counter this likelihood, one marketing vice president made it a point, when he entered a new situation, to explain to his staff that in order to learn the business he wanted to be a part of their day-to-day decision-making process for at least ninety days. Then, to make sure that there were no misunderstandings, he wrote a brief memorandum to each person, listing decisions which he wished to participate in. The explanation minimized the possibility of hurt feelings; the written statement prevented misunderstandings; and at the end of ninety days, most of the decision-making powers were delegated back to the subordinates as promised.

ATTACKING PROBLEMS

Every turnaround leader is anxious to get in the batter's box and start swinging. The take-charge actions I have discussed are designed both to serve as symbols and to set the correct operating environment. The question now becomes whether to attack substantive core problems as part of taking charge. Usually the major problems facing the firm must be evaluated before decisions are made. This doesn't mean that you have to call in a battery of management consultants and start a year long study. As Robert Sackman stated: "A real tough turnaround situation is almost like arriving at the scene after the horse has been stolen."

When the situation allows it, you should perform an evaluation of your problems before you act. If things are critical, a turnaround leader may have to fly by the seat of his pants. If he is any good, he'll make a minimum of mistakes. Robert Wilson had to take drastic action at Collins Radio, but nearly three decades at General Electric had taught him what to do. Wilson admits he probably made a lot of mistakes and let go of a lot of good people in the process. He simply had no other choice, and he realized it.

Total Financial Control

Sometimes the taking-charge stage, the evaluation stage, and the emergency-action stage are compressed to a matter of weeks, even days. In cases requiring immediate action on substantial company problems, taking charge and beginning the emergency stage blend together. In a company facing the danger of bankruptcy, taking charge usually consists of instituting total financial control. The chief executive takes personal charge of the cash flow pipeline. An example of this total takeover is seen in Michael Moscarelo's first few days at International Video Corporation:

> When I came on board, I immediately imposed absolute financial control. I had a meeting with my staff and outlined some of the procedures which invoked financial control. I guess they thought I was kidding. So, a couple of days later, I put out a memo to them. When they saw it in writing, they all went into a state of shock. They said I was going to inhibit them from doing their business. The shop was going to come to a screeching halt. They went on and on and on. I had invoked total financial control, and there was no question about it.
>
> This means an awful lot of extra work for you. Every morning people were outside my door with requests of all kinds. They brought them in by the wheelbarrow. You have to be patient and question everybody as to what they are doing. This is the only way you can indicate that you really mean it. There is one great thing about invoking financial control and getting everyone's attention. It's the best way to find out where a company is going and where its money is going.[6]

What Is Going On?

In organizations facing losses but not in imminent danger of collapse, substantive take-charge actions usually center on the following: first, finding out what is going on; second, evaluating key lieutenants; third, taking obvious steps toward profit improvement; and, fourth, initiating actions to generate information for evaluations. Finding out what is going on is merely a way of determining where you are and where you are heading. Such a determination requires that you immediately come head-to-head with your information systems. You can probably find out what the fiscal condition of the company is from the annual report and the 10-K statements. That's not enough to pull a company out of a downward trend. Thomas Wilcox found this out at Crocker National Bank. His first challenge at Crocker was merely to find out what was going on. The bank's management information system was so primitive that he could not even get answers to basic questions on costs, profitability, and management responsibilities. You've got to take charge of the information flow and get the ball rolling on improvements. Improving information flow will probably mean getting outside help if your key manager in the information area is weak.

Key Managers

Every experienced manager knows the importance of having a group of top-flight key managers. As you move into your new job, you will naturally observe how your senior staff think and act and apply to them whatever standard is necessary, no matter how demanding. You should be sensitive to two points that apply to your senior staff solely as a result of your appointment. One is whether the incumbent managers have the proper attitude with respect to some of the changes that will be required of them. An individual may have all the qualifications to do an outstanding job; yet he may impede progress simply because he resists change. Some discerning executives I have known make a point of informing all incumbent managers within the first weeks that an attitude receptive to change is a vital prerequisite for future success.

The second point concerns whether any key managers who are considered vital for the future are thinking of leaving. As Robert Brown says, "You need certain key people to keep the business running. You can push them, shove them, bang them around, whatever, but you have to be gentle enough so that they don't quit before you get your arms around what they are doing."[7]

Getting a feel for your key managers means working closely with them. To evaluate your management staff, you must work closely with them, plan with them, think with them, get a feel for what they are. Are they results-oriented? Are they commitment-oriented? You only learn these answers after having worked closely with them for some period of time.

An evaluation of key managers usually uncovers weak sisters or incompatible approaches to the large changes that have to take place. There is generally fallout in the executive suite. A good example is William Anderson's actions when he took over at NCR. His reputation as a tough taskmaster was confirmed. It was obvious that he came in to clean up a mess, and his attitude that "everyone was guilty until proven innocent" caused a great deal of apprehension. Altogether, nineteen high executives took early retirement, were demoted, or found other jobs. Anderson put everyone under a magnifying glass, and about half passed muster.

The turnaround leader usually comes alone but soon tightens his control by bringing in key people loyal to him. They may not be his friends or may not even like him, but they are loyal to the person who hired them and have no loyalty to the existing management. In this way the turnaround leader keeps the circle tight, and this helps him keep very tight control. Selection of the right people to staff the organization is an absolute prerequisite for success. Technical competence is important, but more important are personality traits which conform to the style and tempo the leader wants to achieve.

Profit Improvement

In a loss situation there are probably a number of profit improvement actions that can be taken early on without the benefit of detailed analysis. If expenses are too high, start to cut them when you get the first indications. Don't withhold action until you develop the perfect expense-reduction program. If inventory is too high, start cutting the input right away; if receivables are too high, collect at least one past-due immediately. An example of just such an obvious cost drag, that also happened to be an organizational problem, was the excess layer of review in eight regional headquarters at Crocker Bank when Thomas Wilcox came aboard: "There were 465 people in those regional operations." Wilcox asked, "What do those people do?" It turned out they were reviewing things that had already been done. So Wilcox said, "They're gone."

Gathering the Facts

It takes time to gather information and assemble basic facts from which to make decisions. The best you can do in the short term is set in motion or stimulate fact-gathering activities and mechanisms so that later the necessary data will be available. You don't, however, want to set in motion any new expenses for fact gathering for two reasons. First, you don't yet know the relative significance of the key policy questions, and, therefore, you don't know which ones you will want to concentrate on or what facts will have what value. Second, and of more importance, you can't afford any new expenses at the present time. Your major attention must focus on reducing costs and increasing sales.

Taking charge of a mediocre company that is neither losing money nor facing imminent danger of collapse is quite a different process from that of the two types of companies already discussed. Usually the symbolic actions of taking charge resemble each other under all three conditions. It is substantive actions that are different. In a larger company that is mediocre and not in imminent danger, as new chief executive you take a great deal more time in performing evaluations. You take symbolic take-charge actions and make obvious improvements, but usually you study a great deal before acting.

KEEPING CHARGE

If the turnaround executive successfully takes charge and has the organization responding to his commands, he has greatly alleviated his problems in preparing the organization for rapid change. He has to remember that maintaining the momentum of change will require constant pressure by him. This constant pressure is necessary to bridge the performance gap that has developed in his organization between a dynamic environment and a stagnant organization. A turnaround is not corporate evolution, but corporate revolution. A turnaround executive may find that keeping charge is more difficult than taking charge.

Changing Power Continuum

As the organization heals, the turnaround leader usually comes under pressure in terms of his relative position on the power-distribution continuum. In its initial stage, the organization generally responds most readily to change implemented with an emphasis on the authority of the turnaround leader's hierarchical position in the company and on the force of his personality. Solutions to the problems at hand are specified by him and directed downward through formal and personal control mechanisms. At this stage changes are usually introduced in three forms: by decree, by replacement of key people, and by change of the organization's structure. The use of unilateral action is the most common prescription in the early stages of a turnaround, but the turnaround leader soon realizes that he must institutionalize change by sharing power. Over the long run most organizations respond better to shared power.

The turnaround leader has to be keenly sensitive to how much pressure he can apply to the system without making it crack. If he pushes too hard, people may prematurely desert the ship. He cannot run the company alone, nor can he allow the company to continue on its previous track. It is a difficult and sensitive situation. He has to be sensitive enough to know when he is about to put on the last straw and break the camel's back.

Even though the turnaround leader has established that he is in charge, other executives in the company will continually try to expand their sphere of influence. The question becomes: How can the turnaround leader keep the pressure on, keep charge, through all the stages of a turnaround? The answer lies in his degree of flexibility and his commitment to hands-on management. If a turnaround leader is insensitive to the changing nature of the power-distribution continuum, he will eventually have problems with the board of directors above him and key managers below him. The turnaround leader is in constant danger of repeating the mistakes of the autocratic one-man reign he probably replaced.

Power Sharing

By emphasizing power sharing, good turnaround leaders manage to keep charge within the confines of a hands-on management style without running into the problems of organizational stress. This style can be used through all the stages of a turnaround and can even be utilized in an organization of some size that has healthy growth. It can be done without the enormous central staffs, the labyrinthine reporting procedures, and the huge mounds of computer data with which bureaucratic managers hope to gain some measure of control over their far-flung operations. It takes a leader of unusual energy to carry it off single-handedly, but there is at least one large company whose top management continues to rely on plain, old fashioned, face-to-face contact. Richard B. Loynd, the president and chief operating officer of Eltra Coporation, a diversified manufacturer with sales over $1 billion, visits each of Eltra's thirteen divisions as many as eight times a year and puts the managers through formal grillings that last several hours at a time.

SOME PARTING THOUGHTS ON TAKING CHARGE

Attempts to solve all of the problems at hand at the same time are a sign of an amateur or freshman leader. His attack perimeter becomes increasingly large until, finally, his logistics requirements for solving the problems exceed his conceptual capacity. He will fail. Successful managing of problem arrays is a discernible factor that differentiates the amateur from the seasoned professional. When taking control of an organization, there are certain moves to be studiously avoided if the new leader wants to use time and neutralize potential criticism that he is "overdoing" the job.

Focusing on the Relatively Unimportant Too Quickly

Never squander your limited time on matters that can generate only marginal or minimal return. As a turnaround manager, you must take whatever steps are appropriate to ensure that you spend your time only in those areas and on those subjects which affect the organization as a whole—particularly those that affect profits. This is an exceedingly difficult requirement to meet, and although it seems to make all the common sense in the world, no one in your organization will see that you meet it except you. And sometimes you will be your own worst enemy. You will tend, for example, to give too much time to those problems you're most familiar with. If your functional specialty is, say, marketing, you'll be tempted to spend too much time on marketing problems.

After you have enumerated the problems facing your organization, select those that truly affect the entire firm and rank them so that you can, in turn, allot your time. Seek out the high-impact problems and give preference to short-term rather than long-term problems. They are easier to solve, and their solution guarantees your continued presence to face the longer-term problems. The primary criterion for ranking must necessarily be effect on profits.

Allowing Oneself to Be Swallowed Up in Extraneous Meetings and Activities

A prime example of wasted time is the common practice of asking the sales force to congregate at key regional locations to meet the boss who has just come aboard. You don't have much to say to a sales group in the first place. Managers spend horrendous amounts of time in meetings. Meetings, formal and informal, are probably the most used, and abused, channels of communication in the business world. Nothing is so sad and tragic as an opportunity unexploited or a gain unrealized.

Permitting Early Confrontations with Key People

In all probability, you will not have all the facts, or, in the organization's eyes, the seasoned judgment to take on all matters of policy and industry practice in the first month or two. Making premature decisions increases the likelihood of making erroneous decisions. At best, you'll be viewed as a meddler. At worst, you'll rupture normal chains of command and confuse the organization.

When you first come into a turnaround situation, don't expect to have the luxury of time to plan your moves in detail. The first moves, mostly symbolic or obvious improvements you make without study, should be instinctive. If you're any good, in the first thirty days you can make both symbolic and obvious moves to cut fat without a plan. Your involvement in day-to-day decision making, your understanding of the company's financial picutre, and your initial findings on the company's position in the marketplace should help you formulate definite plans for improving performance.

The take-charge period is one of hope and hard work. As Michael Moscarello, former president of International Video Corporation, says:

> What do you do? You pray a lot. There is nothing like being in the red to give you religion. It's really hard work. You've got to make up your mind you are going to roll up your sleeves. It requires total dedication,

> and I mean absolute dedication. You are going to have to sleep it, eat it, everything you do has to be wrapped up in your recovery situation. Just think of your golf game. How often have you messed up by picking up your head too soon? Don't pick up your head until the company is in the black, and even then keep your eye on the ball.[8]

In a turnaround, the leader must have the commitment to perform his job better than anyone else ever has, or ever will. Leadership, a degree of selflessness, competence, and integrity are essential ingredients. The ability to build a team and lead it to the achiement of the firm's goals is critically important. Finally, enthusiasm, a lack of cynicism, and a reach toward ideals provide the uplift and spark needed to mold and move an organization. In addition to being a good problem-solver, motivator, and manager, the chief executive must be fair with all members of his organization, highly dedicated to achieving the business's objectives, and tough-minded enough to see that those objectives are achieved. The leadership the chief executive exercises in determining what are reasonable and suitable objectives for the business will go a long way toward moving that business in the right direction. To achieve the objectives, however, he must gain the cooperation of all members of his organization and build employees' confidence in his personal desire and ability to get the job done.

REFERENCES

[1]Niccolò Machiavelli, *The Prince* (Franklin Center, Pa.: The Franklin Library, 1978), p. 133.

[2]Interview with Robert C. Brown, president, R. C. Brown & Co., San Francisco, Calif., February 1978.

[3]Interview with Roy Woodman, president, International Video Corp., Sunnyvale, Calif., February 1978.

[4]Interview with Ransom Cook, chairman and president (retired), Wells Fargo Bank, San Francisco, Calif., February 1978.

[5]Interview with Glenn E. Penisten, president, American Microsystems, Santa Clara, Calif., February 1978.

[6]Michael A. Moscarello, "The Anatomy of a Turnaround," address before Western Association of Venture Capitalists, San Francisco, Calif., June 19, 1974.

[7]Brown, interview, February 1978.

[8]Moscarello, "The Anatomy of a Turnaround," p. 14.

16
MOTIVATING THE ORGANIZATION

The test of an organization is the spirit of performance.[1]

Peter Drucker

Every organization has a problem motivating its people, but a turnaround company is an especially difficult case because its morale is generally at rock bottom. The president of Volvo, Pehr Gyllenhammer, estimates in his book, *People At Work,* that most companies have between 20 and 50 percent more workers than they would actually need if everyone came to work and was properly motivated. In order to survive, a troubled company often has to be ruthless in determining its "extra employees." It can survive by eliminating extra people, but it will not prosper in the middle and longer terms unless it motivates its employees. It is very difficult for a company to sustain a turnaround unless it can turn its people around.

THE IMPORTANCE OF MOTIVATION

The turnaround leader can only do so much himself. He can diagnose the strategic and operational problems of the firm. He can cut away losing operations and restore positive cash flow in the short run. He can restore a measure of profitability to the firm. To the outside world, these actions can create the appearance of a company turned around. It's important to realize, however, that these prescriptions are halfway measures and can only succeed in getting the company halfway turned. Unless the basic motivation of the people in the company changes from that of a defeatist attitude to one of confidence, it is doubtful that the company can stabilize its gains and return to healthy growth.

The attitudes of these people are more critical in a turnaround situation than at almost any other time in a company's life span. As Robert Wilson, president of Memorex, says about his experience at Collins Radio: "The most significant problem of all was the attitude of Collins personnel. They were function-oriented and, in many cases, negative or even defeatist. Many of the good people were leaving. The negative attitudes were massive and deep-seated but were the kinds of problems that lend themselves to solution with the application of established managerial techniques."[2]

The importance of employee morale is further stressed by James Hawkins, president of Hewitt-Robins, a division of Litton Industries. The Reston, Virginia, maker of bulk handling systems was in a bad way when Hawkins came aboard. He reports: "If you had to put your finger on the biggest problem—after several years of consecutive losses—the morale of the organization was absolutely terrible. It's like being a salesman. If you can't sell yourself, you can't sell anybody else. And that was our first big problem, to turn the morale of the people around and get them to believing in themselves again."[3]

THE STAGES OF TURNING PEOPLE AROUND

The stages in the motivation level of people in a company parallel the turnaround stages a company experiences. Although this is not a scientific observation, I've observed this similarity in reaction levels on numerous occasions. This comparison is shown in Table 16-1. The first and last stages in the people-motivation cycle are obvious. On the negative end, when a company is declining, the motivation level is deteriorating, although there is a lagged effect. On the positive end of the spectrum, there are a limited number of companies (I think less than 5 percent) whose employees are enthusiastic about their work. IBM has sustained a near-enthusiasm level for a number of years. The people pulse of an organization is a difficult thing to measure precisely. Richard Madden, chairman of Potlatch, says: "The reason I made people motivation one of the first of my criteria was because it's the hardest to get a handle on. People can make slick and professional presentations, and

TABLE 16-1
People-Motivation Cycle Versus Company-Turnaround Cycle

Corporations	*People*
Decline stage	Deterioration stage
Unprofitable stage	Demoralization stage
Change-of-management and evaluation stage	Honeymoon stage
Emergency stage	Neutral stage
Stabilization stage	Commitment stage
Return-to-growth stage	Enthusiasm stage

you still don't know what their motivation level is. The brighter they are, the harder it is to tell."[4]

Attitude was deemed so important by Robert Wilson that he had a monthly attitude survey conducted at Memorex. Official surveys can be misleading. Less formal indicators can give clues. A key barometer of company health is employee attitudes regarding profits, and the astute manager can learn about these attitudes without official survey questionnaires (which employees tend to answer the way they think management wants them answered). Playing detective by asking the right questions and by keeping one's ears and eyes open pays big information dividends.

One of the best summaries I have heard on the motivation cycle comes from Ransom Cook, retired president and chairman of Wells Fargo Bank:

> First thing in a turnaround situation is that everybody is blue because there is something wrong with the company. Who is going to be fired? What part of the 20 percent are they? How good is this new fellow? Is he going to make this a decent company that I want to work for? They evaluate him. If he is dynamic and makes positive decisions that they respect, then they turn on. Next you create incentives to sustain the turn-on because people are working harder than they did before. They will drop down if you don't get incentives going. Next, training and giving them the opportunity to advance is important.[5]

The Demoralization Stage

In this stage, the employees are demoralized and generally have a defeatist attitude. They are no longer primarily concerned with their work but, instead, are primarily concerned with their own basic security. As Roy Woodman, president of International Video Corporation, says: "In an unprofitable subsidiary or division of a profitable parent, as long as they get their paycheck they don't worry about their work. You cannot motivate those people in that kind of situation. If you have employees working in a loss operation, they are not very productive; they are demoralized."[6]

Instead of concern for the job, employees drop down to worrying about whether they'll be eliminated from a very important group (the work group) and whether their financial safety will be impaired. Few people today in the United States are worried about the basics of food, shelter, and clothing, and employees don't want to be one of those few. They're worried about themselves, not their work effort, and demoralized employees don't perform very well. They exacerbate the troubled company's already severe problems. Gary Friedman, former vice chairman of Itel, says, "By definition, in a turnaround you go through a motivation cycle. Because a troubled company is a bad place to work, people ask themselves, 'What am I doing here?' "[7]

The Honeymoon Stage

This is a brief stage when the new leader comes in. People are usually thirsting for good leadership. Robert Sackman, president of Rodal Corporation, says:

> In most troubled companies, people recognize bad management. Even though they are participating in it, they are upset, and so they are delighted that someone is coming in who will change that. You sometimes go through a strained period, but it can very quickly be followed by a feeling of euphoria if they are not fired. They feel that "by God, if this thing is now under control and this company is going to grow, I'd like to stay." So much depends on how long the bad period has lasted and how hardened the people have become to statements like "This is going to be the greatest company in the world," etc. The employees worry about what's going to happen to them, but they may be very happy to see that something positive is happening to their company.[8]

The time it takes for new leadership to get the company out of its demoralization stage up to the neutrality level depends on a number of factors. The type of company plays a role in the length of time required. If the company is a humdrum place and has been going downhill for a long time, it will be more difficult to make the motivational turnaround. On the other hand, if the company is a great company in the sense of being a good place to work, it can more rapidly develop the feeling that "we are on the way again, so let's really start moving." Another time factor is the amount of shock that was required to get the company through the emergency stage. In a company that has severe shock, where many people were replaced, demoralization is more difficult to remove.

In turnaround situations the leader must have a positive attitude and transmit this to the rest of the organization. This development of a positive attitude is a key element in turnaround success, and it starts at the top.

The Neutral Stage

This stage is better than the demoralization stage, but people still lack commitment. Those that survive the shocks of the emergency stage get their minds off themselves and onto the job. They are willing to give the new leader a chance but are still skeptical. At best it's just a place to work. Their effort still lacks commitment. People think about their jobs, but they don't think about the company objectives. They are not profit-oriented, but rather, job-oriented. Sometimes, although not in danger of collapse, a corporation is losing money, and the people in this situation couldn't care less. This neutral, mediocre stage must be changed in order to sustain the turnaround.

The Commitment Stage

In this stage the company's people feel confident enough to be committed to the organization's goals. As Chauncey Schmidt, chairman of the Bank of California, says, "The third stage is when you start to get the spark ignited." Such a commitment, however, does not take place automatically. It usually coincides with the stabilization stage of the turnaround and requires two things. The first is continued company success. Roy Woodman feels:

> You can't push employees beyond the "just-a-place-to-work" stage without success. You can possibly push them for a short period of time, but then they come around and bite you. You are not leveling with them. I think when you have them on a plateau—if you have temporary failure—you'll keep their morale up a lot longer if you tell them. But if results keep going down, I don't know any way to keep morale up.[9]

The second factor required to sustain motivation is the establishment of a success climate or culture in a company. As Glenn Penisten says:

> You don't get people committed and enthusiastic until you have really effected the change in the culture in the company. I think the cultural change has to start at the top, and it has to work its way down into the company. You can't come in and say if I fix that manufacturing operation you will fix the problem. Hell, that isn't what started the problem. The problem is the wrong culture in the company.[10]

When a commitment level is attained, it is like radar to the ear of the turnaround leader. He must constantly have his antennae up to spot signs of commitment. As Richard Madden of Potlatch indicates:

> You have "a good meeting." You hear someone making a talk and think he would not have said it quite that way the other day, so you have a feeling the team is gelling. People are getting excited. You are ultimately betting that people logically organize their facts, make calculated judgments, have the courage of their convictions, and run a good ethical shop. It is the people's commitment that makes the company prosper.[11]

When the commitment and employee attitude changes are perceived on the inside, there usually is an accompanying improvement in relations on the outside with customers, vendors, bankers, and shareholders. Changing the attitudes and culture of a company requires both an external and an internal effort. It's not just the people inside a company that matter, but all the constituencies involved in corporate well-being. If commitment can be sustained by continued growth, it will, in many cases, turn to enthusiasm on the part of people concerned.

BASICS OF MOTIVATION IN A TURNAROUND

This is a practical book of very broad scope, so in these few pages you cannot expect a psychological treatise on motivation. What I hope to do is to combine some sound academic basics (mainly those of Frederick Herzberg) with my practical experience in order to develop a structure for motivating people in a turnaround. You might think that if you take a man on and give him a guarantee of employment, a fair salary, and a well-defined job, you can assume from then onward that he will work for the good of the corporation which is employing him. Perhaps there are some who would. But on the whole it is safer to assume that, while the good of the corporation will always be an important consideration, it will not be his first loyalty. The concept of what it takes to motivate people is by itself difficult, but can you imagine how this conflict is amplified in a troubled company that cannot guarantee most of the above-mentioned conditions?

Strong Leader's "KITA"

I believe the first requirement for motivation is the presence of a strong leader. In Frank Grisanti's opinion:

> You don't turn people around; they turn themselves around. Create the environment, and people adapt. If the new leadership is strong, those people who really are sensitive to good leadership will recognize it quickly and change their ways. Without a strong leader, companies fall apart a lot faster. People say, "Managements come and go, and one of these days, we'll get the right guy in here and then we'll beat our problem."[12]

The question is: "What is this leader going to do?" More often than not successful leaders shock the system, give the whole system a "kick in the pants"—a KITA. Now, there are different kinds of KITAs: there are the negative, physical KITA (not used much today), the negative, psychological KITA (used more often), and the positive KITA (used most often today). The positive KITA is a conglomeration of benefits that often have nothing to do with work.

In the beginning of a turnaround, the chief executive doesn't have many positive, physical KITAs to pass around, so he generally uses the very direct approach—he uses negative, psychological KITAs—and he usually winds up weeding people out of the organization. He uses both symbolic and substantive shock to shake the company out of its lethargy. This is not all "bull-in-the-china-shop" mentality. It's partly based on some sound psychological underpinnings. As Herzberg states, "Every audience contains the 'direct-action' manager who shouts, 'Kick him!' And this type of manager is right. The surest and least circumlocuted way of getting someone to do something is to kick him in the pants."[13]

Movement Not Motivation

A lot of turnaround leaders initially rule through fear. But fear cannot motivate a company, it can only move a company. Movement is not motivation. In the emergency stage of a turnaround, movement is enough. In the later stages, it takes genuine motivation to sustain progress. As Robert Brown, president of R. C. Brown & Company, says, "Initially you can make the big stick work, and the big stick is what makes the tough part of the turnaround. You only start motivating after you start showing success. Then you start the whole friendship routine."[14]

Frederick Herzberg puts it another way: "Why is KITA not motivating? If I kick my dog (from the front or the back), he will move. And when I want him to move again, what must I do? I must kick him again. Similarly, I can charge a man's battery, and then recharge it, and recharge it again. But it is only when he has his own generator that we can talk about motivation. He then needs no outside stimulation. He wants to do it."[15]

Motivating Factors

A turnaround company needs motivation to sustain its progress. How can it be achieved? The solution begins with concentrated effort on the motivating factors that Herzberg has demonstrated in dozens of studies. Herzberg's key finding is that, of all the factors contributing to job satisfaction, 81 percent were motivators. And, of all the factors contributing to the employees' dissatisfaction over their work, 69 percent involved hygiene elements.

The key question for turnaround management is how to use the findings. In order of importance, we want to concentrate on advancement and growth, responsibility, the work itself, achievement and recognition of achievement. The first two motivators, advancement and growth, can take place in only a limited fashion in a declining company. You don't start using motivators until after the blood bath. So these motivators cannot be used in the emergency stage and can barely be used in the stabilization stage. In those stages they must wait for the chief executive to reestablish a climate of success. Remember, you can't move people beyond the just-a-place-to-work stage without first achieving some success.

Next on the hierarchy of motivators are work itself and responsibility. These involve more participation in job decision making, but, more specifically, they mean giving employees a complete natural unit of work and granting them authority—job freedom.

Other factors in the hierarchy are recognition and achievement. These involve increasing the accountability of individuals for their own work and acknowledging outstanding performance through awards and promotions. These processes require, respectively, formal communication of results in the reporting structure and the formal communication that outstanding achievement has taken place.

Summary

Motivating people usually works a lot differently in a turnaround than in a more stable situation. It usually relies less on psychological coddling of employees than on the approach described below:

1. A prerequisite is a strong, positive leader of high integrity who demands superior results. He must be a tough evaluator who isn't afraid to act for results.

2. Getting a company turned around from its emergency stage usually requires a shock, a kick in the pants (KITA). This usually includes the weeding out of unnecessary or uncooperative staff.

3. Motivation cannot start until some level of achievement has been reached. Before then, in an emergency situation, management relies on movement rather than motivation.

4. The motivators of growth and advancement are actuated by reestablishing a climate of success.

5. The motivators of responsibility and work itself are actuated through participation.

6. The motivators of recognition and a feeling of achievement are largely actuated through written and verbal communication.

In other words, to motivate people in a turnaround:

- First lead them.
- Then kick them in the pants.
- Reestablish a climate of success.
- Get them to participate.
- Communicate during all stages of the turnaround.

STRONG LEADERSHIP

The appointment of a new chief executive officer is the first step the board takes to change the downhill direction of the company. He has to begin by changing the company's working climate and the attitudes of its employees. He must rebuild employee spirit and ability to produce the results he wants. Before he gets their full cooperation, he must convince them that he is setting reasonable objectives. By example and close follow-up on results, he will have to work constantly at building cooperation. He has to let them know that he means to achieve his objectives—preferably with them, but without those who do not provide suitable alternatives or who hinder progress toward the results he wants. This determination to work together is vital because the only way he will accomplish his objectives is through his organization.

The charismatic leader, who by virtue of his personal magnetism, energy, and force influences his followers to make efforts they would not otherwise make, is providing a personal contribution to the turnaround which the less conspicuous administrator cannot offer. He personifies purpose as well as personal power. Although it is not necessary to be flamboyant or eccentric, the turnaround strategy is well served if the leader is a man whose personal purposes are known and whose commitment to organizational purposes is conspicuous. The "sheep-in-sheep's-clothing" may be quietly effective, but he does not inspire. When adversity obscures the prospects of success and organizational morale falters, dynamic and articulate leadership—centered upon achievement rather than personality—can make the difference between success and failure.

Toughness

People want a leader, and they respond to toughness in the beginning stages of a turnaround. This reaction stems partly from their state of demoralization and partly from their lack of alternatives. Robert Brown agrees:

> They are demoralized and say, "I don't give a damn. I'll just come to work, do my thing, keep my nose clean, draw my paycheck. I'll just do my eight to five every day." Then comes the Star, and he shocks the system, gets control, and has no people sensitivity. They all hate him and say, "As soon as I can find another job, I get out of here." But they never do because they have no other alternatives. Therefore, he can make the big stick work.[16]

Brown's opinions would terrify most organizational development people, but they have the clear ring of reality to them. A case in point is the response of NCR Corporation to William Anderson's demanding leadership. Anderson is a perfectionist, and he seldom praises, for, he says, it used to be just the opposite—"Good Old Joe" was patted on the back no matter how poorly he performed. NCR was a company badly needing a dose of his uncompromising discipline. He rarely meets with a group to thrash out a problem, and one vice president called his style "threat of punishment." These methods occasionally spin off unpleasantness. Whatever the defects of Anderson's style, he has restored pride in the company, and the morale at NCR has improved. As one employee said, "I don't always like Anderson, and I don't always agree with what he does, but I sure would hate to lose him."

What Anderson realizes is that, if you're going to achieve excellent results, not only must you perform excellently, but also layer upon layer of your organization must perform at a high level. The minute you accept mediocrity, you lower the performance levels of your entire organization. Unswerving enforcement of this demand for excellent performance will lead to unpleasant circumstances. There will be people who won't understand and, despite your best efforts at communication, never will understand why you set the levels of performance you do. But it isn't necessary that they all understand! You run the risk of becoming ineffective if you waste time attempting to achieve 100 percent understanding in your organization.

Set the Example

You cannot expect more in performance or commitment than you yourself are willing to deliver. Therefore, the yearning for excellence, the drive for improvement, and the commitment to seek out more responsibility must start with you. But once it does, it is not only fair and appropriate, but expected, that you demand similar levels of performance of everyone in your organization. The effective turnaround leader is perceived by subordinates as unswerving, uncompromising, and unrelenting in the pursuit of excellence. That perception cannot be based on a mere image; it must reflect a genuine, deeply personal commitment to excellence. Robert Wilson of Memorex is demanding of his people, but no less demanding of himself. Wilson spends an incredible amount of time on the job, working six or seven days a week from early in the morning to late at night. This dedication produced a remarkable turnaround at Memorex in the mid-1970s.

The Challenge

But even more basic is the concept that a turnaround leader sets the example himself and throws up a challenge that effective people will accept. The less effective, those fearful of vulnerability, will offer only minimum commitment and will be eliminated. Most people respond positively to a challenge. As Roy Woodman says: "A challenge is even more important in a turnaround situation. People want to be challenged, they want to be part of what is going on, and if you don't give them that feeling, you can't really expect them to produce a hell of a lot. The name of the game is getting things done through people."[17] The turnaround leader shouldn't be afraid to establish challenging objectives for the organization. The stimulation such objectives can provide, the rewards they can produce, and the sheer joy they can provide in their achievement are all well worth working for.

THE ORGANIZATIONAL KICK IN THE PANTS

The biggest organizational kick in the pants that I've run across is that performed by George S. Trimble of Bunker Ramo in dealing with problems at his information systems division. Trimble literally closed down a division to get what he wanted, throwing 1,100 people out of work. He brought in new management and then recalled 800 of his furloughed workers. In the process, Trimble eliminated members of management and staff that disagreed with his new direction for the division.

Robert Brown says, "The turnaround leader has got to make people feel, 'Either you yank your oar or you're out.' But he doesn't have to go one-on-one with guys to say that. That feeling must emanate from him, and it must be a very positive force in the turnaround. If it isn't there, he is dead because the organization will kill him."[18] A turnaround is a time to make tough decisions about people. Kicking the organization usually means moving or replacing people and bringing new people in.

The New Culture

Usually people deficiencies are spotted at the top, first, and turnaround leaders shock the organization by using the replacement theory there to effect change. Normally this high-level replacement is done for two reasons: first, the desire of the turnaround leader to build his own team and, second, the inability of certain high-level managers to adapt to the new conditions (the new culture) that the leader is implanting. Glenn Penisten, president of American Microsystems, says:

> You've got to bring the team together and set the new culture, and it should happen quickly. There were some top managers who would never play that role. They were too deeply ingrained in the other cultural approach, and you very quickly have to unplug them and plug somebody else in. I had to do that with 50 percent of the staff. Adaptability is the only criterion you can make a quick decision on. We didn't have much time. We had four straight quarters of losses, $16 million in debt, and the bankers were nervous. The market was beginning to react negatively to our selling efforts because they lost faith in the company as being financially viable.
>
> The cultures really had to change, and it was a case of both showing and forcing. It was forcing them to live together. It was beginning to show through discussions of problems, trying to determine what was wrong, setting objectives, listening to this guy and that guy, and forcing all of them to participate. I had to force the manufacturing guy to critique the marketing guy, and force him to do it in a constructive way.[19]

The Big Stick

Robert Brown sees an unusual psychological reason for why the turnaround manager can initially use the stick in a troubled situation:

> The guys who are left are the hard core. They've usually got personal or financial problems; they can't afford to be without a paycheck. The big stick works because you can push them and pile it on. But you've got to be careful. You've got to be people sensitive. Generally those that ride with you down to the bottom are there because they have no choice.[20]

There are some excellent operating managers left in the hard core. Usually there are some excellent younger managers that are turned on by the challenge of a turnaround. These should form the backbone of your rebuilding team. Robert Townsend recalls that when he took over Avis, he was assured that no one at headquarters was any good. Three years later, just after Avis had been acquired by ITT, ITT's demanding president, Harold Geneen, met with and listened to Avis headquarters personnel for a day and said, "I've already spotted three chief executive officers!" But these were the same people that Townsend was told were no good just three years before.

Head Cutting and Motivation

It is generally feared that when large staff cutbacks have to be made, motivation will be adversely affected. The common prescription is to get the staff reductions over as soon as possible, and to make them all at once. Staff reductions can be difficult, but may be advantageous to management despite possible negative effects on employee motivation. There is variation with the situation and the person, but layoffs apparently do not have as severe an impact as some executives intuitively believe. These questions were studied in some detail by Mauritz D. Blonder in his doctoral dissertation at City University of New York. Blonder found that high numbers of layoffs had a milder impact on retained employees than expected and that layoff frequency had no noticeable effect on morale.

I disagree with Blonder to some extent. My experience indicates that head-count reduction does not reduce morale much in very sick companies but can drag down morale in less severe cases. The timing of head-count reduction should await the turnaround plan unless the situation is critical.

Jerking the organization hard and fast requires a concerted effort in the communications area if morale is not going to sink further. The turnaround executive must cope effectively with the uncertainty, anxiety, and fear felt by the work force and management alike if he is to achieve a successful turnaround. The answers to uncertainty, anxiety, and fear are that the leader's personal integrity, his personal management standards, and, above all else, his ability to communicate. Whether he wants to accept it or not, the turnaround executive is communicating all of the time that he is with another person. It is important that he appear cheerful, assured, and poised at all times. If he appears despondent or out of his depth, the effect on morale may be shattering.

REESTABLISHING CLIMATE OF SUCCESS

The purpose of reestablishing a climate of success is to provide a climate of growth and achievement for your people. Reestablishing a climate of success in a demoralized organization is a difficult feat. As I mentioned previously, the heavy stress on motivating the organization should not take place until the traumatic emergency surgery has been performed. In every stage, the turnaround leader must display a positive, forceful, and decisive manner.

In order to change the climate of an organization from that of demoralization to one of success, a leader must demonstrate success, establish an environment of change, orient the company to success, and work to motivate the three key levels of the organization. The way a leader takes charge and the way he performs during the evaluation and surgery stages of a turnaround must demonstrate success. When this is accomplished, the organization will be more positively postured to accept the additional changes that will come in later stages.

You must remember that, as a manager, you can't make all the changes by yourself; you have to get other people to do them. Otherwise, the changes will tend to be transitional ("When he goes, we go back to the old ways") or superficial ("We do it this way for the boss, but it really gets done this other way."). Supervisors and managers cannot accept the fact that the old system has outlived its usefulness. The way to break this thinking is to replace the real zealots, get the organization off the defensive, and teach positive improvements so that the personnel have a stake in the new order.

Personal Example

I believe that the best device for creating an environment of change in the organization is to set a personal example. To motivate people to make a special effort, you have to make a special effort. To encourage them to work more than the eight-hour day, you have to work more than eight hours. To stimulate them to come up with ideas, you have to come up with ideas. By making yourself visible and by constantly talking to your people up and down the line, you will cause the organization to emulate the positive traits you are showing. Most importantly of all, by showing your subordinates that you are eager for change, you will help them overcome their own inhibitions.

New People

Another way to effect change is to bring in new people. The issue of bringing in your own team of managers versus working with the existing team is very controversial. I think the decision depends entirely on your evaluation of the present management team and their ability to move fast enough in the direction you want them to go. New people have distinct advantages: they are loyal to you; they don't have a vested interest in existing people or procedures; and they have a fresh viewpoint to bring to the problems at hand. On the other hand, new people have one major disadvantage: they need time to learn the operation, decide what has to be done, and begin doing it. I don't subscribe to the old cliché that it takes a whole week for a new manager simply to find the restroom. Top-flight professionals are like shock troops: they can move into action immediately. But shock troops are hard to find, hard to attract, and often don't have staying power. A new management team, like their shock troop counterparts, should only be used in specialized and isolated situations that require their type of expertise.

Make sure that when you bring people in, they're good. As Chauncey Schmidt said:

> When we brought new people into senior management, they were of such first-class quality it almost awed the people here. Of course, we had some good people already in the organization. They stopped thinking about themselves and began thinking about the newcomers as good people coming in to help them. Then they started focusing on the job. They didn't view the newcomers as competitors, but began to think of making it together as a team.[21]

A turnaround leader must orient a company away from failure and toward success. He must start with the optimistic belief that goals can be met; he must impress people with the need to think about profit today; he must turn a troubled company away from a problem orientation toward an opportunity orientation. The personality of a company is its attitudes. Even in this era of "scientific management," the attitudes of management play the most decisive role in the success or failure of a company.

In troubled companies, conditioned to mediocre performance or to outright losses, profit consciousness is minimal. As William Anderson points out:

> As I said at the first management meeting I called in 1972, the Company's basic objective would be to make money, and that objective would transcend all others. It might appear that I was stating the obvious, but in an organization which for years had been only marginally profitable, many of our managers had forgotten that basic concept.[22]

Profit Orientation

Profit is not a dirty word. It is a very necessary ingredient of corporate survival. Getting employees to keep this fact in the forefront can be a difficult task. Many employees do not associate their own goals with the goals of the business in which they work. To think profit, it is important that employees develop a proprietary interest in the business and feel that if it succeeds, they will succeed.

Since your primary objective is to make a substantial improvement in your profits, I suggest you look at all the costs associated with your own position. Cut out unnecessary costs. Seeing how hard and long you work, others in your organization will be motivated to work with you and pull their share of the load and even more. It is up to you to set the tone and pace for your staff, as well as for the whole organization. Demonstrating what you can do will be quickly noticed. It will revitalize morale, help develop a strong team, and, most importantly, produce desirable results. To turn a troubled company from problem orientation to opportunity orientation, you will have to gain the cooperation of your top executives, motivate your line managers, and win the confidence of the other employees.

The place to start is with your top management team. I suggest these steps in dealing with your top management group:

1. Tell them the truth about the current business situation, concentrating on facts and figures, not opinions and criticisms.
2. Map out what has to be done to restore profitability and success, concentrating on monthly goals in each layer of the company.
3. Convince them that these goals are reasonable.
4. Specify to each key manager what is expected of him.
5. Provide for daily, weekly, and monthly reporting formats for your key managers.
6. Help them in developing profit improvement projects. This is largely a job of teaching and coaching.
7. Motivate your managers through pride, incentive compensation, and performance feedback.
8. Show the key managers how to work as a team.

Persuasion

Getting line managers to help you meet your objectives is largely a question of persuasive leadership abilities. Point out that you are merely asking for a return to the success of prior years. Another effective means of motivating and getting the most from your line managers is taking a one-on-one approach—as opposed to the committee approach—to problem solving. When you have a particularly sticky problem that seems to defy solution, instead of organizing a committee, personally visit and discuss the problem with each key person involved. Your managers should do the same in their problem solving efforts. In committees, people can be reluctant to call a spade a spade, whereas on an individual basis they will talk much more freely and openly. You, of course, will have to sift and sort out what you have learned, come to a conclusion, and develop a course of action for resolving the problem.

As the leader of your company, you should strive to gain employee confidence in your ability and in your determination to achieve the goals you have established. At the same time, it is vital that you be fair with your people in attaining your objectives. To do this, I suggest that you let them get to know you personally and that you get to know them. You are probably thinking that you can't possibly do this with over 500 employees. You can, and it is well-worth making the effort and taking the time.

PARTICIPATION AND COMMUNICATION

The purpose of participation in a turnaround situation is to diffuse the profit-performance motivation among as many people as is feasible. There must be a considerable diffusion from the chief executive officer to the rank and file. It is generally believed and sufficiently proven that if middle-level managers and the rank and file have greater responsibility in decisions about their jobs, positive motivation results. Possibly because the prospect of waiting years for results lacks appeal for senior executives striving to generate near-term profits, participative management in its classic form is seldom seen in North American industry. Rather, it is translated—or distorted—into the straightforward proposition that lower-level management should be given a bigger share in making important decisions. What this mostly comes down to in practical terms is increased delegation of decision-making authority and responsibility to middle and even junior managers.

There have been a number of case histories of participative management success in turnaround situations. One such case was Bunker Ramo, where George S. Trimble did a remarkable turnaround job. In 1976, Bunker Ramo performed a stunning $23 million about-face, turning a $13.8 million loss to a $9.4 million profit. Faced with division chiefs accustomed to operating alone, Trimble instituted a philosophy of teamwork (imposed, paradoxically, by his autocratic fiat) that led at first to numerous defections. He now has a ten-member executive council that meets with him monthly in no-holds-barred, shirt-sleeve sessions.

What kind of participation seems to work in a turnaround? Success seems to revolve around two notions: first, organize people into business units that they can readily identify with and, second, try to get solutions to operating problems from the people themselves. Roy Woodman has a unique but common sense approach to participation:

> You've got to be able to listen and get the employees' inputs—and half the problem is just listening. Basically, I will go with the operating people's ideas when you have two alternative courses of action. You get better results. The commitment is there to implement. You will never prove how much better one idea is than the other. If you use that as a guideline, you will get better results. The people have lots of ways to improve the company. We have done this here, and it produced outstanding results.[23]

Most turnaround leaders seem to agree that employee communication is an important part both of holding a company together during the difficult period and of motivating people later as the company achieves success. The communication is not usually the fancy, big-corporation type but a concentration on face-to-face meetings. Such communication can mollify fears during the difficult part of the turnaround.

Roy Woodman feels this way about leveling with his employees:

> I try to meet with as many people as I can, by groups if the company is large. Downward communications always seem to be a problem. People working down the line don't know what is going on, and obviously there are some things which don't make sense or the company wouldn't be losing money. My basic policy is, if I have any doubts about whether or not I should communicate it, I communicate it. I give them as much information as possible—tell it as it is.[24]

Accomplish First – Motivate Second

I began this chapter by stressing the importance of motivation. But as important as motivation is, the turnaround manager must to some extent subordinate his concern about motivation and members' personal needs to the dominant and inescapable requirements of his role as judge and critic of results. He must insist upon the accomplishment which has been projected and must apply the measures, rewards, and penalties available toward this end. In this role he is not the supportive figure who listens sympathetically to all the reasons why something cannot be done. Rather, he holds fast to his requirement that it will be done. When a decision is finally made that reasonable accomplishment can and must take place according to plan, individuals who fail must, if necessary, be replaced. At some point, to preserve commitment and to remain on course, the needs of the organization must be asserted as primary. Commitment must be tested under adversity before it can be known to be effective.

REFERENCES

[1]Peter F. Drucker, *Management: Tasks, Responsibilities, Practices* (New York: Harper & Row, 1974), p. 455.

[2]Robert C. Wilson, address before Business School, Arizona State University, Mar. 13, 1975.

[3]"A Winning Attitude Produces a Turnaround," *Industry Week*, Aug. 5, 1974, p. 36.

[4]Interview with Richard Madden, chairman, Potlatch Corp., San Francisco, Calif., February 1978.

[5]Interview with Ransom Cook, president and chairman (retired), Wells Fargo Bank, San Francisco, Calif., February 1978.

[6]Interview with Roy Woodman, president, Inter-National Video Corp., Sunnyvale, Calif., February 1978.

[7]Interview with Gary Friedman, vice chairman, Itel Corp., San Francisco, Calif., February 1978.

[8]Interview with Robert Sackman, president, Rodal Corp., Palo Alto, Calif., February 1978.

[9]Woodman, interview, February 1978.

[10]Interview with Glenn Penisten, president, American Microsystems, Santa Clara, Calif., February 1978.

[11]Madden, interview, February 1978.

[12]Interview with Frank A. Grisanti, president, Grisanti and Galef, Los Angeles, Calif., February 1978.

[13]Frederick Herzberg, "One More Time: How Do You Motivate Employees?" *Harvard Business Review Classic*, 1968, p. 82.

[14]Interview with Robert C. Brown, president, R. C. Brown & Co., San Francisco, Calif., February 1978.

[15]Herzberg, "One More Time," p. 84.

[16]Brown, interview, February 1978.

[17]Woodman, interview, February 1978.

[18]Brown, interview, February 1978.

[19]Penisten, interview, February 1978.

[20]Brown, interview, February 1978.

[21]Interview with Chauncey Schmidt, chairman, Bank of California, San Francisco, Calif., February 1978.

[22]William Anderson, "NCR: A Presentation to the Financial Community," NCR Public Relations Release, Dayton, Ohio, October 1977.

[23]Woodman, interview, February 1978.

[24]Ibid.

PART FOUR

MANAGEMENT STRATEGIES AND PRACTICES IN A TURNAROUND

How we live is so different from how we ought to live that he who studies what ought to be done rather than what is done will learn the way to his downfall rather than his preservation.

Niccolò Machiavelli, *The Prince*

17
THE EVALUATION STAGE

The viability of a company isn't just something you feel in your bones; it is more than that. A turnaround manager, almost by definition, by temperament and by character has already made that decision the day that he decided to be the guiding spirit behind the turnaround.[1]

**Thaddeus Taube, former Chairman,
Koracorp Industries**

STRUCTURING THE EVALUATION

The evaluation stage of a turnaround entails making a viability analysis of the business and preparing an action plan to solve the problems of the company in the short run. The analysis is usually performed right after a turnaround executive has symbolically taken charge of the company. The first order of business is to recognize the nature and magnitude of the company's problems. Does the company have anemia or has it got cancer? This should be done within a very few days. The turnaround leader is then ready to make his next moves. Remember, troubled companies fall into three general levels of seriousness. These are:

1. *Survival.* In this situation a company's very survival is at stake. There is imminent danger of bankruptcy if drastic action is not taken. The company may be contemplating Chapter 11 protection or may already have filed for protection.

2. *Continuing losses.* A company may be in a loss position that has not yet threatened the existence of the firm. If the losses continue, the firm will face a threat to its existence at a point in time clearly visible on the horizon. The current losses are adversely affecting confidence. Although not in danger of collapse, the company must quickly become profitable.

3. *Declining business position.* In this situation a company is not sustaining business position. Market share, profit margins, and profitability have been steadily declining. Market leadership was lost a few years ago, and if the company continues trends

of the last few years, it will lose money. Its return on equity and on employed assets is near the bottom of its industry group.

Gut Feelings

Most turnaround executives have usually made this basic classification of the situation even before they walk in the door. Along with a preconceived notion of overall viability, they have a pretty good idea of how serious the problem is. What they haven't done in most instances is segmented the company's problems in sufficient detail to take immediate action. In the instances I recall where action was immediate (on the first day or two) and substantive in nature, either the problems were extremely acute or the turnaround executive had some detailed prior knowledge of the problems. If the problems are acute, the alternatives are few in number and obvious. Robert Wilson had some prior knowledge of Collins Radio and acted immediately to effect drastic change.

The first real decision that has to be made is how much time and effort are to be expended on evaluation. This depends on prior knowledge, the seriousness of the problem, and the size of the company. If the company is small and in serious trouble, the evaluation should take from two days to two weeks. If the company is of medium size and is not in imminent danger of collapse, usually thirty to ninety days are needed. If the company is a large, dead-center company, anywhere from three months to one year (A&P case) is required for evaluation. Usually, larger, stagnant companies such as Addressograph-Multigraph take about six months to evaluate. Even in larger companies though, such as NCR Corporation, immediate action is often necessary. Because of the seriousness of NCR's crisis, William Anderson's only logical course of action was to wade right in, tackle the day-to-day crises, and simultaneously make the big changes that had to be made.

The viability analysis requires a lot of numbers work and on-the-spot fact-finding. Just what factor or combination of factors is causing the problem? How deep is the wound? Will emergency first aid be enough? Can the company itself apply the first aid or should it seek outside help? Contrary to popular belief, diagnosis of business problems is not a simple matter. The distinction between symptoms and problems is often subtle.

Getting Information

One of the key actions in taking charge of a company is ordering the preparation of reports and data for evaluation. No matter how serious or secure the troubled situation is, this action should be taken almost immediately upon arrival. The turnaround executive has got to define clearly all the information he needs for his appraisal. In all but the largest companies he'll be making the viability appraisal on his own. In the larger companies he'll organize internal task forces to evaluate special parts of his analysis or he'll call on the resources of outside consulting firms. For example, Arcata National used the Boston Consulting Group extensively, and A&P used Booz Allen Hamilton. Most turnaround leaders are skeptical of the use of outside consultants. They feel they can do the analysis themselves, and at this stage they want to test the internal capabilities of their organization.

I find that the viability analysis really has two major parts, even when it is of a very short duration. First, a preliminary viability analysis is done that goes beyond a turnaround leader's initial feel but falls short of a detailed, segmented analysis. This preliminary viability analysis focuses on the company's management strategies and tactics which have led to the current state of affairs. By balancing company strengths and weaknesses this analysis weighs the company's ability to survive. This analysis usually takes only a very few days, regardless of the size of the company. The second type of viability analysis is more nitty-gritty and is more detailed in its segmentation of problems. It goes well beyond published information and normal top-level reports. It usually involves a lot of face-to-face, on-the-spot evaluation. It utilizes special reports rather than the standard fare.

THE PRELIMINARY VIABILITY ANALYSIS

This evaluation is usually, but not always, performed after a turnaround leader comes aboard. Frank Grisanti calls it a "horseback ride" through the company. At this point, the viability analysis is still centering on the company as a whole rather than on specific people, divisions, and products. The analysis goes beyond feel and utilizes concrete data and some interviews with a few key people. In one unusual case, Robert Wilson, then of Collins Radio, sent one of his trusted lieutenants, under Bank of America auspices, on a scouting party to Memorex. The preliminary findings of the scouting expedition were that Memorex's executives felt the company could be saved. This feeling was largely based on the fact that the company was still generating a substantial sales umbrella with which to work.

Strengths and Weaknesses

In the most general sense, the viability of a company as a whole is viewed by its leaders as a series of strengths and weaknesses. As Thaddeus Taube, former chairman of Koracorp Industries says:

> The strengths are those that are going to have to be maintained come hell or high water. If you have an operation that's making money, you have got to do everything humanly possible to insulate that operation from what is going on, so that it can continue to make the money because it is what is financing the turnaround. The weaknesses are those elements that involve having to perform surgery where surgery is necessary. In some cases, the weaknesses involve operations that absolutely cannot be viable no matter what, and they have to be cut off immediately. It is like someone who has a malignancy on his arm—if you don't cut that off immediately, it could consume the whole body, and so it is with malignant operations. Not all weaknesses are malignant, however, and in some cases the decision between the amputation and the transfusion is a very delicate one.[2]

In the broad sense, the strengths and weaknesses that William S. Anderson found when he took over as chairman of NCR Corporation were as follows:

1. The marketing organization was product-oriented rather than systems-oriented, with the sales force geared to the mechanical era rather than the electric era.
2. The R&D program was slow in bringing out new electronic products, output per dollar was poor, and too often it was a case of too little, too late.
3. An unwieldy corporate organizational structure was so diffuse that no one appeared to be in charge of anything.
4. Information systems, especially in the financial control area, were either nonexistent or inadequate. Ironically, this was a case of the shoemaker's children going barefoot.
5. Parkinson's law was in full flower; NCR had become a classic example of a company grown fat and complacent.
6. Finally, the once-proud company had a serious morale problem.[3]

Anderson's elucidation of NCR's problems masked an underlying optimism shared by nearly every turnaround leader. He felt that NCR had great strengths and that the reports of NCR's impending demise were premature. The financial, marketing, and technical strengths of the company, given strong leadership, were to win the day.

Analyze Key Factors

From this preliminary evaluation of strengths and weaknesses, the turnaround leader must zero in a little more precisely on the viability questions. Remember, there are three key elements to accomplishing a turnaround. They are:

1. A willingness of the board and senior management to face up to the consequences of the troubled situation and to take drastic action
2. A viable core operation that can provide the internal financing required to sustain a company through its turnaround stages
3. A willingness of the company's lenders to provide the bridge financing needed in the initial stages of a turnaround while the company turns its dormant or poorly performing assets to cash

Since the board has already acted to change management (see Chapter 13) and since the new management has taken charge (see Chapter 15), the preliminary viability analysis centers on the existence of a viable core and on the availability of bridge financing to accomplish the turn.

A Viable Core. A viable core is needed to provide a large enough sales umbrella at decent margins to sustain a firm while its troubles are defined and corrected. The core must have a positive cash flow or the ability to be postured for positive cash flow quickly. It usually has competitive products, equipment, and locations. The initial evaluation will probably center on results that the core is achieving rather than on details about it, if it does not appear to be a major problem.

The identification of the core, or "motherlode," around which the turnaround will center is critical. Remember, the turnaround core is not always the largest or founding business of the enterprise. As in the cases of the Penn Central Railroad, Bangor Punta Corporation, Republic Corporation, Dart Industries (Dart sold Rexall Drugs, its original core), and a number of other turnaround firms, the core was not the original business of the firm. In about two out of three cases, though, the original business is the turnaround core. Any emergency planning must include plans to protect the vital core business from the tribulations and stresses of turnaround effort.

If the viability of the core business is in doubt, more detailed evaluation is required. Methods for performing this evaluation are presented in the next section of this chapter. For the moment, let us assume that the core has been identified and deemed viable. The turnaround leader's next overall viability question concerns the availability of bridge capital to provide cash flow while the company's problems are in the process of being off-loaded. In some rare cases the viable core is such a cash cow that there is little question of where the cash is going to come from to finance the turn. One such case was the redwood lumber division of Arcata National. Although comprising a small percentage of the gross revenues, the redwood business provided substantially all the positive cash flow of the corporation. The cash throw-off was so substantial that lender cooperation was not a critical issue, as it is in most cases. Another even less severe turnaround case is that of Dart Industries. Dart had large write-offs in its real estate and cosmetics divisions, but its Tupperware division threw off enormous amounts of cash during this period.

Lender Support. In most cases, however, the core, when identified, is a weak motherlode, and cannot offset the cash flow problems of the company. In this case, it is absolutely essential that the company get lender support for its turnaround effort. If the lenders agree to restructure the debt, then the potential for basic viability of the business is greatly improved. Often the debt restructuring is the first order of business of a new CEO. Sometimes, as in the case of Robert Wilson of Memorex, debt restructuring is a precondition of taking the job. Wilson's first—and most significant—single action was restructuring the debt in order to provide sufficient cash to run the business properly.

Without lender support for bridge financing while a company turns its unproductive assets to cash or to debt elimination, the viability of a company is in serious doubt. A turnaround leader faced with poor lender support is making a crapshoot; he is spinning the wheel of fortune based upon his assessment of the odds. A savvy turnaround expert will probably avoid such a situation or seek Chapter 11 protection under the Bankruptcy Act to help his odds of success.

Case Examples

Richard Madden, chairman of Potlatch Corporation, describes the preliminary viability analysis in two turnaround situations during his career:

> One operation I ran had good people, and the parent company was willing to support it. The technology was reasonably good. The problem was that the predecessor/owner had merely been directing them to move volume rather than to be profit-conscious. It was fairly easy to size up in a week or two what the essential problem element was there. In that

> particular case it was one of the easiest turnarounds I've done. All you had to do was take bright, aggressive people who wanted to do what the policy of the company was and make it evident that the policy was to have a growing profit and a reasonable rate of return. I told them profit was what they were after, and they went after that variable rather than the volume variable. They began to focus more on profit circumstances. We were losing about $2.6 million in the first year, but we went to $2 to $3 million of profit in the second year. It was really a very quick turnaround.
>
> In another circumstance, I had very old equipment in a very noncompetitive type of industry, but the industry was beginning to change. The key there was to recognize that we didn't have much time; the parent company was not going to tolerate those huge losses. In these cases, the parent or the bank says, "Sorry, there is no more money." That takes about two seconds to size up. The financial variable was, therefore, the critical one. This made us focus on which of the portions of the organization we could high-walk and do something with and which had to go. There were so many things wrong that what we ended up doing was selling off about 55 percent of the business to one major company. The trouble was, we were number three in the industry, and this could have created a ferocious antitrust problem. We had to talk to the antitrust people in Washington and get permission to sell. They gave it because they finally realized we were going to shut down and throw thousands of people out of work if we were unable to sell.[4]

THE DETAILED VIABILITY ANALYSIS

The detailed viability analysis is based on two general approaches: first, segmentation and, second, evaluation of available resources—financial strength, market competitiveness, and people.

Segmentation Techniques

There are four general rules of segmentation that I have found useful in turnaround situations:

1. The rule of three. As this implies, in most aspects the segmentation process divides the whole into three parts; for example, divisions are divided into retain, divest, and hold-for-turnaround-effort categories. The traffic light analogy of green, red, and yellow is appropriate. Yellow is borderline.
2. The "80/20" relationship (otherwise known as Pareto's law). I have seen this relationship proven time and again. Basically

it says that 80 percent of the output usually comes from 20 percent of the input. This condition of imbalance is not a state of nature, in my opinion, but rather a symptom of lax management.

3. The current/future breakdown. Simply stated it says: break down all expenditures and asset tie-ups into those absolutely needed for current, day-to-day requirements and those present because of future potential requirements.

4. Importance-ordering for revenues, costs, problems, etc.

The Rule of Three. I have found that the rule of three applies time and again in segmentation efforts. This does not mean that an entire company is broken down into only three divisions, but it does mean that at any one time a thirty-division company probably has three types of divisions from a performance standpoint. Usually the operating divisions in a turnaround fall into three categories: those that are viable, those that have to go, and those that are borderline. It means that people can be classified into A, B, and C categories, where A is absolute retention, B is better to retain, and C is cease to retain. It means inventory can also be classified into A, B, and C categories. It means that divisions are either cash cows, cash neutrals, or cash sinks. The point is that the three categories differentiate performance in a readily distinguishable and easy-to-understand manner.

Pareto's Law. The rule of three also ties in with the 80/20 rule. It is a well-accepted fact that a few employees file most of the labor grievances or experience most of the lost-time accidents, that a minority of policyholders file most of the insurance policy claims, and that a small proportion of product-line items produces a majority of the sales in most organizations. These 80/20 relationships can help management pinpoint where the greatest opportunities for improvement in performance lie. As an example of this, a few years ago James L. Heskett et al. examined the inventory turnover rates (unit sales per year compared with averaged inventories in units) for a sample of fast-, moderate-, and slow-selling items in a wide variety of manufacturing companies. The results, shown in Table 17-1, suggest that items with the highest volume of unit sales turn over from two to eight times faster than those with the lowest volume of unit sales in the same respective product lines. Each of the companies surveyed used roughly the same inventory-management and item-location rules for all items measured within a particular line.

The major reasons that the three categories come into existence are overexpansion and the attempts to be all things to all people. You may start out with one product line, but because of estimates of customer

TABLE 17-1
Relationship between Sales Volume and Inventory Turnover Rates

	*Annual turnover rate**		
Product line measured	*Fast moving items*	*Moderately moving items*	*Slow-moving items*
Cereal-based food	64.8	13.5	8.8
Wire and cable, tubing	18.5	9.8	6.4
Small appliances	5.5	4.5	1.6
Small appliance parts	1.9	1.6	1.4
Grocery paper	21.3	19.3	8.9
Writing paper	21.9	7.0	5.4
Automotive window glass	4.7	1.7	0.5
Grinding wheels	2.6	2.3	0.7
Chemicals	24.4	14.1	7.0

Source: James L. Heskett, Nicholas A. Glaskowsky, Jr., and Robert M. Ivie, *Business Logistics* (New York: Ronald Press, 1973), p. 457.

*Rates are based on an average of annual turnover for three selected items falling into each volume sales category for each product line. Fast-moving items are defined as those in a particular line comprising the top 20 percent of unit sales volume; moderately moving items are those in the next 30 percent; slow-moving items are those in the bottom 50 percent.

demand and because of general pressure, you begin to proliferate. Soon you have ten product lines and you can't tell which is contributing what; however, as a whole you feel you're doing okay, so you get complacent. Eighty percent of the sales volume is often generated by twenty percent of the line items. The trick is to stop and find out which 20 percent is contributing 80 percent of your objectives, scrap the others, and pare down the lines. Many companies, particularly those run by founders, refuse to trim back and kill "their babies." Trimming the size of the company is only a temporary cutback. You have to redirect your energies and strengthen your position in those segments of the business that will produce the greatest profits.

Current/Future Analysis. A third type of segmentation technique involves making a detailed classification of expenditures and asset tie-ups according to whether they are absolutely needed for current operations or are based on a future promised payout. In this simple classification arrangement two other categories should be included. Items that are not absolutely needed for current operations but that have a clear and sizable current payout should go in the former group. These might include certain automation or quality-control equipment. Items whose payout is speculative, such as public relations, advertising, and sales promotion, should go into the latter group. The objective of this classification system should be intuitively obvious to the reader.

After segmenting operations into winners, losers, and maybes, the turnaround executive will want to take a closer look at the losers and maybes divisions. Losers should be retained only if the rock-bottom expenditure levels, as determined by the current/futures classification, show sizable fat present, or if the turnaround leader knows intuitively that a poor marketing job is being performed. The doubtful retention divisions should be viewed in the same way.

Importance Ranking. A fourth segmentation technique, which is a variation on the 80/20 rule, is to break out detailed expenses in order of importance. One way to do this is to obtain detailed operating reports, expense breakdowns, and any other relevant company reports or cost studies. On the basis of this information, rank the major expense items to determine where to concentrate your time and efforts at the outset, e.g., the top 20 percent of expense items that account for 80 percent of the expenditures. Then, prepare a second ranking in terms of each expenditure's impact on profits, or else evaluate each expenditure's impact as being high, moderate, or low. Compare the expenditure analysis with the impact analysis. Your prime cost-reduction targets will, of course, be big expenditures with little impact. For example, recently, at a large consumer-products company, the thirty-nine-man public relations department was eliminated in a cost-reduction program. At a major electronics company all executive salaries were slashed by 10 percent. Starting with the prime targets, look at the major activities being carried out within each expense category in order to identify ways and means to cut costs immediately without seriously affecting your company's long-term performance.

Evaluating Available Resources

The next step in a detailed viability analysis is to evaluate your financial strength, market competitiveness, and people resources, utilizing the segmentation techniques I mentioned above. The three areas are analyzed in the order mentioned because at the start of a turnaround the financial variable above all is critical to survival. In the intermediate term, competitiveness is important, and people resources will determine the longer-term outcome.

1. Gain a personal understanding of the company's current financial position (balance sheet; cash flow) and an under-

standing of "how to make money" in the business, in plants, and on product lines. This is an evaluation of the company's financial resources.

2. Develop a point of view on what is achievable in the marketplace and when it can be achieved. This viewpoint centers on the evaluation of both market strategy and position, as well as on the actual current results achieved. This is an evaluation of the company's overall competitive position.

3. Evaluate the organization in terms of individuals and overall structure. Here the only valid benchmark is the capacity to accomplish significantly more than what is being done. This is an evaluation of the company's people resources.

EVALUATING THE COMPANY'S FINANCIAL STRENGTH

There are hundreds of books dealing with financial analysis. In these few pages I want to highlight those aspects of financial analysis that are important to the turnaround executive in the evaluation stage. The four key issue areas are:

1. The state of the company's balance sheet and the ability of the company to finance the turnaround from internal sources
2. The difference between operating-statement profits and cash flow
3. The need for the turnaround leader to gain a personal knowledge of how money is made in the type of business he's in
4. The state of the company's information systems in the financial area

State of the Balance Sheet

The turnaround leader has to make a hard-nosed evaluation of his cash and cash flow positions. If the company is currently in negative cash flow, he must quickly gain an understanding of the sources and sinks for cash in his company. The key to this understanding is the company's balance sheet, which can be a trap for any inexperienced executive who thinks a turnaround effort is going to be easy. Usually a company in trouble has a terrible balance sheet position. On the surface a casual observer may look at a couple of key ratios and deduce that things really are not that bad. A closer look usually uncovers all the dirty financial linen that accumulated in the decline stage of operations. Assets may be overvalued, particularly intangible assets. Inventories are probably overvalued and subject to large write-downs later. Data processing systems may be capitalized. A number of current expense categories may be capitalized. Future revenue streams may also be discounted and capitalized on a current value basis. I would caution anyone who is evaluating a troubled company's balance sheet to look at every asset category with a jaundiced eye. Many an inexperienced executive has counted on accounts receivable that were uncollectible. Of course, goodwill is a pipe dream. In some industries, such as the apparel industry, inventory reacts to age about the same way a woman does, not very gracefully. Changing patterns of style can seriously erode the ability of apparel companies to translate their inventory values into good receivables. Levi Strauss learned this fact the hard way in Europe, where it wrote down about $30 million in out-of-style inventory in the early 1970s.

Liabilities may be understated. Sometimes payables can be accounted for in such a manner that there is a perpetual time delay in recognizing them, creating a payables "float" that understates your real liability position. The balance sheet is the company closet where all the skeletons of past mistakes are usually hidden. I caution you, as turnaround executive, to review the balance sheet with the cold, hard eye of a pawnbroker. Each major account should be reviewed in detail with the company's controller. If he doesn't have the answers, you know where your staff surgery has to begin. Also, reviewing the balance sheet this way may give you insights into dormant assets that can be turned to cash. In all fairness, I've seen assets understated as well. Usually, land purchased many years ago has a market value in excess of that carried on the books. As another example, if a company has a substantial LIFO inventory account, the unit value of inventory is probably understated compared with its market value. Don't forget to take obsolete merchandise as a haircut. There are usually a lot of "dogs" hidden away in the inventory account.

Cash Flow

Once you feel comfortable with the balance sheet realities (usually they make you feel less comfortable), it is time to determine the difference between operating-statement profits and actual cash flow. In many businesses, this can be substantial. Substantial differences crop up in companies in the financial service, natural resources, and technology areas. I helped turn around a financial services conglomerate whose shining star was supposed to be its domestic insurance company. Because that company had begun utilizing GAAP (Generally Accepted Accounting Principles) even before the industry started, and because it was a young, growing company, there was little resemblance between the GAAP statement and the statutory (cash flow) statement. GAAP allowed front-end commissions to be amortized over the expected life of the insurance contract, thus overstating cash profitability. Although the GAAP statement showed tidy profits, the statutory statement was in deficit, forcing the parent to provide additional cash on a regular basis. A similar situation occurs in leasing companies that discount the value of long-term leases. Actual cash flows are less than those shown. The opposite effect often occurs in resource-rich companies that are depleting their resource position. On an annual basis at least, these companies often generate more cash than the operating statement reflects. My point is this: the operating statement and the cash flow statement are often worlds apart.

In order to get a true picture, order up a cash flow analysis and review the change-in-financial-position statement. These statements, in addition to your balance sheet profile, should allow you to get a picture of the current cash flow situation and of the future prospect for wringing cash out of the dormant or losing assets you are carrying. The thrust of this effort is to determine the internal cash flow capabilities of the firm. If the firm is in a negative cash flow position, surgery of some kind will be called for. Your objective should be to have the firm generating a positive cash flow in a short period of time. Although most firms ultimately have enough resources within themselves, you probably will need external funds to bridge the gap while you turn fallow assets to cash.

It is unlikely that a firm in serious trouble can return to positive cash flow without surgery of both an operational and a strategic nature. Operational cutbacks usually mean head count reduction. Sometimes positive cash flow can be achieved solely by head count reduction, but usually this is not sufficient. Strategic surgery, which is usually strategic divestment, requires a longer period of time to achieve than does operational surgery. Cash flows from divestments may take several months to obtain, hence the need for bridge financing from the lending group. Getting the cooperation of the lenders is a key part of the turnaround leader's job. Essential to this process is the presentation of an emergency plan (a subject of the next chapter). If such a plan is well thought out and well-presented, the company has a good chance of getting lender support.

In very serious cases, after divesting its problems the company may shrink back to a size at which it cannot support its current debt load, even when it has positive cash flow from operations. This particularly severe case requires that the debt be restructured. Restructuring requires a whole new plateau of lender support because it generally requires loan conversion to shaky equity, and sometimes outright forgiveness of debt, which will appear as a loss on the lender's books. You need the support of the lender group in either converting debt to equity, forgiving some debt, placing some debt at very low interest rates, or stretching out debt repayment on an interest-only basis for a number of years.

It is critical that the turnaround leader make a realistic appraisal of his internal cash capabilities and of his bridge financing requirements. I suggest being very conservative in your estimates, allowing plenty of room for error. In the early stages of a turnaround, negative surprises constantly appear, and it always seems to take twice as long as expected to close deals. I've found that bankers don't mind negative perspectives half as much as they mind negative surprises. If you leave plenty of room to make the targets you have agreed to with the bankers, you will go a long way toward solidifying a working relationship built on mutual confidence.

Profit Rationale

Every different type of business has a different profit rationale. Profit rationale is something that operating statements usually don't bring out. The rationale is the marketplace reason for the existence of a business. Larger businesses have multiple rationales. It is imperative that the turnaround leader personally understand the business rationale (s) of the company he commands. Believe it or not, the incumbent people in the company may not understand the rationale or may have in mind an outdated rationale which does not match the realities of the marketplace. What you are really doing is finding out how to make money in the business. Before you can understand the business as a whole, you've got to understand how money is made at the plant and/or the product line level.

This profit rationale analysis can pay handsome dividends. In one case, following a financial analysis of a product line for which margins were declining as a result of decreased prices, a new president determined that field-pricing authority was making a mockery of price discipline. His response was to take pricing authority out of the field and to centralize it at headquarters under one person with a sound set of ground rules to go by. The result was that profits began to improve almost immediately. In another case, the CEO of an industrial products company carefully looked at the profit and loss statement of a plant and spotted a scrap rate of well over 15 percent on a major item. Manufacturing told him it would take a year before the plant could consistently and economically produce the item, which was under a major sales push by the company's marketing staff. This push was immediately curtailed and the money redirected to other products.

In your first day on the job, get the normal financial statements produced for the previous three years and for the current period. You should find these broken down by company or division, product line, and plant, although many troubled companies do not have such financial breakdowns. The real key is for you personally to pore over each item on the statement and to identify trends and relationships among elements of cost, volume, and profits. Break-even charts, value-added calculations, and balance sheets should all be analyzed. From these analyses, a list of questions and tentative conclusions should be prepared for discussion with others in the company.

Financial Information Systems

Your request for financial information will probably uncover a number of weaknesses in the information systems of the company. Remember, these weaknesses reflect not only on the information systems department but on all functional departments that are not paying attention to their business. Most troubled companies have all three possible types of deficiencies. These are: Out-and-out lack of information, overreliance on accounting statements that do not resemble operating realities, and basic traps in presentation due to faulty conceptualization.

When I first arrived at a major private steel company, I was appalled that the company had been running without basic cost and sales-inventory information. There was no organized sales history by product, region, salesman, or division. The inventories, which were kept by hand, were inaccurate, and were not tied together with the order book. Cost information was scanty and certainly didn't break down costs by product, even though cost variations among products were significant. In this case, it took two years to straighten out the problem. The new systems had a very favorable impact on company operations. The systems did not make enough difference, however, to offset the difficult problems of import competition, an aged plant, and a featherbedded labor contract. They did point out why the company was noncompetitive, and they subsequently made possible an orderly shutdown of manufacturing operations which saved the shareholders' equity. I learned from that experience that the lack of controls and information can get you into trouble more easily than the presence of proper controls can get you out of it.

Some of the more common information problems often stymie financial analysis. Basic company reports are not organized in a manner that assists analysis. For example, profit-and-loss statements are kept solely by market, rather than by plant or product line. Usually, standard costs are poor and out-of-date. As a consequence, it is almost impossible to ascertain from profit-and-loss statements how sound margins are, information which is critical for day-to-day pricing. I once saw the president of a company descend on a plant that was losing money and, within an hour, come up with the reason, which others had failed to discern. He took the outdated standard cost sheet of the major plant product, which was generating unfavorable manufacturing variances, and reconstructed it, using the working knowledge of the manufacturing group present (i.e., employees required, per shift, machine productivity rates, material costs, etc.). A comparison of the new approximate standard with current prices clearly showed that either prices had to be raised or the line had to be dropped. Some of the existing staff were unable to make that type of required analysis. This deficiency is not unusual in troubled companies.

Another problem I have encountered is overreliance on accounting numbers. There is not one manufacturer anywhere in the world who knows what the actual cost of one of his products is. Business numbers are generated by a firm's accounting system. At best, they represent the closest available approximations of the "real" numbers, based on generally accepted principles consistently applied, and those approximations must necessarily be widely employed. Calculations of month-end accruals are, at best, only averages or estimates. The accuracy and reliability of business numbers depend on the extent to which purposeful, dedicated effort is expended, and even under optimal conditions business numbers lack real-time and real-world accuracy. But the magnitude of the reliability gap is important. The goal must be to continually narrow that gap.

The audit report from your independent public accounting firm is only your first step toward obtaining hard numbers. Their report deals with tests of accounting practices and principles. But the numbers you will seek with which to evaluate a decision alternative frequently lie outside the accounting system. They won't even get the scrutiny of an outside, disinterested professional. Examples of these numbers abound: square foot availability; "cube" utilization in warehousing; plant capacity utilization; machine loading; tons shipped; forward-aged order-backlog data; number of orders, invoices, or time tickets; and so on. The basic problem is a company's relying on accounting information to delineate closely the requirements for managerial accounting, even though such information is designed for the requirements for financial accounting. Managerial accounting must be tailored to the business in question and sometimes even be personalized to the man in power. At best, financial accounting has to rely on a basic model—generally accepted accounting principles—for all businesses of a given type. Never let the tail wag the dog and accept only financial accounting information in trying to operate a business. What you need is tailored managerial accounting, plus eight to ten key nonfinancial statistics.

Sometimes I've run into outright misstatement of the facts in systems improperly conceptualized. In one case, a steel company had several finishing divisions that were fed by a basic steel-making division. The problem was that the accounting department was pricing steel from the basic steel division to the finishing divisions, on the basis of out-of-date costs—and I mean way out-of-date. The result was that the finishing operations looked much better than they actually were, while the basic steel-making operation looked much worse than it was. The accounting department knew the current costs, and the two people creating this absurdity were one desk apart. After ordering the numbers to be recast, I recommended to the company president the elimination of one of the finishing divisions. It took us three months to complete the divestment.

Another example took place in the banking business. As the turnaround leader of the bank involved described it:

> Everyone's P&L looked as if they were making tremendous amounts of money because they had all the revenue and only half the expenses. If you add it up, the profits of all of our branches and our international banking system, in a year in which we made about $5 million pretax, was about $40 million. I used to go around saying, "You guys must be great because you're earning $40 million, but I've got to tell you that somewhere around here there is a son-of-a-bitch who is spending $35 million! Sooner or later I'm gonna find him, fire him, and all the problems will be over." But we didn't have that guy spending $35 million.
>
> Typically a branch guy would go out and sell a service because he got all the revenue, and all the expense went to corporate. The more business that the guys out in the branches sold to get more fees, the more expenses in operations. If you try to explain it, it is so ludicrous on the face that nobody could possibly justify it, but, nevertheless, that was the system. One of the very first things we did was to allocate all the expenses back out to the branches to show people what their overall operations looked like.[5]

These two cases illustrate why a turnaround executive has to be keenly aware of the numbers at which he is looking. He has to be able to separate reality from fiction, and he might run into a lot more fiction than he expected.

EVALUATING A COMPANY'S COMPETITIVE POSITION

After sizing up your financial strength, you should next evaluate the fundamental competitiveness of the business. You have to determine quickly whether there is a place in the market for your product or service, with an adequate gross margin that will permit you to compete on a profitable basis. Time is of the essence in your evaluation of competitive position. At the outset you should determine how much time you have available, decide to use every bit of it, and use it efficiently.

The evaluation of a company's competitive position should center on three types of issues:

1. The company's competitive strategy in the market segments in which it operates
2. The company's market position
3. The effectivenss of the company's marketing organization

Competitive Strategy

A company's competitive strategy may be forcing it into an uphill battle against insurmountable odds in the marketplace. Take for instance the issue of market share. While a large body of research findings and practical experience points to the necessity of a high market share in order to achieve a high return on investment, market share is often incorrectly defined so as to encompass too broad a market segment. A large number of turnaround leaders agree that market share is a key issue and that generally the larger your share, the more competitive you are. More important, however, is the proper positioning of the company in a profitable market niche. As Frank Grisanti says:

> What you do first is to look at the size of the market. There's lots of room in every market. The question is, what's your niche and how are you prepared to handle it. There's nothing wrong with having 2 percent of the market, if you can support it. But nine times out of ten, when you have an infinitesimal piece of a market, there is no way you can support your position. The likelihood is that you are scrambling for a piece the big guy has put aside because they can't service it. But because you are scrambling and there is price pressure, you can't win. For the most part, if you are down among those ten or twenty companies who are struggling for 10 to 20 percent of the business, it's hard to make a buck.[6]

On the other side of the coin, blindly going after additional market share can pose serious risks. There are appropriate strategies for success in low-market-share situations. These usually include segmentation of market niche, control of R & D costs, control of growth rates, and use of strong leadership. The turnaround leader, in his assessment of competitiveness with regard to product line strategy, should not condemn small market-share size or small company size as a competitive disadvantage out of hand.

In a similar vein to the unlimited market share strategy is the blind acceptance of the product-life-cycle concept. This is a particularly important issue in regard to a turnaround situation. Again, a turnaround leader must not accept with blind faith the premise that the reason his company is in trouble is because his products are in the down part of their product life cycle. If that is in fact the case, then he should be able to milk these products for cash flow. Often, however, belief in a product life cycle proves to be a self-fulfilling prophecy.

A number of troubled companies have had such a fascination with new products that they have moved into new fields without fully analyzing the potential of their existing product lines. Yet, building profitable add-on volume in existing product lines may well offer the lowest risk and highest potential return. This is particularly true for turnaround companies that have unused production capacity and need only a modest amount of new working capital for expanding market coverage. I caution the reader here that I am not talking about gaining new business in existing lines by marginal costing or price decreases. Lowering prices is a common error that troubled companies make in such a situation.

The fundamental structure of a particular market can often defy the logic of general textbook strategies. Size alone is a shallow criterion for competitiveness. A classic example of this is the dire state of the Consolidated Rail Corporation. Plagued by high labor costs and uneconomic routes, Conrail convincingly proves that six bankrupts merged together do not add up to a winner.

Size relative to industry may also be completely immaterial. If you have a single $1 billion refinery sitting on top of a marvelous set of oil wells in Texas and you have 300 service stations on big superhighways scattered around Oklahoma, Arkansas, etc., you don't have to be a $30 billion company. You can be a $4 billion company and wipe anybody else off the map. Fundamental competitiveness has to be looked upon not in terms of absolute size, but in terms of the viability of economic units and the ability of those units to compete against other units.

Market Position

The strategic aspects of competitiveness give a turnaround executive a broad view of where he is. Very quickly he has to face the naked truth about his current competitive position relative to what it should be. This means that a turnaround leader has to focus on the current reality of his marketing effort. This is usually done by obtaining market-position reports. Each of the various market or product managers should be assigned the task of preparing market-position reports for review and discussion. Market-position reports will, of course, vary by business, but by this stage, standard content is fairly well known. To make reporting meetings most productive, however, the turnaround leader should remember to cover these points:

1. Historical information on sales, profit, market share, and the like. Current year information is not enough.
2. Reasons (by product, channel of distribution, end-use customer group, and geographic area) for changes in market share.
3. History of innovations in product, market, promotional approach, and price over the last three years.
4. Strengths and weaknesses of market information and of demand projections.
5. Assumptions being made about future size of market, product trends, and likely competitive moves.
6. Plans for each market.

Marketing Organization Effectiveness

Given an assessment of the market position of a company, the evaluation should next center on the effectiveness of the marketing organization itself. A lot can be gained by observing the people in the organization and by reviewing their response to requests for information. I would recommend two other types of evaluation if time permits: a structured audit of company effectiveness and a trip into the field to talk to a few key customers.

There are any number of detailed rating systems for marketing effectiveness. As a minimum, make sure your system includes the following questions:

1. Does management acknowledge the primacy of the marketplace and of customer needs in shaping company plans and operations?
2. Does marketing management generate innovative strategies and plans for long-run growth and profitability?
3. Is the marketing organization staffed and integrated so that it will be able to carry out marketing analysis, planning, implementation, and control?
4. Are marketing plans implemented in a cost-effective manner and are the results monitored for rapid corrective action?

5. In order to monitor the results, does management receive the kind and quality of information needed to conduct effective marketing?

Making customer calls is very time-consuming but also very enlightening. After spotting a particularly thoughtful and damning complaint letter from an important customer, Roy Ash of Addressograph-Multigraph flew off to discuss the problem personally with the customer. Ash's move was oriented to the problem at hand and served the symbolic purpose of letting his organization know it should be customer-oriented. There is absolutely no substitute for hearing firsthand what customers think about a company's performance. Poor deliveries, slow responses to quotations, or poor handling of credits contribute to unfavorable results. One sales head, after listening to customer after customer complain about the lack of stocks of popular items, traced the complaint back through inventory control to the plant; to many people's chagrin, it turned out that production scheduling was producing against an outdated estimate of industry popularity—there had been a marked shift in popularity of the items. Incredible? Not really. In fact, after a thorough search, it would be surprising if one didn't find potential improvements in the responses of quite a few companies to the day-to-day handling of their customers.

EVALUATING YOUR PEOPLE RESOURCES

Evaluating the character of your organization should take no more than thirty to ninety days. This evaluation should include not only the skills of individuals but also the structure of the organization. People, both as individuals and in organized groups, have to be good if the organization is to perform. Many chief executives have difficulty in evaluating this area properly. This difficulty often stems from the failure to evaluate people against a very demanding standard. In a turnaround situation, the standard should be: Can the organization and its people do significantly better to improve results than they are doing?

This is a very difficult process if the turnaround leader is coming from the outside. He can assess historical financial information affecting sick operations much more accurately than he can the people in the organization, because he really doesn't know the people. Because the assessment of people by others in a turnaround is not an accurate assessment, the turnaround leader has to make the assessment himself, and, unfortunately, this is a slow process. If an insider is making the turnaround, his knowledge of the people obviously gives him a leg up on the outsider who comes in.

Once a useful framework for thinking about the evaluation of an organization has been developed, the actual process should be based upon your judgment and experience wtih people. Some approaches that work are:

1. Apply segmentation and ranking techniques to each group of your organization in the probable order of its importance to the success of the business. This means that excellent people may become expendable because of their organizational group. I would attempt to transfer outstanding performers to other organizational groups.

2. Once you have "importance-ranked" your groups, evaluate quantitatively whether the group measures up to its tasks ahead? In one financial services company, such an analysis suggested that most of the old-line mutual fun salesmen were likely to be converted to successful insurance salesmen. Sales management zeroed in quickly to find out who had the necessary skills and then recruited new people for some of the key posts.

3. Conduct an actual survey of customers to learn both their attitudes toward the company and the reasons for these attitudes. Often more information can be developed if this survey is conducted by an outside organization. It can be very informative on a variety of points in short order, at reasonable expense. Recently, an organization I was involved with found out that its lease brokerage operation enjoyed a good reputation as being innovative and aggressive, but that the operation was hampered by the company's slow payment on leases and mileage allowances. The survey indicated that when these faults were corrected, the company would have an excellent chance to increase its market penetration.

Decisions on people are usually made on the basis of three different criteria. Usually simple numbers requirements are used in rank-and-file decisions, tempered by union seniority rules, affirmative action programs, and company policies. Crocker National Bank got into a great deal of litigation when it did not consider affirmative action programs in firing its people. Middle management is usually judged by knowledgeable upper management. Senior management is usually judged by the top man himself. Usually senior people are judged upon their projected ability, or lack thereof, to adapt to the new culture rather than upon their technical ability. Glenn Penisten of American Microsystems stressed this cultural fit, and other turnaround executives mentioned the fact that senior management must to pull together as a team during the difficult turnaround period.

Don't be overenamored with axing people because replacing people isn't the only solution to poor performance. In a demoralizing situation, motivation training and job restructuring should be considered in all but the most serious instances. Make certain that the key managers you bring in don't try to sack everyone. In one case, a new vice president of a division recommended replacing 70 percent of his key managers. Some were obvious candidates for dismissal, but others were intelligent and had solid track records. I indicated that the new executive was making a mistake by not paying enough attention to alternatives to replacement. It is a lot easier to motivate and train an incumbent with brains than it is to find replacements.

When replacement is decided upon, turnaround leaders' methods vary from the benevolent to the arbitrary. The most arbitrary approach I've heard of was that of James Hawkins in the serious Hewitt-Robins situation: Hawkins's technique: junk the 'yes men.' His procedure: "You say something to them that's almost right. But it's wrong. If they agree with you, you can them."[7] I'm not an advocate of this approach, but good people decisions are critical.

So important were people decisions to Robert Di Giorgio, chairman of Di Giorgio Corporation, that "marginal" divisions were divested if they lacked people who could effect the turnaround.[8]

PUTTING IT ALL TOGETHER

Before the turnaround plan can be formulated, the various evaluations must be integrated into an overall assessment of the company position and into the most appropriate actions in the light of the situation. The factors considered earlier—the general level of seriousness of the company's situation; the leader's gut feelings; the existence or nonexistence of the key viability factors in the turnaround; and the company's finances, competitive position, and people—should all lead through their evaluation to the ability to judge the company's current strategic health and the company's current operating health. The company's strategic health should be rated as strong, average, or weak. The company's current operating health should also be ranked strong, average, or weak. These two assessments create a three-by-three matrix with nine possible cells as to the location of a company's overall performance position. Such a matrix is shown in Table 17-2. Obviously a company that has both a strong operating position and a strong strategic position does not need a turnaround. Just as obviously companies that have a weak position in both these categories not only are turnaround candidates but also are the

TABLE 17-2

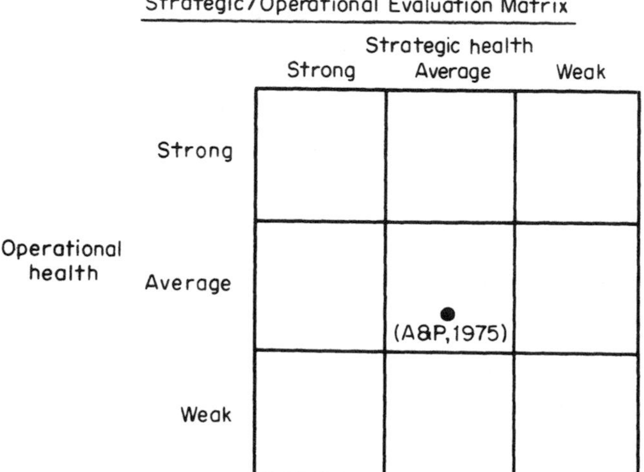

most serious candidates for potential bankruptcy. Most companies fall somewhere in between. For instance, A&P had average strategic health and below average operating health before beginning its turnaround efforts in the mid-1970s. Generally, when both operating and strategic factors are weak, liquidation is probably the best option unless the firm has another business in which it can invest.

When there is a weak operating position and moderate or strong strategic position, an *operating* turnaround strategy is usually needed. Liquidation is sometimes reasonable when the business's strategic position is only average and an operating turnaround is required.

When there is an average operating position and an average or weak strategic position, a *strategic* turnaround is normally indicated. In practice most firms that have failed in their turnaround attempts have usually tried an operational turnaround when in fact a strategic turnaround plan was called for. When a firm has a strong strategic position and an average operating health, a turnaround is seldom needed. Such firms could improve their earnings, however, by undertaking aggressive action plans for improving operating efficiencies. When a business is strong operationally but weak strategically, strategic turnaround is indicated but usually not attempted.

Operating Turnaround Strategies

There are three basic types of operating turnaround strategies: cost-cutting, revenue-generating, and asset-reduction. A decision as to which of these strategies to use is often based on pro forma cash flow projections and a cash flow break-even chart. In addition, a net income break-even point is also useful for indicating the required magnitude of the turnaround effort. If a firm is realtively close to its current break-even point or if its sales are between 60 to 80 percent of break-even and it has visible overhead fat, high direct labor cost, high fixed expenses, and limited financial resources, then cost-cutting strategies are usually selected. Cost-cutting actions produce results more quickly than do revenue-generating or asset-reduction strategies.

If the firm's sales are between 30 and 60 percent of its current break-even point, then the most appropriate turnaround strategies are normally revenue-generating and asset-reduction strategies. Usually there's no way to reduce costs efficiently in order to reach a break-even point under this situation, so revenue-generation and possible asset-reduction efforts are required. The use of asset-reduction strategies in this range will depend on the financial position of the firm. If the firm is in a strong financial position, it can undertake revenue-generating strategies that will utilize its resources in the intermediate term. If finances are critical and capacity is already utilized, then the firm will probably have to consider a combination of revenue-generating tactics financed by an asset-reduction strategy.

At the opposite extreme, if a business's current sales are less than a third of its break-even, then usually the only viable option is an asset-reduction strategy, especially if the business is close to bankruptcy. As a rule the only assets that should be kept are those that the firm will definitely use within the next year or two. The sale of the remaining assets should be done in deliberate fashion to avoid write-downs below book value.

When a firm's current sales are between 50 and 80 percent of break-even point, combination strategies are usually the most effective. If the firm has low fixed indirect labor costs, then revenue-generating strategies are most useful. Although balanced strategies are preferable, they produce a higher level of complexity and may not be successfully handled by a weak organization. They should be pursued only when the organization is deemed capable of successful implementation.

Strategic Turnarounds

Strategic turnarounds center on off-loading business that from an operational viewpoint cannot be saved or whose divestments are needed to finance the turnaround of viable units. A decision is required as to whether the company will attempt to increase its market position in the businesses it has chosen to retain. Strategic moves usually require financial and nonfinancial resources that firms in a poor operating position cannot normally generate on their own. In these situations, one source of funds may be a corporate parent that is willing to fund heavy investments in the areas of relative competitive advantage, over long periods of time, as Philip Morris has done with Miller's beer.

Envision a company's strategic position in a business segment as that of either a leader, competitor, follower, or dropout. It takes substantial financial and nonfinancial resources to move up two levels—for example, to move from a dropout position to a competitor position, Therefore, strategic turnarounds center either on one-level increases in share position or on segmentation/niche strategies, which utilize the strong product position areas at the expense and elimination of weak products. Segmentation and niche strategies usually provide little or no opportunity for eventually seizing leadership in the overall industry involved. Unless the new niche is focused on and unless it grows substantially, such strategies usually produce lower dollar sales and lower net income totals than do successful one-level, share-lifiting turnaround strategies.

It must be remembered that the strategic turnarounds are usually not attempted in weak firms facing emergency turnaround conditions. Usually management responds to turnaround situations with operating strategies, even when these are not called for. In many cases where turnaround attempts fail, management attempts an operating turnaround when a strategic turnaround is needed. In some cases the wrong type of operating turnaround is attempted. Management seldom adopts strategic turnarounds because strategic actions take longer to pay off. Equally importantly, a firm may miss a strategic window in the marketplace. Unless it has unusual strategic resources, it must wait until a competitor slips before it can make its move. Usually, turnaround situations are not so time-forgiving. In less severe turnaround situations, strategic turnarounds and operational turnarounds emphasizing revenue-generating strategies have proven successful.

Strategic turnarounds are usually attempted by companies in strong operating positions. Before a strategic turnaround is begun, an investigation should be made of conditions in the industry, of its stage of evolution, and of its competitive structure. Shifts in relative competitive position occur only during times of rapid change in the industry. These periods are called strategic windows. During most of those times it is almost impossible to make major shifts in competitive position with the limited resources available in firms requiring turnaround action.

REFERENCES

[1]Interview with Thaddeus N. Taube, former chairman, Koracorp Industries, San Francisco, Calif., February 1978.

[2]Ibid.

[3] William S. Anderson, "The Turnaround at NCR Corporation," address at Beta Gamma Sigma dinner, Wright State University, Apr. 19, 1976, p. 6.

[4]Interview with Richard B. Madden, chairman, Potlatch Corp., San Francisco, Calif., February 1978.

[5]Interviewee remains anonymous due to sensitivity of material.

[6]Interview with Frank A. Grisanti, president, Grisanti and Galef, Los Angeles, Calif., February 1978.

[7]"A Winning Attitude Produces a Turnaround," *Industry Week*, Aug. 5, 1978, p. 14.

[8]Interview with Robert Di Giorgio, chairman, Di Giorgio Corp., San Francisco, Calif., February 1978.

18
PLANNING STRATEGIES IN TURNAROUND SITUATIONS

Most large companies in the UK have had formal corporate-planning procedures for at least ten years. One tangible benefit from this should have been the virtual elimination of turnaround situations. . . . However, there is no evidence of any noticeable improvement of this kind.[1]

Barrie Pearson

Most turnaround leaders interviewed agreed that the traditional approach to planning doesn't work in a turnaround. Traditional corporate-planning efforts are too ponderous, have a basic reality gap, and concentrate on trends rather than on the growth/decay packages that are the reality of corporate life. Turnaround executives are not antiplanning, but the name of the turnaround game is change. The challenge is to keep the turnaround plans dynamic and, more importantly, to execute the plans. This chapter outlines practical planning essentials that are appropriate to turnaround situations.

THE NEED FOR PRACTICAL PLANNING

In seven out of ten cases turnaround moves are *at first* based on intuitive action with either no plan or a very informal plan. A formal plan is utilized at some point in eight out of ten cases, but five out of ten of these formal plans came after the emergency stage (See Appendix Table P for details). In most cases major moves are necessarily based on intuition or on informal plans growing out of a quick evaluation. Turnaround executives intuitively know how much evaluation time they can afford and they make their moves accordingly.

Planning and Doing

In a turnaround situation, too often the urge to begin doing something is so compelling that we fail to define completely just what it is that we are about to do. Doing offers an immediate tangible satisfaction—results!

We want to "get on with it." Planning is an inglorious task—almost always a "staff function," something we "really should formalize" and "should do more of." However, productive, meaningful planning is at least as important as the challenge of "doing." It's ridiculously easy to make on-the-spot decisions—if you have previously thought out and evaluated all of the feasible alternatives. In a turnaround, "hard" questions such as the following are required:

1. Is the part of the company under review a drain on the company's cash? Will it be so in the future? How much cash will be involved? Can the company afford the cash drain?
2. How much capital does the segment of the business tie up that could be freed for other uses?
3. Is a given product or division contributing adequate profits now? What are the prospects that it will do so in the future?
4. What opportunities are there to utilize (at higher rates of return) resources made available through a divestiture?

Operating people are likely to spend a great deal of time trying to improve a product or business which they should devote little time to or drop altogether. Top management must channel valuable time and effort away from thse unprofitable areas toward products which have a future. Planning, properly carried out, provides the guidelines to prevent such waste. In order to accomplish this phaseout, the plan should specify those activities to be placed on "milking status." When this is done, managers can limit their phaseout efforts to those which are adequate to keep the operation running until the final shutdown takes place.

Rehabilitation often requires that management risk a large capital expenditure for product development in order to keep a particular product line competitive. When there is little real planning, management may be tempted to try to ride out a temporary decline in sales. All too often, unfortunately, such a decline becomes permanent. When a divestment takes place, it should be conscious and planned—not forced because of neglect and poor management.

Turnaround Plan Characteristics

A turnaround company needs more than plans of the "back-of-an-envelope" type. And more than any other type of company, it must avoid the basic planning errors that make planning just lip service. Its plans must be simple and realistic. They must involve line management and must concentrate on segmenting the business into its strong and weak elements. The turnaround company must concentrate on decisions.

Simple Plans. Turnaround planning must be simple, not ponderous. It is not unusual for a division of a large company to produce a corporate plan which is over 200 pages long. By definition, long-range plans are prepared by senior managers and staff specialists, and the amount of time involved is frightening. Time is spent by individual managers preparing their contributions and subsequently rewriting them to meet their superior's approval; then there are the inevitable briefing and coordination meetings. The trap here is that these massive planning efforts often consume valuable time needed for action and reflection. I agree with Barrie Pearson who says: "Ideally, the planning document should be so brief that the chief executive of the division has time to write the whole narrative himself, following a planning meeting with his management team to establish individual commitments. There is no reason why the divisional planning document should be longer than 20 pages."[2]

Realistic Plans. The ponderous approach leads to the reality gap. Not surprisingly, in some instances the divisional corporate plan is largely written by a business-school-educated staff man who has little real product or customer knowledge in the particular markets involved. The real motive for the delegation of duty is to let the line managers concentrate on running and developing the business while still appearing to meet headquarters' planning requirements. Such evasion is a powerful condemnation of the effectiveness of corporate planning in those companies. As one CEO remarked, "Strategic planning is just a plaything of staff men." Another said, "It's like a Chinese dinner: I feel full when I get it, but after a while I wonder if I've eaten at all."

Line Management Involvement. The problem of reality stems from the plan preparers. In many cases there is a yawning chasm between the broad scenarios of the staff men and actual company problems. In order to be meaningful, planning must get down to the line management level and must pay attention to the concerns of the people actually running the business. This downward movement requires a push from the company's chief executive officer. It is part of the overall cultural change required for a full turnaround.

In a substantial number of cases, even where the top management has been actively involved in preparing the plan, copies of the document are simply filed away after the review meeting with headquarters and not referred to again. Plans that concentrate on hundreds of accounting exhibits and thousands of numbers usually substitute uncritical forecasting for planning. If anyone still suffers from the delusion that man is able to forecast beyond a very short time span, let him look at the headlines in yesterday's paper and ask which of them he could possibly have predicted a decade ago. In fact, planning, by its very nature, is supposed to prevent managers from uncritically extending present trends into the future. Sloughing off yesterday is a much more important element in companies going through a turnaround than it is in more stable companies. Instead of numerical forecasts planning must concentrate on the strong and weak parts of the business.

Finally, observations of companies wrestling with planning suggest that the lack of real payoff from planning is almost always the result of one fundamental weakness, namely, the failure to bring planning down to current decisions. As Lou Gerstner says:

> All too often, the end product of present-day strategic planning activities is a strategic plan—period. Nothing really new happens as a result of the plan, except that everyone gets a warm glow of security and satisfaction now that the uncertainty of the future has been contained. Unfortunately, warm feelings do not produce earnings or capture market share. Neither do graphs of five-year earnings projections, gap charts, or complex strategy statements.[3]

Most of us have seen companies face-to-face with survival properly analyze strategic issues, map out detailed action plans, and then fail to act because the chief executive officer cannot bring himself to make some tough decisions.

THE BASIC PLANNING ELEMENTS

Any plan, whether it be a plan for a high-growth company or for a company in difficulty, should contain four basic elements. These are objectives, strategies, tactical action plans, and provisions for follow-up review of implementation results.

Objectives

Without an objective, the organization is like a ship without a rudder, going around in circles. It's like a derelict; it has no place to go. Developing and communicating an objective, a unified sense of direction, to which all members of the organization can relate, is probably the most important concept in management for top-level consideration, and yet it is frequently overlooked. Unless the organization, its people and management, have an objective, a corporate identity, a philosophy of what they are in business for—and some plans to achieve these objectives—then there is not unified direction that management can use to relate to day-to-day decisions.The responsibility for setting objectives lies with the chief executive officer and the board of directors.

Strategies

The current methods of developing strategies have two fundamental problems that severely limit the likelihood of good decisions coming out of the process. The first problem is that strategic planning requires reasonably accurate long-term forecasts, and yet such forecasts are almost always impossible to produce. The second problem is that most strategic plans are, in practice, not much more than financial hopes filled with "nice" numbers. Usually they are quantitative extrapolations of the past. Instead, they should center on pinpointing the strong and weak parts of the business and spelling out what actions are to be taken to eliminate weakness and to build on strength.

In troubled companies particular caution must be exercised to ensure that the selected strategies are appropriate in light of the limited resources available. For example, when the old Underwood Corporation decided to enter the computer field, it was making what might have been an extremely astute strategic choice. However, running out of money before it could accomplish anything in that field turned its pursuit of opportunity into the prelude to disaster. This is not to say that the strategy was bad. However, the course of action pursued was a high-risk strategy. Each company must decide for itself how much risk it wants to live with.

Tactical Plans

The third element in any plan is to figure out how to "get from here to there." This requires tactical plans. Since only quantitative measures can be communicated without ambiguity to all managers involved in the planning function, quantitative measures have become in practice the focal point of the typical business plan. Thus management's conception of the future of the company is in terms of financial needs. These financial needs are then compared with the results of forecasts of sales and profits from the organization's existing products. Since the needs estimates usually are somewhat pessimistic, this comparison almost always discloses a disparity between the bullish financial goals of top management and the best expectations of middle management about the future of current products and operations. This disparity is often called the "strategic gap" and represents what strategic planning is supposed to contribute to attaining the company's goals.

When the future is analyzed in terms of alternative actions that the company can take to close the gap, the odds favor diversification as the method. Diversification can be accomplished either by innovation through internal development, by acquisitions, or by a combination of the two. However, as one examines the growing list of companies that have become entangled in financial misfortunes because of decisions apparently made in accordance with the principles of strategic planning, it seems that strategic planning may not always produce the expected results. Here are some well-publicized examples:

- General Foods attempted to diversify through acquisition (Burger Chef). The 1972 annual report indicates a write-off of $39 million.
- Rohr Industries attempted to diversify through internal development (urban mass transit). The 1976 annual report indicates a write-off of $52 million.
- Mattel attempted to diversify through acquisition (Ringling Bros.). The 1975 annual report indicates write-offs of $25.5 million.
- Outboard Marine attempted to diversify through internal development (snowmobiles). The 1975 annual report indicates write-offs of $42 million.
- Singer attempted to diversify through internal development (business machines). The 1976 annual report notes a $325 million provision for discontinuance of that division.

Follow-Up Reviews

Profitable growth doesn't just happen; the surest way to achieve it is to identify and pursue specific business divestment and development projects and to make an individual executive accountable for each. What business are we not involved in today which we should plan to enter by creating a new division or by acquisition? Should any division be divested or closed down? The most important part of the corporate plan is the list of key milestones to be achieved along each major projection within the next year. It is essential that each milestone be expressed in a measurable way and that a specific executive be accountable for its achievement by a deadline date. For a typical division, there may be between five and ten key milestones which are to be achieved during the year. The action plans should spell out:

1. *What* is to be done.
2. *Who* is to do it.

3. *How* it is to be accomplished.
4. *When* it is supposed to be complete.

The commitment to key milestones ensures that each member of the top management team has a specific accountability to contribute to business development and that he or she is not allowed simply to concentrate on operational problems and fire fighting. The addressing of accountability, that is, the periodic review of what is actually done versus what was planned, is extremely important. I recommend quarterly planning reviews where managers develop a formal report card as a minimum requirement. Without accountability, planning is just a gesture in the right direction.

PLANNING CONTRASTS BY TURNAROUND STAGE

While the key elements of planning are common to most company situations, they take substantially different forms in a turnaround company. They are shorter, more direct, and subject to more frequent revision. When a turnaround leader takes over a troubled company, his objective is often very simple: survive and return to positive cash flow. He has simple objectives but very limited resources. He suspects, but does not know for sure, that the company as a whole is viable. First, he must perform a viability analysis in order to ascertain whether the company is viable. This evaluation and the subsequent plan that emerges from the evaluation are critical.

There are three distinctly different plans during the turnaround cycle. The first is the emergency plan, which usually is formulated in from five to ninety days after the turnaround leader arrives. Its objective is to get the company to positive cash flow and thus ensure its survival. Next is the stabilization plan, which usually takes a company from the point of positive cash flow through its first year of turnaround. The stabilization plan does not usually have a planning horizon of more than one year. Third is the return-to-growth plan, or redevelopment plan, which takes a company from its solid profit base back to normal growth. This plan usually covers from one to three years. Not all turnaround companies require an emergency plan or a stabilization plan. Companies that are merely declining in margins and market share probably will require only a redevelopment plan.

Operational Gaps

I have found a simple concept very useful in understanding a troubled company's situation. By definition, a troubled company has a sizable performance gap between what the board of directors expects and what the company actually achieves. It is useful to break this performance gap down further into two distinct types of gaps. The first is a strategic gap. A troubled company is often in businesses (products or services) in which it doesn't belong. In Part 1 of this book, I discussed the problem of overdiversification, overexpansion, and excessive leverage. These are the causes of a troubled company's strategic performance gap. The root cause of this strategic performance gap is the inexperience of the company's management or its inability to operate a given type of business, because of a lack of financial and management resources. Strategic gaps can occur from being in the wrong businesses as well as from not being in the right businesses.

A troubled company nearly always has a second type of performance gap called the operational gap. The operational gap means a company is legitimately capable of running a core business, but is not running it very efficiently. It is not operating its core business up to potential. In one glaring example, a medium-size company had a subsidiary which was losing $150,000 per month. The CEO's reaction was to divest and he began a campaign to do so. I told him that whether we kept or sold the loser, we had to take a shot at turning the subsidiary around first. I took charge, wrote a turnaround plan, and executed against the plan. The loser broke even within sixty days and was earning $250,000 per month within six months. A $400,000 per month positive swing changed the CEO's thinking about divestment.

The operational performance gap is therefore the difference between the actual and potential performance of existing businesses that should be retained. My survey of turnaround company CEOs indicates that they felt that 65 percent of the performance gaps in their companies had been operational and 35 percent had been strategic. For a further discussion of this concept, see my article in *Managerial Planning* magazine.[4]

In my mind, the strategic performance gap is more critical in most cases than the operational performance gap. A business can tolerate a truly enormous number of errors in detail if the strategic direction is relevant and correct. No person or organization has ever done or will ever do anything of significance in the most efficient possible way. The inefficiency tolerance level of a business is surprisingly high. The profit margin for a new product may be only 31 percent instead of a planned 40 percent, but the firm will survive and continue profitably.

Contrasting Planning Elements

The objectives, strategies, tactics, and review methods incorporated in a business plan vary from one stage of the turnaround to the next. An outline of these contrasts is shown in Table 18-1.

TABLE 18-1
Contrasting Elements in the Business Plan by Turnaround Stage

Planning	*Emergency plan*	*Stabilization plan*	*Return-to-growth plan*
Objective(s)	Survival, return to positive cash flow	Profit improvement, earn acceptable ROI	Growth and development, growth in market share
Strategies	Liquidation/divestment, product elimination, head count cuts	Divestment, product-mix enhancement, improve operations, reposture the business	Acquisition, new products, new markets, increase market penetration
Tactics	Numerous, see Chapter 19	Numerous, see Chapter 20	Numerous, see Chapter 21
Review and control	"Hands-on" management, daily and and weekly cash reports	Managerial accounting emphasis, weekly operations re-reviews, monthly profit and loss reviews	In addition to stabilization controls, quarterly planning reviews

There are a multitude of tactics used by turnaround companies. Table 18-2 shows a typical set of marketing strategies for the various stages of the turnaround.

THE EMERGENCY PLAN

An emergency plan is formulated from the information gathered during the evaluation stage. Usually in turnarounds there are a limited number of options available, and they are often readily apparent. Stick to the critical problems that have turnaround leverage and are the cornerstones of your action plan. Don't try to cover every problem. Don't bring up problems without pointing out solutions and corrective action. It's more important to solve 80 percent of the problem with imperfect solutions than to go after the last 20 percent, but in doing so take three times as long to produce results. I feel that a reasonably detailed written plan (twenty pages) is essential in order to get a company through its emergency phase. In a smaller company, the plan may only be in your head because you are changing the rules so quickly that any plan that you dared set forth might not be in effect the following week or month. A typical example of an emergency plan is John Byrne's approach in turning GEICO around. Byrne's "war plan" called for the firing of 3,000 of

TABLE 18-2
Marketing Strategies for Turnaround Stage
(Strategy adopted for division or product line)

Marketing decision area	*Emergency stage*	*Stabilization stage*	*Return-to-growth stage*
Business goal integration	Manage for immediate cash	Manage for earnings	Invest for future growth
Market share	Forego share development for improved profits, protect current franchises	Target efforts to high-return segments	Aggressively build across all segments
Pricing	Raise even at expense of volume	Stabilize for maximum profit contribution	Lower to build share
Promotion	Avoid	Invest only as market dictates	Invest heavily to build share
Existing product line	Eliminate low-contribution products/varieties	Shift mix to higher-profit product categories	Expand volume, add line extensions to fill out product categories
New products	Add only sure winners	Add products selectively and in controlled stages of commitment	Expand product line by acquisition, self-manufacture, or joint venture

his own troops and the dropping of 300,000 bad risk policy holders in New Jersey.[5]

Required Time

The time that is spent on the emergency plan depends on the size of the company and the urgency of the situation. If you are losing money hand over fist, you have to start divesting and liquidating almost immediately. Various turnaround leaders have various approaches, but a number of them, including Chauncey Schmidt of the Bank of California and Roy Ash of Addressograph-Multigraph, simply make up lists. Schmidt compiled a list of fifty-six problems facing Bank of California. Ash kept jotting down what he saw as the issues that had to be resolved. Those notes became what he calls "my brick pile" for redesigning A-M. They include some 200 items, ranging from problem products to organizational difficulties. Summing up his overall goal in his own form of mental shorthand, he wrote: "Rethink, redesign, rebuild, and re-earn." In the same spirit, he says that he wanted to make the company's executives "re-question everything."[6]

Problem Segmentation

Once the problems are identified, you have to find a way to sort and organize your ideas. In a complex situation I find segmentation techniques helpful for focusing the results of evaluation. (See Chapter 17 for several segmentation techniques.) You will find that segmentation will speed up the formation of your emergency plan considerably. The mass of information that you have developed during your evaluation may overwhelm you unless you can organize it in a segmented fashion.

Segmentation means a breaking down of the company into its most relevant profit/loss contribution elements. Ideally a company should be segmented by legal entity, by responsibility areas, and by product lines or products. In reality most troubled companies have not been segmented at all or, if they have been, they have been segmented improperly. The Gould Battery Company was operated as one unit before William F. Ylvisaker took over, even though it had four distinct businesses.

In my own experience, detailed breakdowns below the profit or cost center level are not necessary in the initial stages of the turnaround. Product breakdowns can be limited to product lines rather than to individual products. Because of the lack of information and because of time pressures, a great many specific mistakes are made for the sake of the overall good. If the time is available, detailed breakdowns should be made. Roy Ash insisted upon product profitability breakdowns at Addressograph-Multigraph, but he had the time and resources available to avoid the emergency stage altogether. William Ylvisaker found, as I have, that initial segmentation can provide some surprising insights. As he stated:

> Gould had been making its own [rubber cases for batteries] cases in three plants and losing a lot of money. We found we could buy cases more cheaply. We also found we could cut the number of plants making batteries from nineteen to nine without any loss of output and with a lot less overhead. Steps like that began making the business profitable right away.[7]

Once the company's problems are understood, a written action plan should be prepared. In serious situations the game plan is really a cash flow plan because serious situations are negative cash flow situations almost by definition. The plan in such a case should outline how to return to positive cash flow. As Frank Grisanti says, "The first thing you have to do is stop the bleeding." This type of plan in so serious a situation is largely intuitive and put together quickly. Since time is of the essence in a bleeding situation, no more than thirty days should be allotted to this plan, even in large companies. In small companies ten days to two weeks "max" is advisable. The core of the emergency plan focuses on cash flow improvements. This cash flow plan calls for manpower surgery, purchase order surgery, and necessary liquidation of losing subsidiaries. The plan in essence is a cash flow tourniquet to stop the bleeding.

The tourniquet approach works best in small to medium-size companies that are without multiple product divisions. It is helpful but not entirely effective in larger, multibusiness companies. In more complex cases, the turnaround executive should identify his strategic losers and borderline cases, that is, businesses that he should not be operating in light of management or financial resource limitations. He must also look for inefficient operation of his core businesses, as well as for overhead fat in his headquarters.

Lopping off losing businesses usually means eliminating large chunks of the cash flow problem. On the other hand, divestment and even liquidation can take months to accomplish. Closing strategic gaps generally involves time as well as planning that must be initiated immediately. Closing operational gaps usually can be done much more expeditiously because it is an internal process. Unlike strategic moves, which require dealings with a group of potential buyers of the sick divisions, operational efficiencies are a matter of internal action, usually based on executive fiat.

Plan for Closing Strategic Gaps

As I pointed out in Part 1 of this study, the most common error of commission that managements of troubled companies make is expansion beyond their managerial and financial resources. Usually this can be characterized as overdiversification. In many cases a company finds that it is not only the wrong size but is out of balance with respect to the deployment of its assets compared to the returns it is earning. Closing strategic gaps at this point in a turnaround is mostly a function of asset divestment and liquidation, since about six out of ten turnaround companies are facing immediate cash difficulties. The primary reason for these moves is to turn unproductive assets into cash or to stop the cash flow bleeding of losing operations.

Asset-Redeployment Strategies. There are four major asset-redeployment strategies that can be utilized. They are divestment, shutdown, acquisition, and transfer of assets. One thing to keep in mind in consid-

TABLE 18-3
Use of Various Asset-Redeployment Strategies during the Turnaround

Strategy	*Percentage use*
Divestment of operating divisions	57
Divestment of substantial operating assets	31
Shutdown of facilities	37
Acquisition of companies	10
Acquisition of operating assets	5
Other	1

Source: Donald B. Bibeault, Survey of eighty-one turnaround company chief executives, April 1978.

ering redeployment strategy is the degree to which an asset can be separated from the rest of the enterprise. A business, product line, product, market, or other component of the corporate enterprise must be clearly identifiable as a measurable unit that can be separated from the rest of the organization for purposes of problem identification, evaluation, and implementation. This is always a problem but is often compounded in a turnaround situation. As a rule, divestment decisions cannot be effectively made unless management deals with segments that can be physically separated (for purposes of cash recovery or its equivalent) from the rest of the organization.

I surveyed the turnaround companies to find out how often they employed the major asset-redeployment strategies I mentioned above. Results are show in Table 18-3.

Classifying Subsidiaries. The evaluation of divisions and product lines should allow management to place each of these segments in one of three categories: must retain, must divest, or borderline case. The borderline cases are the ones that must be further evaluated. Usually there is a bias toward retaining borderline cases if the cash is not absolutely needed. But remember, this is the time to be totally ruthless in regard to getting your company back to positive cash flow. Borderline cases are usually subdivided into those that with operational surgery can be retained and put on a milking status and those that need a rehabilitation effort. Usually the tough turnaround leader does not want to waste his time rehabilitating a borderline-type case. Some divisions or product lines that are put on cash flow milking status during the emergency stage may be rehabilitated during the stabilization stage. If rehabilitation of a borderline case is attempted and fails during the emergency stage, that division is usually divested in the next stage. Many borderline cases that are put on milking status during the emergency and stabilization stages are divested during the return-to-growth stage.

Rehabilitation takes a lot more management effort than milking does, since it is a miniturnaround within the larger turnaround. In a lot of cases, management is under severe pressure and would rather milk or divest for cash flow than rehabilitate. On the other hand the core, or motherlode, is not only retained but is definitely protected during the turnaround. Table 18-4 explains the various retention/divestment alternatives and how they change by stage.

As Table 18-4 shows, the retention/divestment plan during the emergency stage is made up of the following substrategies:

1. Retain and protect the core business, the motherlode.
2. Retain other profitable divisions and product lines unless forced to sell.
3. Retain certain borderline cases on a cash-milking status.
4. Retain other borderline cases for rehabilitation only in rare cases where cash flow is not a problem and near-term prospects are bright.
5. Wait to divest borderline misfits, usually after long-range plan is in place.
6. Divest losers to stop the bleeding, and poor performers to get cash.
7. Avoid acquisitions.

Divestment. It is interesting to contrast the different reasons given for making divestments by turnaround companies with those given by non-turnaround companies. These are shown in Table 18-5. As the table shows, turnaround companies divested much more frequently for poor performance reasons than did companies in general. In addition, their resource needs were greater than other companies. Together, poor performance and capital needs accounted for 74 percent of the reasons for divestment. Although changes in plans or in objectives accounted for 20 percent of the reasons for divestment, my experience indicates that such changes are usually a factor in the later stages of a turnaround.

Typical of the kind of divestment I have been discussing was Chock Full O'Nuts Corporation's divestment of its Rheingold Breweries Division, a division which cost the company more than $21 million in pretax

TABLE 18-4
Retention/Divestment Alternatives during Turnaround Stages

*Type of company**	*Emergency stage*	*Stabilization stage*	*Return-to-growth stage*
Retained:			
Core business ("motherlode")	Protect	Improve profitability	Develop
Other profitable divisions	Run in current form	Improve profitability	Develop
Borderline:			
Retained in milking status	Milk for cash	Consider rehabilitation	Usually divest
Retained for rehabilitation	Rehabilitation rarely attempted	Try to rehabilitate	
Divested as misfit	Not usually	Yes	N/A
Divested:			
Early divestments	Divest for cash or to stop losses	Divest as misfit	N/A
Later divestments	N/A	Divest for poor ROI	Divest as misfit
Acquisitions	Not done	Usually not done	Modest program begun

*During preliminary and detailed evaluation stages respectively, these categories and subcategories are formulated.

TABLE 18-5
Factors in Decision to Divest

	Nonturnaround companies (%)	*Turnaround companies (%)*
Poor performance	26	42
Changes in plans & objectives	23	20
Need to raise capital	10	17
Excessive resource needs	19	15
Constraints in operations	15	5
Antitrust conflicts	7	1
TOTAL	100	100

Source: Nonturnaround company statistics based on Leonard Vignola, Jr., *Strategic Divestment* (New York: Amacom, 1974), p. 52; turnaround company statistics based on Donald B. Bibeault, Survey of eighty-one turnaround company chief executives, April 1978.

losses and three years of constant trouble. The divestment ended what Chock's president, Seymour S. Mindel, called a "3½ year nightmare."

The value received for divested assets is shown in Table 18-6.

The results indicate a somewhat orderly divestment policy, although the value received was less than book in 30 percent of the cases, thus contributing to the substantial write-downs during the emergency stage. Previously I mentioned that turnaround leaders often write down assets below what they ultimately receive during the emergency stage in order to get all the bad news out of the way and to leave themselves with a performance cushion on the upside.

TABLE 18-6
The Value of the Divested Assets Received

Value	*Percent receiving*
Full going-concern value	7
Less-than-going-concern, more-than-book value	10
Book value	53
Less-than-book, more-than-auction value	5
Auction or liquidation value	25
TOTAL	100

Source: Donald B. Bibeault, Survey of eighty-one turnaround company chief executives, April 1978.

Plan for Closing Operational Gaps

Usually, divested assets do not recover enough cash to close the cash flow gap. A turnaround executive must calculate how much cash flow can be saved by better operations in the retained companies. If this number, together with his original cash-recovery numbers from divestment, still leaves a shortfall, he will have to cut deeper. There is a practical limit to how far he can cut. Usually profitable divisions are not sacrificed for cash flow or balance sheet reasons during this part of the turnaround, but sometimes the situation makes that alternative necessary.

Closing operational gaps at this point in the turnaround is mainly a function of imposing drastic cost management, making obvious operating efficiencies, and auditing key factors in the marketing operation. The emergency plan should reflect a realistic appraisal of what is achievable in regard to improving operating results in the short run. This is not a time for timidity, but rather a time for planning how to carve as much out of your operation as is needed to achieve positive cash flow. Plan on achieving your objectives regardless of the alibis and gnashing of teeth within your organization. Don't be surprised if you wind up with a leaner, more effective organization than you had before. The "doomsayers" will all be telling you that you can't possibly operate that way, but instead you'll find that you are operating better.

You should initiate most elements of cost avoidance and cost prevention as part of taking charge of the company. By cost avoidance, I mean postponing spending wherever possible. This means that you must take control of the cash flow pipeline, principally the purchasing area, and institute tough review and approval routines. Remember, don't postpone expenses now if postponement will increase costs later. You can't postpone necessary equipment maintenance, for example, but all equipment maintenance is not necessary. All new projects, staff additions, other actions and programs are usually put on the back burner until the emergency plan is ready. The point is to not spend the money until objectives have been clarified.

The emergency plan centers on cost elimination and cost reduction. It is amazing how much energy is wasted in trying to reduce costs on products that should have been eliminated in the first place. Cost elimination centers on doing away with operations that are not profitable or are only marginally productive. Eliminating or planning to eliminate divisions, plants, or product lines or implementing shutdowns of outmoded facilities must be reviewed in a hard-nosed fashion. Every company has a few "sleepers" and "sacred cows." Get rid of them.

Head-count Reduction. Most cost-reduction efforts center on retained operations. There's usually plenty of room in which to maneuver. John

Thompson, senior vice president of planning at Crocker National, states flatly that there is at least 20 percent fat in any corporation. I don't doubt it, but that doesn't mean that you should enforce a 20 percent across-the-board cut in costs. You have a choice of the "meat-ax," across-the-board approach, the selective surgical approach, and the cost-reduction program approach.

I've found that, although it takes a little more study, the selective surgical approach works best. There are cases when the situation is so severe that the meat-ax approach is required. If your subordinates hedge or delay in cooperating with the selective surgical approach, take out your meat-ax and start swinging, yourself. Cost reduction starts with head count reduction, and there is great reluctance to lop off heads. The turnaround leader doesn't like it any more than anyone else, but he realizes it's necessary. The company in trouble is like an overloaded lifeboat: either every third person has to get off or the boat will sink.

Cost-reduction programs are a "cop-out" unless you've just got a mild case of mediocrity. Methods improvements, goals, etc., sound nice but take too long and seldom meet expectations. At this stage, selective surgery is your best bet. Remember that selective surgery doesn't mean that you don't go after a goal of 20 percent reduction. In fact you go after whatever you've determined that you need. If it's 50 percent, go after it. "Selective" means that the cuts are not across-the-board cuts. Cost reduction in most businesses, except very capital-intensive ones, usually means people reductions. In most companies you can count on about a $2 reduction in total costs per dollar of employee cost reduction, but evaluate your own situation and plan according to your company's individual conditions. I polled the turnaround companies to see how they made their staff reductions. The results are shown in Table 18-7.

Hiring freezes and attrition usually are not high enough in numbers to meet most staff-reduction requirements in a turnaround. The situation usually demands active efforts to reduce head-count. If possible, avoid terminating people during the first sixty days because a piecemeal approach to head-count reduction has a devastating effect on morale throughout the business in a turnaround situation. Nonetheless, if the situation is sufficiently serious to warrant action being taken earlier, then take it. The surgical-cut approach is based upon a distinction between those functions that are absolutely necessary to run the business and those that have a future payout but are not immediately necessary.

In looking for further manpower reductions, ask all managers to approach their cost-reduction work by determining if they can (1) eliminate an entire activity, or any element of the job activity; (2) reduce the frequency of performing an activity, or the frequency of performing any element of a particular job; (3) change the methods, procedures, equip-

TABLE 18-7
Strategy Utilized in Making Staff Reductions

Strategy	*Percent utilized*
Functional department decreases after analysis	66
Across-the-board percentage decrease	12
Attrition only	7
Attrition and hiring freeze	6
Hiring freeze only	5
Percentage cuts based on organizational level	4
TOTAL	100

Source: Donald B. Bibeault, Survey of eighty-one turnaround company chief executives, April 1978.

ment, or personnel used in performing an activity; (4) eliminate overlapping or duplicate work, idle time, and overtime; (5) establish work standards of performance for each person on their staff. I think you will find that getting specific answers to these questions from all your managers can do a great deal to stimulate their thinking on how manpower levels and other costs can be reduced.

If you don't get the cooperation you need, then you may have to order reductions based on your own evaluation of the needs of the company. What level of reductions can you plan for? In headquarters administrative areas I've seen some drastic prunings. In one case, I made surgical cuts to reduce a headquarters staff from 571 to 356 in one year's time. Four years after the first cuts, total company revenues were 2½ times what they had been the day I walked in. The headquarters staff had shrunk to only 247 people. The head count reduction had taken out $5 million of personnel costs and $4 million of other expenses. From a pretax loss of $4.2 million the company had gone to earnings of nearly $5 million pretax.

Some departments were eliminated altogether. Data processing was cut back 65 percent. Accounting was cut back 15 percent, while some direct marketing staff increases were made. The point is that drastic cuts in overhead can be made. In another case, Jim Hawkins of Hewitt-Robins found his headquarters extremely overstaffed. The 250-person staff was cut to 17. Most of that drastic change was staff reduction, but some people were placed in operating departments. The point I'm trying to make is that you have to take whatever action is necessary to stop the bleeding.

Operating Improvements. I'm not going to spend much time here on the various operating improvements that can be made. Details of these will be discussed in the coming chapters. In one case, I saw a company turning inventory over three times per year. Previously the company had averaged about four turns a year—the industry average. By instituting an inventory management approach and by forcing sales and manufacturing to communicate better, the company was able to increase inventory turnover to 4.5 turns per year within six months. This netted a $3 million inventory reduction and decreased borrowing costs by $450,000 per year. The program cost $20,000 to implement and took no extra personnel.

Marketing is often called the "whipping boy" of the turnaround. As Robert Brown says:

> Marketing really doesn't have much of a place in the early stages of turnaround. There is usually a retrenchment, and marketing is always the third leg on the stool; it is the last one you do anything with. The first is financial, the second is operations, and the third is marketing. Usually, you chop the advertising budget to zero and get rid of all the stuff you can do without, and that is always at the expense of marketing.[8]

But tampering at all with the current selling expense level will mean working in a very sensitive area. Selling activities are close to the customer, and many an emotional case has been presented for not cutting selling expenses for that reason. Don't let selling expenses be a sacred cow to you or anyone else in your organization.

Besides expense reductions, your emergency plan should focus on other aspects of marketing that have substantial bottom-line effect. The turnaround companies which I polled had pricing problems in 45 percent of the cases, product problems in 39 percent, promotion problems in 10 percent, and distribution problems in only 6 percent. I've found time and again that troubled companies do a terrible job of pricing. They usually underprice, sometimes giving away a substantial chunk of money that accounts for a large part of their operating losses. In fact, one of the symptoms of an ailing company is that they are out of pace in pricing. In 45 percent of the cases troubled companies priced too low compared with competition; in only 13 percent of the cases did they price too high. The lesson here is that your company is probably underpricing. You can go a long way toward closing the operation gap by pricing properly.

Another problem is product proliferation. As Frank Grisanti says, "Trying to be all things to all people. Get the marines because the customer controls you, and you don't control the customer." Fully 92 per-

cent of the surveyed companies pursued a policy of eliminating losers from their product lines. On the average, 17 percent of their products were eliminated. I know of one company that went from 250 different models to just 33 and yet had a substantial increase in sales. In addition, 72 percent of the turnaround companies surveyed consciously dropped unprofitable customers during the emergency stage.

THE STABILIZATION PLAN

Stabilization planning is based on the premise that the corporation will survive and that it has proven it can do so. During this period, the corporation begins to look beyond the day-to-day crisis and the requirements of survival. It knows it can survive, but it does not know how dark or how bright its future will be. It has come in from the rain, but dark clouds still are on the horizon. Stabilization, by definition, implies a settling-down process that allows time for giving the future more thought—because now everyone believes there will be a future. The overriding objective of the stabilization period is to provide a sound platform for future growth.

Planning Strategies

This requires a stabilization plan, a definition of the future of the company over some time horizon (usually one year). During stabilization, emphasis is on a three-pronged strategy:

1. Improving the profitability of retained operations by improving margins
2. Running existing operations more efficiently by improved systems and techniques
3. Reposturing the company to provide a stable platform for future growth

Profit improvement is done in a more deliberate and well-thought-out manner than was done in the emergency stage. The emphasis is no longer purely on cash flow, but on profitability and on the relative return on assets employed. A product, a division, or an operation must provide something more than just positive cash flow to be retained; it must provide profits relative to the capital invested. In the emergency stage the basic strategies are defensive, while in the stabilization stage I would characterize the basic strategies as conservative. Contrasts in the basic strategies are shown in Table 18-8.

TABLE 18-8
Contrasting Planning Strategies during the Stabilization Stage versus the Emergency Stage

	Planning strategies	
Decision area	*Emergency stage*	*Stabilization stage*
Basic thrust	Take defensive steps	Maintain conservative posture
Products	Prune product line drastically	Prune product line, prune individual products
Costs	Reduce costs drastically, "meat-ax" cuts if necessary	Reduce costs, improve overhead value
Capacity	Cut capacity, disinvest	Limit risk focus and defer investments
Financial management	Manage for cash flow, even at expense of profit and less statement	Strengthen balance sheet, develop strong bank relationships
Dividend	Eliminate dividend	Consider reinstating small dividend

Source: Ideas for this structure based on Donald K. Clifford, B. A. Bridgewater, Jr., and Thomas Hardy, "The Game Has Changed," *McKinsey Quarterly Review*, Autumn 1975, p. 16.

Profit Improvement. Improving profitability in the stabilization stage centers on two fundamental tactics: first, making retention/divestment decisions and, second, cutting costs and increasing prices to achieve higher margins. The retention/divestment decision differs markedly from the emergency stage. In the emergency stage, liquidation is more often the case rather than is divestment. Also, when the situation is serious, a company in an emergency situation may be forced to sell one of its winners, a course of action seldom taken in the stabilization stage.

Profit improvement tactics in the stabilization plan center on rigorous enforcement of margin requirements. One of the more surprising characteristics of troubled companies is their amazing lack of price discipline. By allowing their prices to lag behind cost increases, many companies lose precious margins, particularly during inflationary periods. (One glaring example is an automotive original-equipment manufacturer that let its margins shrink by 50 percent even though it enjoyed a 100 percent market share.) During stabilization, the tactics employed are concentrated on margin improvement rather than sales volume growth. Robert Di Giorgio emphasizes this tactic. "In your stabilization planning you go for margins, not volume. Our volume stood still for three years. We went from several million dollars lost to several million dollars profit in that same period with the same volume. It was the mix and quality of the business that improved."[9]

Improving Systems. Another stabilization plan entails trying to run the day-to-day business more efficiently. This involves a major emphasis on increased control, both financial and nonfinancial. It involves developing better information for decision making. There is a deliberate effort by management to take a new, fresh, and detailed look at every facet of how it operates its basic businesses. In regard to running the operation better, Frank Grisanti says: "At this point in time we are talking about firming up the organization, making sure that everybody is in proper position, laying the foundation for routines—the normal operating routines—systems and procedures instituting and tuning up the organization and stabilizing the people."[10]

Reposturing the Business. The third major strategy of the stabilization plan is to reposture the business. After the company has completed its planned withdrawal from unprofitable products, services, market segments, and territories and is running its basic business more efficiently, it must look toward business areas which are more attractive from the standpoint of future profitability and growth. Before it can launch full-scale development programs, it must redeploy its financial assets and clean up its balance sheet in order to provide a stable financial platform for growth.

The balance sheet clean-up is a major tactic used in the reposturing strategy. Usually a company going through a turnaround develops a very unorganized balance sheet, both in terms of its debt structure and in terms of its deployment of major assets. This imbalance has its roots, most often, in the poorly managed expansion of a business. Over the years, many a company has expanded its operations forward toward its consumers or backward toward its raw materials without considering explicitly the asset-distribution balance it was striking between short-term profitability and the long-term stability of the organization. Management often has simply allowed the asset balance between divisions to seek its own level, like water.

What frequently happens is that top management, in the name of integration, allows assets to gravitate to the segments of the company that have the greatest mass and activity, and hence the greatest attractive power. Over time, other areas suffer from shortages of assets, and these very segments may be the ones that have the greatest profit potential, especially over the short term—yet they tend to remain in a semistarved and neglected condition.

Imbalance is also likely to occur as a company's market situation changes over time, e.g., when the relative profitability of the segments of a business shifts or when a maturing market or life cycle diminishes the risk of market fluctuation. Ideally, as such shifts occur, a company should alter its asset distribution so as to reflect its new market environment. However, such market changes often evolve subtly over time and are not recognized until a significant imbalance has already occurred.

Once imbalance has occurred, the financial benefits of shifting—either forward or backward—may substantially outweigh the risks. In soft goods, the primary profit leverage comes most often from the marketing area, with manufacturing returning value that is low by comparison. Companies such as Mattel, Incorporated, have therefore subcontracted a large part of their manufacturing, which they had formerly performed themselves, and applied the assets thus liberated in the more profitable retailing segment. Because Rexall drugstores were providing an unsatisfactory return on the company's investment, Dart Industries decided to liquidate them and to put the assets into the more profitable ethical drug manufacturing segment of the business. As Justin Dart said, "It was a bit like selling Mother."

Perhaps no better example exists of a firm's constant search for security through reposturing than the dramatic shifts at W. R. Grace over the years. The balance of net sales by business sector for W. R. Grace is shown in Table 18-9.

TABLE 18-9
Reposturing of Business Sectors at W. R. Grace, 1950-1977
($U.S. in millions)

	1950	*1962*	*1977*
Latin American operations	$132	$110	$ 0
Shipping, etc.	56	73	0
Agricultural chemicals	12	94	513
Natural resources	0	85	235
Specialty chemicals	0	212	1,671
Other consumer products & services	0	0	1,057
Restaurants & stores	0	0	500
Total net sales	$200	$574	$3,976

Source: "There's Always Something New at W. R. Grace," *Fortune*, May 8, 1978, p. 119.

Table 18-9 shows three stages in the company's transformation under the grandson of the founder. Serious change started in 1950, five years after Peter Grace was named president. By the midpoint in his tenure, in 1962, he had firmly established chemicals as the core of the company and had made the first acquisitions of consumer businesses. By 1977, not a single piece of the old W. R. Grace was left.

THE RETURN-TO-NORMAL-GROWTH PLAN

If a turnaround company successfully implements its stabilization plan, it should be ready to plan for a redevelopment of its growth pattern on a sustained basis. One would hope that the lessons of overexpansion, overdiversification, and overleveraging, which got the company into problems earlier, will not be repeated by management. The redevelopment plan is a very useful step in ensuring that the modest growth objectives toward which the turnaround company can now strive are balanced by its available resources. Usually this plan covers a period from one to three years long.

During the emergency stage, a turnaround company usually has both strategic and operational performance gaps of a severe nature. During the stabilization stage, a turnaround company continues to have performance gaps, but these are usually less severe and generally are operational gaps. This is especially true if the misfit businesses have been divested or liquidated. In the return-to-growth stage, the turnaround company usually starts out by pushing internal development efforts and later emphasizes external diversification efforts.

Planning Strategies

If a company has successfully implemented its stabilization effort, it has wrung out most of the profit-improvement potential from its existing businesses, products, and balance sheet restructuring efforts. Now the turnaround company must plan to develop new thrust areas on a modest basis. Overemphasis on the operation of the existing business without an appropriate amount of effort being directed toward the discovery and development of new products, processes, and services to replace those which are obsolete can result in the stagnation and eventual decline of the enterprise. The turnaround company has been forced earlier by the severity of its problems to be internally oriented and to place less emphasis on change in the world around it. Now it has to address that change, on a planned basis. The change in emphasis between the strategies utilized in the stabilization stage and those used in the return-to-growth stage is shown in Table 18-10.

TABLE 18-10
Contrasting Planning Strategies during the Return-to-Growth versus the Stabilization Stage

	Planning strategies	
Decision area	*Stabilization stage*	*Return-to-growth stage*
Basic thrust	Maintain conservative posture	Take aggressive action to seize advantage
Products	Prune product line, prune individual product	Extend and improve product line
Costs	Reduce costs, improve overhead value	Invest in productivity (automate, improve overhead value, etc.)
Capacity	Limit risk focus and defer investments	Increase marketing thrust to hold or build volume, drive for increased share
Financial management	Strengthen balance sheet, develop strong bank relations	Obtain external funding in modest amounts
Dividend	Consider reinstating small dividend	Reinstate dividend

Source: Ideas for this structure based on Donald K. Clifford, B. A. Bridgewater, Jr., and Thomas Hardy, "The Game Has Changed," *McKinsey Quarterly Review*, Autumn 1975, p. 16.

Growth Strategies

Any company, but especially turnaround companies, must give careful attention to the management implications of development moves as outlined in Table 18-11. In the early part of this stage, it is wise for the turnaround company to stick fairly close to its existing technologies, products, and markets. Certainly it should avoid superdiversification (the lower-right-hand corner of Table 18-11) at all costs.

In contrast to the stabilization stage, where existing markets and technologies are nurtured to their fullest, a turnaround company in the return-to-growth stage should be postured to move toward product improvement and market expansion. It may go so far as to diversify into new customer markets and new products, but it should do so after a great deal of soul-searching. The boundary condition, in terms of risk for the turnaround company attempting to increase its growth rate in these ways, is difficult to define precisely. Of utmost importance is the realization that any diversification should not be able to sink the company

TABLE 18-11
Strategic Growth Alternatives

New Markets	*New products & technologies*		
	No technological change	Improvement or adapt product	New technology or product
Existing markets	No change	Product improvement	Product replacement or new production technology
New regional markets	Market expansion—geographic	Market expansion—geographic-improved product	Market expansion—geographic-new product technology
New customer markets	Market expansion—customers	Market expansion—customers-improved product	Diversification: Market expansion—customers-new product technology
New international markets	Market expansion—international	Market expansion—international-improved product	Superdiversification market expansion—international-new product technology

Source: Warren J. Keegan, "Strategic Marketing: International Diversification Versus National Concentration," *Columbia Journal of World Business,* Winter 1977, p. 125.

financially. The consideration of management resources is more important that that of financial resources. Overdiversification takes place when the management of a company cannot test the quantitative and qualitative information coming from a subsidiary against its concrete experience. Judgment then becomes abstract, and inaction or improper decisions are likely to follow.

Development Expenses. Another helpful concept is that of isolating all corporate-development expenses in a company. Most companies fail to do this. I advocate separating out all "must" expenses in the emergency stage of a turnaround, so a turnaround company in a rebuilding stage should be able to isolate development expenses. In the early part of this stage most turnaround companies opt to concentrate on internal development. Later the redevelopment plan concentrates on external acquisition programs. An example of this is the growth approach taken by Bangor Punta Corporation. Before making new acquisitions, chairman David W. Wallace first concentrated on ridding Bangor of twenty failing or so-so operations, a legacy of an earlier acquisition binge.

Although the pace of small acquisitions and mergers decreased in the early 1970s, there are currently more larger-company mergers in the news. Turnaround companies, on the other hand, tended to make smaller acquisitions, less far afield of their basic core businesses. An exception to this is Amcord, a company that is not shying away from external growth even though once bitten by a growth strategy. Most of Amcord's competitors feel it is difficult to diversify out of cement and are sticking to their knitting.

Although Amcord has been very successful in its basic businesses as a result of a cement shortage, it is diversifying away from the capital-intensive cement business into other areas where it sees higher growth at lower capital risk. This redevelopment plan has been questioned by a number of observers on one strong premise—it proved a dismal failure under the prior management. Whether the plan will work will depend on the operational and acquisition ability of Amcord's management. As I write, Amcord has not yet shown that its return-to-growth strategy can work.

Growth Strategy Case

The interplay of strategy and planning in a successful turnaround is best illustrated by the case of a small ($60 million sales), once-profitable maker of industrial plastics. Acquired in 1973 by a giant, diversified company, it suffered a serious downturn in 1974. Top management knew that the profit decline since 1974 was due partly to the rising price of one major raw material, a petroleum derivative, and partly to the deteriorating production economics of their old plants. They were less confident about the validity of the division's strategic assumptions.

The initial situation analysis was an eye-opener. First, division management's optimism about the commodity end of the business turned out to be ill-founded: the specialty plastics side was clearly more promising. An analysis of end-use markets, coupled with detailed projections of likely profit economics, pointed to a slow-growing but genuine opportunity in selected segments. But to capitalize on that opportunity, the company would have to modify the product line and marketing effort.

Accordingly, management decided to convert the division, over a five-year period, from a minor factor in many sectors of the industrial plastics market to a strong competitor on a much narrower front. The specialty product line was to be tailored to customer requirements, the sales force upgraded, and the marketing approach refocused. As demand for the specialty line grew, the division was to gradually withdraw from the commodity business. At the same time, exposure and risk were to be reduced by closing the older of the two manufacturing plants, by cutting working capital, and by eliminating near-term capital expenditures.

Eighteen months after these decisions were made, the division had already realized profit improvements of better than $4 million, almost doubling its profits and performing well above the corporate ROI target—so well, in fact, that a proposal to replace the remaining manufacturing plant with a modern, efficient facility was approved. Discernible in the division's profitable new strategy were four characteristics that can be observed in most high-payoff strategies. Any return-to-growth plan worth its salt should pay attention to these fundamentals.

First, the plastics division concentrated on the most profitable and exploitable product families and types, customer industries and specific customers, and channels of distribution. Analysis showed that well over half of the division's 200 specialty plastics lines were making only a marginal contribution to fixed costs or were actually losing money. Nearly forty were competing in markets where they were clearly inferior; for example, one line that was being pushed for outdoor application did not stand up well to weathering and the many colors offered often meant short, uneconomic production runs.

By pruning unprofitable products and consolidating product recipes, the line was cut to just thirty-three items with better-than-average performance characteristics, each targeted at end-use markets where competition was not yet severe and where demand was likely to grow. Prices were increased, based on the price differential with the nearest competitive material and on the calculable effect on the customer's production costs.

Second, in its drive for expanded market share in the commodity sector, the plastics division had unwittingly embraced several high-risk strategies. Despite its precarious position as a marginal competitor, it had failed to plan for such contingencies as a proposed federal regulation that could have wiped out one major product application. Moreover, the company would have risked sharply increasing its financial exposure had it proceeded with the proposal to replace the two obsolete plants. Risks were reduced by withdrawing from the commodity business, during the period that the phaseout of the older factory was shrinking the asset base and cutting working capital. To put the strategy on a pay-as-you-go basis, the company set up specific financial and market-development objectives for specialty plastics, and tied replacement of the second plant to their attainment. At the same time a targeted sales effort and a tough manufacturing cost-reduction program were launched.

Third, often businesses plan market and sales initiatives, product development programs, and the like that are unrealistic or inconsistent. The plastics division, for example, had been trying to penetrate the specialty market with a sales force that only knew how to sell commodity plastics to a few high-volume customers. Unable to help with new applications, they soon lost the few prospects that turned up for the specialty line. The new strategy, in contrast, explicitly identified target customers, analyzed their potential, and laid out programs for upgrading the sales force and providing applications support.

Again, though the division was plagued with cost problems and loaded with new products it couldn't sell, its R&D staff had been hard at work developing new specialty products. But four out of the twelve new products under development were technological long shots, and the total potential market for the rest was estimated to be less than $50 million. Under the new strategy, a watchdog group of managers—from marketing, customer applications assistance, and R&D—was set up to keep all new product projects and applications projects geared to the new market priorities.

Fourth, the redevelopment plan specified tasks, responsibilities, and timetables. Specific goals, responsibilities, and completion dates were assigned to each major product group and business function for three years ahead. Objectives for volume, profit, and market share were translated into specific targets such as the percentage of trial customers to be converted into repeat purchasers and the breakdown according to product and customer of the amounts and timing of price increases.

REFERENCES

[1]Barrie Pearson, "Is Corporate Planning a Waste of Time?" *Management Accounting (London)*, vol. 55, April 1977, p. 156.

[2]Ibid. p. 157.

[3]Louis V. Gerstner, Jr., "Can Strategic Planning Pay Off?" *McKinsey Quarterly Review*, Winter 1973, p. 35.

[4]Donald B. Bibeault, "Corporate Growth: A Conceptional Framework," *Managerial Planning*, July–August 1975, pp. 1–10, 29.

[5]"GEICO: Insuring the Profit Picture by Spreading Out and Slowing Down," *Business Week*, October 16, 1978, p. 182.

[6]Louis Kraar, "Roy Ash Is Having Fun at Addressogrief-Multigrief," *Fortune*, Feb. 17, 1978, p. 47.

[7]"Turning a Troubled Company Around," *Nation's Business*, December 1976, p. 22.

[8]Interview with Robert C. Brown, president, R. C. Brown & Company, San Francisco, Calif., February 1978.

[9]Interview with Robert Di Giorgio, chairman, Di Giorgio Corp., San Francisco, Calif., February 1978.

[10]Interview with Frank A. Grisanti, president, Grisanti and Galef, Los Angeles, Calif., February 1978.

19
THE EMERGENCY STAGE

We had to let go large numbers of people at our Dayton plant. If there's a lesson here, perhaps it is that business is not the field you should be in if you want to be a perpetual local hero. Throughout your business career, you will probably be under intense pressure to make popular decisions rather than the right decisions. That is a temptation which must be studiously avoided. It often can be fatal for the very enterprise you are seeking to protect.[1]

William S. Anderson, Chairman,
NCR Corporation, 1976

EMERGENCY STAGE BASICS

In the emergency stage, a company does what is necessary to ensure its survival. If cash flow is not a problem, the emergency stage is only mildly traumatic. In most cases, however, corporate surgery is as traumatic to the corporation as medical surgery is to the human body. A company can be put on the operating table just a few days after the turnaround leader arrives. In the case of Collins Radio, Robert Wilson had a $40 million-a-year cash flow problem, and he let 2,000 people go from the payroll within two weeks of his arrival. Wilson readily admits that many of those people were good people, but the priority at Collins had to be stopping the bleeding.

Even in less severe situations, the evaluation phase takes a matter of weeks, and surgery begins rapidly. At Crocker Bank the action plan was ready in forty-five days after Thomas Wilcox's arrival, and a lot of the surgery was complete within ninety days. Because of less pressing cash flow problems, Roy Ash could take his time at Addressograph-Multigraph. "This company has a big flywheel that gives us the time and cash throw-off to other things. The corporation's ample hoard of cash allows us to deal with this task deliberately rather than frantically."[2] The real deciding factor about how fast or slow and in what fashion to move is the state of your cash flow. If you've got plenty of cash and your pile is not being depleted at an alarming rate, then take out your planning book, get your analysts, and study. If you are bleeding, pull out your scalpel; if you're in danger of not surviving, get out your ax.

In this chapter I'll discuss turnaround tactics and action examples that have proven successful in each functional area of management. The functional areas to be discussed are strategic asset redeployment, financial management, marketing management, operations management, and human resources management. The emergency stage generally means shrinking back to those segments of a business which have achieved or can achieve good gross margins and can compete effectively in the marketplace. This means reorganizing to reduce expenses to a new, low level of business. It means converting all the nonworking assets into cash. If at all possible, the emergency stage should be based on a carefully conceived emergency plan.

ASSET REDEPLOYMENT IN THE EMERGENCY STAGE

There are four main practical consideration that I am going to cover in this part of Chapter 19. These are:

1. What do you do with borderline divestment candidates?
2. What do you take into account in planning the divestment?
3. Whom do you try to sell to?
4. What do you do when your plans don't work out as expected?

Borderline Divestment Units

Try to divide your operating divisions into viable retention units, divestment units, and borderline cases. The retention units are easy to decide; the divestment units are easy to decide; it's the borderline units that cause problems. Depending on the company situation, borderline units are probably going to have to go unless you can make a quick fix. Usually a seasoned executive is sent from headquarters on a "cure or kill" mission. If things are tough in the company as a whole, rehabilitation is hastily performed or simply not attempted.

The basic criterion for making the borderline decision is that, in serious cases, anything that cannot contribute positively to cash flow within a very short period of time must go. You must perform the surgery, divesting the company of the noncontributing segments of the business, then converting their assets to cash that can be used to reinforce your financial resources. Make a short-term plan that tells you the amount of cash you will require in order to reach positive cash flow. Include the value of your definite divestment units, and assess the value that would result from selling outright or liquidating your borderline units. Usually the loss taken by selling borderline units would be less than the loss which would be incurred if you were to hold on to the borderline unit and attempt to turn it around.

The critical determination here is how much loss you would incur before you were able to turn the borderline operation around. You have to make a very simple and fundamental set of calculations. For example, if the subsidiary has a volume of $12 million per year, or $1 million per month, you have a decent sales umbrella. Assume the industry gross margin is 32 percent and that you cannot do any better than that. Fundamentally, you have got to develop a plan that at least gets you to a 32 percent margin, because that is what you have to work with. The basic question is, can you rapidly cut your overhead cost down to a point where you can live within the 32 percent margin. In order to do that, how many bodies have got to go, how many fixed expenses must be cut? Start with a zero-based budgeting kind of program. The results might say that breaking even is impossible with only a volume of $1 million per month, that a volume of $1.5 million is required as a minimum for the business to be viable. The question then becomes, "Can we reach it?" Even if the answer is yes, it still may take two years, and the loss along the way to the break-even point might be greater than the liquidation loss. And in that case, the subsidiary would be a candidate for immediate divestment or liquidation.

Frank Grisanti elaborates on this theme:

> If it's a cost-cutting and a reorganizing fix and you have the volume base to work within, you go. But if you don't have the volume base to work with, all the cost cutting doesn't get you there. Then you've got to say, "How long will it take me to get the volume basically, to realistically get there?" Okay, you have to make that volume judgment. If it's a marketing fix, you've got to assume that it's going to take a while to do. If it's a cost kind of fix, you can do that in ten days. The question is: "How much of a licking can we afford to take before it's fixed?"[3]

Typical of the head scratching, soul-searching, and divisiveness that a major divestment program can cause is what occurred at G. D. Searle, which announced early in 1978 that it would be divesting about twenty divisions and writing off $100 million in losses. For five months management under Donald Rumsfeld debated the fit, profitability, and cash and management needs of every Searle business before announcing its decisions. Donald Rumsfeld remembers, "I would come home at night with a big briefing book, and my wife would say, 'Put your book down and say hello!' "

Main Divestment Considerations

In a crisis situation, trying to unload a loser can be difficult. If you can't afford additional cash flow losses, liquidation may be the only alternative. You can expect a substantial haircut relative to book value in a liquidation situation. A company should try to straighten out a loser by doing some quick surgery and then should attempt to sell it as a going concern. Even more painful to a company than having to liquidate a borderline case is being forced by circumstances to unload a winner. Just such a difficult situation was Rapid American Corporation's forced sale of Playtex to Esmark. For Rapid, the sale of Playtex was the price of survival. Rapid received $210 million from the sale and used the money to pay off $150 million in bank debt and to buy $67 million of its public debt—selling at a deep discount—for $35 million.

A turnaround company usually requires cash payments for divestment and liquidation. According to Leonard Vignola, author of *Strategic Divestment*, 60 percent of sellers want and need cash. Before a company can count cash as being in the till, it must realistically evaluate a number of practical considerations. Management must consider: (1) the true value of the divestment/liquidation candidate, (2) the degree of convertibility, (3) the ease of convertibility, and (4) the time span necessary for conversion. Computation of the cash recovery, or its equivalent, from a particular divestiture requires determining these factors.

1. *The true value of a divestment/liquidation candidate.* This may not be known until the divestiture/liquidation actually takes place. It is important that the use to which the asset will be put be carefully specified. In some cases the value of the resources that will be put to another use is impossible to assess accurately. In other cases payment is made in a manner that provides a flow of cash over a considerable period of time.

2. *Degree of convertibility.* This reflects the extent to which a business, product, market, or fixed asset can be converted to cash or in some other way made available for other use. In some cases resources may have no cash value after disposal. This occurs when the cash proceeds recovered in the divestment process are less that the cash costs incurred in disposing of the asset.

3. *Ease of convertibility.* This refers to the managerial effort, time, and other costs needed to divest segments at a decent price, often as going concerns. Plants and other facilities which are difficult to convert generally must be sold piecemeal or scrapped. Often disposal, particularly of specialized equipment, is difficult, owing to excess productive capacity within an industry. Demands of government regulatory agencies may result in a divestment being an involved, time-consuming, and expensive process.

4. *Time span for conversion.* Another problem is caused when not all of

the resources involved can be converted to cash within a prescribed time period. Will the proceeds from the disposal or divestiture be received immediately, or will they be paid to the company over a period of years? What form will such payments take?

Another prime consideration is whether the divestiture unit can make a positive contribution to a prospective buyer. As a going concern, a divested unit could be worth more to a purchaser than to a seller. In these cases the economic realities of divestments purchased below book value can be favorable to a buyer. The divested unit would therefore be viable to the buyer, if not to the seller. This improved viability is usually derived from conditions in the new setting that did not exist or were not possible in the old one. In one case, a seafood company had gone into bankruptcy. In order to discharge certain obligations, it sold several of its losing operations, consisting of fishing fleets and processing facilities. High lease and capital costs made a profitable return on those operations impossible for the divesting company. However, at the price that the new owners had to pay for the facilities, the annual costs became absorbable, and a reasonable return could be shown. A new economic reality may cause the divested unit to have substantially lower overhead costs. Such a realignment may be achieved when a former subsidiary is set free and is no longer subjected to arbitrary allocations of corporate overhead charges.

Once the company has made the determination of what has to go and how large its write-offs will be, it has to decide on the best prospective buyers. For companies in trouble, the best buyer is often a direct competitor of the troubled division. As Robert Brown says:

> Very simple. You find the guy who is killing you, the guy that is beating your brains out, who is causing you all the problems. He is now bashful in his attitude, because now you have sold him your market share. The easiest way to get out of business is to have him buy you out. He can make a hell of a good deal for himself; he is the natural buyer; it is clean, it is neat and it is all one package. Out it goes and it is instant cash. GE wanted to get out of the computer business. Where did they go? Right to a competitor. Generally, if you are such a crappy operation, there is no antitrust problem.[4]

Justice Department approval can be attained if you can argue that competition will suffer even more if you are forced to shut down than it will if you sell out. You'd better be prepared to defend that argument. The Justice Department took on Revere Copper in just such a case and won a court order blocking the proposed sale of its aluminum plant to Alcan Aluminum Corporation.

The next best value can be obtained from customers who want to integrate vertically. As Robert Brown says:

> The second place to go is to the integrators. Let's say that your division has been supplying a component to another manufacturer. So you go to him and say, "Look, we don't want to be in the business any longer. We have been supplying you for twenty years, why don't you buy us and supply yourself?" A good number of divestitures go that road. Companies can either backward- or forward-integrate, and that is a great place to sell companies.[5]

When Things Go Wrong

When sale of an asset is not proceeding smoothly, more drastic action is necessary. In the case of smaller medium-size companies that are under severe pressure, there is a downgrading from the originally expected receipts of the sale. For instance, if the company tried to get going-concern value early on, it probably would retreat to book value. More than half the divestments go through at book value. But 30 percent go through at less than book, and 25 percent go through at liquidation value. Another tactic is to set a definite target date that says, "Okay, if I haven't sold it as a going concern by this date, then I should liquidate it. It's cheaper for me to start liquidating than it is for me to try to make it a going concern." The saga of disposing of a poorly performing division may take years in larger companies that are not under severe pressure. Such a case occurred when Rohm & Haas Company had its fibers business up for sale. It took over two years for Rohm & Haas to find a buyer, in this case Monsanto Company.

Some corporate asset disposition takes interesting forms. In a recent turnaround effort I broke the back of the company's critical cash flow problems by disposing of the corporate Lear jet, thus providing an immediate net cash injection of $600,000. The creative entrepreneur who had gotten the company rolling had also gotten a little ahead of himself in the company plane area. The company was clearly not large enough to require a Lear jet and could hardly support the expenditures. It was difficult to pry the Lear loose, and the ego blow caused one of the few direct disagreements between us that surfaced at board level.

FINANCIAL MANAGEMENT IN THE EMERGENCY STAGE

The main practical considerations of financial management during the emergency stage of the turnaround are:

1. Cash flow analysis and control

2. Debt restructuring
3. Working-capital improvements
4. Profitability analysis support
5. Cost reduction support
6. Elimination of creative accounting

In each of these areas, the chief financial officer and his staff have an important role to play in supporting the turnaround effort.

Cash Flow Analysis and Control

Before you can do anything about a severe cash problem, you've got to understand the steps necessary for solving that problem. Cash is the lifeblood of any business. You must treat negative cash flow the way that you treat the human body that is bleeding. First you've got to control the bleeding by applying a tourniquet; then you must analyze the nature of the wound and perform the surgical procedure necessary to stop the bleeding on a permanent basis. Cash flow problems must be treated in much the same manner. First, you must take control of the cash flow pipeline, then you must analyze your total cash flow problem, and finally you must perform surgery to solve the problem on a more permanent basis. I mentioned several approaches to taking control of the cash flow pipeline in the chapter on taking charge (Chapter 15). In fact, one of the ways of taking charge of a company is by controlling its cash flows. "Control" should be direct, personal control in smaller companies and centralizing control in larger companies.

Putting a hold on the corporate cash flow pipeline involves controlling what goes out and stopping anything from coming in. That means that accounts payable will be frozen until you have analyzed where you stand. There is no need to pay someone for things you have already gotten when critical items that you desperately need are being put on a C.O.D., "collect on delivery," basis. The real key to controlling what comes out of the pipeline is to control what goes into the pipeline. That means that you have to take personal control of purchasing. Automatically freeze all purchase orders. Basically, you stop everything from coming in that could affect cash, and you stop everything except payroll from going out of the cash pipeline until you can flush out your system. Then you can control exactly what is going on with your cash flow situation.

After the pipeline is under control, you must analyze in detail where you stand. In a cash situation turnaround (as opposed to an earnings turnaround, with good cash reserves) you forget about the profit and loss statement, and you focus strictly on your application-of-funds timing. There are a lot of invisible cash traps in analyzing this timing. The big thing that most people overlook, in large and small companies, is prior-period obligations that confuse the analysis of your current requirements. People fail to pay attention to vendors out there that are overdue, the balloon payments that are coming up on bank debts, and other prior-period obligations. You have got to assess all of these obligations before you can make legitimate promises to your creditors and vendors. Creditability and candor are necessary with your vendors to get their assistance in the emergency phase of the turnaround.

Candor with vendors and bankers does get results, as James C. Miller, president of Intermatic, Incorporated, learned:

> Paying bills in 180 to 210 days meant higher prices, poor delivery, and interrupted production. "On my first day, I called the principal of each major vendor. I explained what we were trying to do and asked for their cooperation. In every case, I got it willingly," Mr. Miller points out. Intermatic also established a new vendor relations policy. "First, we're never 'out' when a creditor calls: someone always talks to him. Second, we make realistic promises and never fail to keep them. Finally, if a supplier has problems which require more prompt payment, we try to make an exception," Mr. Miller explains.[6]

In very critical cash situation turnarounds, daily control of cash is an absolute requirement. In critical situations you cannot sit in your office waiting until you get an IBM run which is after the fact. A better hands-on approach is to put your finger on the pulse of two or three key activities daily. The first of these is collections because someone is getting *x* thousands of dollars every day and putting it in the bank. Get the report on this. Secondly, somebody is shipping items from your company every day. Get reports on those figures every day. In critical situations, you must know every day what has been shipped, what has been collected, and what the balances are in the accounts receivable. The fact that you are looking at this gets a better performance from a lot of people in two areas. One is getting things out the door so that they can be added to the shipments, and the other is getting the credit manager to make sure that he is following up on receivables.

In companies facing this acute cash flow situation, a weekly cash flow plan must be prepared. Monthly cash flow plans are insufficient because they do not pinpoint the lean cash flow weeks when a company can run out of money. Every feasible source of additional cash must be explored, and all cash that can realistically be anticipated must be incorporated into a detailed cash flow plan. Table 19-1 shows a sample cash flow plan by

TABLE 19-1
Sample Cash Flow Plan by the Week
(In thousands of dollars)

Elements of cash flow	*Week 1*	*Week 2*	*Week 3*	*Week 4*
Cash at start of week	52	24	(6)	64
Cash inflows:				
Accounts receivable collections	8	14	90	68
Royalty payment	...	...	...	10
Sale of surplus fixed assets	...	...	...	60
Total cash inflows	8	14	90	138
Cash outflows:				
Salaries and wages (net)	12	12	12	12
Raw material purchases	10	12	8	8
Supplies	2	2	...	2
Miscellaneous expenses	4	4	...	...
Rent	8	...	...	...
Income tax (refund)	...	...	...	(24)
Payroll taxes		14		
Total cash outflows	36	44	20	(2)
Cash at end of week	24	(6)	64	204

weeks and indicates the problem weeks. The timing of cash flows is critical and must be closely monitored.

Debt Restructuring

Debt restructuring is a key to turnaround success to those companies in serious trouble. Certainly Bank of America's help was key to Memorex Corporation's turnaround. The bank agreed to convert $30 million of its debt into preferred stock and convinced other lenders to exchange an additional $10 million of debt for preferred stock. The agreement also allowed the company to credit bank purchases of Memorex equipment against its debt and to request the bank to buy even more preferred stock when Memorex redeemed its 5¼ percent convertible subordinated debentures. Finally, Bank of America provided Memorex with a new $35 million line of credit. As one analyst said, "Bank of America provided the financial framework to turn the company around, and Bob Wilson did it."

In addition to negotiation with lenders to restructure debt, debt reduction through such measures as divestment, cash conservation, and cash concentration is required to reduce a sometimes intolerable load. Boothe Courier dedicated all available cash from depreciation and earnings to repaying its debt and converted $14 million of subordinated debentures to preferred stock. Boothe's debt was cut 80 percent to $18.8 million, and equity rose to a solidly black $24.5 million in an eighteen-month period. Joseph Alibrandi, president of Whittaker Corporation, also took decisive steps toward debt reduction when he first arrived by selling off or liquidating more than 55 percent of his predecessor's purchases. With the $114 million cash and $22 million in notes realized from the sales, he reduced debt at Whittaker by 45 percent.

Working-Capital Improvements

Working-capital improvements frequently provide the most readily available short-term opportunity to improve the financial position of turnaround companies. For many companies, simply rounding up cash from far-flung divisions and dormant bank accounts, as well as tightening up on cash controls, has provided a cash boon: Foremost-McKesson, in San Francisco, claims that it has squeezed an extra $30 to $35 million out of operations in recent years, simply by tightening up on internal controls and by setting up a form of of internal, electronic funds transfer system.

Case Examples. The management of working capital deals mainly with cash, receivables, payables, and inventories. I have found that troubled companies are full of cash-improvement opportunities. I was appalled to learn, in one company, that invoicing was delayed up to 2½ weeks after shipment. I ordered a quick fix that knocked this down to about three days. Within a few months, an integrated order-processing system was computer invoicing and mailing on the evening of the shipment day. Receivables increased initially $1.5 million on the same sales level. At the same company there were about 2,500 different items in the main warehouse. Production and sales were at odds with each other, and, consequently, the inventory was serving as an expensive buffer between the two warring parties. I knew that the inventory had some "dogs" in it, but a quick match-up of annual sales and inventory levels showed an appalling out-of-balance condition.

Often each area of working capital has been mismanaged or undermanaged, leading to an overall condition that can have significant bottom-line impact. Take, for example, the case of an industrial equipment company with approximately $50 million in annual sales volume. An audit of the working-capital position of this company showed that the cash percent of sales was running 3.1 percent above that of selected major competitors whose business most closely paralleled that of the company. Receivables were increasing and as a percent of sales were currently averaging 8.2 percent above that of the competition; the accounts payable percent of sales was running 5.1 percent below the competition's, a gap which aggravated the problem. Inventories were rising sharply, and at that point their percent of sales ran nearly 8 percent above the competition's. A project team was organized to correct these working-capital problems. The project team succeeded in relieving nearly $10 million of working capital by taking action in four areas:

1. All bank accounts were scrupulously held to the levels dictated by compensating-balance agreements with the banks. The team reduced cash balances over $1 million.

2. Receivables were cut by nearly $3 million. This reduction was achieved through a number of actions, the most important of which were these: the team sharply reduced slow-pay receivables by curtailing the salesmen's practice of granting extended terms to customers. To be sure that payment concessions were granted only when they were a competitive necessity, the project team instituted new procedures to charge the cost of extended terms to sales-district profit and loss statements and to make related reductions in the salesmen's incentive payments. The team analyzed, by customer location, the time required for payments to reach the home office. It found that it could speed the collection of customers' remittances by strategically locating three additional lockboxes around the country.

3. Payment policies were selectively adjusted. The project team was able to increase accounts payable by just over $2 million, which brought them more in line with industry practice and allowed an offsetting reduction in short-term debt.

4. Inventories were reduced by $3.2 million. To effect this, the project team carefully analyzed and updated purchasing practices, order quantities, and production scheduling.

As a result of these working-capital improvements, the company was able to sharply reduce short-term bank borrowing. This had a threefold impact: (1) the company avoided refinancing at higher cost; (2) pretax profits increased over $900,000 per year, owing to reduced interest payments; and (3) the company was able to increase working capital by an additional $1.7 million because of sharply lower compensating balance requirements.

Accounts Receivable. Often, the quickest and best source of cash is your accounts receivable. An intelligent analysis can be made without knowing much about the details of the business. If the book figure for accounts receivable is higher than the equivalent of forty to fifty days of company sales, you may be sure that there is work to be done. In poorly managed companies, the job is often neglected. If the company has not earned a profit, there has been no income tax incentive to write off uncollectible accounts. As a result, these uncollectibles continue to clutter up the balance sheet, making it harder to identify the accounts you should be working on.

Study the accounts receivable records to see whether the financial department is doing a good job. If you find a host of small, unpaid balances in the receivables and, at the same time, many unmatched credit entries, then you know that procedures don't exist or aren't being followed for matching cash receipts with the appropriate invoices in order to straighten out any discrepancies. Examples of the latter are when a customer pays for a product but doesn't pay for the freight, or takes an unauthorized discount, or in any way pays less that what the invoice calls for. If these discrepancies are ignored for long, it becomes almost impossible to straighten them out without writing off your loss. If you can find time to be your own credit manager and to do some of the telephoning to delinquent accounts, you will be rewarded with new insights into your business. When you talk to a customer who hasn't paid his bill, you find out why he isn't paying. Often it is because your own company has made mistakes that no one has done anything to correct.

Fixed Assets. Managers are likely to neglect looking into their fixed assets for hidden capital. Somehow, land, buildings, machinery, and equipment seem sacred. If the company has been in existence many years, these assets are usually deeply depreciated on the books. However, because of inflation, these assets are likely to be worth far more than book value. (Land, although it is not depreciable, usually is inflated in price too.) If you find this hidden capital, you should seriously consider whether you need all of it and whether you are using it effectively.

Profitability Analysis

Profitability analysis is important in making divestment and control decisions. I have been amazed at the number of troubled companies that have failed to measure their lines of business or that did a very inadequate job of measuring them. In one case, a $50 million steel company with four divisions only measured two of them. The two new divisions had grown larger than the old divisions to which they were wedded, but no one had bothered to segment out the new profit centers. A year later this had been done, but no one was bothering to break out the effect of transfer-pricing. I ordered the break-out and was amazed to discover that two divisions were getting substantial transfer-pricing benefits to the detriment of the supplier division. When this was straightened out, we found that two were big losers. In a case already mentioned, a $4-billion-asset financial institution was charging branch operations only direct expenses. Every branch looked terrific because over $35 million in expenses was unallocated. After legitimate service charges and allocations were made, the winners and losers among branches became a lot clearer.

In the emergency stage, you must quickly and correctly segment your business unit, if that has not already been done. You should also get P&L information by product line. You may have to settle for product-line margins. Except in rare cases, profit and loss breakdown to the individual product level will have to await the stabilization stage. James Hawkins's experience at Hewitt-Robins indicates a typical situation:

> The company's cost accounting system was a disaster. They didn't know, when they bid a job, whether they were going to make a profit." In contrast, today "you know you are going to make a profit, or you don't take the job. We have not yet got it to a product-line P&L (profit and loss), but we can take it to a product-line margin, which is very close to it.[7]

When segmentation by division is difficult, the use of the direct-costing approach can develop data by business segment on contribution or estimated profit and loss. A good example is the case of Acme Industries, shown in Table 19-2. The company, losing $90,000 a year on declining volume, was clearly on the doorstep of disaster. The direct-costing approach provided important insights into the locus of the company's problems. Table 19-2 shows the contribution method of direct costing, segregating the business into three divisions by product line.

Allocating nonassignable period expenses on the basis of volume or simply looking at contribution by segment, it can be seen that Division C was losing substantial sums, Division A was losing smaller amounts, and Division B was showing a profit. The slim product-line contribution of Division A was a surprise, but the extent of Division C's losses came as a shock.

TABLE 19-2
Acme Industries, Inc.: Direct-Cost Profit Analysis by Line of Business
(In thousands of dollars)

	Division A	*Division B*	*Division C*	*Total*
Net sales	$400	$1,300	$800	$2,500
Direct costs				
Material	50	190	130	370
Direct labor	100	330	250	680
Various O/H	44	100	100	244
Selling			40	40
Total direct costs	$194	$620	$520	$1,334
Net marginal contribution	$206	$680	$280	$1,166
Assignable period expense	$48	$8	$60	$116
Product line contribution	$158	$672	$220	$1,020
Nonassignable period expse.				
Manufacturing (% of volume)	108	353	217	678
G & A & sell (% of volume)	74	240	148	462
TOTAL	182	593	365	$1,140
Profit	$(24)	$79	$(145)	$(90)

Cost-Reduction Support

Cost-reduction support is an essential role of financial management during a turnaround. Simply controlling the cash flow pipeline and identifying costs by relative size and type can make a significant contribution to the turnaround effort. Cost-reduction support was explained in more detail in the last chapter.

"Creative" Accounting Elimination

Eliminating "creative" accounting practices is necessary to get a true picture of where a company stands. In one of my first turnaround efforts, the prior management had been overcapitalizing many items that would normally be expensed. I reversed this practice but had to take a one-time, half-million-dollar bath to do so. Here are some other practices to watch out for:

1. Capitalized research costs

2. Lease arrangements with "side letters" that still remain off the balance sheet
3. Capitalized items such as training costs, interest costs on loans, computer set-up and software costs
4. Lack of routine maintenance on plant and equipment, causing potential major renovation
5. Treatment of extraordinary income as ordinary and ordinary expenditures as extraordinary items
6. Valuation of inventories at market, rather than at cost
7. Increasing of annual results by upstreaming greater-than-legal share of partially owned subsidiary's income
8. Valuation of assets at inflated values
9. Improper statement of dividends from subsidiaries
10. A "department 99" to invent customers (Equity Funding case), ammonia, or vegetable oil

It's tough enough to figure where you are even when the rules are used properly, let alone when creative accounting practices are allowed. During the first few weeks of the turnaround take strenuous action to eliminate all such activities.

I have also seen accounting practices that hurt a company's profitability. In one case a company had long-term maintenance contracts it was reserving for. It had neglected to write off fixed plant costs against its reserve (a legitimate accounting practice) and had thereby decreased legimate earnings by $1.2 million a year. After cleaning out all the "bad" accounting practices I was able to increase legitimate book earnings by $800,000 per year, with the concurrence of our "big eight" public accounting firm.

OPERATIONS MANAGEMENT IN THE EMERGENCY STAGE

Truly significant results can be achieved in cutting operational costs when the pressure is on. Since operations exist in hundreds of thousands of specific forms, it's difficult to provide general approaches. There are numerous texts written about closing operational gaps. Of the many hundreds I have reviewed, I feel that these four will give an adequate starting point for your own operations-management improvements:

- *Cost Reduction from A to Z,* by Lindley Higgins[8]

- *Controlling Production and Inventory Costs,* by Albert Raymond & Associates[9]
- *Raising Productivity,* by Frederick Hombruch[10]
- *Handbook of Cost Control,* by Richard Wilson[11]

Operational costs are eliminated by divesting whole divisions or product lines, by shutting down operations, by significantly reducing manpower, by reducing inventory investments, by controlling purchasing, and by significantly increasing productivity. I have already discussed strategic divestment earlier in this chapter.

Shutting Down Operations

Two classic cases of shutting down operations come to mind. The first is Bethlehem Steel's massive shutdowns, announced in late 1977. Bethlehem closed two aging plants, reducing its overall steel-making capacity by 10 percent and cutting 7,300 workers from its payroll. Bethlehem estimated that steel-making costs at the aging facilities were 30 to 40 percent higher than at the company's newest mill. Outside analysts estimated that Bethlehem saved more than a $100 million a year by the move. The second example is the massive plant shutdowns in the U.S. auto industry. While many of these were part of the industry's dematuring and slimming down program, many others were necessitated by retrenchment and the requirements of increased productivity.

Reducing Manpower

Manpower reductions are the biggest single component of operating improvements during the emergency stage. Companies or divisions in trouble have produced significant results, both at the direct-labor level and at the overhead level, when pressed by circumstances.

Direct-Labor Reductions. Take the case of General Motors's Hyatt Bearings Division in Sandusky, Ohio, which was losing money before a change in management was effected. The division was losing money, orders were falling behind, productivity was lagging, and the payroll was overloaded. How do you go about correcting the situation? In this case, Phillip B. Ziegler was brought in with only one instruction: "Fix it." Ziegler did just that, and between 1970 and 1975, employment at the division's three plants decreased from 12,300 to 8,000 employed. The division not only became profitable, but also began producing more sales dollars and, more importantly, more goods with a smaller work force.

GM's tightening up of its Hyatt Bearing Division demonstrates the enormous reductions that are possible in manufacturing when tough discipline is applied. Aggressive manpower reductions by elimination usually result in greater cost decreases than more studied approaches do. But when wholesale cutting is not possible, significant gains can be achieved by creative approaches. In a recent turnaround I did, labor productivity was increased 250 percent over nine months by a combination of sound management action and work force incentives.

Overhead Reductions. Every businessman knows that his overheads have grown prodigiously in recent years. Between 1950 and 1980, for example, the number of nonproduction workers in the United States manufacturing industry increased six times as quickly as the number of production workers, and today nonproduction workers account for 40 percent of all payroll costs. Typically, 70 to 85 percent of overhead is payroll-related, so overhead reduction is not a painter's procedure because most of the savings comes from work force reductions. Almost every organization in the world automatically does three things that tend to encourage the automatic inflation of overhead costs:

1. It establishes clear organizational boundaries. A manager who requests a service rarely knows the costs to the company of creating it and consequently cannot properly weigh its ultimate value to the company against the value of his receiving it. The result is that services frequently continue to be provided long after the need for them has diminished or disappeared.
2. The professionals who run these service-performing departments tend to encourage demand for additional services and to perform most services to a level of quality all out of proportion to the actual need.
3. Managers tend to be rewarded more for pleasing their superiors than for running a tight ship. So, very naturally, to avoid being caught short they tend to overstaff or overspend. The managerial instinct for self-protection further encourages overstaffing.

Manpower reductions are usually more severe in a company's overhead and staff departments during the emergency stage. I previously mentioned a 65 percent overhead cut in a company that I helped turn around. That company was very fat, due to a continued staff buildup over a number of very profitable years. The actual head count by department

TABLE 19-3
Headquarters Employee Head Count by Function and Subsidiary

Function/Subsidiary	*1-15-70*	*1-15-71*	*1-15-72*	*1-15-73*
Chief executive office	10	8	5	5
Legal department	16	8	6	6
Treasurer/controller	81	46	37	35
Information services	67	38	29	26
Management science	5	5		
Personnel department	11	5	4	4
Investor services	112	109	61	51
Investment research	38	19	12	16
Total parent	340	233	154	143
Retained subsidiary X	40	55	57	69
Retained subsidiary Y	149	49	35	33
Retained subsidiary Z	28	6	2	2
Total retained subsidiaries	217	110	94	104
Divested subsidiary	14	13		
TOTAL HEADQUARTERS	571	356	248	247

Note: Name of company withheld for reasons of confidentiality.

is shown in Table 19-3. It's amazing what you can do without, when you're forced to.

Reducing Inventory Investments

Inventory is a typical operations area that can be substantially improved. A common error in evaluating inventory is the mistaken opinion that the only wasteful inventory expense is associated with having too much inventory. Excessive inventory costs can be associated with both having too much and having too little. Pity the poor company that has both adverse conditions.

Out-of-Balance Inventory. I witnessed this at a steel company that had $13 million in finished inventories. The company was concerned because inventory turnover had slipped from four times to three times per year. The total inventory numbers masked a problem of being stuck with a large number of slow sellers and at the same time of being very short on fast-moving items. The company had never matched sales against inventory position. When I ordered my data processing staff to do this, the results obtained showed a severe imbalance position. This is shown in Table 19-4.

The company was nearly out of inventory of its fast-moving items and was turning away profitable business. On the other hand, it was stuck with nearly $6 million worth of slow movers. This is the most severe case of imbalance I have yet encountered. The problem was solved in the short run by liquidating the slow movers, even though an inventory write-down had to be taken. Part of the funds freed up were used to retire bank debt and part were put into usable inventory in the fast-moving item area. The longer-term solution was an order-entry system that matched up orders, inventory and production schedules by product code.

Segment Inventory. The reader may find it hard to believe that such condtions exist or can come into existence until coming face-to-face with the reality of them. One cause of these conditions is the provision of undifferentiated service levels. Service should be provided at higher levels in those items that make up the major percentage of sales. Often companies do not differentiate.

Thus, a company with half of its stock tied up in items representing only 20 percent of unit sales and with its highest-sales-volume items selling four times faster than the lowest-sales-volume items has a great deal to gain by reducing inventories of slow sellers to the point where their turnover rates approach those of fast sellers. It can reduce inventories of its slow-moving items by 75 percent for an overall reduction of 37.5 percent. How can the reduction be accomplished? One way is to reduce inventories of slow-moving items at all locations at which they are stocked. This, of course, greatly reduces both the availability of each item and the overall service level. An alternative is to concentrate all available stocks of slow-moving items at a single location. This requires only one reserve stock for unusually large customer demands and offers greater

TABLE 19-4
Inventory Imbalance Situation

Movement level	*Annual sales, $ millions*	*Percent of total sales*	*Inventory, $ millions*	*Percent of inventory*	*Months supply of inventory*
Fast	$25.2	60	$2.1	17	1.0
Moderate	12.6	30	4.2	33	4.0
Slow	4.2	10	6.3	50	18.0
TOTAL	$42.0	100	$12.6	100	3.6

control over a greatly reduced inventory. This type of differentiation recognizes that customers hold varying levels of expectations. Fast-moving items often are standardized models or parts that customers expect to be in stock and supplied rapidly. Slow-moving items often are off-sized or nonstandard items for which many customers will expect to wait longer periods of time.

As one appliance retailer told me, "If manufacturers would recognize the fact that customers expect to wait up to six weeks for nonstandard appliances with unusual features, they could save a lot of money. Instead, they provide the same level of service on orders for all items in the line." Of course, this philosophy has to be applied selectively, according to the characteristics of a particular product line. Certain automotive parts, for example, call for a high level of service regardless of sales volume because they are critical in the repair of idled equipment. Differentiation in this type of business may have to be based on categories of items, measured in terms of both unit sales volume and the criticality of the part.

Pareto's law, the 80/20 rule, also applies to the amount of time and money spent on inventory control. The amount spent on inventory control should be in proportion to its profit potential. One method would look like this: arrange inventory items in descending order by annual dollar sales or annual usage. Classify the items as follows: Class A items, representing the top 80 percent of total dollar sales; Class B items, representing the next 15 percent of total dollar sales; Class C items, representing the remaining 5 percent of dollar sales. The items would fall in approximately the same categories, if the distribution were made on the basis of gross profit contribution. Spend more time and effort controlling the 20 percent A items that account for 80 percent of the sales. They should get 80 percent of the effort. Don't disregard B and C items, but give them far less emphasis. Segment your inventory and don't concentrate on total inventory. The rule to follow is that proportionately more inventory dollars should be invested in finished goods as the engineering content of the finished goods approaches zero. The less engineering content there is per unit of marketable product, the more important availability becomes as a buying influence. This is particularly true for industrial products because the smaller the engineering content of the product, the less the preplanning exercised by the user in anticipating its replacement. The manufacturer who provides the most consistent availability will obtain the sale and, eventually, the greatest market share.

Controlling Purchasing

Another important element of cost is controlled through purchasing activities. Usually a few items will account for the bulk of the dollars involved in purchasing. Have these commodities sorted out, and have the kind of material, the suppliers, and the suppliers' most recent quotations all charted. Ask for new quotations from these regular sources as well as from new sources. And if you haven't been taking the cash discount for prompt payment, and in fact have been keeping your suppliers waiting up to ninety days, you're probably paying higher prices than the other customers. Point out to your suppliers that you realize they have been financing you, and within a given period (i.e. ninety days), you'll be back to discounting. Put all of them on a payment schedule to catch up to prompt payment and stick to this religiously. Put them on notice that you'll treat them fairly and you expect competitive quotes.

Incoming Inspection. Another profit leak in connection with purchases could be failure to inspect incoming materials. Too many companies assume that everything they buy is okay, but only if they examine incoming materials can they determine how much is usable or if they've received what they paid for. Draw on your suppliers for their assistance in trying to reduce manufacturing costs. Many times, variations in the materials create problems in feeding machines, causing out-of-tolerance assemblies and even extra material handling, all because of the way in which the stock is supplied for use at production stations. Variations in materials are especially detrimental where there is automated equipment because uniformity of the material is vital to efficient operation. Many times product scrap and reject costs are attributable to poor incoming material control.

Outgoing Inspection. In one of the more incredible profit leaks I have discovered, a major railcar maintenance facility was underbilling its customers. I became aware of this when I noticed that the material input to the shop was less than the material billed out. With an inspector along with me I asked to see the billing cards on several finished cars. We found two $1,200 paint jobs unbilled as well as other discrepancies. The cause of all this was an almost ludicrous procedure of billing from the initial railcar inspection sheet. The shop did other repairs and thought "someone else" would pick up the changes. There was no in-process billing check sheet, nor was there a final inspection. We immediately corrected this deficiency and increased revenue per car by an average of $150 with this fix alone. The shop was at that time averaging about fifty railcars per week, so that plugging this profit leak was very significant.

Increasing Productivity

At this same maintenance facility, we engineered a 100 percent increase in productivity within three months. Admittedly, productivity was lagging when we began, but by introducing better and more simplified billing procedures, better plant supervision, and more experienced shift supervision and by telling the work force where it stood and what we expected of it, we were able to garner truly outstanding productivity results in a short period of time. This quick "management"-type fix was followed later by incentive programs for the work force, thus making another quantum jump in productivity possible. The overall effect on productivity with this combined program increased our throughput capacity of the plant by almost 300 percent on a unit basis.

The main point I want to stress is that in operations and cost control truly remarkable levels of achievement are possible. For those who dare to be creative, who have the guts to cut hard and deep, who have the courage to challenge the conventional wisdom, and who possess the drive and leadership to see that improvements happen, the results are there for the taking.

MARKETING MANAGEMENT IN THE EMERGENCY STAGE

During the emergency stage of a turnaround there is a great deal of pressure to demarket rather than to market. The heady expansion and flamboyance of an earlier period both of which may have been factors in getting the company in trouble give way to a retrenchment based on factual bottom-line considerations. I'm going to review the areas of marketing in order of their problem magnitude in a turnaround. These are the four P's of marketing: pricing, product, promotion, and place (distribution).

Pricing

Underpricing. Underpricing seems to be a perennial problem with troubled companies. As strange as it may seem, troubled companies usually underprice—through sheer neglect, timidity of management, or incorrect assessment by their sales force. Underpricing occurs four times as often as overpricing. I once was called in to investigate a company that had a $1.2 million pretax loss. The company had competitive products but a poor cost structure. However, two-thirds, or $800,000, of the operating shortfall was due to underpricing relative to competition. Underpricing seemed to have settled at a constant 4 percent. With the price advantage the sales force had an easy time selling and, in fact, were order-takers rather than salesmen. After thorough discussion, we decided to raise prices by 5 percent in each of two increments six months apart in order to catch up with the competition. Although the company was not the industry leader, it was felt that higher prices had a good chance of sticking without loss in volume because of sources of supply were few and because the lengthy new-source approval process followed by customers. The price increases came off without a hitch, and the company broke even by the third month and was solidly in the black by year-end.

Underpricing in this case was due to sheer neglect, sheer neglect coupled with the proclivity of sales people to make life easy for themselves by underpricing. Sales people are the last people to want to raise prices. The solution to the problem is to centralize pricing authority and administer the company's pricing policies strictly. In this way, the company steps in to prevent salesmen from giving away the store.

Poor Pricing Strategy. Not all pricing problems are due to sheer neglect or to the misguided efforts of salesmen. In some cases, pricing strategy errors are made right at the top. In 1972 A&P, already smarting from losses, decided to go into the discount food business. The result was near disaster, leading to the costliest price war in the history of the food industry. A&P touched off a series of events that were partly responsible for an industry profit slide of $4 billion and an A&P loss of $41 million in just six months.

In another case, I saw a steel company misread the market and make a near-fatal error in pricing. The company's prices, as well as those of its two domestic competitors, were being undercut by Japanese imports. All three domestic competitors were operating below breakdown capacity at the existing price levels. In order to increase volume above the break-even point, the company chose to attempt to meet the Japanese prices. In the days before trigger pricing, the Japanese simply kept going lower, thus maintaining the same relative price advantage. The other two domestic companies were forced to match the third's lower prices. The result was a minimal volume increase and more red ink at the bottom line. Trigger pricing, plus a realization of the two-tier situation, led to a quick reversal of the pricing strategy.

Poor Pricing Theory. The pressure to increase volume in order to offset high fixed costs often leads to frustrating results. Unfortunately, in most cases marginal income accounting and break-even accounting—so popular in business school textbooks—fail the test of real life applicability.

The theory is that, for a short period, additional sales can be profitably added to the normal sales volume, even at prices too low to cover a proportionate share of fixed overhead. Managers often do this because they presume that 100 percent of the fixed overhead of the company is borne by their regular business anyway. However, pricing your product so that it does not cover a full share of overhead is dangerous. Except for rare and well-controlled exceptions, marginal business taken to keep the operation going incurs the same overhead costs as the regular business and, by adding to the complexity of the total operation, often requires more than normal overhead.

During a short period of overcapacity, if the overhead really cannot be cut, it may make sense to take added business at prices that will pay less than full overhead expenses. Even a modest contribution to paying these expenses for that period may be better than none. The danger is that an emergency measure often becomes standard practice. It is an easy way to go broke.

The fallacy of break-even accounting is the assumption that expenses are easily divisible into fixed and variable. Overhead is rarely as fixed as accountants are inclined to think, except for very short periods. In any long-range analysis of a business, there is no such thing as fixed overhead—it is all variable to some degree, even such items as rent, heat, light and power, depreciation and amortization, professional services, and executive salaries. The terms "variable overhead" and "fixed overhead" would be better called "overhead that varies immediately with the level of activity" and "overhead that varies in the long run with the level of activity."

One able executive of a large merchandising company recently said, "Our biggest problem is sales. Our industry has high fixed costs, and we have to promote hard to maintain a rate of sales to cover these costs." This is a typical, mistaken business attitude: assuming that the cost and price structure is a given and that, therefore, the company must grow to cover all the overhead. In many situations costs can be cut dramatically to increase margins. Where there is good reason to believe that an increase in price would bring about only a small reduction in sales, a price increase is a good tactic to employ. An example of this is the pricing strategy of a major oil company in regard to automotive windshield-washer fluid. This product is largely water with a small amount of detergent and a little antifreeze added. Originally it was offered at a reasonable markup over costs and sold for a relatively low price. However, it was noted that motorists buy washer fluid infrequently and have no clear notion of the price they paid the last time. Consequently, when they want or need it, they will pay what is asked with little thought or resistance. The product has since been priced several times higher than originally, with no measurable decrease in demand and with a nice, fat profit margin that has helped in the promotion of other items where there is price competition and margins cannot be as wide.

Product Line

Product line proliferation is one of the more common diseases of a company out of control and in trouble. Unfortunately, product or product line proliferation is synonymous with growth in many a company. I've found that this misguided belief can cause a great deal of trouble. The most common cause of trouble is the widely held belief that the only road to success is through growth. Many businessmen see growth of sales as the solution to all problems. It seldom is. Growth is not synonymous with capitalistic success. In fact, shrinking the number of products or product lines is usually the surest route to better profit and higher return on investment.

In simplifying a business, the best place to start is usually with the products. This is where the ball game is really played. Take each product line and analyze it separately. In most companies with more than one product line or group of products, there are some that are contributing to its growth and success and some that are dragging it down; it takes a careful study to tell the difference. If the company has adequate product-line cost information, so much the better. Learn how the information is developed and analyze whether the cost allocations between product lines are reasonable. Look for the low-margin product lines that represent a substantial part of the volume. In troubled companies, don't expect to have detailed information on individual products.

The Old Mainstay. If a line has been a company mainstay for a long time, your people are likely to tell you that, despite its low margins, keeping this line is absolutely necessary because of the overhead it absorbs. You will probably also be told that it carries more than its share of overhead and that it really does better than the figures say. In my experience, this is usually not true. In fact, such a line may be doing worse than shown on the statement and may have more actual indirect expense than is charged to it on the accounting books.

Often one line is holding a company down. In one major company, I found that a major product line had been the backbone of the company for almost a generation. The line showed a minor loss year after year, while gradually declining in volume, both in absolute terms and in relation to a newer line marketed through other channels. This old line was being marketed to original equipment manufacturers (OEMS) in an industry where the smaller customer manufacturers were gradually being driven out by a few large survivors, who had become demanding buyers of components. The company's newer line of products, however, was sold to the consumer market through several thousand distributors. And it was growing profitably every year.

Management was told that the company could not service without the old OEM line because the overhead the line carried made the profits on the distributor line possible. But that was not true. The OEM line required extensive engineering in annual model changes for each separate customer, had generally more stringent requirements for quality performance, and had a greater variety of more complicated mechanisms. Yet the customers' demand for immediate response to up-and-down schedule changes made production scheduling beyond a few days almost impossible to achieve.

The company sold off the OEM line. And, by so doing, it was able (1) to cut the overhead more than proportionately, (2) to free funds tied up in a nonprofit program, and (3) to turn the company from a big loss to a big profit in less than a year.

Product Elimination. In studying product lines, management should ask seven basic questions:

1. *Is the sales volume of the product or product line rising or falling?* Most products have a life cycle of from five to twenty years (depending on how you define "product"). If sales are on the downtrend, spend little or nothing at this point to keep a product from dying a premature death. My approach here is usually to try to milk the product for cash flow. Keep raising the price and see if it can be made high enough to justify milking the product. If a product is losing money and is past its peak, chop it out. You should spend your money on the product that is on its way up. Indeed, if this product already has a good margin, its margin probably can be increased even more.

2. *Is the product line making a profit?* If the product is not profitable, as shown by the company's existing cost system, don't lightly accept the arguments that it is really doing better than the figures show, that it doesn't use as much overhead as is allocated to it, and that if only such-and-such were done, it would start making money. In particular, don't listen to such arguments for a product line which the company has had for years and which once made money. Better than revive it, let it die quietly.

3. *What are the gross margins of the different product lines?* There is no fixed rule for a satisfactory gross margin (the difference between net sales price and the total cost of material, direct labor, and applicable factory overhead). One manufacturing company had a material cost which alone was over 90 percent of the sales price, yet the product had a very satisfactory profit. The reasons: the material was expensive but not bulky, and the company made only a slight addition to the product before selling it to a few larger users; in addition, operating expense was negligible, and the company didn't pay for the raw material until after it had collected for the modified product from its own customers. Consequently, almost all the gross margin went directly to the owner's salary and profit.

In general, however, in the manufacturing business, if you are to have a profit of at least 10 percent on sales before federal income taxes, your gross margin should be no less than 35 percent and preferably well over

45 percent. If your gross margin is low, unless you can raise selling prices (the first place to look), you face a long struggle to improve operating efficiency because while you are battling to reduce manufacturing costs, you can be sure that your competitors are plowing that field too. You may find later that your hard-won improvements have only kept you from losing more ground.

4. *Is the sales department determining the pricing?* If so, you can bet the prices are too low. Salesmen rarely believe that they can get a higher price for the product, until they are told by management that they have no choice. (Overly marketing-oriented officers have the same failing.) It is amazing how often the customer will pay more with little or no complaint, despite all the salesmen's warnings that to raise the price is suicide.

5. *Is your sales department's pitch, "we have to have a full line"?* Only the "full line" approach justifies continuing to make and sell low-volume items which are expensive to tool and manufacture and which, per unit sold, cost a fortune to catalog and carry in stock. If your competitor carries a full line, your sales people will insist that they cannot compete unless they have all the items too, because the buyer wants to purchase from one supplier.

Offering one-stop purchasing is a good sales gimmick but often is not good business. The Crane Company had the most complete line in the plumbing industry, but its losses mounted until Thomas Mellon Evans acquired it, eliminated the low-margin items, and thus put it back in the black. Another case is the Simmons Company, which drastically cut back the number of product styles the company offered: hide-a-bed styles were reduced from 250 to 45 and mattress styles were reduced from 200 to only 50.

6. *Does your sales program offer a wide variety of options, extras, and specials?* Custom products always cost more, and unless the volume is large enough so that some economics of scale can be realized, they are certain to lose far more money than the books show. Many companies gradually add more and more variations to their line in order to suit the particular specifications or whims of various customers. These specials are ordered as a matter of habit for years thereafter, even when the customer can do just as well with a standard product. If you rigorously cut out the specials, you can usually convert the customer to a standard item. If you can't, you are probably better off losing his account.

7. *Is the "book-to-bill" ratio acceptable?* The book-to-bill ratio is the ratio of unfilled sales backlog to shipments billed. As a product line matures and competition comes in, the ratio will drop off even though shipments continue. Break down book-to-bill ratios by product line, since overall ratios aren't a good basis per companywide assessment.

Please keep in mind that you don't need to be all things to all people to prosper. Posh Abercrombie and Fitch failed when it tried to court the mass market. Now the venerable New York retailer's snobbishness is being restored by former May Company California president Geoffrey Swabe, who's also trying to recapture its fickle clientele. Peck and Peck, the conservative, eastern-based women's apparel company, which catered mainly to the basic-black-with-pearls set, like Abercrombie and Fitch tried to snare a younger, hipper buyer and eventually went bust.

Asking all the foregoing questions should aid you in cutting out low product lines. If you are lucky, you can sell off a low line to a competitor or to someone who wants to get into the business. If you are not able to do this, just stop making it. One way to stop is to put into effect a large, across-the-board price increase. If the line has been grossly underpriced, you may not lose much business and may have turned a bad line into a good one. But even if you lose most of the business, a few of your customers, although they may object noisily to the price, may continue to buy from you—at least for a while—permitting you to favorably dispose of your inventory.

When you cut out a line entirely, several things happen. Because your sales volume is reduced, your accounts receivable in that line turn into cash. You stop buying inventory and stop putting in direct labor, and these save you more cash. You terminate all personnel involved in the line except those necessary for the final salvage operation, saving still more cash. You simplify your total operation, producing even more savings. You will probably need less machinery and may be able to sell off the surplus for cash. Finally, even if you can't sell all the inventory, you can scrap the rest, thus you free up space which you can put to better use or even no use at all.

Closing down a product line is usually recorded on the accounting books as a loss. However, you are merely recognizing losses that were actually incurred some time ago but don't show on the books yet. You might as well bite the bullet. When a company is a single-product company and its core product slips, it has very little choice but to milk that product and use the resulting funds to bring out a new product. This is a very risky strategy, but the only alternative is shutdown. A case in point is Arctic Enterprises, Incorporated, a maker of snowmobiles that was forced to move to other products by the decline in industry sales.

Promotion

Promotion costs in most troubled companies are out of balance with the profit goals of the company and sometimes out of touch with reality. Usually, the bottom 20 percent of any sales activity chews up a disproportionate amount of time and cost, and can be neglected or eliminated with a much larger effect in terms of reducing costs. Pareto's law—that in all human endeavor, 20 percent of the aggregate activity produces 80 percent of the final useful effect—applies to sales activities as much as to any other human activity.

Most companies are saddled with the heritage of 100 percent promotional coverage that comes largely from the "smother 'em" marketing concept of consumer goods marketeers who want to sell to and through every outlet and want to sell their full line to and through everybody. This is a luxury that few people can afford, particularly troubled organizations. To get quick, short-term results, try grabbing on to the top 20 or 30 percent of customers, orders, products, or whatever can produce much more than its share of volume of profits. Concentrate on this top group, eliminate the bottom 20 or 30 percent and neglect the middle until you have time to make a detailed analysis and can decide which, if any, of the customers or products you have been purposely neglecting deserve to be put back on your active list.

Salesmen's Incentive. I knew of one company that changed all its marketing management to a salary-only status during a crisis. The results were expectedly devastating to initiative, since there were no rewards for selling, except at the sales representative level. Fixed costs were very high, and the situation did not change until the lack of incentives was eliminated. As in that case often a company simply lets its compensation strategy remain the same long after the nature of the business changes. In another case a troubled Chicago company had break-even ratios in its losing sales offices that were from 2.0 to 3.6 times current revenues. The nature of the business had changed from a situation where salesmen had provided nearly every customer service to where they were simply order-takers. Although their costs had gone down drastically, the salesmen's commission rate had not been adjusted downward for fifteen years. Attempts to cut rates were met with a great deal of resistance but finally were implemented with dramatically positive bottom-line results.

Placing the sales force on a reasonable incentive plan seems like such an obvious business basic that it's hard to believe that companies fail to handle this matter properly. Time after time I've seen troubled companies neglect basics in many areas, not just that of sales-force incentives. Simmons Company, the troubled mattress maker, has attempted to make its salesmen more aggressive by placing them on a compensation program of straight, incentive-based commissions in line with the rest of the industry. Before, 70 percent of the salesmen's compensation was salary and only 30 percent was incentive-based bonuses. Gregory O. Berquist, vice president and treasurer, said: "Some salesmen stood out like sore thumbs, so much so that they didn't last long under the commission system." Explaining why the salary system did not change sooner, Grant Simmons just shrugged and said, "It had been that way for 50 years."[12]

Other Promotion Costs. Besides getting cost-effective control of the direct sales activity, short-term marketing improvements center in the emergency stage on decreasing or eliminating current expenditures that have no measurable current or future payout. In some severe cases, where survival is at stake, current dollars must be saved even when there is the prospect for a measurable future payout. Soft expenditures such as public relations, community image building, and advertising are usually chopped to the bone. On some or all products, the advertising effort, like the sales effort, is often aimed at least in part at long-term image building. The advertising effort can usually be safely suspended and the money saved used in a number of other ways that should stimulate sales—in price reductions, in commission increases to salesmen, or in wider margins for wholesalers or retailers.

The marketing and sales people will protest mightily against most of such moves to cut promotion expenses. Half of their arguments are usually a smoke screen and the other half bear merit. The half that bear merit, however, are lacking in a feel for the overall picture. This is where the turnaround leader earns his pay, and this area is usually where his tough guts are put to the test. Be prepared for the threat of a mini revolt among the sales personnel if tough measures are needed. In the face of such revolt, one company lost control of its sales force for years through constant capitulation. The turnaround leader must be sensitive to the front-line needs of his promotion effort, but he must not allow his corporation to become a captive of narrow interest. He must be sure of his direction, sensitive to its ramifications, but tough and determined to see his decisions carried out.

Place

Place, or distribution, decisions in the emergency stage are a variation of the 20/80 theme used in a number of different areas. Basically the turnaround company stresses its strong customers and strong locations and weeds out its weak customers and weak locations. A company that is going through an emergency stage must concentrate its scarce resources on the strong. It cannot afford the time or expense to rehabilitate the weak. It cannot afford current cash flow sinks that have a risky future payoff. About 72 percent of the turnaround companies surveyed eliminated unprofitable customers as part of their marketing turnaround efforts. An average of 23 percent of the customers were eliminated. A case in point is Simmons Company (mattresses, hide-a-bed sofas, etc.). The number of retailers carrying Simmons products was reduced to 5,000 from 8,000, eliminating dealers who contributed little to sales, so that Simmons's 150 salesmen could devote more time to their best customers. Safeco insurance eliminated 155,000 policyholders (9 percent of its casualty insurance sales) in New York and New Jersey because it had lost $25 million on underwriting in those states over a five-year period. Safeco's fanatic devotion to underwriting profits—as opposed to sales or investments—earned the company a well-deserved reputation as one of the industry's star performers.

There is no need to belabor the general pattern of tightening up that I'm advocating. You'll have to apply this general principle judiciously to the particular situation at hand. Every analysis of salesmen's use of time that I have seen indicates that considerably less than one-half of the eight-hour day is actually devoted to face-to-face selling. The salesman spends most of his time traveling, waiting, and performing nonselling activities, such as making service calls and doing other "busy" work.

On the basis of your experience, you can eliminate or neglect parts of a typical salesman's day, at least in the short term, without any long-term impairment of customer relations. Certain types of customers can be handled by long-distance telephone calls for two out of every three contacts, rather than by traveling and making a personal visit. Probably a substantial amount of time has been devoted to sales-development calls: calls aimed at informing potential customers and getting them in a frame of mind to ultimately make a purchase. No short-term harm would result if these were neglected for six months.

Most salesmen have a favorite group of small customers. These may be people who once purchased a lot but don't now, or people who have recently started to buy and promise later to become big customers. In any event, whatever the reason, small-volume customers entail an expensive use of a salesman's time. For example, in a major oil company, the industrial sales force was soliciting oil and grease business in manufacturing plants, mostly metalworking operations. Analysis showed that 68 percent of the total number of accounts were unprofitable and were producing only 10 percent of the volume. By company edict, most of the small companies were dropped peremptorily; sales increased 76 percent as a result of the more effective use of the selling effort thus freed, and marketing expenses for the industrial sales department were reduced by almost half—from 22.8 to 11.5 percent of sales. What had been a net loss of 2.9 percent was turned into a net marketing profit of 15 percent.

HUMAN RESOURCES MANAGEMENT IN THE EMERGENCY STAGE

I devoted Chapter 18 to discussing when and how to motivate a company going through a turnaround. This section of the current chapter is not about motivation but rather is mostly centered on making staff reductions, normally a demotivator, in the emergency stage. Making staff reductions is a difficult process. In his first three years at NCR, William

Anderson cut the work force in Dayton from 12,000 to 2,000. Needless to say that caused a lot of bitterness in Dayton against NCR. Although Anderson counted these cuts as the toughest part of his job, he felt that they were absolutely necessary to create a strong NCR in order to ensure the jobs of a great many more NCR people.

The majority of staff reductions are not done on an across-the-board basis but on a functional department basis. If you have to cut across the board, you can eliminate 20 percent of indirect people and 10 percent of direct labor without hurting your organization in a turnaround. Beyond that, you need to study groups and departments separately in order to come to your final determination. In a crisis, support functions in a company are greatly curtailed. Engineering is an area that during normal times always seems to be padded. People are usually self-motivated in engineering, but a great number of activities are carried on that do not have a current or future payout to the company. You can probably do away with a lot of data processing projects. You can probably get away without a lot of financial analysis. The point of all this is that you must get hard-nosed about every extra person on the payroll. It's no time to play Caspar Milquetoast. If at all possible, plan and make your cuts all at one time. If the situation is desperate and you have any doubts, make the necessary cuts.

Employees in Divested Operations

Employees in divested operations are a special case. The impact of divestment on the employees of a divested activity can range from quite minimal to very substantial. If the divested operation continues to function in much the same way, employees may notice little, if any, effect of the divestment. Conversely, if the divestment brings with it substantial changes, including the shutdown or transfer of part of the operations, employees may feel a great impact. If part of the activity is to be relocated, some provision for transferring the employees who are willing to move should be made. Existing employees can be given a chance even when the new owner intends, with good reason, to shake up the activity once control has been gained. Finally, some employees just will not fit into the revised operations, though they might want to. Severance arrangements will vary with the intentions and the economic capabilities of the selling and buying companies.

Executive-Level Cutbacks

Executive-level cutbacks usually account for the highest percentage of cuts by category. At American Microsystems 50 percent of the executive group had to be let go. This is fairly typical of most turnaround situa-

TABLE 19-5
Turnover Rates during Turnaround Compared with Historical Rates

	Percentage of companies		
Employment level	***Higher (%)***	***Same (%)***	***Lower (%)***
Executive management	57	38	5
Middle management	43	43	14
Rank and file	28	62	10

Source: Donald B. Bibeault, Survey of eighty-one turnaround company chief executives, April 1978.

tions, but I've seen the top executive ranks subject to nearly 100 percent turnover in many cases. Eighty percent of the top level executives were cut at Crocker Bank. In Table 19-5 turnover rates in my survey companies are compared by organizational level with historical rates.

Table 19-5 shows that turnover was higher in executive management ranks in nearly six out of ten cases. Barry Diller, chairman of Paramount Pictures Corporation, also conducted a massive bloodletting in the executive ranks. All but a few of the top twenty-five officers were replaced. Few corporate chores performed by executives are more painful than firing other executives. If they are one's colleagues, the process is even more painful. That's why outsiders are often chosen to perform the painful surgery that accompanies a severe company decline. Firing production workers or low-level white collars is unpleasant enough, but generally those who make the decisions are shielded from direct contact with the victims.

In most cases the turnaround executive is obliged to wield the ax personally. He cuts deep and decisively. Usually a clean break is made, that is, the dismissal is made effective immediately. Little is gained and much can be lost by letting a man stay around. He can't work effectively, he challenges authority, and he demoralizes other people. Today, in most cases, executive-level firing is cushioned by sweetening the terms of separation and by assisting the executive in placing himself in another position. For an excellent article on this see "The Art of Firing an Executive," in the October 1972 issue of *Fortune*.[13]

Middle-Level Cutbacks

Middle-level cutbacks are a mix of both numbers and personal considerations. There is definitely a ranking process that goes on, but in drastic cutbacks a lot of mistakes are made. Basically you've got to rely on your division heads to make the cutbacks, since it's unlikely that you can develop a personal knowledge of the affected people in any but the smallest companies. Give them your objectives and allow them to make the specific choices. My method is to have managers rank their people in a simple A, B, C system when forced to make cutbacks.

People in the C category are going to get the ax. B-category people are people who are good, but are borderline in terms of need. Until a decision is made they will be kept on to do business. A-category people are people you cannot lose from the organization. The middle management ranks are going to carry the brunt of the turnaround work load, and they are an important group because they are close to the production and administrative groups. In order to minimize middle management resentment, companies are beginning to utilize out-placement assistants, coupled with more generous severance pay. John Thompson of Crocker National Bank believes Crocker was able to minimize resentment in its middle ranks because it spent a lot of money on an effective out-placement program. He says that it was able to place most of its people into better positions outside of Crocker than they had with the bank in almost every case.[14] As Gary Friedman, former vice chairman of Itel, says, "The key is cutting off the dead weight immediately rather than having a fraternity or club where you say, 'Let's keep all the good ol' boys around for old times sake.' That's like eating a cancer sandwich."[15]

Rank-and-file Head-Count Reduction

Rank-and-file head-count reduction is more of a numbers game, but that does not mean that the turnaround leader is not making a mistake if he handles the situation in an impersonal manner. The key to making large-scale reductions rests on three sound premises:

1. Make the reductions fairly and equitably.
2. If time permits, make the reductions based upon sound analysis.
3. Communicate the actions and why they must be made to both the outgoing employees and those that remain.

Segmenting the Group. After the rank-and-file percentage cut-by-function has been decided, each member of the management team should be asked to produce a list of people to be either terminated or transferred internally. The information required, in addition to the names of people to be terminated, is their job title, length of service, annual income, contract of employment, and cost of termination. The turnaround executive, reluctantly responsible for this task, must do his utmost to ensure that people are treated as fairly, as generously, and as compassionately as possible. Failure to recognize the need for a head count reduction, however, can only result in putting the jobs of everyone employed within the business at an even greater risk, because the continued survival of the whole enterprise would be in jeopardy.

At the beginning, no across-the-board cuts should be made unless survival is at stake, even though it's clear that the payroll is too high for volume. Instead, each function should be analyzed to determine how many people are required to perform it efficiently. For example: Suppose there are seventeen people in the customer service department, and it takes three days to acknowledge an order. The manager might say that he needs perhaps two more people to get the job done within twenty-four hours. Analysis proves that the nine best people, using a better system and better forms, can do it in twenty-four hours. Thus there are eight too many, not two too few. Announce that the nine will stay and that, unfortunately, eight must go. That boosts the morale of the nine; tells them that they have weathered the storm that everybody feared.

Communications. Communicating the cutbacks is important. The manner in which they are communicated is even more important. Detailed planning should be carried out to ensure that all terminations are announced and executed at the same time, so that uncertainty and anxiety among the remaining personnel are minimized as much as possible in the difficult circumstances which exist. Equally important, appropriate notification should be given to trade unions and government departments, in accordance with the highest standards of custom and practice of the particular country. Also, consideration should be given to providing interviewing and counseling activities through either government or private employment agencies, to assist the terminated employees in finding suitable alternative employment as quickly as possible.

Many managements don't believe in telling employees about business matters, especially when the companies are in trouble. However, most employees get to know what is going on through the grapevine and many know simply because they talk to vendors. The trouble is, no one gets the full picture and rumors are rampant. I suggest explaining your exact plans and the effect that these will have on each employee individually, even when it means eventual termination of the employee involved. Candor like this can pay off, as James C. Miller, president of Intermatic, Inc., found out when Intermatic cut its work force 41 percent in the first year of the turnaround. Despite the cuts, Miller got full cooperation, even from the ones who knew they were going to be terminated. Miller said, "They are much happier knowing what was going to happen, rather than fearing an unknown future."

The tough people decisions of the emergency stage fall squarely on the shoulders of the turnaround leader. He must take that long and hard-boiled look at his company. If changes are needed, he must make the first moves. He can't expect his managers to do the housecleaning chores, particularly in a sizable company, where the cover-your-butt syndrome is so strong. Nobody wants to work himself out of a job. The basic elements of crisis management differ from the basic elements of normal, sound management practice in kind and certainly in intensity. However, the "troubleshooting" analytical techniques, by themselves, accomplish nothing. It is leadership—the determination to implement a realistic emergency plan and to press it to completion—that in the final analysis makes it happen.

REFERENCES

[1]William S. Anderson, address at Beta Gamma Sigma dinner, Wright State University, Apr. 19, 1976, p. 8.

[2]Louis Knoar, "Roy Ash Is Having Fun at Addressogrief-Multigrief," *Fortune*, February 27, 1978, p. 48.

[3]Interview with Frank A. Grisanti, president, Grisanti and Galef, Los Angeles, Calif., February 1978.

[4]Interview with Robert C. Brown, president R. C. Brown & Co., San Francisco, Calif., February 1978.

[5]Ibid.

[6]"A Winning Attitude Produces a Turnaround," *Industry Week*, Aug. 5, 1974, p. 46.

[7]Ibid, p. 47.

[8]Lindley R. Higgins, *Cost Reduction from A to Z* (New York: McGraw-Hill, 1976).

[9]Albert Raymond & Associates, *Controlling Production and Inventory Costs* (Englewood Cliffs, N.J.: Prentice-Hall, 1977).

[10]Frederick W. Hombruch, Jr., *Raising Productivity* (New York: McGraw-Hill, 1978).

[11]Richard Wilson, *Handbook of Cost Control* (New York: Wiley, 1975).

[12]"Simmons: A Turnaround Proves Hard to Bring Off," *Business Week*, June 5, 1978, p. 150.

[13]"The Art of Firing An Executive," *Fortune*, October 1972, pp. 88–91, 178.

[14]Interview with John S. Thompson, senior vice president, Crocker National Bank, San Francisco, Calif., January 1978.

[15]Interview with Gary Friedman, former vice chairman, Itel Corp., San Francisco, Calif., February 1978.

20
THE STABILIZATION STAGE

In the emergency stage you've identified the plan for the renovation of the company and you've cut out the cancers. Usually you still have a sick patient who is recovering from surgery, and you're not sure about the company in the long run. In the stabilization stage you've got to go back to your existing and remaining corporations. And you want to go back to them with the view of whether they are capable of long-term survival—not just can they produce a decent cash flow right now, but are they worthy of being kept over the long haul?[1]

Jeffrey Chanin,
former Executive Vice President,
Daylin Corporation

STABILIZATION STAGE BASICS

Stabilization entails definitely settling down after the trauma and surgery of the emergency stage. The patient is no longer in danger of demise but is hardly a robust, healthy company. The settling-down process does not imply that the turnaround leader's task is complete. It is far from complete because his principal task now is to rehabilitate the company. In contrast to the emergency stage, where company executives concentrated on cash flow and survival, the emphasis now is on profit improvement. The company is probably no longer rapidly shrinking, but neither is it growing. It can be at dead center, from a revenue standpoint. Profit improvement is primary; cash flow next in importance; and sales volume revenue growth third. The objectives of the company during the stabilization stage are achieved by the adherence to a three-pronged strategy:

1. Concentration on profit improvement by continued attention to margin achievement
2. Enhancement of profitability by the running of the existing operations more efficiently
3. Reposturing of the company for increased profitability and return on investment on assets employed

Profit improvement tactics in the stabilization plan center on rigorous enforcement of margin requirements. One of the more surprising characteristics of troubled companies is their amazing lack of price discipline. By allowing their prices to lag behind cost increases, many companies lose precious margins during inflationary periods. (One glaring example is an automotive original-equipment manufacturer that let its margins shrink by 50 percent, even though it enjoyed a 100 percent market share.) Another company, with a highly complex product line of 40,000 items, ran weekly cost/price reviews. During 1974 and 1975, it eliminated more than 20 percent of all items for inadequate profitability. As a result, the company's operating margins grew to be 10 points higher than those of its leading competitors.

Emhart Corporation's strategy of cost control, efficient operations, and off-loading losing pieces of the business is typical of a company in the stabilization stage. These measures enabled Emhart to cut over $100 million from the combined debt of its once floundering USM subsidiary. By trimming the work force, raising prices, holding down wage increases, and making modest new product additions, USM came through its stabilization period successfully.

ASSET REDEPLOYMENT IN THE STABILIZATION STAGE

Asset redeployment in the stabilization stage centers on reposturing the business to achieve greater profitability and return on investment. This is achieved principally by making a number of retention/divestment decisions that will, in the opinion of the turnaround leader, lead to improved returns in the intermediate term, as opposed to the short-term returns sought during the emergency phase. At this point in the turnaround the long-term planning perspective is not set. Divisions, plants, product lines, and facilities are judged from a different perspective than previously. There is less emphasis on short-term cash flow and considerably more attention to whether the operation "fits" the managerial concept of the enterprise or has an acceptable rate of return. Company growth, business vitality, and managerial efficiency depend as much on the proper "pruning out" of assets and activities with poor performance records as they do on the inflow of new investments and on the successful operation of those segments that justify retention.

Retention Divestment Packages

The retention/divestment-decision packages are key parts of the stabilization plan. These decisions have to come from the top because they seldom come from the bottom of the organization. While such a disinvestment program often makes eminent sense from a corporate point of view, it is a rare division or product manager who willingly plans himself out of business. Most managers will argue that new growth is just around the corner; all they need to get the payoff is a little more investment "up front."

One simple but powerful approach some multibusiness managers are using today is to sort their individual businesses into three broad portfolio categories: sources of growth (future earnings), sources of current and intermediate earnings, and sources of immediate cash flow. A classic example of the divestiture plan was the announcement by G. D. Searle early in 1978 that it planned to divest itself of twenty of its unprofitable businesses, totalling $100 million in annual revenues. At the time President Rumsfeld indicated that Searle wanted to concentrate its management efforts and financial resources in areas where Searle had strength and experience. He also felt that the divestitures would relieve areas of operating loss, simplify the continuing businesses, and better position the company to take advantage of future growth opportunities in its core businesses. Searle's strategy was developed after a six-month appraisal and sorting out of its operating subsidiaries.

In this stage of the turnaround, misfits and poor-return-on-investment operations are divested rather than liquidated. A company can expect to receive book value or better under these circumstances. The unsuccessful misfit should be put out of its misery as soon as possible. Otherwise it becomes a drain on a company's resources and a crushing burden on its management. For the majority of successful misfits or partial fits, financial as well as managerial divorce is the right thing. An old proverb says, "In looking for a husband for your daughter, don't ask: 'Who'll make the best husband for her?' Ask instead: 'For which kind of a man would she make a good wife?'" This is the right rule for the divestment of a successful or promising misfit or partial fit. An example of a strategic misfit was Potlatch Corporation's position in the brown stock business. It divested because its puny market position palled next to that of giant Weyerhauser and International Paper.

Increasing Liquidity

Usually in the stabilization stage, companies do not make a dollar-for-dollar trade-off because their balance sheet needs strengthening. The reposturing usually includes provisions to increase financial assets, clean up the balance sheet, and provide a stable platform for growth. The reposturing approach looked something like this at Di Giorgio Corporation, according to Robert Di Giorgio:

> We were in twenty-five businesses and identified the ones that were the least rewarding. Most of the ones that were the least attractive were also

> profitable. We had two or three that weren't profitable that we decided to stay in. The opportunity was there, but we had not been taking advantage of the opportunity. The problems in these businesses centered on either the wrong strategic thrust or the wrong people. In one business, we made three changes in management in about fifteen months before we found the type of manager we wanted. Finding that right guy was the key element in the turnaround. With good management in place, we could change the strategic thrust of the business and complete the requirements for the turnaround effort. In our current long-range plans, we identify areas where we want to hold our position, where we want to retrench, and where we want to grow.[2]

Kaiser Cement and Gypsum Corporation sold its gypsum operations in 1978 for both strategic and return-on-investment reasons. Since 1973, Kaiser's annual return on its gypsum operations had been less than 2 percent because of the loss of $16 million accumulated from 1974 through 1976, but its cement operations returned 20 percent. Since late 1974, Kaiser's president, Walter E. Ousterman, had been trying to repair the damage at the gypsum division by streamlining operations. Some 972 of the company's 3,500 gypsum employees were laid off including 9 vice presidents. As Ousterman says, "Like an old car, we had to paint it up before we could sell it." The sale of the West Coast gypsum operations brought Kaiser more than $70 million to redeploy into acquisitions and into expansion of its existing and highly profitable cement operations.

FINANCIAL MANAGEMENT IN THE STABILIZATION STAGE

Financial management in the stabilization stage varies in direction and intensity from the emergency stage. Rather than cash objectives at the expense of profits, profitability takes on a stronger role; rather than debt liquidation, the emphasis is on balance sheet enhancement; rather than cost reduction, the emphasis is on profit improvement. In addition, the company in this stage has the time and resources to develop better control systems and managerial accounting systems. Thus the main financial management activities are:

1. Liquidity improvement
2. Balance sheet cleanup
3. Control system development
4. Managerial accounting development

Liquidity Improvement

Liquidity improvement in the stabilization stage is achieved more by the institution of sound management practices than by the wholesale wringing out of cash flow from unproductive assets. There is still some divestment activity but during this stage the principal focus is not on getting cash flow positive as much as it is on improving profitability. Cash flow is still intensely managed, but management is far less likely to sell a high-performance subsidiary for cash flow purposes, as it might have been forced to do in the emergency stage. Part of the liqudity improvement activity involves strategic moves to improve liquidity, and part reflects operational improvements.

One key strategic move that a company can make in regard to its core business is to slow the growth rate in order to moderate the demand for new capital. Typical of companies in this stage is one that decided to aim for drastically improved margins while sharply restricting its sales growth. It aggressively weeded out less profitable businesses and products, selectively increased prices on high-value lines, and pushed product and profit improvement programs. Another company, by controlling its growth rate, improving margins, and avoiding costs associated with acquisitions, improved earnings and cash flow by 75 percent over three years.

Companies in this situation find it of vital importance to manage their cash more tightly from an operational standpoint by finding ways to minimize float: by changing banking and lockbox configurations, by utilizing international cash flow more effectively, by selectively extending payables, by aggressively reducing inventories and receivables, by making judicious use of leasing in place of direct capital investment, and by exploiting a number of other devices for maximizing mileage from working capital. Typical of the results that can be achieved is a railroad that showed a cash balance of only $9 million, but drew a total of $17 million out of its cash gathering and disbursing system to help finance a major equipment acquisition program. In another case, an oil company reduced the cash in its gathering and disbursing system by 25 percent, providing over $25 million for marketing and refining expansion. Some common characteristics of a loosely run system that give clues to improvement opportunities are:

1. Decentralized responsibility for processing cash receipts, disbursing funds, and maintaining relationships with banks
2. Absence of a reasonably accurate, daily cash forecasting system
3. Use of gathering or concentration banks in cities which are non-Federal Reserve or have no bank wire facilities

4. Lack of current figures on float in major disbursing accounts and on cash-in-transit in parts of cash-gathering system
5. No record for individual accounts showing purpose, activity, tangible and intangible services, and average bank ledger balance
6. No current analysis of the cost to company, and of the profitability to the bank, of each major banking relationship
7. Limited use of the administrative services provided by banks, such as draft-payment payments, lockboxes, depository transfer checks, zero-balance accounts, and automatic wire transfer
8. Maintenance of balances in a large number of banks and/or accounts for disbursing purposes

Balance Sheet Cleanup

Balance sheet cleanup that centers on debt restructuring during the emergency stage must be pursued vigorously. Rather than relying on hard-pressed lenders to ease credit arrangements, including outright debt forgiveness, a company in the stabilization stage usually relies on its own financial resources for restructuring. By smart asset redeployment, a company can significantly ease its liquidity problems and its long-term debt burden. A case in point is the takeover of the sluggish Irvine Company by a more aggressive development group headed by Albert Taubman. Although the group was originally saddled with $240 million of package debt, it was able to clear up $190 million in just one year by mortgaging property and selling off a small percentage of assets. It was left with over 90 percent of its property intact as a very manageable short-term debt position.

Control System Development

Effective controls must be implemented beyond the cash flow pipeline controls of the emergency stage. During stabilization, these controls must be institutionalized by setting up effective control procedures that are implemented at all levels of the organization. These include the invoicing, inventory, purchasing, and cost controls that are absolutely essential for sensitive management control. One of the key things that management wants to eliminate in the stabilization stage is the plethora of surprises so common during the emergency stage. That's why Glenn Penisten calls his stabilization stage the "year of consistency." As he says, "I don't want any adverse surprises popping up this year."[3]

Three basic types of controls should be emphasized during the stabilization stage. These are: overall controls, cash controls, and cost controls. Cash controls were put into effect in the emergency stage.

Overall Controls. Overall controls apply to strategy and commitments. Three examples point up the huge losses that can occur by neglecting overall controls:

- After investing $21 million in Executive Jet Aviation, Inc., Penn Central has been found to be illegally in control of an airline by the Civil Aeronautics Board. Further, the holdings were worth less than $1 million, and legal action was taken against "inside" operations.
- Diner's Club lost over $70 million in two years both as a result of poor control over credit card processing expenses and associated fraud and as a result of competitive forces.
- Losing ventures in computers, nuclear power, and jet engines cost General Electric more than $500 million in aftertax profits.

An out-of-control situation is typified by the experience of Hesston Corporation, which got caught with huge inventory write-downs in 1976. As late as the spring of 1976, the company's factories were running at full throttle to meet heavy orders, but the shipments were primarily replenishing dealer inventories that had been severely depleted in the previous few years. No one at Hesston seemed to notice that the farmers, who actually used the products, had stopped buying. And because they were basing their estimates on dealer orders and not on actual retail sales, Hesston's marketing specialists were making demand forecasts that did not bear even a remote resemblance to reality.

Cash Controls. Cash controls include control over loosely monitored transactions. In one company I helped turn around, I was amazed by the lack of controls on shipping and invoicing. A truck laden with $10,000 worth of steel could get by the guard gate with a bill of lading filled out by the shipping department. However, there were no controls on the bills of lading themselves, that is, there was no follow-up to ensure that the steel that went out the gate was ever invoiced. An improperly made out bill of lading was simply crumpled up and tossed in the wastebasket. I quickly instituted a bill of lading control that matched all bills of lading to invoices on a computer listing. All mismatches had to be physically accounted for. Troubled companies often exercise low scrutiny over bills as Roy Woodman, president of International Video Corporation, illustrates:

> People overlook some of the biggest possibilities for savings, simply because it has been done over and over again. One big cost of doing business is property taxes, inventory tax, etc. I ran into one situation in the first year I got the property tax bill. Property taxes were $180,000 to $190,000. I signed the check. I assumed that this had been carefully followed up. The second time it came along, I had a little bit more time, so I had the property taxes checked on similar businesses in the city and in the area, and I was able to reduce that figure by 30 percent. Just because the dollar figure is large or because people have done it before, doesn't mean that there isn't a possibility there for savings. Everything you look at is a possible savings to the company.[4]

There isn't a troubled company around in which the accounting department isn't overpaying bills from the utility company, the telephone company, or other major suppliers. Minimum cash controls must include control over cash commitments, expenditures, and disbursements.

Control Systems Effectiveness. Control systems effectiveness is easy to lose sight of. When you install your control system, be sure that, if anything, it is somewhat tighter than necessary. If it is only somewhat tighter than necessary, there will be no inordinate adverse reaction on the part of management; but if your control system is insufficient, you will have no alternative but subsequently to tighten it, and if you do this, expect managers to complain because they will sense that you really aren't the sure-of-yourself leader that they expected. After gaining control and asserting your leadership role, you can ease back on controls and give your managers more independence.

Another common pitfall is the overreliance on quantitative controls only. Litton's earlier poor performance can be traced to the nature of their control system. They had a microscopic checking of performance on a quantitative basis that was textbook perfect. However, one of Litton's operating vice presidents admitted that top management was not getting the right information. He said: "Litton has very fine quantitative reporting techniques, but not qualitative. They must rely on their divisional managers to tell them that they are taking care of things qualitatively—whether they are keeping up with the field, with their customers' needs, with technology." TRW, another conglomerate that has had relative success in comparison to Litton, does have qualitative controls. Its executives insist that what happened to Litton couldn't happen to them. Their reasons include: (1) a strict reporting procedure that puts every division manager on the carpet once a month; (2) strict insistence on accurate projections; and (3) a mandatory informality that makes the best information in the company accessible to everyone. This informal approach includes both review sessions among peers and a company-wide policy of open-door access to top management. Each business is different and requires operating statistics that are tied to the business itself. As Gary Friedman, former vice chairman of Itel Corporation, says:

> You can get away with six to eight basic statistics per business; for example, how many salesmen do you have, how many customers do you have, how many offices do you have, what percentage of the market, how many units did we ship, how many units new or ordered and what's the backlog? I'd say if you've got more than ten, then you've got a bunch of theoretical guys running around.[5]

Another aspect of control is the continuing debate over who should control the division controller in a company. As a result of illegal practices, increased reporting demand, and the failure to give warning of impending difficulties, many companies are giving their corporate controllers greater authority over their division controllers. Given the potential for friction, misunderstanding, and ineffectiveness, inherent in greater corporate control over division controllers, top management must carefully weigh the advantages and disadvantages of such a move. Most of the turnaround leaders interviewed felt that turnaround situations (generally) require that the division controllers report to the corporate controller. Their conclusion does not minimize the real problems inherent in such an arrangement, but, on balance, they felt that such a relationship is necessary in a troubled company. A good controller will feel that way too.

Managerial Accounting Development

Managerial accounting does not exist in most corporations. Accountants still get all hung up in procedures, debits, credits, GAAP principles, and tax refinements, and often leave management holding the bag on the information it requires to manage. Ultimately, this is management's fault because it allows itself to be shortchanged by these technical experts, who often owe their profession more allegiance than they do the man providing their paycheck. This does not imply that financial accounting standards must not be conformed with. In most troubled companies, managerial accounting is a nonentity. In several cases I've seen, financial accounting requirements were patchworked together to stand in for managerial accounting, and gave misleading and even false information.

At the very least the accounting department seems to be an orchard full of "yes-but's."

Company presidents want information that can be used for decision making without any side issues being raised about the quality of the information. They know that if the information can be questioned, to any degree, the decision-making process can break down into a debate about the reliability of the information, no matter how trivial the question might be. Glenn Penisten's attitude typifies the frustration company presidents have in this regard:

> If you ask the accounting department to design your financial control system, they design you an accounting system. An accounting system is very nice and neat but doesn't tell you what you need. All it tells you is the bottom line and the balance sheet that fulfills the public and regulatory needs. You can't manage with those accounting numbers. I fuss with the accounting people all the time about sending up operating systems that satisfy the accounting firm. Set up the minimum amount that is necessary to satisfy the accounting firm relative to being a public company and from there on get away from accounting altogether in determining what kind of financial control data you need, because it's meaningless.[6]

The key to ending the frustration felt by management is to apply sufficient resources to the managerial accounting function. It also means that managerial accounting should be linked to financial accounting only if it can avoid being contaminated by it. The requirements of the accounting profession should play no role in the numbers required by management.

I have found that five types of managerial accounting information are most useful to me. These are:

1. Cost profiles of total costs
2. Budgetary build-downs from top to bottom
3. Product profitability analysis
4. Responsibility accounting
5. Standard costs by product or service

Cost Profiles. Cost profiles of total cost by major categories help a great deal in understanding the business. Sort cost categories from the largest to the smallest to help in the cost-reduction effort. What I am suggesting here is a systematic approach to understanding where the cost leverage is in the business. For example, some accounting systems have so much

TABLE 20-1
Cost Control Profile for a Chemical Company
(In thousands of dollars)

	Product group		
Cost element	***Resins***	***Specialties***	***Total plant***
Direct materials	$18,166	$4,057	$22,223
Burden	2,740	1,676	4,416
Direct labor	1,063	431	1,494
Indirect labor	757	511	1,268
Indirect materials	581	435	1,016
TOTAL	$23,307	$7,110	$30,417

detail that you can barely see the forest for the trees. I know of one system where expense categories were not segmented out for the whole company. This relatively small company, it turns out, was spending over $700,000 per year on professional fees—accountants, lawyers, and consultants. When that was pointed out, action was taken to hire inside legal people and to cut down on consultants. The accounting system had not shown the break-out. Breaking a business down into simple cost components and constructing a cost profile can be a rewarding exercise. Such a profile for a chemical company is shown in Table 20-1.

Examination of Table 20-1 leads to the suggestion that direct materials are a more fruitful area for cost-reduction efforts than direct labor or indirect labor. Burden also seems to be more important than either direct or indirect labor. By developing a cost profile, it's easy to determine the more important costs. Similarly, each category shown in Table 20-1 can be broken down into its own profile to get a clear picture of where efforts should be expended.

Budgetary Build-Downs. Budgetary build-downs from top to bottom are a means I've used to detect problem areas. By build-down I mean a search for problems that usually starts at the top level of reporting breakdowns, say, the divisional level. The problems are then tracked down successively from a division to an operations to a department and, finally, to the lowest collection level, the cost center. In this way a perspective on the magnitude of the problem can be maintained. Actual performance versus budget can be quickly evaluated.

Product Profitability Analysis. Product profitability analysis is an essential building block of profit improvement. In one medium-size steel operation, the costs of over 2,500 items were lumped together under averages. I guessed that the averages hid large cost differences that would considerably affect management's decisions on products. Very quickly, by using average mill hours, I got the accounting department to calculate averages for each of the three major product lines, rather than just one average. Results are shown in Table 20-2.

As Table 20-2 shows, the original conception of product contribution changed drastically by a simple analysis that took about three days' effort. Management had suspected these results but had never buckled down to face reality until the company faced trouble. This type of analysis is often lacking in troubled companies. Below the product-line analysis was an underlying need to evaluate individual products. In the case shown in Table 20-2, product line B contained 2,000 of the total 2,500 products. Although the whole product line looked shaky, a more detailed analysis using standard costs indicated that there were some distinct winners and losers within the product line. Although the line's average cost was $325, some products could be made for $240, while others cost $500 to make. In many cases the marketplace was not provided adequate pricing on the more costly products.

I know of another case where a large paper division of a major company failed to allocate $40 million of expense in a $110 million revenue operation because of simple laziness on the part of successive controllers. As a result, every product looked like a winner. The new division head refused to tolerate this and forced the proper allocation through. This

TABLE 20-2
Results of Product-Line Costs Analysis

Product line	*Base cost*	*Finishing cost*	*Total cost*	*Average revenue*	*Margin*
BASED ON USE OF ONE AVERAGE FOR ALL PRODUCT LINES					
A	$275	...	$275	$250	$(25)
B	275	...	275	280	5
C	275	$60	335	340	5
AVERAGE	$275	$20	$295	$290	$ (5)
BASED ON USE OF A SEPARATE AVERAGE FOR EACH PRODUCT LINE					
A	$240	...	$240	$250	$10
B	325	...	325	280	(45)
C	260	$60	320	340	20
AVERAGE	$275	$20	$295	$290	$ (5)

action revealed that many products were being sold under cost. One product that was grossly underpriced was being made by that division alone and thus had no competitors. Its price was increased substantially to a point where it showed a profit but was priced below a substitute product. Product costing, like all managerial accounting, should be based upon what is practical and doable. Don't spend more money on accuracy than is necessary for good decisions. Basically, if you don't know your costs, you can't make a profit—except by accident. Product economic analysis will show how product costs are physically generated and where the economic leverage lies, details usually masked by financial accounting systems.

Responsibility Accounting. Responsibility accounting requires that each responsible manager get reports on those areas and business results that he has under his control. A cost center manager will probably get only budget variance reports; a department head will get budget variances but also production and unit-cost information. An operations head will need the combined information of his departments and an overall measure of his productivity. And, finally, a division head will see revenue and profit and loss for his division presented against a plan. The managerial accounting system should be flexible enough to provide proper information on every area for which a manager is responsible, even in a dynamic and changing business environment.

Standard Costs. Standard costs for products or services should not be an accounting albatross, hung around managements's neck for a whole year so that variances can be neatly reversed at the end of the accounting period. Where an annual standard makes sense in a stable climate, use it and integrate it with the accounting system. In other cases, because of inflationary pressures or technological advancements, other standards—such as those based on an escalator curve or a learning curve—may be appropriate. Standard costs, if based on company realities, can be a valuable tool in management's evaluation of its winners and losers, and can replace the acceptance of overall averages that mask reality.

To be effective managerial accounting needs a distinct organizational location. You can't get what you need out of one group. You have to have designated financial accounting people and designated managerial accounting people. Marry the results of those two groups to make sense because you can't get that all out of one group.

OPERATIONS MANAGEMENT IN THE STABILIZATION STAGE

Operations management in the stabilization stage differs from that of the emergency stage in several respects. Profit improvement is achieved by systematic programs rather than by one-shot cost reductions; remaining plants are made more efficient, rather than being shut down on a wholesale basis; manufacturing efficiencies are achieved by brainpower rather than by surgery; inventory management is intensified, and overhead is evaluated on a cost/benefit basis rather than simply lopped off.

In the stabilization stage, operations management often makes the difference between whether a company will survive in mediocrity or continue to improve so that a basis for sustained growth can be provided. Operations efficiency often makes the difference between a less-than-adequate profit performance and an outstanding one. In industry after industry, differences in manufacturing costs go far toward explaining why a gap separates the industry leaders from the also-rans. These significant variations from company to company in the same kind of business challenge the complacency of any management content with the proposition that it has been doing as well as it can with its manufacturing operations.

This was demonstrated recently when a well-known industrial equipment company found its return-on-investment falling far behind that of the competition. The critical factor turned out to be a 14 percent difference in cost of manufacturing, a discrepancy not immediately revealed in conventional accounting data or operating reports. Because the root of the problem had not been readily apparent, management had spent a good deal of time and effort strengthening its product line and sharpening its marketing effort. Sales volume accelerated, but profit margins continued to sag. Analysis finally disclosed that competing companies had 25 percent more production per employee, 32 percent more production per square foot of plant space, and 66 percent faster inventory turnover.

This explained the difference in profitability. Bringing the cost of manufacturing down to the average of the company's three major competitors—in this case not an unreasonable or unattainable objective—would, it was revealed, raise the company's return on investment from 7 to 22 percent, about the level of the more successful organizations in the industry. And additional improvements in manufacturing (for example, reduced in-process inventories) would boost earnings by another 11 percent, bringing the company's return on investment to a handsome 33 percent. Results like that are achieved by:

1. Organizing ongoing effective profit improvement programs
2. Developing manufacturing efficiencies in labor productivity, technology, maintenance, distribution, and purchasing and inventory control, to name a few
3. Performing overhead value analysis

Profit Improvement Programs

Profit improvement programs, as opposed to cost-reduction programs, should be focused upon in the stabilization stage. Cost reductions are usually one-shot programs aimed at expendable activities. While this one-shot, cost-reduction approach can get you some immediate savings, improving efficiency usually requires longer-term programs. For example, the president of a major publishing company recently reduced his company's staff from 354 to 304. Shortly thereafter, a number of key vice presidents convinced their boss that they "just had to have additional personnel." Within a year, the staff was above 350 and was still increasing, yet they were handling the same activities at the same level of business.

Roadblocks. There are two major roadblocks to launching an effective profit improvement program:

1. *Failure to appreciate the size of the profit improvement potential.* Many people look for 10 percent improvement levels when overall improvements of 25 to 30 percent can be expected, and 60 percent savings in some departments are possible. Typical managers are content with achieving marginal savings, if any, as long their departments are running smoothly. They tend to see the importance of their jobs as related to the number of people under them. Managers have to be pushed very hard to admit fat is there, even when documented proof is available. Often, in the final exasperating analysis, authority and the "big stick" have to be used far more extensively than professional organizational development experts would ever care to admit. I have seen departments function with one-third their previous manpower after eliminating a superstructure of bureaucracy, titles, and private secretaries. If you really want to have a turnaround, you've got to strip away the veneer of ego gratification and get down to the hardwood of shirt-sleeve performance.

2. *Lack of profit consciousness, particularly in overhead activities.* Let's face it, very few people have their identifiable destinies linked to the bottom line in a typical corporation. Most people, even conscientious ones, identify with a smooth, trouble-free workday that allows them to get home to their families with a minimum of stress. This consciousness usually leads to chronic overstaffing. Moreover, there are few cost or efficiency standards applied to nonmanufacturing activities, as much as we'd like to think otherwise. Profit consciousness is not the normal diet in most companies, particularly troubled companies. Most people have a junk food mentality; they know a low-fat, high-profit diet is better for them and the corporation, but they usually wind up eating a high-fat, overstaffed, low-profit diet. Good profit consciousness, like good nutrition, has to be almost force-fed.

One inevitable result of this attitude becomes apparent when the net effect of across-the-board cost-cutting drives has been evaluated. What company has not had the experience of launching one of these drives, rejoicing in its immediate impact, and then noting a year or so later that either the same excessive costs have reappeared or new and equally unnecessary costs have crept into the operation? If profit improvement remains a "here today, gone tomorrow" objective, if it emerges from the chief executive's office from time to time in the form of an edict that orders everyone to cut all costs by 10 percent next Monday, then steady and permanent improvement in profits simply does not take place.

Some Arbitrary Cost-Cutting Drives. Some arbitrary cost-cutting drives have actually resulted in the elimination of profitable activities. In one company, the order to reduce costs led to the elimination of a fifty-man work group that maintained and repaired certain mechanical equipment. The president had ordered a reduction in the work force, and the plant manager complied by arranging to have this work done on contract. Two years later a close analysis disclosed that the cost of maintenance had almost doubled because of the higher charges paid to the outside contractor. These charges were buried in a cost account separate from that of maintenance labor.

To overcome such obstacles and launch an effective continuing program for improving profits, top management must do four essential things: (1) condition itself for major change; (2) stimulate a greater sense of profit consciousness throughout the entire organization; (3) develop the conviction among all members of management that the job of profit improvement is a never-ending one; and (4) make sure that the profit improvement job is approached in a fresh, skillful, comprehensive way.

Enough Successes. Enough successes have been placed on the record to prove how useful profit improvement efforts can be when they are systematically organized and planned. One of the nation's largest and most profitable consumer foods manufacturers, widely known for outstanding marketing achievements, merits praise for its approach to profit improvement. Facing increasing costs after World War II, this company adopted all the usual approaches to cost reduction: elimination of unnecessary reports, running of cost-cutting contests, and the like. They were only modestly successful. After eight years. management took stock and found that new savings averaged less than $2,000 a year per manufacturing manager and supervisor.

The company then did an about-face and began a systematic effort to instill the responsibility for profit improvement into its line management and supervisory group. It was made clear to each line manager that a successful career with the company would be directly related to ability to improve operations and reduce costs. The responsibilities of the staff group were also redefined; from that time on they were charged with delineating the profit improvement responsibility of line management. Having launched this program, top management took every occasion to reward outstanding performance. In five years, the company raised its new savings to an average of well over $10,000 a year for every line and staff member of manufacturing management, a fivefold improvement over the previous level.

In summary, cost reduction is best implemented by executive fiat in the emergency stage. The project-team, or flying-squad, approach works best in the stabilization stage. Finally, profit improvement can be spread down to many layers in the organization by implementing an effective management by objective (MBO) approach in the return-to-growth stage of the turnaround. When a company is forced to face tough realities and is managed by a turnaround leader relentless in his pursuit of the bottom line, attitudes about improvement often shake off the lethargy of the past. Executives see for the first time the extraordinary results that can come about from these programs. Mental attitudes change, and people become open-minded, creative, and enthusiastic in their approach to solving management problems.

Development of Manufacturing Efficiencies

Developing manufacturing efficiencies in various areas can have a decided impact on profitability improvement. Labor productivity improvements of significant magnitudes can be achieved by utilizing improved management and the application of technology. I mentioned earlier that more efficient management at General Motor's Hyatt Bearings Division in Sandusky, Ohio, reduced the work force from 12,300 to 8,000 in five years, while production increased. Updegraph and Person, point out some outstanding examples of technology improvement:

- A plastics producer recently installed a new type of automatically controlled equipment, permitting this company to maintain production while cutting its work force by over 80 percent.
- A new manufacturing process recently doubled the capacity of one plate glass manufacturer, with a labor force increase of only 15 percent.
- In another plant, a new insulation system uses recently developed materials and an inert gas to produce a home refrigerator having 28 percent more capacity without any increase in exter-

nal dimensions. This company will begin with a marked competitive advantage in its marketing effort.

- One major steel company has reported that its new oxygen steel furnaces pour 491 tons of steel an hour, almost five times the rate of a typical open-hearth shop.

In a turnaround of a railcar maintenance facility that I worked on, labor productivity was improved an average of 30 percent per month, for a total of 256 percent over an eight-month period compared with its dismal former level. Prior management had offered every excuse known to man as to why productivity could not be improved even marginally.

In a classic case, technological obsolescence and union featherbedding caused a steel company to close operations. One of its rolling mills will serve as an example of the companywide problem. The rolling mill had a contract crewing level of thirty-nine men per shift, down from forty-two men per shift a decade before. Each man was costing $30,000 per year in 1978. During a strike a decade before, when the contract crewing level was forty-two, twelve supervisors, alone, had run the rolling mill very successfully for six months. Assuming that the twelve supervisors were smarter and better-motivated, and therefore equivalent to fourteen of the crew, we can estimate the union featherbedding rate at twenty-five men per shift or $750,000 per year per shift. On top of that, newer mills were doing the same function with only five men. The company had a technological gap of $270,000 per year per shift, coupled with a featherbedding gap, to total a gap of over $2 million per year for a two-shift operation in this one mill alone.

Maintenance. Maintenance, often a stepchild in the past, is important today because of its effect on the utilization of costly production equipment. The cost of equipment magnifies the cost penalties of downtime. An unnamed paper company, for example, recently found that reducing downtime by one percentage point was worth as much in added profits as a $200,000-a-year increase in the value of added production capacity. In a company that can sell all the paper it produces, the impact of maintenance on profitability will obviously be substantial, but even in companies with excess capacity, downtime can cause a sizable increase in costs. Perhaps because they have led in automation, oil refining companies now are among the first to upgrade maintenance. Many years ago one such company, beginning to realize the importance that maintenance would play, embarked on a ten-year program of developing management skills in maintenance. The payout of the long-term program has been dramatic. Over a ten-year period, while production has gone up 70 percent, maintenance forces have been reduced 55 percent. At the same time, the refinery's on-stream record has been significantly improved. The increase in profits directly attributable to this change in maintenance management has been estimated at close to $15 million a year.

Transportation Efficiency Improvements. Transportation efficiency improvements can also be substantial. Monfort of Colorado was losing $2 million per year on its trucking business before it recruited Joe Breitenstein, an experienced trucking executive, to run its transportation unit. Breitenstein soon replaced Monfort's older trucks with new, more fuel-efficient models. At the same time, he concentrated on backhaul business-hauling goods for outside shippers on return trips to Colorado. Today 80 percent of the trucks returning home carry loads, up from 40 percent a year or so ago. The transportation division is now running profitably.

Inventory Investments. Inventory investment management can be substantially improved over the level achieved in the emergency stage. NCR decreased its inventory levels from a horrendous peak of 42 percent of sales in the first quarter of 1975 to less than 25 percent of sales a little over two years later. The reduction of over $300 million in inventory had a substantial positive impact on NCR's balance sheet improvement program. Philips Industries was carrying $65 million in inventories in 1974 but was only carrying $40 million by 1978, even though sales in fiscal 1978 were $46 million above the level of four years earlier.

Bucking the Trend. Bucking the trend in the adverse steel industry is exactly what Nucor Corporation has been doing over the last few years. At a time when most of the steelmakers are moaning over the erosion of profits and the loss of market share to the European and Japanese steel manufacturers, Nucor is setting earnings records. There are several reasons for the company's superior profit performance. First, Nucor's entire work force is nonunionized. Its wages are competitive with unionized mills, but its workers' productivity is greater. Nucor employs a bonus or incentive system, whereby workers who exceed specific production goals can receive bonuses that often exceed 60 to 70 percent of their base pay. The incentive plan is highly conducive to productivity. It takes Nucor less than five man-hours to produce a ton of steel. This total includes clerical, sales, and management personnel. If we include only hourly workers, labor input is under three man-hours. The result: it cost the company about $45 to produce a ton of steel in 1977 versus about $115 for the rest of the industry.

Overhead Value Analysis

Overhead value analysis (OVA) is a way of extending the one-shot, cost-reduction actions of the emergency stage. In traditional value analysis, a study team determines what a selected product or item must accomplish, and then either develops a better, lower-cost design or develops an engineering method of accomplishing the same results without sacrificing the required level of quality. OVA simply adapts the same principle to overhead functions and their costs. It provides an efficient mechanism for scrutinizing rapidly and in an organized way all the many thousands of activities that make up overhead, identifying all the areas where cuts can safely be made and pointing to the right cost/benefit trade-offs where quality is concerned. Overhead staff that are lacking in technical competence, are poorly managed, and are not directed toward specific profit improvement objectives are a pure cost drag. Overhead staff that perform routine but necessary functions are cost-neutral. Overhead staff that are technically competent, properly managed, and directed toward specific profit improvement objectives are cost-positive. Overhead staff can thus be a cost drag, cost-neutral, or cost-positive. It is a function of management to make the staff effective.

MARKETING MANAGEMENT IN THE STABILIZATION STAGE

Marketing management in the stabilization stage is part of the overall settling down and refinement process that characterizes this stage of the turnaround. Marketing was the third leg on the stool during the emergency stage, after finance and operations. In this stage, marketing becomes the second leg on the stool after operations. This shift is exactly what happened at White Consolidated after it acquired Westinghouse's losing appliance division and conducted an emergency cost turnaround. For the first time the company began vigorously advertising its White-Westinghouse appliances, spending nearly $1 million in 1977's first quarter, versus $35,000 for all of 1976. WCI, now the third-largest appliance maker after General Electric Co. and Whirlpool Corp., also became aggressive in pricing its products.

Marketing management in this stage concentrates on profit improvement strategies like these:

- Careful targeting of efforts toward high-return, high-growth segments
- Continued protection of current franchises
- Stabilization of expense; commitments to maximize profits

- Investment only as market opportunities dictate
- Shift of mix of higher-profit product categories
- Addition of products very selectively in controlled stages of commitment

Some cost-reduction strategies include:

- Restriction of objectives and of targets for the company's marketing program to areas where risk of loss is low
- Minimization of the marketing payroll
- Subcontracting of nonrecurring functions
- Sharing of costs whereever possible
- Selection of the most cost-effective marketing techniques

The tactics utilized in pricing, products, promotion, and place (distribution) issues are shown below.

Pricing

Pricing is an area that needs refinement during the stabilization stage. The problem of underpricing, relative to one's competition, should have been cleared up in the emergency stage. Clearing that problem up still leaves two areas that need additional attention. The first is the relative pricing among the mix of product offerings. My experience has been that pricing in the mix may be a victim both of historic relationships in the industry and of outright neglect. The real losers were eliminated earlier, but some products may only be marginal because of problems in relative mix pricing. Many companies that set out deliberately to rectify these mix irregularities often have outstanding success. That process requires boldness and industry leadership. It doesn't require that you be the biggest company in your industry, but rather that you know what you are doing and why. If you have sound reasons for selective increases, and maybe even for a few decreases, the industry pricing practices will adjust unless someone is an irrational price leader. I saw this work in the steel industry, the valve industry, and a number of other cases. The overall result is that the average pricing yield will increase and some products will pull out of the marginal category into passing status.

The second factor that must be resolved is the industry pricing practices in regard to customers. One of the most striking research findings is that the vast majority of industrial firms believe that their prices are either about average for their industry or above average. Only 7 percent believe their prices are below average. These findings, based on a sample of 220 companies, were obtained by Richard Skinner.[7] See Appendix Table Q for details. The implications of this apparently illogical pricing attitude are far reaching. One consequence of this attitude is that whether different industries enjoy reasonable or tight profit margins may depend on historical factors over which the present generation of marketing managers seemingly has little control.

The practical application of all this is that turnaround firms may have to take the lead in increasing the whole structure of their industry's pricing. Albeit such a move requires analysis and a lot of guts, it also has a high payout. I've participated in two companies that have successfully made such a move. A third is Mark Controls, where Gary MacDougal changed the pricing structure of the valve industry. When costs started to escalate rapidly in 1974, MacDougal insisted that customers bear some of the increase on contracts already made and also demanded escalator clauses be included in all new contracts. "Had we been in the industry longer," says MacDougal, "we couldn't change the pricing terms of the contracts." MacDougal's success is typical of that of turnaround leaders who wind up doing what everybody else says cannot be done. They eliminate the reasons why things cannot be done and push until they are accomplished. In another example John J. Byrne, CEO of troubled Government Employees Insurance Company, exploited the widespread fear that his company might go under, in order to wring maximum rate increases out of state insurance regulators. In 1976, for example, the regulators granted GEICO a 38.5 percent average rate increase, compared with a 21.5 percent increase for the industry as a whole.

Products

Products underwent a major pruning in the emergency stage to eliminate sure losers and cash flow sinks. In the stabilization stage, the meat-ax is put away and the scalpel comes out for a refining process. Instead of looking at product lines, managers now scrutinize individual products. Typical of such a process is that which occurred at Mark Controls. The company set up a computerized costing system that calculated the precise cost and profit margin for each of the 15,000 products that the company sold. Since then, about 15 percent of those products have been dropped from the company's line because they were insufficiently profitable. MacDougal also shifted the company's product line toward those markets that he thought would grow most quickly.

Product Strategy. In addition to the strategy of taking a closer look at products, the basic product line strategies in the stabilization stage include: eliminating marginal products, pushing a more profitable mix, exploiting existing products, and making some modest product-line extensions where low risks are perceived. Typical of moves to eliminate marginal products are those of Colt Industries. Colt abandons cyclical products that don't emerge from normal cycles on a profitable basis. A few years ago when the company's large power transformers proved cyclically unprofitable, Colt quickly dropped the line and focused instead on smaller-distribution transformers.

The company has also gotten rid of a raft of products simply because they failed to meet the criteria of market leadership. In machine tools, Colt's Pratt & Whitney Div. (unrelated to United Technologies Corp.'s aircraft-engine subsidiary of the same name) dropped profile milling machines, reamers, and gage blocks in order to concentrate on producing lathes for medium-size job shops, a segment of the market where the division had a much stronger position.

New Products. Because of the fascination of new products, a surprising number of troubled companies move into new fields as a source of growth, without fully analyzing and exploiting the potential of their existing product lines. Yet building profitable add-on volume in existing lines may offer the lowest risk and highest potential return. This is particularly true in businesses that have unused production capacity (a common situation in troubled companies) and that need only a modest amount of new working capital for expansion. Companies that set out to exploit their existing products find their major opportunities in two areas: selective marketing strategy and profit improvement.

One company that earlier made the mistake of ignoring existing product potential, and that now is returning to its brand names is Warnaco, Incorporated. Warnaco, Inc., one of the nation's largest apparel manufacturers, learned a painful lesson about the troubles that can beset a company when it starts taking its major brand names in vain. The company owns some of the strongest names in the garment business, including Hathaway (men's dress shirts), Puritan (men's sport shirts), and White Stag (men's and women's sportswear). But a few years ago, when Warnaco introduced a host of new apparel products, it did not market them through its major brand name divisions.

After record profits in 1973, Warnaco's performance steadily deteriorated. Though sales grew almost 40 percent to $393 million by 1976, the company showed a staggering $24 million loss that year. Although trimming product lines has kept the company's revenues relatively flat ever since 1976, with its return to its brand names, Warnaco is now back to profitability.

Exploiting Existing Products. Exploiting existing products inevitably brings up the question of product life cycle. The blind acceptance of the product life cycle concept is for amateurs only. The real world, where hard-nosed decisions are made and behavior governs outcome, is replete with products that have been given a premature burial to the detriment of the undertaker (corporation). As Roy Woodman says:

> I don't give quite as much credit to life cycles in products as maybe other people would. My experience has been that a product will be on the downside of the life cycle if you convince yourself it is. And you've got to prevent people from doing that. In other words, if you are convinced that sales are going to slide on any given product 10 percent a year and it is going out of business in three years, then it is going out of business.[8]

Di Giorgio Corporation off-loaded its losers and began concentrating on exploiting existing product lines that showed promise. It sought to capitalize on Di Giorgio's successes in food processing and wholesaling by injecting marketing know-how into its other companies' operations and by building brand recognition for its products. Never known for its marketing prowess, Di Giorgio recruited more than a dozen marketing stalwarts from Procter & Gamble, Bristol-Myers, and Consolidated Foods. When Chairman Robert Di Giorgio said, "You can't grow profitably unless you market intelligently," he sounded almost like a convert to a new religion.[9]

Another product strategy is product line extension, that is, adding new products to existing customers, markets, etc. The urge to increase volume so as to utilize plant and marketing facilities and personnel more economically frequently causes a company to add new products to a line. How far the combined selling of products may be extended economically depends on several factors. If these new products appeal to similar consumer groups, sell through the same channels, move through the same markets, and require equal amounts and similar kinds of selling efforts, adding them may be profitable. But a company should move slowly because there are many traps in this seemingly simple volume-building effort. Subtle differences in customer groups, channels, markets, or selling activities can create substantial management problems. What may seem to be an advantage of more complete utilization of facilities and personnel can, in fact, be offset by the difficulties of training salesmen to sell a different type or a larger number of products.

Promotion

Promotion activities are refined and modestly upgraded during the stabilization stage. Just as the stabilization marketing efforts in the product area concentrated on the winners, so should promotion efforts be conducted by winners and concentrate on winning products and accounts. You'll probably find a grossly out-of-balance situation in a troubled company emerging from the emergency stage. It's not uncommon to be carrying a large number of unproductive salespeople, selling low-profit items to low-purchase-level customers. Just how serious and wasteful this problem can become will be graphically illustrated by the following cases.

Weak Salesmen. I was asked by the CEO of a medium-size financial services firm to help turn around its direct sales force after the parent had emerged from its emergency stage. There were numerous problems and many solutions, but among the most striking features that I found was the sales distribution of the 300 salesmen in the field. It was a classic case of the 20/80 law and a case highly susceptible to the ABC rating scheme. The actual percent-of-sales breakdown by groups of fifty salesmen is shown in Table 20-3.

TABLE 20-3
Distribution of Sales Revenue by Salesmen Group

Sales group	*Percent of total sales*
Group A:	
Top 50 salesmen	61
2nd 50 salesmen	21
Total Group A	82
Group B:	
3rd 50 salesmen	9
4th 50 salesmen	5
Total group B	14
Group C	
5th 50 salesmen	3
6th 50 salesmen	1
Total group C	4
Total 300 salesmen	100

Note: Company name withheld due to confidentiality requirements.

TABLE 20-4
Matrix of Salesman Income versus Likelihood to Raid

Income	*Very likely*	*Likely*	*Not likely*	*Not raider*	*Total*
0–5,000	5	8	21	31	65
5–10,000	4	12	45	29	90
10–15,000	11	20	30	19	80
15–20,000	25	10	3	2	40
20,000 plus	20	3	2	0	25

Note: Company name withheld due to confidentiality requirements.

I determined, after study, that 150 salesmen had to be dropped (many were part-time anyway). I won't go into the multitudinous reasons, but the head of the sales subsidiary fought the move vigorously. He didn't fancy having only 150 troops compared to 300 troops. His biggest argument was that the 150 dropped salesmen would raid the captive mutual funds and insurance policy holders. To find out if that were true, I conducted a survey of the sales force based on a questionnaire filled out by the first-line supervisors and reviewed by regional managers. One of the more striking findings was the correlation of the likelihood of raiding with the income of the raider. The results shown in Table 20-4 clearly show that low-income salesmen were very unlikely to raid, while the higher-income salesmen were likely to raid. The low-income raiders would probably be ineffective in their efforts and, thus were not a source of concern. Armed with all the evidence, the CEO, the VP Marketing, and I spent a whole day out of the office coming to terms. The sales force was reduced over six months time. Each manager had fewer bodies to worry about, the malcontents and losers were eliminated, and expenses were cut. The sales subsidiary went from a $250,000 loss in the previous year to a $300,000 profit and continued to be profitable. More surprisingly, to some people at least, overall revenues increased 20 percent rather than declining 10 percent, as expected by the "soothsayers."

Directing Selling Effort. In my business career, I have seen this case just mentioned repeated time and again with predictable results. The lesson is clear that a company must concentrate on the strong. This general principle may be extended to the effective use of salesmen's time in terms of both product promotion and customer accounts.

Some estimates have placed the average sales-call cost for industrial companies at approximately $75, and it appears that one of the most

TABLE 20-5
Product Line Productivity Analysis

Product category	*Total sales $ millions*	*Company sales, %*	*Company contributed margin, %*	*Company selling effort, %*	*Ratio of $ cont. margin to $ selling effort**
A	$ 6	15.0	23.1	18.0	8.33
B	4	10.0	12.3	17.0	4.70
C	16	40.0	36.9	25.0	9.60
D	2	5.0	9.2	14.0	4.21
E	12	30.0	18.5	26.0	4.61
Totals	$40	100.0	100.0	100.0	6.50

*Total direct selling effort equals $2 million

pressing challenges facing today's marketing executive is the achievement of adequate market coverage without "pricing" the direct sales force out of existence. Selling effort must be directed toward those product and customer segments that produce the highest contribution to the firm. Table 20-5 shows how these concepts can be married to produce a product-line productivity analysis that can be used to make decisions about promotion effort concentration. Table 20-5 indicates that product line E could be a candidate for some combination of price-increase or selling-reduction effort. Profiling your promotion efforts in a similar

TABLE 20-6
Account Productivity Report
(Targeted and nontargeted)

Customer account category	*Number of calls*	*Calls, %*	*Sales dollar value, $ millions*	*Sales, %*
Targeted accounts:				
1	70	11.2	$26.0	5.8
2	94	15.1	96.0	21.3
3	366	58.7	284.4	63.0
4	42	6.7	8.6	1.9
5	52	8.3	36.0	8.0
Subtotal targeted	624	100.0	$451.	100.0

fashion for advertising, sales promotions, and distributors can point the direction toward practical improvements.

Place (Distribution)

Making place (distribution) decisions in the stabilization stage continues to be a refinement process. John Byrne, CEO of Government Employees' Insurance Company, brought the company through its emergency stage with meat-ax cuts. For example, after only a week at GEICO, Byrne announced that the company would hand in its license to sell insurance in New Jersey—and not renew 250,000 policies on which the company was losing $30 million a year. Soon after, Byrne made a similar move in Massachusetts. In GEICO's stabilization stage, Byrne made some additional refinements.

> Byrne also did away with a computerized system that allowed policyholders to renew their insurance coverage without providing any new information, even on matters that would increase the cost of insurance, such as a change of cars or a recent traffic accident. When Byrne required such current information to be submitted on renewals, he found that GEICO was underpricing 9% of its renewal policies. When those were repriced, some 400,000 policyholders on which GEICO was losing money decided to get their insurance elsewhere. "For a year and a half it was like a two-minute drill of a football game around here," says Byrne. "Now we're back working on the basis of blocking and tackling."[10]

A customer account-productivity report, similar to the product-productivity report mentioned earlier, can be of substantial assistance in directing a company's sales-promotion efforts to the highest yield accounts. An example of such a report is shown in Table 20-6. Targeted account sales in customer category 3 have produced 63 percent of the salesman's total sales. The other customer account categories have a much lower percentage of productive calls. Also sales-to-customer account categories 1, 4, and 5 are substantially below the dollar commitment value. If such a pattern does not hold for the entire region, the problem may be isolated at the individual-salesman level. By comparing percentage of total calls with percentage of total sales a field sales manager can obtain an initial warning as to whether a salesman is allocating his time properly and/or whether a product category's other marketing mix elements, e.g., pricing or product redesign, need investigation. These types of profiling can be extremely useful in developing profit improvement results in turnaround companies during the stabilization stage. The general principle in the stabilization stage is to develop the strong and eliminate the weak.

HUMAN RESOURCES MANAGEMENT IN THE STABILIZATION STAGE

The major human resources management issues faced during the stabilization stage of the turnaround are:

1. Improving the capabilities of your organization by improving the people mix
2. Dealing with organizational conflicts and the centralization/decentralization problem
3. Implementing compensation programs that support the turnaround effort
4. Getting people to think profit

These efforts are in addition to the motivational concerns covered in more detail in Chapter 16.

Improving the People Mix

Improving the people mix means off-loading personnel who cannot or will not support your turnaround effort, and spotting willing and able winners who will rise to the challenge. During the emergency stage, the emphasis on staff reductions was largely a numbers game. Although I do not advocate across-the-board, meat-ax approaches, at times they may be necessary. Functional cuts are hardly the meat-ax approach but are certainly not the fine-tuned incisions of a brain surgeon's scalpel. During the emergency stage, you've probably gotten to know your executive group closely, along with key staff members. Your emphasis during the stabilization stage should be on pushing your people standards as far down the organization as possible. Like a pebble dropped in a pond, the amplitude of your efforts unreinforced will decrease to ineffectiveness at a distance from the source.

The Executive Group. You have to start by making performance decisions about your executive group, and then you must ensure that high standards of achievement are pushed down to every layer of the organization. In all likelihood, the executive group purge was completed in the emergency stage. If you have not spotlighted your executive group sufficiently or if you have some marginal people whom you decided to test out, now is the time to make your move. Never accept poor performance from your executive group, and accept mediocre performance for only a short period. Clean out your executive group and bring in the needed skills and motivation to fill the gaps where necessary .

After you shape up your executive group, two other actions are necessary. First, you must establish meaningful standards of performance and, second, you must take direct action to ensure that the performance spotlight is put on every layer of the organization.

Performance Standards. The standards for profit center managers are obviously tied to the substantial improvements required in their operations. I have found that leaving them entirely to their own devices in achieving these standards, using the existing mix of people, can be insufficient in a tightly scheduled turnaround effort. It is difficult to transmit your sense of urgency to the typical manager. There just aren't that many turnaround-oriented people around. For that reason, profit improvement and people improvement, at the rate at which you want them achieved, mean hands-on involvement by the top man. Even though your key people may make all the right noises, you've got to make it happen. This means they have to be led, pushed, dragged, and even badgered into making the necessary moves as rapidly and as decisively as you know is required by the situation.

The philosophy that I've seen work best is what I call the "hit 'em high, hit 'em low" method. "Hit 'em high" means that your emergency plan and your stabilization plan must set attainable but significant improvement goals for the company. Let your key people take part in formulating these goals. They also have to tell you how they are going to achieve them. This is where the timidity starts to creep in. Make sure that their operational plans are tough enough and decisive enough to reach their goals. Accomplishing that still isn't enough because, in the emergency stage and the stabilization stage, you'll have to be on top of them at all times. Now, how does that relate to people?

Hands-On People Decisions. You've got to hit your organization low in the people department. You've got to use hands-on methods to ensure that marginal people are weeded out. It's going to take constant preaching, beseeching, and impeaching, but after a while they'll get the idea. A sales-force example is a case in point. The head of the sales subsidiary had to be forced to weed out his men and swallow the medicine that turned his subsidiary around. From time to time you'll run into profit center executives who will want to go further than is necessary, but for the most part that is not the case. Open resistance and defiance are not customary and should not be tolerated; valid arguments, however, must be listened to. Remember, only your constant pressure to weed out the marginal people will get the job done.

In much the same manner, your hands-on attention to bringing in capable people will be required. Weeding out marginal people in the stabilization stage will create gaps that must be filled. Each gap is a good opportunity to increase your organizational capabilities. Before filling these gaps, from the outside, make sure that people currently in the organization have a fair shot at bettering themselves. A turnaround effort usually creates a lot of voids that need filling. You'll usually find that there is a small core of motivated people who are "turned-on" by the challenge of a turnaround. As Robert Brown says, "They'll work their butts off for you because they see the turnaround as a great opportunity to prove their abilities."[11] Be on the lookout for these people, use them to the fullest, and reward them for their efforts.

The important ingredients in filling people gaps are technical competence and attitude. Of the two, attitude is far more important at this stage of a turnaround. This doesn't mean that technical competence is forgotten. You usually don't make your number two marketing man your vice president of finance, but you do have to stay open to cross-functional changes and to giving youthful or older producers their chance to run. The main requirement is results, and results may come from surprising places. I think every turnaround leader is surprised at how a handful of people become fired up with enthusiasm and sparked by the challenge of a crisis situation.

Using experienced insiders is preferable to bringing in outsiders, but promoting from within is not a hard-and-fast policy of turnaround companies. Use insiders when you can, but go to the outside if you must. Outsiders will not be tainted by the prior experience of the declining years but on the other hand they will lack knowledge in detail about the company. It will take them longer to get up a head of steam. They will need some coaching and reinforcement. On the other hand, fresh insights, objectivity, and prior experience can well make up for the other problems in an experienced pro. Bring in proven performers only. Either get people you already know personally, or get unknowns who are excited about the turnaround. Turnarounds are not that hard to sell to good people seeking a challenge. If they have been through a turnaround before and have a realistic view of the circumstances, so much the better.

In improving your people mix, I've found two techniques of substantial value. First, you must insist upon top-to-bottom ranking of personnel within an area or function. "Who is my best accountant, who is my worst? Is the worst still retainable?" Quantitative rankings or English verbiage only serves to muddy the waters at this juncture. Later, all the niceties of organizational and personnel development can be brought in, but at this point the company is still in a crude Darwinian personnel situation. Insist on rankings, realizing that you'll have to question and modify the initial results.

Second, you must identify the successor in each key area of the company. This should, but may not, fall out of your ranking approach. For one reason or another, the turmoil of a turnaround is going to cause a lot of situations characterized by the question, "Who's going to run it now?" Within functions or across functions, you had better have the answers in mind ahead of time. In one case, I chopped a seventy-person data-processing department down to seventeen people in two years. The department's line of succession was always clear cut. The end result was that the department wound up being run by a young, cooperative, shirt-sleeves former systems analyst with plenty of smarts. When I started my effort, the department was run by an older, uncooperative, pompous vice president, replete with private secretary. We found we could do the job with far less expenditure. The layers of fat in this case were peeled away one at a time.

Dealing with Organizational Conflicts and Centralization/ Decentralization

Organizational conflicts and centralization/decentralization problems have to be resolved in a company proceeding through the stabilization stage. The centralization/decentralization problem must be resolved first before organizational conflicts can be resolved. Generally, in a turnaround situation the locus of power is highly centralized. The needs of an organization for unified direction in solving its obvious problems take precedence over the vaunted independence of the functional or divisional heads. Centralization is the byword in the emergency stage. In the stabilization stage, the age-old debate between the two forms begins to take shape again.

In smaller fair-size companies, the centralization of services such as purchasing, accounting, data processing, personnel, etc., usually continues through the stabilization stage, but profit center managers are given back some of their autonomy for decision making. Their overall goals and objectives, while ostensibly a cooperative effort, are still imposed by the turnaround leader. There is close and frequent followup to insure that these goals are met. The profit center managers continue to be in the grip of centralized hands-on management, and that usually means the top man. This state of affairs can continue in companies that make the Fortune 1000 list, but it seldom remains that way in the larger firms.

Organizational Conflict. Closely related to the problem of centralization is the one of organizational conflict among the functional heads of a company or division. Most fledgling management men expect a business to run smoothly, be well coordinated, and have a minimum of internal friction or conflict. But businesses do not run smoothly. In business, conflict exists. Moreover, it exists between certain organizational elements, regardless of the nature of the business. For example, the man responsible for sales would like to sell everything to everybody, whereas the man responsible for credit would like to permit sales only to customers with top credit ratings. This is a natural conflict, because the salespeople are charged with the responsibility of selling the most products at the best price, whereas the credit people have the responsibility of determining whether the customer can pay for the merchandise.

Another natural conflict exists between the people responsible for sales and the people responsible for production. For example, sales might like to have the product in a wide variety of colors, styles, and models, whereas production would like to have as little variety as possible. This conflict is easy to understand when we remember that variety increases sales but reduces production efficiency. A second natural conflict between sales and production lies in delivery schedules, because salespeople would like to have every order filled instantly, whereas the production people have to fit each new order into existing schedules. In every organization still other natural conflicts arise between quality control and production, between engineering and sales, and between engineering and production.

Every company exhibits evidence of functional orientation and bias. Rarely, for example, do salesmen or sales managers have kind things to say about the production team, and production people and their managers rarely have kind things to say about their sales force. Each group believes that without its contribution, the company would have been out of business long ago, and each is convinced that if it weren't for the ridiculous demands of those other groups, the company would be far better off.

Conflict Solutions. Before any corporation can have external success, it has to achieve some degree of internal tranquillity. The magnitude and direction of internal conflict have to be recognized and dealt with. If conflict has been rampant within the organization for some time, department heads are probably ready to have some sort of order and stability imposed from above. Few status quo leaders take the decisive move that Glenn Penisten, president of American Microsystems, took in ordering his whole executive group to leave their offices in separate buildings and move into a set of offices near his own. After spending day and night together in the same conference room for weeks on end, they came away a united management team, each having a much better understanding of the others' problems.

One way or another, the turnaround leader must resolve these conflicts in a decisive manner. The greatest weapon in the hands of the turnaround leader is the real or imagined external threat. Focusing on a competitor's activities can get the whole organization pulling in the same direction. Production people will happily digest and attack a competitor's probable production techniques. Salespeople will happily analyze the competitor's marketing techniques for their strengths and weaknesses. During this analytical and introspective process, polarized functions will be united for a common purpose. Then, too, during this process internal conflict can be made to look like a form of corporate treachery. Either of two arguments—the competitors are hot on our heels, or we've got to catch up—can be used to refocus any functional outbursts. The tendency to magnify competitors' strengths has to be controlled. Too often we view competitors with an awe that is unjustified. They may view us the same way.

Implementing Compensation Programs that Support a Turnaround Effort

Implementing compensation programs that support a turnaround effort is the primary direct motivational tool of the stabilization stage. I go by the concept that "if you pay peanuts, you'll only hire monkeys." I believe that a few highly qualified people, well-compensated, can be more effective than an army of also-rans. One friend of mine once had an investment management department of forty people with average performance. The parent in a turnaround situation forced such austerities on him that he quit, saying he couldn't run with twenty people what he ran before with twice that number. Yet a few years later, in another situation he managed the same large sum of money, using only six people, and had outstanding results. His people were proven performers and were very highly compensated. He paid up to twice the going rate, but his overall costs were lower, his people were motivated; and his results were outstanding. This example is a specific case carried to an extreme, perhaps, but the general principle is still valid. Run with as lean a staff as possible, and pay them well.

Incentive Tied to Targets. In a turnaround situation, you are stressing activities that probably have a short-term focus—for example, staff reduction, inventory realignment, and asset disposal. The trick is to gear the incentive program to those activities, that is, to judge the operating groups on a number of factors, only one of which is profitability. Extraordinary items that are under the control of management—for example, the selling of certain government contracts or the disposal of certain parts of the business—should be taken out of the formula. In one company the traditional type of bonus formula permits each unit to provide for incentive payments in its budget so that it can, in fact, earn its own rewards. The leader works with the manager of each group to determine an appropriate-size bonus pool for his key people. This amount is included in the manager's financial plan for the year, and is accrued as certain events occur or targets are achieved. Thus, for example, 20 percent of the bonus fund might be credited to the accrual when certain staff reductions are accomplished; perhaps another 20 percent is credited when certain unprofitable accounts are closed or made profitable; 30 percent is added when a warehouse consolidation program is completed. Tying incentives to short-term objectives makes a lot of sense and reinforces everyone's desire to get things done.

If you are in a division turnaround, your division's compensation should not depend on corporate performance during a turnaround. For example, many older plans have formulas that limit incentive-award pools to some percentage of income after taking out a stated return on stockholder equity. In a turnaround, many things have to be accomplished that may not relate to near-term shareholder interests. Such plans tend to be written from the top down and you will probably find that your incentive program should be developed from the bottom up. This system, like any other, can be prostituted and made to become a means of overpaying fat cats at the top. The temptation to do this should be resisted by any fair-minded CEO who knows what drives people and organizations.

Getting People to Think Profit

Getting people to think profit is separate from, but related to, motivation. People don't automatically think about the cost of the things they waste, especially when they are surrounded by evidence of waste. An employee may be quite concerned about where the dollars go when he is spending his own hard-earned money. But his employer's money is another matter; to him there seems to be a never-ending supply of that. No wonder our business bankruptcy is so high.

If an employee were to leave and open up his own restaurant, he would see to it that his people worked diligently at all times, that his lights were turned off at closing time, that employees weren't putting too much soap in the dishwasher, that the food portions were controlled, and that the quality of the food was up to his standard of excellence. The turnaround leader's task is to instill this same concern in each employee and to keep him from feeling like a small cog in a very large machine.

Communication, participative goal-setting, and visual demonstrations all have a place in profit-consciousness. To create real profit excitement, the turnaround leader has to open up new lines of communication. One envelope manufacturing company vividly demonstrated waste control by collecting all the wasted paper and envelopes from a day's run and suspending this waste from the ceiling in a fishnet. A contest was held and Thanksgiving turkeys were offered as prizes for the three employees who came closest to guessing the dollar value of this one day's scrap if it were converted into finished product.

IN SUMMARY

In summary, the stabilization stage is a time to:

- Take a hard and fresh look at everything the company is doing—from cash management to cost accounting; from purchasing to production; from design to distribution—with an eye toward making significant improvements in efficiency and effectiveness.
- Make basic changes in measuring management performance. Make sure the profit center concept does not lead to decisions that will affect individual units favorably but have a dreadful effect on the company as a whole.
- Establish financial and nonfinancial control procedures, including new market forecasting systems which, in effect, serve as early-warning systems for potential problems.
- Finally, look outside and try very hard to see yourself as others see you. Don't become complacent. Don't become ingrown. Don't fail to ask yourself the big, hard questions like:
  —Why is it that competitors can make products similar to ours and sell them for substantially lower prices?
  —Why did we lose a particular order? Was it because the customer was stupid, or was it because we were not as good as we thought we were?
  —How did our service compare with that of our competitors? Did we think it was good simply because our people said it was good?

Become more interested in what your customers tell you about your company than in what your own people tell you about the company. If you do these things correctly, you'll be positioned to return to normal growth, the subject of the next chapter.

REFERENCES

[1]Interview with Jeffrey Chanin, former executive vice president, Daylin Corp., Los Angeles, Calif., February 1978.

[2]Interview with Robert Di Giorgio, chairman, Di Giorgio Corp., San Francisco, Calif., February 1978.

[3]Glenn E. Penisten, speech before Corporate Planners Association, San Francisco, Calif., Jan. 19, 1978.

[4]Interview with Roy Woodman, president, International Video Corp., Sunnyvale, Calif., February 1978.

[5]Interview with Gary Friedman, former vice chairman, Itel Corp., San Francisco, Calif., February 1978.

[6]Interview with Glenn E. Penisten, president, American Microsystems, Santa Clara, Calif., February 1978.

[7]Richard Skinner, "Pricing Strategies to Cope with Inflation," in B. Atkin and R. Skinner (eds.), *How British Industry Prices* (London: Industrial Market Research Limited, 1975), p. 72.

[8]Woodman, interview, February 1978.

[9]Di Giorgio: A Food Processor Pushes Its Name Brands," *Business Week*, Oct. 9, 1978, pp. 70, 75.

[10]GEICO: Insuring Its Profit Picture by Spreading Out and Slowing Down," *Business Week*, Oct. 16, 1978, p. 182.

[11]Interview with Robert C. Brown, president, R. C. Brown & Co., San Francisco, Calif., February 1978.

21
THE RETURN-TO-GROWTH STAGE

The mistaken notion that only errors of commision involve risks is too readily accepted. . . . Failure to initiate action aimed at growth is a far more serious failure than running slightly over on expense budget in order to bring in a needed program.[1]

Richard S. Sloma

THE BASICS OF THIS STAGE

The yearning to return to a growth posture is deep within the bones of most executives. In companies that have recently been through the trauma of a turnaround, this return must be balanced against the realities and limitations of a recently sick patient. Like a human on the mend after a serious operation, a corporation may outwardly have the appearance of total recovery without having its old capabilities intact. The patient may look well, but he cannot go out immediately and run the back-to-back 100-meter sprints. In fact, it would be downright detrimental if he chose to do so. Instead, he must start training to return to his old form, and this training starts out slowly. By the end of the training period, the patient should be at or near the level of his previous abilities. At this stage of the turnaround, the corporation's primary objective is longer-range development, positioning the company for ten or fifteen years of future development. This development objective usually includes the following strategies:

1. The redeployment of assets from slow-growth areas to faster-growth areas in a way consistent with high margin and return-on-investment standards, thus closing strategic performance gaps
2. The positioning of the company's financial capabilities to support increased growth
3. The investment in internal operational capabilities to provide increased productivity and capacity
4. An increased emphasis on marketing that allows modest mar-

keting expansion through new customer markets, improved products, and some new products

5. A renewed emphasis on developing human resources by initiating both motivation and development programs

ASSET REDEPLOYMENT IN THE RETURN-TO-GROWTH STAGE

Asset redeployment in this stage of the turnaround consists mainly of redeploying assets to faster-growth/higher-return areas by off-loading poor return-on-investment operations and by making selective acquisitions. In cases where operations cannot easily be divested without incurring substantial write-offs, they are usually deemphasized or placed on a cash flow milking status. Assets employed in working capital status should have been squeezed hard during the previous stages in the turnaround. Typical of an asset-redeployment program aimed at higher growth and higher returns is that begun at Foremost-McKesson, Incorporated, in 1977. One aim of that asset-redeployment program was to move the company into proprietary products and away from commodity-type products such as feed-grade whey, which is dependent on the corn crop and cattle market for profitability. Foremost currently is concentrating on products which give it control over its own destiny and which yield gross margins that are not at the mercy of nonmanagerial factors.

The direction makes sense for Foremost, which had stagnated in the distribution business, with its accompanying thin margins. At the same time, the company reorganized operations into profit centers and substituted return on investment for return on sales as the primary gauge of performance. Return on sales is an inadequate measurement in the distribution business because it does not focus on the efficient use of assets. Applying return-on-asset analysis, Foremost discovered that operations employing $199 million of assets and generating sales of $523 million earned only $1 million in net profit. The company started disposing of some of those operations.

Most, if not all, of the acquisitions made at this stage of the turnaround consist of successful companies. There are notable exceptions to the rule. In a move that appeared to be a classic case of overpaying for assets, Allegheny-Ludlum acquired ailing Chemetron Corporation, which was selling for half of book value in the market. Allegheny-Ludlum won a bidding contest that boosted the price to book value, leaving many to doubt A-L's move. But A-L moved quickly to turn around its new acquisition. It:

- Absorbed Chemetron's money-losing Tube Turns Div. into its specialty steel operations, slashed overhead, and turned a profit.

- Swapped part of Chemetron's industrial gas business (about $80 million in sales) for a one-third ownership of Liquid Air Corp. of North America, which boasts $350 million in annual sales and pays a generous dividend.
- Found three bidders for Chemetron's pigment business who were willing to pay "well over book value." Allegheny has other Chemetron chemical divisions on the block as well.
- Sold its own Jacobsen Mfg. Co., a maker of lawn mowers and tractors, to Textron, Inc., to raise cash to pay down some debt.

Allegheny-Ludlum bought Chemetron with a turnaround plan in mind and turned a loser into a winner. More typical of turnaround company acquisitions are those that were made by Memorex Corporation during its return-to-growth stage. Memorex chose to grow by internal as well as external moves and by this plan currently makes one or two selected acquisitions each year. In 1977, for example, for $8.6 million the company acquired Business Systems Technology, Inc., a manufacturer of peripheral equipment for small business computers. It then bought Lencor International, which makes CFI brand memory products, for $7.6 million. The $14 million purchase in 1978 of Telex Corp.'s marketing subsidiary in Europe strengthened Memorex's position overseas and added $7 million worth of equipment to its lease base.

My advice on making acquisitions at this stage of the turnaround is:

- Be opportunistic and, if possible, concentrate your efforts on acquiring cash-rich, high-debt-capacity companies.
- Don't overreach, trying to make a marginal deal seem like a good deal just to be doing something.
- Be patient; there are thousands of deals, so wait for the ones that are ideally suited to you.
- Don't overleverage to make acquisitions.

Remember, the real value in an acquisition comes after the deal has been made and it's time to run the new company. Robert Brown says:

> I think there is real growth and there is window-dressing growth. To me, true growth is internal growth, not external growth. I give high marks for internal growth and nothing for external growth. The reason for that is, if you have enough financial horsepower and good custodial management, you can grow very quickly for a while by acquiring. At some point, you have to stop acquiring and you've got to start operating

> what you've got. The great darling of business a few years ago was a conglomerate run by a salesman with great external capabilities. He went out and bought a lot of companies, some good companies and some lousy companies. And when he put them all together, he couldn't make them work. When he ran out of money, he went bankrupt. Then they threw him out of there and got somebody to turn it around.[2]

A few years ago, as part of an acquisition, Hooker Industries acquired a business that had a strong market position in its industry. For the previous ten years, the business's sales volume had been steady with good profit margins, but the business had experienced an overall declining trend in total profits. The management had a clear but narrow vision of its business. The organization was technically competent and aggressive but, because of its narrow field of concentration, it had actually been losing market share. Management was oriented to current problems, with little concept of future goals or of the strategies to achieve them.

Within the organization, however, there was knowledge on which a bigger and more profitable future could be built. Moreover, there was desire for greater achievement. Immediately following the acquisition, meetings were held to familiarize the managers of the new division with long-range planning concepts and to help them develop these concepts in their business. Within a few months time, enthusiasm grew within the division for this approach to running its business. The managers raised their sights from yesterday's practices and performance, and focused on tomorrow's opportunities.

After ten years of no growth in sales volume, volume in the next five years increased at a rate of 14 percent yearly—doubling in that period and all a reflection of growth from within. Whereas for ten years profits had been declining slowly at a rate of 3.5 percent yearly, in the next five years profits almost tripled, increasing at a rate of 21 percent yearly.[3]

FINANCIAL MANAGEMENT IN THE RETURN-TO-GROWTH STAGE

Financial management in the return-to-growth stage of a turnaround is not as critically important as it was in the emergency and stabilization stages. In its approach and outlook, financial management in this stage of the turnaround more nearly resembles that of a normal company. The main financial management activities are:

1. The development of sound and creative financing schemes to support a modest acquisition program
2. The maintenance of tight financial disciplines throughout the company

3. The use of special techniques to forecast, isolate, and track development expenditures
4. The financial evaluation of strategic growth decisions using simple financial models

Creative Financing Schemes

Creative financing schemes will be necessary to support a company just coming through a turnaround, because cash resources will probably be short. I recommend internal development programs rather than external growth programs at the beginning of this stage of a turnaround. Opportunities-availability often takes precedence over timing in many turnaround situations. This situation usually leaves the CEO and his chief financial officer scrambling for leverage points in a cash-poor company whose products may not yet have regained market acceptance. Creative financing through workout arrangements can sometimes enable you to stretch beyond your apparent financial strength.

Typical of the creative approaches that can be applied is that used by two food wholesale executives that took over a struggling company and tripled its volume to $60 million in sales in two years. This growth was accomplished by taking over four wholesalers with a combined volume in the $40 million category. The wholesalers typically turned their inventory from twelve to eighteen times a year and earned a return on sales of 2 percent or better before taxes. Usually, the companies that were acquired were free of any debt because they never had any need of borrowing. One creative financing approach used was to utilize a maximum amount of debt secured by the inventories of the acquired firms. At the time the acquisitions were made, commercial lenders were willing to offer secured lending at an interest rate of 12 percent. This did reduce the pretax earnings of the acquisitions substantially, but as long as interest rates remained below 20 percent, the business broke even on its acquisitions. The final step in the strategy, however, was to make a public offering for equity money, thereby retiring the debt in order to ensure that the acquisitor's earnings and return on equity positions were similar to those of other companies in the industry. Although this approach is risky, the entrepreneurs met with success by carefully timing their acquisitions, by leveraging, and by running the business efficiently.

Tight Financial Discipline

The tight financial discipline that was established in the prior stages of the turnaround is maintained, but is usually decentralized in this stage. Successful turnaround companies focus on using capital efficiently, and they successfully fight margin deterioration in the face of growth pressures. What sets the outstanding performers apart is the discipline they exercise in this regard. This discipline includes constant attention to prices and costs.

It also includes rededication to the balance sheet and return on capital. It takes many forms, including building balance sheet performance factors into personal objectives and management incentive plans, setting objectives for increasing suppliers' warehousing of raw materials, expanding use of lockboxes and new remittance procedures to cut receivables, installing and enforcing highly selective guidelines for extending payables, and requiring higher hurdle rates for new capital investment while replacement costs were taken into account. The overall budgetary controls established earlier are expanded and enhanced.

Special Techniques

Special techniques to forecast, isolate, and track development expenditures are needed. I've found that most companies fail to recognize the total scope and cost of their development programs, which may be spread over one hundred departments or more. A good start at isolating these costs was recommended earlier in the "current/future" breakdown performed in the evaluation stage. Nearly every turnaround company in a rebuilding stage should be able to isolate development expenses. In addition to the operating-statement impact of development and sales growth, companies often fail to take into account the balance sheet, or working-capital effect of such growth.

Forecasting Working-Capital Requirements. The working-capital effect can best be forecast by using financial ratios to relate inventory, accounts receivable, general cash, and accounts payable to either average sales levels or marginal sales increases. In a hypothetical company how much inventory increase will be necessary to ensure that products are available? Use the inventory turnover ratio. If sales volume is $100 million, and inventory levels average $25 million, then inventory turns over four times a year (net sales divided by inventory). If the sales budget calls for a sales increase to $125 million, then inventory will have to increase by $6.25 million to $31.25 million.

Accounts receivable also can be expected to increase as sales volume increases. By using the day's receivables-outstanding ratio, one can estimate the increase that can be expected. If the hypothetical firm has $100 million in sales and average receivables of $11 million, it has a receivable collection period of 40 days [(accounts receivable divided by net sales) × 365]. If volume is increased by $25 million, receivables will increase by $2.75 million.

As sales increase, so does the amount of cash the company must have on hand for general operating purposes. This is usually expressed in the cash/sales ratio. If average cash balances of $10 million were needed to maintain a $100 million sales level, then $12.5 million would be needed if sales increased to $125 million.

Offsetting some of these increases is the fact that, as sales rise, so do accounts payable. The hypothetical firm has $8 million in payables of current sales level. These are measured in the same way as accounts receivable. If 36.5 days payables-outstanding is normal, a sales increase from $100 million to $125 million will increase payables by $2 million. To summarize, we find that an additional $9.5 million of working capital is necessary to support a $25 million increase in sales:

Cash	$ 2.50 million
Inventory	6.25
Accounts receivable	2.75
Accounts payable	(2.00)
TOTAL	$ 9.50 million

If the company pays 10.5 percent interest for short-term borrowing, then an additional expense of $1 million, pretax, should be considered in determining the cost of the sales increase. The financial planning that goes along with the sale planning must provide for the $9.5 million in extra funds. Otherwise, the firm may find that it doesn't have sufficient cash on hand to pay its current obligations. The increased cash flow from sales usually cannot be expected until one or two months after the goods are sold, and all the suppliers and employees must be paid before that time.

The LIFO Trap. Another management technique that has been used and abused by companies is the valuation of inventory by LIFO (Last-In-First-Out) means. The overall implications of such an approach have been misunderstood by many companies, and LIFO's use has actually hurt the overall position of troubled companies. For some companies, particularly larger ones, LIFO can indeed be very useful in an inflationary period. To determine their selling costs, LIFO firms apply the actual costs they are paying now to produce or purchase the goods they sell. They match current costs with current revenues—get rid of unreal inflationary inventory "profits." That's obviously good. LIFO is an effective way to reduce taxes and improve cash flow—this is important—in an inflationary environment.

But LIFO does something else that isn't good for many troubled companies. It creates an artificially low inventory valuation. At the time of the switchover, the firm's inventories in effect are frozen at the then-existing level. They are carried in "layers" of historical cost on the books. Increases in inventory, thereafter, are brought in as new layers. LIFO thus reduces, not only the income statement, but the balance sheet as well.

When a troubled company goes to the bank for a loan, the banker looks at the bottom line. In this case, he sees smaller profits at greater losses. He also sees a smaller net worth and smaller working capital. Thus, LIFO can have the effect of reducing a company's credit-worthiness. And credit is the lifeblood of a growing or troubled firm trying to keep up with increasing receivables, payables, and inventories. LIFO can be very rough on companies that are in volatile industries, where there are apt to be sharp run-ups and run-downs in inventory levels. Deferred tax has to be paid after the firm has grown from a very small firm and is in a higher tax bracket. If and when the business is sold, the tax finally comes due (though not if it's a tax-free exchange of stock).

Financial Modeling Techniques

Financial modeling techniques have gone through several periods of high expectations accompanied by low results in the last fifteen years. I advocate the use of simple models for overall financial planning at this stage of the turnaround. By keeping the model simple, that is, centered on eight to ten key variables at the most, top financial or general management has a useful tool for making strategic financial and operating decisions. I think a case can best illustrate my point. The company in this case history is a turnaround company that had reached the return-to-growth stage. It had cleaned up its balance sheet in the stabilization stage and had relatively low fixed-capital needs and a favorable debt/equity ratio at the outset; however, it was facing the potential threat of margin pressure. Also, it wanted to grow rapidly through entry into a new market segment.

The company knew that it could meet its capital needs if sales remained static. The problem was to expand volume rapidly and, at the same time, to increase earnings-per-share at a favorable rate, to avoid excessive debt, and to retain equity control. Therefore, in order to develop sound guidelines for financial decisions the company chose to test several alternative assumptions on rate of growth, profit margins, levels of working capital, and sources of additional financing. The first test case was based on the company's operating plan for the next five years. It contained these key assumptions:

- Sales would increase from $50 million in 1980 to $90 million in 1985.

- Profit margins would remain static at current level—8.5 percent of sales before interest and taxes.

- Current assets would remain at the 1980 level of 89 percent of sales, current liabilities at 14 percent of sales. The company's high current ratio had come from off-loading a number of losing businesses.

Running the financial model for the first case, the company found that it would need close to $40 million in additional equity and debt to finance growth. The company assumed that all new outside financing would be in the form of debt. Therefore, with equity increasing only by the amount of retained earnings after paying a dividend of $1 per share, the company estimated that it would have to take on $33.2 million in new debt. Based on this model:

- Earnings per share would rise from $2.10 to $3.12, an acceptable but not exciting growth.

- The debt/equity ratio would rise to 1.33, which was double the 0.67 that the company had set as its guideline.

- Interest coverage at 2.7 times and return on equity at 14.6 percent would be adequate.

To test the effect on using less leverage, the company reran the model on the assumption that the debt/equity ratio would be retained at 0.67, with additional capital being raised by selling common stock at fifteen times earnings. The result was to:

- Cut the increase in earnings per share by more than one-half

- Generate equity dilution of 29 percent, an unacceptable level, which would threaten control of the company

- Reduce return on equity to 12.2 percent

Strategic Decisions. These analyses led the company to four strategic decisions:

1. It decided to add new volume only if the volume carried a higher margin than the average for the company's current business.

2. It launched a major profit improvement program aimed at reducing purchasing and marketing costs and, thereby, improving margins on present products.

3. It placed top priority on reducing current assets, which at the time constituted over 85 percent of total assets. Simultaneously, the company decided to explore the possibility of increasing current liabilities to a level more in line with competition.

4. It decided to retain its target debt/equity ratio of 0.67 but to allow the ratio to rise to 1.0 if necessary to avoid dilution, provided: (1) the ratio were permitted at that level for a period of no more than one year; and (2) operating profit margins were retained at present levels or higher.

The company then reran the first case with one change: it assumed that current assets could be reduced from 89 percent of sales to 71 percent, and current liabilities increased from 14 to 20 percent. The results of this run were favorable:

- Earnings per share would rise by $2, a very favorable rate of growth.
- All new capital requirements could be met through long-term debt, and the debt/equity ratio would not rise above 0.57.
- All other financial indicators appeared favorable.

The results here suggested that, given these conditions, the company could afford to invest in new products that would provide growth beyond $5 million in volume.

The company ran a number of additional tests to check out and refine its conclusions. These runs dimensioned the problems the company faced in growth and highlighted the critical importance of both margin retention and control over working capital. Armed with this information—potential capital needs—the company was able to do a far better job of communicating corporate strategy for meeting its objectives. In addition, it consulted with its financial institutions well in advance of actual need, which strengthened its bargaining position.

OPERATIONS MANAGEMENT IN THE RETURN-TO-GROWTH STAGE

In addition to the operations-management practices outlined in the two previous chapters, three other dimensions characterize operations management in this stage.

1. The organization and classification of development projects so that they can be dealt with at the summary level by top management
2. The efficient investment of human and capital resources in internal and external development programs
3. The parceling out of overall company objectives to smaller managerial units using MBO (Management by Objectives) approaches

Development Expenditures

The organization and classification of development projects can be a complex task in medium and large companies. A $1 billion per year revenue company found out that it was spending $150 million per year on development projects. The company also found that personnel in more than one hundred departments were engaged either full- or part-time in such projects. These people were scientists, market researchers, product-development specialists, members of new-product teams, designers, engineers, planners, and others. In addition to the staff of the pure development departments, there were individuals throughout the organization whose tasks were largely future-oriented—even when their departments were primarily involved with current business. In fact, there were not many organizational units that did not look past the current-base businesses in some way.

Management also found that the people engaged in development work tended to be some of the best employees in the organization. A company seeking to grow internally must, as a general rule, employ higher-caliber personnel than those of a similar company that is content to maintain the status quo. And these higher-caliber people almost inevitably are assigned to development tasks. This makes the management of the development process more difficult because direction and tight control must be combined successfully with the creativity, imagination, and dedication of innovative people.

New Business Projects. One helpful way to deal with such problems of complexity and control is to categorize activities so that they can be dealt with at a summary level by top management, as well as at a detailed level by operating people. In the company in question, management classified *new-business* projects as follows:

1. Research in the pure exploratory sense. Research comprised only about 5 percent of the total development expenses. These

projects were designed to expand the frontiers of technological knowledge, in the hope of developing new materials and processes for commercial exploitation.

2. Product development. Projects in this category were in the early phases of the development cycle. A project entered this category when the first, crude specifications for the new product were delineated. The project was reclassified into the next category as soon as it began yielding any sales revenue from market tests, even though product-development activities continued concurrently with the initial marketing efforts.

3. Market introduction. This category included all the expenditures associated with launching a new product. The projects were at the loss-reversal stage in their cycle. Losses tended to increase in the early stages of market introduction, but if successful, the product subsequently became profitable.

Existing Business Products. Projects for existing businesses involved a more diverse and diffuse range of activities, but again some broad subcategories were designated:

- Product-modification projects designed to extend the life cycle of existing products by improving and expanding the line (for example, changing of product design, packaging, or flavors)
- Marketing-extension projects aimed at opening new market segments or new geographical areas to existing and modified products (for example, special promotional campaigns)
- Cost-engineering projects designed to improve processes, programs, and other activities

In order to pull the identification, organization, and allocation of development resources together, management needed to modify the planning and budgeting systems of the corporation so as to display these breakdowns.

The Efficient Investment of Human and Capital Resources

Both the efficient investment of human and capital resources in development projects and the enhancement of existing business activities will be assisted by tools such as the development expenditure breakdowns mentioned above. Once the total picture is clarified, the turnaround leader can begin to make future-growth investment decisions. Such a situation occurred at Collins Radio when Robert Wilson took over. Arthur Collins had tremendous confidence in any technological leadership, but had little interest in marketing. He had poured $30 million worth of research and development into the C-system, a complex, general purpose computer designed for sophisticated on-line operations. But the C-System was was introduced long before there was market demand, and sales did not materialize. The computer project was almost dead when Wilson took over. Wilson soon focused the C-System on a specialized but fast-growing segment of the communications market: voice and data switching. That made a good fit with the company's sales engineers. The result was that Collins grabbed almost undisputed leadership in a niche of the computer market that today is growing at the rate of $100 million or more a year.

Management by Objectives

Well-run organizations successfully attain their goals by parceling the goals out to managerial units which employ two management principles: feedback and reward. In addition, the organizations keep checking performance to determine which people fail to meet established standards, and they deal with them by prescribing either further job training or disciplinary measures. Management by Objectives includes the participation of subordinates in establishing these standards, in discussing results, and in getting explanations and future commitments.

In many organizations, however, managers become nonachievers, perceiving their role as simply defenders of the status quo. This may mean that they make sure that the proper forms are filled out, office equipment is available, etc. Their prime priorities become ensuring that nothing is done that might be a source of embarrassment or might make them open to criticism—proving some outside or uncontrollable force is at fault when real problems arise. Examples: "Our performance is off because of absenteeism; the equipment is down because the workers you hire these days are unmotivated; we didn't get the order out because the parts didn't arrive on time. . . ."

Managers who are aggressive in perceiving and attacking problems (not defensively rationalizing them) can cope in a positive manner with an unexpected breakdown—they get repairs made or shift production as quickly as possible; they handle late deliveries of parts by improvising (borrowing from another department) or sending a truck out to get the parts from another vendor.

The extraordinary popularity of MBO indicates that many organizations may use MBO as a crutch. They have lost the elementary insight into the essential functions of a manager. Their managers go through the motions of managing by living up to set procedures—for example, by watching time clocks, granting everyday personnel requests, selecting replacements when someone quits—focusing on minor elements while missing the "big picture." Costly programs with attractive packages and procedures (sort of paint-by-number sets) designed to reinstitute the traditional managerial functions are unnecessary. Once corporate objectives are ascertained and competent managers hired, MBO becomes a natural function. The central role of the manager is to be a goal-attainer and problem-solver. Thus, the manager who has to be taught how to perform this role in an extended, expensive course has never been a manager—nor has his boss, if he failed to recognize this.

MARKETING MANAGEMENT IN THE RETURN-TO-GROWTH STAGE

Marketing management, which was the third leg on the stool in the emergency stage, becomes the first leg on the stool in the return-to-growth stage. In this stage of the turnaround, the marketing emphasis is on increasing revenue growth and profit growth by exploiting existing products and by introducing selected new products. The overall mix of products and markets should grow faster than previously, because of additional marketing promotional activities. I characterized the emergency stage as demarketing and the stabilization stage as status quo marketing. This stage is *remarketing.*

Expanding Margins through Product Mix Changes

A case in point is the moves made by Dean Foods Company to product-diversify out of a low-growth business. Soaring labor costs and intense price competition shaved margins on milk products razor-thin, and per capita sales of milk products dropped steadily. To replace those lost sales, Dean developed a variety of nonmilk-based refrigerated food products, including some that capitalized on the very diet consciousness that was and is killing milk sales. Dean displayed ingenuity with a refrigerated nondairy chocolate drink called "Chocoriffic," which it introduced in 1976. The drink is made in part from whey, a liquid by-product of cheese manufacturing. Whey costs only 30 percent as much as the nonfat dry milk it replaces. In addition to faster sales, Dean's payoff on such new products has been fatter margins: 8 percent or more pretax on the new nondairy products, compared with 2 percent or less on most milk products. The money for the diversification program came largely from Dean's early cost-cutting campaign. Several unprofitable businesses were sold, including a frozen entrée operation and two dairy units in Michigan. Dean then invested heavily in more efficient, high-speed milk-processing equipment. During the first four years of its diversification program, earnings rose at a compound annual rate of 42 percent.

Marketing Strategies and Tactics

I think another case history can best illustrate the type of market strategy and tactics that are employed at this stage of the turnaround. The steps that were actually followed are simplified and substantial data are omitted. RTG (Return-to-Growth) Corporation (the actual name has been withheld) is a manufacturer and marketer of industrial equipment sold nationally in the United States. It has eight product lines and a total sales volume of $200 million. On this volume, it earned $8.8 million, or $4.20 per share in 1980.

The top management felt that product line A, which accounted for close to 25 percent of RTG Corporation's volume, could be exploited better, since its contribution to profits was relatively small and was declining. Concerned about this, top management decided to give high priority to revitalizing A's profitability. It began by making a thorough product/market analysis which led to a new selective marketing strategy for the product line.

Competition Trends. First, an industry profile was drawn up that showed product/market and competitive trends—for example, the size of the total market for the product as well as of each market segment; the growth rate of the market and its segments in the previous five years, and the rate expected in the next five years; factors that might have affected market demand and margin levels (emerging industries, technological advances, and the like); and the market share and share trend of all major competitors. The total market for product line A was $1.4 billion. The market had grown for the past five years and was projected to maintain a 14 percent growth rate over the next five years. It was expected that the lengthening of product-replacement cycles would be offset by a new primary-market demand in an emerging industry segment. The market for product A was dominated by three competitors that jointly controlled 80 percent of the market in 1980, having increased their position from 74 percent during the preceding five years. Table 21-1 shows the breakdown.

RTG Corporation estimated that the market for product A would retain its margins over the next five years, given the relatively small number of competitors, the continued strong growth, and the emergence of an important new market, all of which militated against a price war and allowed opportunities for economics of scale. New market entrants were considered unlikely, owing to the technological and capital requirements of the business. A significant threat to the market was foreseen in four to seven years, however, a threat rising from technological innovations that could provide a wholly new substitute product.

TABLE 21-1
Breakdown of Competitive Market Shares for Product Line A

Competitor	*1975 Market share (%)*	*1980 Market share (%)*
X	30.3	35.3
Y	25.5	24.8
Z	18.3	19.9
Total of top three	74.1	80.0
Six small competitors	21.9	16.5
RTG Corporation*	4.0	3.5

*Actual name withheld for confidentiality.

Market Position Profile. Second, a company profile was prepared that analyzed the profit variables and market position of the product—for example: present and projected break-even economics, market share by segment, and growth in dollar volume and share by segment. The market for product line A was one of the faster growing markets in which RTG Corporation competed, with nearly half again the average growth rate of RTG's other product market. Yet A's market share ranked among the lowest of all RTG products. This ran directly counter to RTG Corporation's corporate goal, which was to build the strongest market shares in those markets which were growing the most rapidly. Further, while product line A's dollar volume had nearly doubled in the past five years, its market share had fallen off 0.5 percent point. A's major competitors had been more aggressive than RTG or the six small competitors and had captured the lion's share of market growth. The profit value of increasing market share by one point was substantially higher for product line A than for RTG's other products, thus, reflecting A's large and growing market and its good 35 percent contribution rate (Table 21-2). Improving market share was therefore worth a significant investment.

Product line A had not built a dominant position in any of its seven major end-use market segments; however, in two segments, its share was nearly double that of the all-segment average and was several times that held in its weakest markets. Furthermore, profit contribution in these two segments ran 3 to 5 percent of sales higher than in other markets.

In analyzing margin and profit deterioration over the previous five years, RTG found that: (1) A would have more than tripled its 1972 pretax profits if it had been able to retain its 4.0 market share; (2) changes in item sales mix within product line A were not responsible for margin deterioration; (3) key cost improvements were essential to the increasing

TABLE 21-2
Pretax Profit Contribution by Product Line of RTG Corp.
(Value of one share point)

Product line	*Percent share of market*	*Pretax profit, $ millions*
C	14.0	.95
D	10.7	.72
B	6.8	2.20
G	5.8	.40
H	5.2	.45
F	4.2	1.65
A	3.5	4.90
E	2.0	2.63

Note: RTG Corporation's actual name withheld for reasons of confidentiality.

of profitability; and (4) variable cost had risen faster than sales, sharply reducing pretax profits. (See Table 21-3).

Competitive Economics. Third, RTG analysts prepared a competitive profile that showed the economics and anticipated strategies of the market leaders—for example, their break-even volume and contribution

TABLE 21-3
Economics of Product Line A over Time Compared to Top Three Competitors
($ millions)

	*RTG Corporation**		*Average of three major competitors*
	1975	*1980*	*1980*
Revenue	$25.0	$49.0	$373.2
Variable cost	14.5	31.8	186.6
Fixed cost	9.0	16.2	141.8
Total cost	23.5	48.0	328.4
Profit	1.5	1.0	44.8
Break-even	21.4	46.2	283.6
% above break-even	17	6	32

*Actual name withheld for reasons of confidentiality.

margins, and the price and product moves with which they were apt to build market share and profitability. The operating scale of the three large competitors gave them better volume economics, placing A at an inherent disadvantage in head-to-head competition (Table 21-3). Competition was operating at 32 percent above break-even volume and had a variable contribution of 50 percent, while A was operating at only 6 percent above break-even volume, with a contribution margin of 35 percent.

Given these competitive economics and the dominant market position of the three leaders, the product manager for A believed it likely that his competitors would aggressively seek not only to maintain their shares but also to build profitability in the larger market segments by:

1. Adding salesmen and increasing incentive payments to distributors
2. Maintaining a high quality of technical service to key accounts
3. Introducing a series of product improvements to increase performance
4. Holding the line on price in order to maintain high profit contribution
5. Achieving cost reductions in the production and distribution of the basic product thus offseting the cost of these programs

Market Strategy for Product A. The next step was the selection of a strategy for product line A from a range of options. The product manager considered an across-the-board marketing effort to compete with major competitors on all fronts, building share by granting larger distributor discounts than the majors. He rejected this approach on the grounds that it deteriorated the basic economics of A and that the company lacked the muscle to implement it against the leaders, who had higher margins with which to meet price competition. Next, the product manager considered a selective approach to the marketplace. He singled out the two market segments in which A had the highest market share and best margins, facts which indicated a product advantage and a reputation for quality. For these key markets, the product manager adopted the following strategy: he reduced prices slightly; he increased the technical service staff in order to provide better customer service to important users; and he took advantage of profit improvement opportunity by: (1) eliminating several marginally profitable items from the line so that the marketing effort could focus on items with the highest profit potential; and (2) initiating the redesign of key items in line A to better meet the distinctive needs of the two priority markets.

For the other five major segments of the markets, which had lower margins, the product manager planned selective price increases. Those increases, netted against the reductions for the two prime markets, brought the overall average price reduction to 5 percent. On the basis of his market research and inquiries among the sales force, the product manager judged that this net reduction would earn A a total market-share gain of one full point. On the basis of an analysis of competitive economics, it was determined that this would not be a big enough reduction in the competitors' market share to provoke competitive price retaliation, but would be sufficient to generate over $2 million in added profits—a 200 percent increase—for RTG.

The product manager got approval for $5 million in new capital in order to purchase new equipment that would improve A's reliability and would reduce production costs by 3 percent of sales. The cost savings alone generated a discounted rate of return higher than the company's hurdle rate of 18 percent. This strategy proved highly successful. Although there is no guarantee that even the most thoughtful course will prove out in practice, the chance of success is higher if a strategy is based on solid knowledge of the facts that are critical to major market decisions.

RTG Corporation Objectives. RTG Corporation objectives were next set to increase earnings per share from $4.20 to $7.00 by 1982. This proposed increase represented a major jump from the relatively static profit position of the past five years. Against this objective, the company dimensioned the need for new products by developing individual product/market strategies for each of its eight product lines, as it had earlier done for product line A. In analyzing the outlook, it found that total earnings from present lines would fall $0.95 short of its $7 per share objective, or $4.8 million short, based on current shares outstanding. This gap had to be filled by new products that were either developed internally or acquired with cash. If stock acquisitions were made, even greater additional earnings would be required to reach $7 per share. At 4.4 percent aftertax profit—the present average for existing products—$108 million in new-product volume was needed to fill the $4.8 million profit gap.

In establishing criteria for new products, RTG Corporation realized that increasing its product lines from eight to twelve would inevitably increase its product/market complexity. To manage this increase, the company decided to seek new products that would build on present corporate strengths to the greatest possible degree. In other words, RTG Corporation chose to confine the increase in complexity to numbers of products only, thus sidestepping the other elements of product/market complexity. This meant avoiding technologically complex products, forward or backward integration, or products with inherently short life cycles; building on current distribution channels and established customer relationships; and avoiding products where competition was entrenched, labor and social pressures were severe, or government regulation was substantial. To those criteria the company added another: any new products should provide a 12 percent discounted rate of return on investment and provide margins at least equal to those of current products. One tool RTG Corporation used to arrive at these criteria was the product/market grid, illustrated conceptually in Table 18-11 in the section on Return-to-Growth Plan.

After screening product/market opportunities against these criteria, RTG decided to examine a major related industrial product area having a 75 percent overlap with RTG's current customers. It hoped this area might contain a segment that would be promising for the development or acquisition of one of the four new products. The challenge was to sort out from a broad band of competing product concepts and technical variations the one approach that would assure the company of good profit economics, a sound competitive position in the marketplace, and a feasible entry vehicle.

RTG analyzed each of eleven market segments against the following yardsticks: (1) market size and growth; (2) competitive market control; (3) product/market profitability; (4) fit with RTG Corporation's present product and market strengths; (5) absence of elements that would cause major increases in complexity; and (6) ease of entry through either internal development or cash acquisition. In making this analysis, RTG followed the same approach it used in developing product/market strategy for existing products. This led the company to a $160 million market segment and to three small alternative acquisitions with potential for providing a foothold for entry.

Overall Strategy. The overall marketing strategy that evolves, and the one that appears to be the most effective for turnaround companies in this stage, is to:

1. Hold the expansion of product/market complexity to a pace and direction that can be managed effectively.
2. Obtain and hold niches in end-use markets where it is possible to maintain a profit performance superior to competition and to avoid retaliatory action from very large competitors.
3. Capitalize on the advantages most turnaround companies have over their giant competitors. These include:
   (a) The ability to grow in small markets. A number of turnaround companies have grown by building on product/market segments of $5 to $20 million annual volume—

segments that are too small to receive higher-level management attention from the industrial giants.

(b) The ability to enter large markets without affecting profitability. Turnaround companies often find that they can enter a very large market and take a one- to five-point market share without seriously disturbing market equilibrium; a giant corporation's entrance into the same market is inevitably disruptive.

(c) The ability to make and attract acquisitions. Turnaround companies frequently have more flexibility in acquisition, since restraints from the Justice Department and Federal Trade Commission are fewer. At the same time, some small companies would rather affiliate with a turnaround company, in which they can have a voice in management, than be buried in a large corporation with its inevitable administrative constraints.

(d) The ability to react quickly to market demands. A number of turnaround companies can take advantage of short-term market opportunities more readily and can meet special customer needs faster than can their larger competitors, whose administrative machinery delays decisions.

4. Avoid markets and products that are simply off limits because of heavy capital requirements to reach economic scale.

5. Avoid fields that for success require long-term, high-cost research or state-of-the-art technology.[4]

HUMAN RESOURCES MANAGEMENT IN THE RETURN-TO-GROWTH STAGE

The importance of motivation and people development becomes even greater at this stage of the turnaround than in the previous stages. William S. Anderson, chairman of NCR, in discussing the company's future challenges, put it this way: "Perhaps the foremost of these challenges is the people challenge. . . . You can take an organizational chart and simply restructure it. You can demolish antiquated plants and build new ones. And you can replace inept managers with those who are competent. But it takes a little longer to transform the skills and attitudes of . . . 65,000 men and women."[5]

Since I have previously discussed motivating the organization in Chapter 16, I'll confine my present discussion to the three other key human resource issues at this stage of the turnaround. These are:

1. Building a successful management development program

2. Reorganizing for faster growth
3. Modifying your compensation programs

Admittedly, this is not an exhaustive list of human resources management issues, and it is not meant to be. I have found that these are the elements that differentiate turnaround human resources practice from that of stable management. The reader is encouraged to refer to the hundreds of other texts on human resource management under stable conditions. At this point in the turnaround, the organization more closely resembles a typical company than at the earlier stages. The three issues require practical interpretation because turnarounds are inherently practical. Grandiose management development programs and reorganization programs are not practical in turnaround situations and are doomed to failure.

Building a Management Development Program

Management development in this stage of the turnaround entails two practical requirements: adequate training in the management ranks, and the identification of those few rare individuals, beyond the original, small turnaround group, that will be required to make the company grow. Concentrating on a whole host of other issues would be self-defeating. Typical of the inadequate management development programs that troubled companies possess is the one Martin S. Kramer found at Gimbels Brothers when he took over as chief executive officer. Kramer marveled at the naiveté of Gimbels' then-incumbent personnel director when the director was asked about his executive development work. The man prided himself on the fact that the program did not cost the company a thing. As the director related, "When we need an assistant buyer, we hire someone right off the street, give them a do-it-yourself training book, and that's how they get trained." This approach, of course, was responsible for Gimbels' appalling lack of executive talent and for a turnover rate that was three times greater than that of its leading competitors.

At this stage most turnaround companies cannot afford the more grandiose management development schemes. Training here means "on-the-job" training for the most part rather than fancy academic training or psychological experimentation. The turnaround company has to seek out those rare individuals who are truly committed to the effort and then build around them. It has been true, it is true, and it will be forever true that "a good man is hard to find." Those individuals are the cornerstone of the corporate growth you are committed to. Selecting individuals for development and more responsibility is a highly subjective task. It's tough, in practice, to rank people because they are not homogeneous. Performance evaluations are of only minor value, since they tend to be biased and since performance looks backwards. In contrast, potential looks forward. Potential can only become visible if the right climate for management development exists. The characteristics of this favorable climate appear to be:

1. Absence of political maneuvering for position, with penalties for unfair personal competition and petty conspiracy
2. Rejection of preference on grounds other than approval of performance—sex, blood relationships, friendship, and ethnic, educational, or social background
3. High standards of performance for work as well as for the evaluation of that work, including disciplined attention to meeting detailed commitments
4. Tolerance of individual differences
5. Willingness to take risk (and acceptance of the inevitability of occasional failure) in delegating responsibility to the relatively inexperienced
6. Acceptance and encouragement of innovation with consequent freedom to act upon ideas
7. High standards of moral integrity, including rejection of expediency even at the cost of windfall profits

The patient establishment and stubborn defense of these values are a practicable undertaking for the leader of an organization. In addition to the development of a favorable climate, I have found the most useful guidelines for executive development in turnaround situations to be:

1. Be prepared to ignore some of the cherished rules of executive development; they can be self-defeating in a short-term program.
2. Fish where the fish are and concentrate on developing people with the greatest identifiable capacity for development regardless of their experience or technical background.
3. Get participation and support from as many key managers as possible, watching for attitudes of profit consciousness.
4. Focus on on-the-job development; it will yield the most productive of results, particularly in the short term.
5. Make sure that the executive development effort supports the

achievement of a business plan which rewards individuals who achieve results and which heavily discounts excuses for failure.

Reorganizing for Faster Growth

Another people issue faced at this point in the turnaround is reorganization. Generally, power has been located very close to the top, for control purposes, up to this point. Although this locus of power and decision making is appropriate for control purposes, it is not usually appropriate for growth strategies. In all but the smaller companies, it will probably be necessary to decentralize decision making and certain staff functions. This control shift is almost analogous to a wagon train that pulls up in a circle for protection when attacked and then returns to its more normal state when the attack is over.

When Robert Wilson reached the return-to-growth stage at Memorex, he restructured the company's organization chart. He scrapped the tightly centralized setup that was installed after he came aboard for a more decentralized structure splitting Memorex into forty-four business teams. In order to get more "spear carriers," under the new setup Wilson gave field managers more responsibility for the earnings of their units. He also gave many day-to-day operating decisions to two executive vice presidents, thus allowing himself more time to spent on long-range planning. "The old setup," said Wilson, "was adequate for the Memorex of today, but I am concerned with the Memorex of tomorrow."

Modifying Compensation Programs

At this point in the turnaround, your compensation programs will probably have to be modified to more typical corporate forms. Be careful that the imbalances that could be supported in prior periods on grounds of rapid improvement do not carry over to hurt you at this stage. Such imbalances have occurred at Memorex where a few top managers received enormous compensation, while most managers had low salaries. Variable compensation is a natural outgrowth of a crisis period, but its perpetuation into the return-to-growth stage definitely leads to low morale. The Draconian working hours, inadequate staffing for projects, and constant pressure must be alleviated at this stage. Memorex and other turnaround companies often lose executives right and left at this point unless they take corrective action on motivation (see Chapter 16) and compensation. The short-term programs that in the past created high incentive for a few key turnaround managers must now be modified to include greater participation. Some short-term programs could be extremely difficult to undo. For example, if earlier you passed out options to a lot of down-the-line executives, others will expect to participate now. If this is not consistent with your long-term philosophy, you may find yourself with haves and have-nots.

By the return-to-growth stage the level of risk has declined; the level of reward will also probably have declined. The emphasis in this stage is again on revenue growth coupled with margin discipline. Objectives change and so must compensation. The key to establishing a forward-looking compensation program is to isolate and resolve the basic issues. These include how much you want to pay your good people; whether you want to use incentives and if so, to what extent. In your business, does it make sense for a division manager to have half of his total compensation variable, at risk with his performance? Do equity-building programs related to your stock performance seem fair? Are you willing to award compensation for potential as well as for performance?

Now is the time to make sure that your compensation programs are interrelated with long-term business objectives and consistent with them. Your incentive reward system must be capable of revision so that it can continue paying off for the right things over the long-term, bright future your company now faces.

At this point the company's long battle to regain robust health should be over. The difficult task of maintaining consistent growth and profitability over the coming years has just begun. Only those who have come through a difficult turnaround can understand the pressures and demands of the task. The corporate turnaround is a management challenge of the highest order. When the turnaround challenge is complete, new challenges to growth and profitability will inevitably take its place. Just as inevitably, corporate executives will meet and beat the new challenges that face them. I wish you luck on your new challenges.

REFERENCES

[1]Richard S. Sloma, *No Nonsense Management* (New York: Macmillan, 1977), pp. 77, 78.

[2]Interview with Robert C. Brown, president, R. C. Brown & Company, San Francisco, Calif., February 1978.

[3]Material on Hooker acquisition adapted and revised from William F. Christopher, "Marketing Planning That Gets Things Done," *Harvard Business Review*, September–October 1970, pp. 128–136.

[4]Material on RTG (Return-to-Growth) Corporation adapted and revised from Donald K. Clifford Jr., "Managing the Threshold Company," A McKinsey Report to Management (New York: McKinsey & Company, 1973), pp. 44–56.

[5]William S. Anderson, "NCR: A Presentation to the Financial Community," *NCR Public Relations Department*, Dayton, Ohio, October 1977.

APPENDIX

TABLE A
Comparison of Organization Type during Decline with Current Type

Organization type	*Structure during decline, %*	*Current structure, %*	*Percent change*
Centralized/functional	44.0	25.6	−18.4
Decentralized/geographic	17.3	17.5	+ 0.2
Decentralized/product division	37.3	57.8	+19.5
Other	1.4	-	− 1.4
TOTAL	100.0	100.0	0

Source: Donald B. Bibeault, Survey of eighty-one turnaround company chief executives, April 1978.

TABLE B
If the Principal Reason for Decline is External—the Subcauses Are....

	Ranked first		*Weighted rank*	
	Number	*Percent*	*Number*	*Percent*
Economic change	13	41	29	42
Competitive change	10	31	18	26
Government constraint	4	13	11	16
Social change	3	9	6	9
Technological change	2	6	5	7
TOTAL	32	100	69	100

Source: Donald B. Bibeault, Survey of eighty-one turnaround company chief executives, April 1978.

TABLE C
The Relative Importance of Various Types of Management Problems in Declining Companies

	First rankings		*Weighted rankings*	
Management problem	***Number***	***Percent***	***Number***	***Percent***
One-man rule	32	44	40	21
Lack of management depth	16	22	39	21
Management change problem	9	13	26	14
Inbred bureaucratic management	8	11	22	13
Weak finance function	1	1	25	13
Unbalanced top management team	4	6	17	9
Non-participative board	2	3	14	7
TOTAL	72	100	183	97

Source: Donald B. Bibeault, Survey of eighty-one turnaround company chief executives, April 1978.

TABLE D
Subrankings of Failure to Keep Pace with the Marketplace

	Number one ranking		*Total weighted rank*	
	Number	***Percent***	***Number***	***Percent***
Competitive change	24	71	49	54
Production/cost improvements	4	12	15	17
Economic change	4	12	9	10
Technological breakthrough	1	3	5	6
Social change	1	3	5	6
TOTAL	34	100	86	100

Source: Donald B. Bibeault, Survey of eighty-one turnaround company chief executives, April 1978.

TABLE E
Rankings of Various Types of Control Problems

	Number one ranking		*Total weighted rank*	
Problem areas	*Number*	*Percent*	*Number*	*Percent*
Budgetary control	22	37	46	30
Product costing	15	25	35	23
Responsibility accounting	9	15	33	22
Asset accounting (valuation)	9	15	19	13
Cash flow forecasts	4	7	19	13
TOTAL	59	100	152	100

Source: Donald B. Bibeault, Survey of eighty-one turnaround company chief executives, April 1978.

TABLE F
Were the Early-Warning Signals of Decline Ignored or Acted Upon?

	Number	*Percent*
Yes, ignored, etc.	60	79
No, not ignored, etc.	12	16
Other	4	5
TOTAL	76	100

Source: Donald B. Bibeault, Survey of eighty-one turnaround company chief executives, April 1978.

TABLE G
Five-Year Predictive Accuracy of the Multidiscriminant Analysis Model of Bankruptcy

Year prior to bankruptcy	*Hits*	*Misses*	*Percent correct*
1st $n = 33$	31	2	95
2d $n = 32$	23	9	72
3d $n = 29$	14	15	48
4th $n = 28$	8	20	29
5th $n = 25$	9	16	36

Source: Edward I. Altman, *Corporate Bankruptcy in America* (Lexington, Mass.: Heath-Lexington, 1971), p. 73.

TABLE H
Z-Score Worst Performance

Company	*Z score*	*Working capital as a % of assets × 1.2*	*Retained earnings as a % of assets × 1.4*	*Pretax income + interest as a % of assets × 3.3*	*Market value of common + preferred at liquidating as a % of debt × 0.6*	*Sales divided by assets × 1*
Memorex (?)	0.74	0.23	−0.69	0.14	0.15	0.92
Mohawk Data Sciences (4/75)	0.91	0.34	−0.20	−0.06	0.03	0.80
Electronic Associates	0.94	0.57	−1.15	0.27	0.13	1.12
Todd Shipyards (3/75)	1.03	0.30	−0.03	−1.12	0.10	1.79
Puerto Rican Cement	1.06	0.04	0.17	0.07	0.08	0.69
IN Pharmaceuticals (11/74)	1.34	0.17	0.10	−0.21	0.08	1.21
Duplan (9/74)	1.37	0.42	0.02	−0.32	0.02	1.23
Sanders Associates (7/74)	1.56	0.53	−0.27	−0.47	0.09	1.68
Cooper Laboratories (10/74)	1.61	0.27	0.06	0.17	0.38	0.72
Amcord	1.69	0.10	0.28	0.26	0.23	0.81
Condec (7/74)	1.69	0.25	0.13	0.20	0.09	1.04
Schaefer, F&M	1.71	0.13	0.08	0.17	0.03	1.31
Arvin Industries	1.77	0.13	0.19	0.23	0.16	1.06
Telex (3/75)	1.78	0.26	−0.27	0.44	0.21	1.12

Source: Arlene Hershman, "How to Figure Who's Going Bankrupt," *Dun's Review*, October 1975, p. 65.

Note: Figures used in compiling table are for fiscal year ending 12/74 except where otherwise indicated.

TABLE I
***Z*-Score Best Performers**

Company	*Z score*	*Working capital as a % of assets × 1.2*	*Retained earnings as a % of assets × 1.4*	*Pretax income + interest as a % of assets × 3.3*	*Market value* of common + preferred at liquidating as a % of debt × 0.6*	*Sales divided by assets × 1*
Taylor Wine (6/74)	304.09	0.62	0.85	0.79	300.87	0.97
American Home Products	169.10	0.54	0.75	1.17	164.99	1.65
Starrett, L.S. (6/74)	125.08	0.72	0.82	0.79	121.58	1.17
Schering Plough	88.39	0.52	0.94	1.00	84.86	1.07
Marion Laboratories (6/75)	78.80	0.56	0.82	1.32	74.81	1.29
Bandag	58.83	0.62	0.71	1.19	54.89	1.43
Eastman Kodak	52.06	0.40	0.82	0.82	49.05	0.97
Nalco Chemical	47.88	0.38	0.91	0.87	44.24	1.48
Polaroid	42.38	0.64	0.88	0.20	39.68	0.98
Merch	38.08	0.35	0.78	0.96	34.92	1.07
Betz Laboratories	37.98	0.41	0.64	0.81	34.63	1.50
Northwestern Steel & Wire (7/74)	37.65	0.54	0.79	0.88	34.15	1.28
Johnson & Johnson	36.60	0.45	0.80	0.68	33.29	1.38
Data General (9/74)	36.32	0.56	0.44	0.89	33.27	1.17

*As of year-end 1974.

Source: Arlene Hershman, "How to Figure Who's Going Bankrupt," *Dun's Review*, October 1975, p. 65.

Note: Figures used in compiling table are for fiscal year ending 12/74 except where otherwise indicated.

TABLE J
Banker's Warning Signals on Company Problems

These signals cannot be classified as early-warning signals; however, K. D. Martin, vice president of the Bank of America, has developed this list of red flags. They are arranged in descending order of frequency, with the most frequent red flags appearing first.

1. Slowness in submitting financial exhibits by the borrower. This can be the result of either unwillingness on the part of the borrower or a lack of experience or manpower in the financial part of the company.
2. Declining deposit balances, overdrafts and/or returned checks. The former, declining deposit balances, may be unnoticed for a period of time, but the latter, overdrafts and/or returned checks, appear with traumatic suddenness.
3. Failure to perform on other obligations, including personal debt of the principals. This information can come from a variety of sources; however, the importance of not allowing split borrowings can be seen in this regard.
4. Inventories become swollen. This flag can usually be found in the financial data supplied by the borrower or as the result of credit inquiries received from suppliers.
5. Loan payments become delinquent with past due periods increasing.
6. Slowness in bank's ability to arrange plant visitations or meetings with principals.
7. Borrower becomes a target of legal process or actions. Such actions would include the filing of security interests by other creditors; tax liens, including those for withheld taxes; attachments and/or levies against bank accounts, etc.
8. Trade payables and/or accruals begin to build. This observation can be prompted by the submission of financial information by the borrower or inquiries and leads from suppliers and others.
9. Adverse information from competitors and customers of the business concern.

Source: K. D. Martin, "Problem Loan Signals and Follow Up," *Journal of Commercial Bank Lending*, September 1973, p. 39.

TABLE K
An Economic- or Competitive-Factor Turnaround's Important Subfactors

	Ranked first		*Weighted rank*	
	Number	***Percent***	***Number***	***Percent***
Favorable increase in industry volume	17	58	22	33
Favorable increase in competitive prices	5	17	20	30
Favorable shift in product mix	2	7	11	16
Breakthrough in product costs	1	4	6	9
Other	3	10	3	4
TOTAL	29	100	67	100

Source: Donald B. Bibeault, Survey of eighty-one turnaround company chief executives, April 1978.

TABLE L
Key Factors in Company Turnarounds in Detail

	Number one ranking		*Total weighted rank*	
	Number	***Percent***	***Number***	***Percent***
People aspects:				
Strong leadership	35	48	54	27
Absolute control by mgt.	9	12	23	11
Change in success attitude	6	8	23	11
Turnaround of people	2	3	15	7
Subtotal	52	71	115	56
Competitive aspects:				
Viable basic core business	9	12	34	17
Developed marketing niches	3	4	8	4
Competitive equipment and processes	0	0	6	3
Subtotal	12	16	48	24
Financial resource aspects:				
Assets to redeploy	7	10	26	13
Creditor/lender assistance	2	2	14	7
Subtotal	9	12	40	20
TOTAL	73	100	203	100

Source: Donald B. Bibeault, Survey eighty-one turnaround company chief executives, April 1978.

TABLE M
Key Management Control Subfactors

	Number one rank		*Total weighted rank*	
	Number	*Percent*	*Number*	*Percent*
Tight budgetary controls instituted	26	40	48	28
Responsibility accounting improved	19	29	38	22
Product margin and costs improved	14	22	34	19
Cash flow forecasting improved	1	2	26	15
Valuation of assets improved	3	5	15	9
Nonfinancial measures improved	1	1	11	6
Other	1	1	1	1
TOTAL	65	100	173	100

Source: Donald B. Bibeault, Survey of eighty-one turnaround company chief executives, April 1978.

TABLE N
Key Competitive Factors in Turnaround

	Number one rank		*Total weighted rank*	
	Number	*Percent*	*Number*	*Percent*
Favorable increase in industry volume	17	59	22	33
Favorable increase in industry prices	5	17	20	30
Favorable shift in product mix	2	7	11	16
Product cost breakthrough	1	3	6	9
Raw material price improvements	1	3	5	8
Other	3	11	3	4
TOTAL	29	100	67	100

Source: Donald B. Bibeault, Survey of eighty-one turnaround company chief executives, April 1978.

TABLE O
Ranking of Manager Characteristics Most Displayed by Turnaround Leaders

	Number one rank		*Total weighted rank*	
	Number	*Percent*	*Number*	*Percent*
Growth-oriented executive	29	39	43	35
Entrepreneur	18	24	29	24
Turnaround specialist	15	20	27	22
Maintenance manager	2	3	8	7
Status quo manager	4	5	6	5
Other	7	9	8	7
TOTAL	75	100	121	100

Source: Donald B. Bibeault, Survey of eighty-one turnaround company chief executives, April 1978.

TABLE P
Were the Major Turnaround Moves Accomplished According to a Formal Plan or Mostly by Intuitive Management Action?

Response	*Percent*
Intuitive action first	19.3
Intuitive action followed by formal plan	50.6
Formal plan followed by implementation	30.1
TOTAL	100.0

Source: Donald B. Bibeault, Survey of eighty-one turnaround company chief executives, April 1978.

TABLE Q
Comparisons with Competitors' Prices for Different Types of Product Sold

	Types of product sold			
	*Capital goods**	*Components**	*Materials**	*Percent of all products*
Higher than average	50	39	28	39
About average	38	48	63	50
Lower than average	8	8	6	7
Not stated	4	5	3	4

*Figures shown are percentages (base 220).

Source: Richard Skinner, "Pricing Strategies to Cope With Inflation," *How British Industry Prices*, eds. B. Atkin and R. Skinner (London: Industrial Market Research Limited, 1975), p. 72.

SELECTED BIBLIOGRAPHY

BOOKS:

Abegglen, John. *Big Business Leaders in America* (New York: Harper and Row, 1955).

Ackoff, Russell L. *A Concept of Corporate Planning* (New York: Wiley, 1970).

Altman, Edward I. *Corporate Bankruptcy in America* (Lexington, Mass.: Heath-Lexington, 1971).

Andrews, Kenneth. *The Concept of Corporate Strategy* (Homewood, Ill.: Dow Jones-Irwin, 1971).

Argenti, John. *Corporate Planning: A Practical Guide* (London: Allyn & Unwin, 1968).

Argenti, John. *Corporate Collapse: The Causes and Symptoms* (New York: Wiley, 1976).

Argenti, John. In Roland Mann (ed.), *The Arts of Top Management: A McKinsey Anthology* (New York: McGraw-Hill, 1971).

Atkin, B., and **R. Skinner,** (eds.). *How British Industry Prices* (London: Industrial Market Research, 1975).

Barmash, Isadore. *Great Business Disasters* (New York: Ballantine, 1973).

Batten, J. D. *Tough-Minded Management* 3e, (New York: AMACOM, a division of American Management Associations, 1978), p. 23.

Beaver, W. *Financial Ratios as Predictors of Failures: Empirical Research in Accounting* (Selected Studies, 1966).

Bensler, Joseph E., Jr. "Rebuilding the Profitability of the Production Effort," in Joseph Eisenberg (ed.), *Turnaround Management* (New York: McGraw-Hill, 1972), pp. 75–102.

Burger, Chester. *Walking the Executive Plank* (New York: Van Nostrand, 1972).

Caswell, Cameron W. "Implementing Near-Term Marketing Improvements," in Joseph Eisenberg (ed.), *Turnaround Management* (New York: McGraw-Hill, 1972), pp. 59–74.

Cooley, W., and **P. Lohnes.** *Multivariate Procedures for the Behavioral Sciences* (New York: Wiley, 1962).

Crozir, Michael. *The Bureaucratic Phenomenon* (Chicago: University of Chicago Press, 1969).

Dale, Ernest. *The Great Organizers* (New York: McGraw-Hill, 1960).

Drucker, Peter. *Management: Tasks, Responsibilities, Practices* (New York: Harper & Row, 1974).

Drucker, Peter. *Managing in Turbulent Times* (New York: Harper & Row, 1980).

Eisenberg, Joseph. "Developing an Ongoing Profit-Improvement Capability,' in Joseph Eisenberg (ed.), *Turnaround Management* (New York: McGraw-Hill, 1972), pp. 103–126.

Eisenberg Joseph (ed.). *Turnaround Management: A Manual for Profit Improvement and Growth* (New York: McGraw-Hill, 1972).

Frahan, William E., Jr. *The Fight for Competitive Advantage* (Cambridge: Division of Research, Harvard Business School, 1972).

Glueck, William F. *Business Policy: Strategy Formulation and Executive Action* (New York: McGraw-Hill, 1972).

Green, P. E., and **D. S. Tull.** *Research for Marketing Decision* (Englewood Cliffs, N.J.: Prentice-Hall, 1975).

Grossman, Lee. *The Change Agent* (New York: Amacom Books, 1974).

Gyllenhammer, Pehr. *People at Work* (Reading, Mass.: Addison Wesly, 1977).

Harris, John. "Major Reason Companies Get into Trouble," *Boardroom's Business Secrets,* (New York: Boardroom Reports, 1977), p. 4.

Herzberg, Frederick. "One More Time: How Do You Motivate Employees," in *How Do Successful Executives Handle People: Harvard Business Review Classics,* (Cambridge: Harvard University Press, 1967), pp. 82–92.

Heskett, James L., Nicholas A. Glaskowsky, Jr., and **Robert M. Ivie,** *Business Logistics* (New York: Ronald Press, 1973).

Higgins, Lindley R. *Cost Reduction from A to Z* (New York: McGraw-Hill, 1976).

Hombrach, Frederick W., Jr. *Raising Productivity* (New York: McGraw-Hill, 1977).

Irwin, P. H., and **F. W. Langhorn,** "The Change Seekers," In *New Insights for Executive Achievement* (Cambridge: Harvard University Press, 1968), pp. 14–27.

Jay, Antony. *Management and Machiavelli* (New York: Holt, 1968).

Lawrence, Paul P. "How to Deal with Resistance," in G. W. Walton, et al. (eds.), *Organizational Change and Development,* (Homewood, Ill.: 1970), pp. 181ff.

Lev, Baruch. *Financial Statement Analysis: A New Approach* (Englewood Cliffs, N.J.: Prentice-Hall, 1974).

Maccoby, Michael. *The Gamesman: The New Corporate Leaders* (New York: Simon & Schuster, 1976).

Mace, Myles L. *Director: Myth and Reality* (Cambridge: Harvard University Press, 1971).

Machiavelli, Niccolo. in Thomas G. Bergin (ed.), *The Prince.* (Franklin Center, Pa.: Franklin Library, 1978).

Mancheski, Frederick J. "The Chief Executive's Role in Managing for Profit," in Joseph Eisenberg (ed.), *Turnaround Management,* (New York: McGraw-Hill, 1972), pp. 1–28.

Maslow, A. H. *Motivation and Personality* (New York: Harper & Row, 1954).

McEachern, William A. *Management Control and Performance* (Lexington, Mass.: Lexington Books, 1975).

Mishkin, William S. *Techniques in Corporate Reorganization* (New York: Presidents Publishing House, 1972).

Morgan, John S. *Managing Change* (New York: McGraw-Hill, 1972).

Murphy, Thomas T. *New York Stock Exchange 1977 Fact Book* (New York: New York Stock Exchange, 1977).

Neuschel, Richard F. *Management Systems for Profit and Growth* (New York: McGraw-Hill, 1976).

Osgood, C. E., G. J. Suci, and **P. H. Tannenbaum.** *The Measurement of Meaning* (Urbana: University of Illinois Press, 1957).

Peters, Ralph W., Jr. "Building an Executive Development Program," in Joseph Eisenberg (ed.), *Turnaround Management* (New York: McGraw-Hill, 1972), pp. 209–232.

Priesing, John W. "Taking Charge to Strengthen Marketing," in Joseph Eisenberg (ed.), *Turnaround Management* (New York: McGraw-Hill, 1972), pp. 29–58.

Raymond, Albert & Associates. *Controlling Production and Inventory Costs* (Englewood Cliffs, N.J.: Prentice-Hall, 1977).

Risker, Paul D. "Launching an Acquisition Program to Increase Company Growth and Profitability," in Joseph Eisenberg (ed.), *Turnaround Management* (New York: McGraw-Hill, 1972).

Robertson, Andrew. *The Lessons of Failure* (London: MacDonald, 1973).

Ross, Joel E., and **Michael J. Kami.** *Management in Crisis: Why The Mighty Fall* (Englewood Cliffs, N.J.: Prentice-Hall, 1973).

Skinner, Richard. "Pricing Strategies to Cope with Inflation," in B. Atkin and R. Skinner (eds.), *How British Industry Prices,* (London: Industrial Market Research, 1975), pp. 95–113.

Sloma, Richard S. *No Nonsense Management* (New York: Macmillan, 1977).

Smackey, Bruce M. "A Profit Emphasis for Improving Sales Force Productivity," in *Industrial Marketing Management,* 1977, pp. 135–140.

Smith, R. A. *Corporations in Crisis* (New York: Doubleday, 1966).

Timoney, James P. "Developing a Compensation Program to Support a Turnaround Effort," in Joseph Eisenberg (ed.), *Turnaround Management,* (New York: McGraw-Hill, 1972), pp. 257–280.

Todd, Michael. In Herbert V. Procknow (ed.), *The Public Speakers' Treasure Ches* (New York: Harper & Row, 1964).

Townsend, Robert. *Up the Organization: How to Stop the Corporation from Stifling People and Strangling Profits* (Greenwich, Conn.: Fawcett, 1970).

Tull, D. S. and **D. I. Hawkins.** *Marketing Research: Meaning, Measurement and Method* (New York: Macmillan, 1976).

Updegraph, John M., Jr., and **Burton C. Person.** "Rediscovering Profits in Manufacturing," in *McKinsey Anthology* (New York: McGraw-Hill, 1971), pp. 120–132.

Uyterhoeven, Hugo E. R., Robert W. Ackerman, and **John W. Rosenblum.** *Strategy and Organization:—Text and Cases in General Management* (Homewood, Ill.: Dow Jones-Irwin, 1973).

Vignola, Leonard. *Strategic Divestment* (New York: Amacom Books, 1974).

West, Christopher J. *Inflation: A Management Guide to Company Survival* (New York: Wiley, 1976).

Weston, J. Frederick. *Merger and Acquisitions Planning and Action* (New York: Financial Executives Research Foundation, 1963).

Wilson, Richard M. S. *Handbook of Cost Control* (New York: Wiley, 1975).

NEWSPAPERS:

"American Science Seeks Market Hike Following Success in Space Effort," *Wall Street Journal,* Dec. 9, 1977, p. 10.

"Bank's Third Chief in a Year Should be a Winner," *San Francisco Sunday Examiner & Chronicle,* Mar. 28, 1976, sec. C, p. 11.

"Boston Co. Complete Streamlining After a Chaotic, Embarrassing Period," *Wall Street Journal,* Aug. 28, 1978, p. 8.

Chase, Marilyn. "Itel's Agony: How a Red-Hot Firm in Computer Business Overheated and Burned," *Wall Street Journal,* Feb. 22, 1980, pp. 1, 27.

Davino, David P. "Pinching the Pennies: Caution about the Outlook for 1976 Extends to Prospering Firms Like Mallinckrodt," *Wall Street Journal,* Feb. 28, 1978, p. 40.

"Doctor Offers Intensive Care for Ailing Firms," *Los Angeles Times,* Business & Financial Section, Tuesday, Aug. 19, 1975, p. 7.

"Drive to Survive: AMC's Bid to Remain an Auto Maker Is Seen Linked to NonCar Lines," *Wall Street Journal,* Mar. 23, 1978, pp. 1, 22.

Gartner, Timothy C. "New Life for Stockton Plant," *San Francisco Chronicle,* Nov. 12, 1977, p. 33.

"Harvester Continues to Have Major Problems Some Analysts Say, Despite Turnaround Signs," *Wall Street Journal,* May 25, 1979, p. 27.

"He Guides Firms from Bankruptcy to Solvency," *Palo Alto Times,* Oct. 19, 1977, p. 14.

Lublin, Joann S. "Brash Don Rumsfeld Tries His Prescription to Turn Searle Around," *Wall Street Journal,* Jan. 25, 1978, pp. 1, 12.

Lublin, Joann S. "What Do You Do When Snowmobiles Go on a Steep Slide?" *Wall Street Journal,* Mar. 7, 1978, pp. 1, 20.

"Mac Andrews Plans to Divest Itself of Textile Business," *Wall Street Journal,* Dec. 23, 1977, p. 8.

MacHalaba, Daniel. "Dumping a Dud, Selling a Troubled Unit Is a Frustrating Task for Many Companies," *Wall Street Journal,* Dec. 30, 1977, pp. 1, 23.

"The Man Behind AMI's Turnaround," *San Francisco Chronicle,* March 30, 1978, p. 17.

Montgomery, Jim. "New Direction: Citizens & Southern Shake-Up University Evolution of Boards: The Outdated Rubber Stamp," *Wall Street Journal,* Mar. 21, 1978, p. 1.

Morgenthaler, Eric. "Swedish Firm Tries Not to Let History Impede Its Progress," *Wall Street Journal,* Oct. 10, 1978, p. 1.

Pasztor, Andy. "Deepening Mire: As Chrysler Corporation Sinks Further, Doubts Grow About Recovery Plan," *Wall Street Journal,* Dec. 12, 1979, pp. 1, 24.

"Revere Copper Is Blocked on Sale of Facility to Alcan," *Wall Street Journal,* Dec. 12, 1977, p. 13.

"G. D. Searle Sets Divestiture of 20 of Its Businesses," *Wall Street Journal,* Jan. 12, 1978, p. 6.

Simpson, Janice D. "Turnaround Artist: Wilson of Memorex Revives Its Profits, Cuts Its Debt Load," *Wall Street Journal,* Feb. 21, 1971, pp. 1, 16.

"Singer Chief Gives Textbook Example of Saving a Firm from Near Disaster," *Wall Street Journal,* Feb. 21, 1971, p. 1.

"Steel's Hard Times: Bethlehem Meets Crises with Drastic Pruning of Plants' Personnel," *Wall Street Journal,* Oct. 10, 1977, p. 1.

"Stumbling Giant: A&P Recovery Drive Takes Turn for Worse, Jeopardizing Dividend," *Wall Street Journal,* Jan. 10, 1978, pp. 1, 22.

"Turnaround Artist: Wilson of Memorex Revives Its Profits, Cuts Its Debt Load," *Wall Street Journal,* Aug. 25, 1977, pp. 1, 16.

Von Hoffman, Nicholas. "Penn Central Boondoggle: Bankruptcy Move Debated," *New York Times,* Feb. 2, 1975, p. 7.

White, Donald K. "When the Going Gets Too Rough," *San Francisco Chronicle,* Oct. 14, 1977, p. 42.

White, Donald K. "Harold Ellis Is Jaunty Jolly," *San Francisco Chronicle,* Nov. 16, 1977, p. 43.

White, Donald K. "Medicine Man Moves to Itel," *San Francisco Chronicle,* Apr. 16, 1980, p. 34.

Winter, Ralph E. "On the Prowl: Conservative Firms Bent on Profit Growth Join the Merger Chase," *Wall Street Journal,* Nov. 2, 1978, p. 1.

PERIODICALS (BY DATE OF PUBLICATION):

Haire, M. "Projective Techniques in Marketing Research," *Journal of Marketing,* April 1950, pp. 649–656.

Buchele, Robert B. "How to Evaluate a Firm," *California Management Review,* Fall 1962, pp. 5–17.

Smith, David C. "Pruning Products: The Move Away from Full-Time Marketing," *Management Review,* October 1962, pp. 10–12.

Berenson, C. "Pruning the Product Line," *Business Horizons,* Summer 1963, pp. 63–70.

Alexander, R. S. "The Death and Burial of 'Sick' Products," *Journal of Marketing,* April 1964, pp. 68–72.

Kotler, Philip. "Phasing Out Weak Products," *Harvard Business Review,* March-April 1965, pp. 109–116.

Neuschel, Richard F. "Profit Improvement as a Way of Corporate Life," *McKinsey Quarterly Review,* Spring 1965, pp. 38–47.

Gardner, John W. "How to Prevent Organizational Dry Rot," *Harper's Magazine,* October 1965, pp. 20–24.

Snuth, David C. "Pruning Products: The Move Away from Full Time Marketing," *Management Review,* October 1967, p. 10.

Lippitt, Gordon L., and **Warren H. Schmidt,** "Crisis in Developing Organizations," *Harvard Business Review,* November-December 1967, pp. 48–58.

Altman, Edward I. "Financial Ratios, Discriminant Analysis and the Prediction of Corporate Bankruptcy," *Journal of Finance*, September 1968, pp. 589–609.

Thain, Donald H. "Stages of Corporate Development," *Business Quarterly Review*, Winter 1969, pp. 33–45.

Christopher, William F. "Marketing Planning That Gets Things Done," *Harvard Business Review*, September-October 1970, pp. 128–136.

Rothe, J. T. "The Product Elimination Decision," *Michigan State University Business Topics*, Autumn 1970, pp. 45–52.

Myers, J. H. "Finding Determinant Buying Attitudes," *Journal of Advertising Research*, Dec. 1970, pp. 9–12.

Sheth, J. N. "The Multivariate Revolution in Marketing," *Journal of Marketing*, Jan. 1971, pp. 13–19.

Schoeffler, Sidney; Robert D. Buzzell, and **Donald F. Heaney,** "The Impact of Strategic Planning on Profit Performance," *Harvard Business Review*, March-April 1971, pp. 137–145.

Hillman, Richard H. "How to Redeploy Corporate Assets," *McKinsey Quarterly Review*, Fall 1971, pp. 43–55.

Eckler, R. W. "Product Line Deletion and Simplification," *Business Horizons*, October 1971, pp. 13–17.

Frahan, William E., Jr. "Pyrrhic Victories in the Fight for Market Share," *Harvard Business Review*, September-October 1972, pp. 100–107.

Vancil, Richard F. "Better Management of Corporate Development," *Harvard Business Review*, September-October 1972, p. 59.

Gooding, Judson. "The Art of Firing an Executive," *Fortune*, October 1972, pp. 88–91, 178.

"Small Firm Adopts Big-Group Shape," *International Management*, vol. 27, November 1972; pp. 37–40.

McLeod, Ian H., and **James E. Bennett,** "When Participative Management Doesn't Work," *McKinsey Quarterly Review*, Winter 1972, pp. 52–62.

Wilcox, J. Review of *Corporate Bankruptcy in America*, by Edward I. Altman, *Journal of Accounting*, February 1973, pp. 92–93.

"They Do Repair Jobs on Small Companies," *Business Week*, Feb. 17, 1973, pp. 50, 54.

Scott, Bruce R. "The Industrial State: Old Myths and New Realities," *Harvard Business Review*, March-April 1973, pp. 133–148.

Greiner, Larry E. "Evolution and Revolution as Organizations Grow," *Harvard Business Review*, July-August 1972, pp. 37–46.

Bayler, Harmon. "Planning for Cost Reductions," *Management Accounting*, vol. 54, April 1973, pp. 31–36.

Shad, John. "Higher Premiums in Corporate Acquisitions," *Harvard Business Review,* July-August 1973, pp. 82–92.

Martin, K. D. "Problem Loan Signals and Follow Up," *Journal of Commercial Bank Lending,* September 1973, pp. 38–44.

Arnstein, William E., and **Ray W. Cheeseman,** "Providing Help for the Company in Trouble," *Management Adviser,* vol. 10, September-October 1973, pp. 31–37.

Toeppen, R. Paul. "Using an Outside Financial Consultant in a Problem Credit," *Journal of Commercial Bank Lending,* vol. 56, September 1973, pp. 46–50.

"Can Brinegar Save the Northeast Railroads?" *Business Week,* Nov. 10, 1973, pp. 170, 174, 178.

Gerstner, Louis V., Jr. "Can Strategic Planning Pay Off?" *McKinsey Quarterly Review,* Winter 1973, p. 35.

"The Troubles That Are Taxing H&R Block," *Business Week,* Dec. 8, 1973, pp. 112–114.

"The Flapjack King Has a New Regent," *Business Week,* Dec. 22, 1973, p. 33.

Buzzell, Robert D., Bradley T. Gale, and **Ralph G. M. Sultan.** "Market Share—A Key to Profitability," *Harvard Business Review,* January-February 1974, pp. 97–106.

"The Miscalculations at Rapid Data," *Business Week,* Feb. 9, 1974, p. 26.

Nekvasil, Charles A. "Unloading the Burden of Past Successes," *Industry Week,* Feb. 18, 1974, pp. 47, 49–50.

Kitching, John. "Winning and Losing with European Acquisitions," *Harvard Business Review,* March-April 1974, pp. 124–136.

Ford, Charles H. "Is Your Company Oriented Towards Success?" *Industry Week,* Mar. 8, 1974, p. 42.

Vanderwicken, Peter. "When Levi Strauss Burst Its Britches," *Fortune,* May 15, 1974, pp. 72–78.

"Why Con Ed Is in Such Deep Trouble," *Business Week,* May 25, 1974, pp. 108–112.

"A Bank Holding-Company's Mix Turns Sour," *Business Week,* June 1, 1974, pp. 82–88.

Lyons, John F. "Can You Be Sure if It's Westinghouse?" *Financial World,* vol. 141, June 12, 1974, pp. 20–23.

"Mounting Troubles for U. S. Industries," *Business Week,* June 15, 1974, p. 36.

"On the Verge of Bankruptcy," *Credit and Financial Management,* vol. 76, August 1974, pp. 32–33.

"A Winning Attitude Produces a Turnaround," *Industry Week,* Aug. 5, 1974, pp. 46–47.

Murray, Thomas J. "The Tough Job of Zero Budgeting," *Dun's Review*, October 1974, pp. 70–130.

Soderberg, Roger K. "Assistance to Financially Troubled Companies," *Journal of Commercial Bank Lending*, vol. 57, November 1974, pp. 43–54.

Altman, Edward I., and **Thomas P. McGough,** "Evaluation of a Firm As a Going Concern," *Journal of Accounting*, December 1974, pp. 50–56.

Clifford, Donald K., Jr. "Managing the Threshold Company in Tough Times," *McKinsey Quarterly Review*, Winter 1975, pp. 2–12.

"Will the Insurance Turnaround Continue?" *Institutional Investor* 4 (February 1975):66.

"Palmieri—Real Estate Doctor," *Business Week*, Feb. 3, 1975, pp. 32–34.

"The Morning After," *Forbes Magazine*, Feb. 15, 1975, p. 38.

"A Turnaround—But Not Quite by the Book," *Industry Week*, Mar. 31, 1975, pp. 36–38.

Howson, B. J. "Prescription for a Sick Business," *Canadian Business*, vol. 48, April 1975, pp. 76–78.

"The Squeeze on Panarctic," *Business Week*, Apr. 21, 1975, pp. 116–118.

Muothy, K. R. S., and **M. S. Alter,** "Should CEO Pay Be Linked to Result?" *Harvard Business Review*, May-June 1975, pp. 66–73.

Patz, A. L. "Performance Appraisal—Useful but Still Resisted," *Harvard Business Review*, May-June 1975, pp. 74–80.

Lyons, John F. "What's Wrong at First Pennsy," *Financial World*, vol. 143, May 7, 1975, pp. 9–12.

"How Chase Hopes to Rescue the Chase REIT," *Business Week*, May 19, 1975, pp. 112–117.

"Help for Financially Troubled Firms," *Industry Week*, May 26, 1975, p. 37.

Kratchman, Stanley H., Richard T. Hise, and **Thomas A. Ulrich.** "Management's Decision to Discontinue a Product," *Journal of Accountancy*, June 1975, pp. 50–54.

Hise, Richard T., and **Michael A. Ginnes.** "Product Elimination—Practices, Policies, and Ethics," *Business Horizons*, vol. 18, June 1975, pp. 25–32.

Neuman, John L. "Time for Lasting Cuts in Overhead," *McKinsey Quarterly Review*, Summer 1975, pp. 12–20.

Worthing, P. M. "Improving Product Deletion Decision Making," *Michigan State University Business Topics*, Summer 1975, pp. 29–38.

"The Benefits of Explaining Your Business to Employees," *Nation's Business*, vol. 63, July 1975, pp. 26–28.

"Genesco Comes to Judgement," *Fortune*, July 1975, pp. 106–113, 17, 180.

"Life in the Toils of the Bankruptcy Act," *Fortune*, July 1975, pp. 142–148.

Bibeault, Donald B. "Corporate Growth: A Conceptional Framework," *Managerial Planning*, July-August 1875, pp. 1–10, 29.

"The Recession Balks Genesco's Turnaround," *Business Week*, July 7, 1975, pp. 66–68.

"Crocker's Tom Wilcox: Tough Management for a Stodgy Bank," *Business Week*, Aug. 11, 1975, pp. 38–43.

"Ryan Homes: Stellar Performance," *Business Week*, Aug. 25, 1975, pp. 48–55.

Clifford, Donald K., B. A. Bridgewater, Jr., and **Thomas Hardy.** "The Game Has Changed," *McKinsey Quarterly Review*, Autumn 1975, pp. 14–22.

Silberman, H. "Bankers of the Year: Gabriel Hauge and John F. McGillicuddy, Manufacturers Hanover's 'Turnaround Twins,'" *Finance*, vol. 93, September-October 1975, pp. 8–14.

Martin, Linda Grant. "What Happened at NCR After the Boss Declared Martial Law," *Fortune*, September 1975, pp. 100–104, 178, 181.

"Colonel Crown vs. a Reviewing Rock Island," *Business Week*, Sept. 29, 1975, pp. 63–65.

Hershman, Arlene. "How to Figure Who's Going Bankrupt," *Dun's Review*, October 1975, pp. 62–65, 107, 108.

Gaffen, Harvey, and Henry Moss, "Multiple Skills Called On When the Question Is Survival," *Journal of Accountancy*, October 1975, pp. 102–105.

"A Calculator Maker's Survival Strategy," *Business Week*, Nov. 10, 1975, pp. 154–155.

"All Was Not Well in the War Room," *Fortune*, Nov. 25, 1975, p. 25.

"How the Directors Kept Singer Stitched Together," *Fortune*, December 1975, pp. 188–189.

Ansoff, H. Igor. "Managing Strategic Surprise by Response to Weak Signals," *California Management Review*, Winter 1975, pp. 21–33.

Dhalla, Nariman K., and **Sonia Yuspeh,** "Forget the Product Life Cycle Concept," *Harvard Business Review*, January-February 1976, pp. 102–112.

Woodward, Herbert N. "Management Strategies for Small Companies," *Harvard Business Review*, January-February 1976, pp. 114–122.

"Star Wars Light Fox's Future," *Business Week*, Jan. 23, 1976, pp. 106, 108.

Tracey, E. "The Loneliness of the Master Turnaround Man," *Fortune*, February 1976, pp. 118–122.

Conn, Robert L. "The Failing Firm Industry Doctrines in Conglomerate Mergers," *Journal of Industrial Economics*, March 1976, pp. 181–187.

Schendel, D. E., and **G. R. Patton,** "Corporate Stagnation and Turnaround," *Journal of Economics and Business,* vol. 28, Spring-Summer 1976, pp. 236–241.

Stevenson, Howard H. "Defining Corporate Strengths and Weaknesses," *Sloan Management Review,* Spring 1976, pp. 51–67.

"Bangor-Punta's Turnaround Could Come Unstuck," *Business Week,* Mar. 15, 1976, pp. 62, 64.

"Bringing Sanity to a 140 Company Conglomerate," *Business Week,* Mar. 15, 1976, pp. 66–68.

"Kramer's Campaign to Rebuild Gimbel," *Business Week,* Mar. 29, 1976, p. 32.

Clive, Thomas. "Chrysler Rescue and Regeneration," *Personnel Management,* vol. 8, April 1976, pp. 27, 45.

Loving, Rush, Jr. "W. T. Grant's Last Days—As Seen from Store 1192," *Fortune,* April 1976, p. 109.

Miller, Ernest C. "A Director's Perspective," *Management Review,* April 1976, pp. 4–12.

Lefrak, Sam. "Real Estate Bargain Hunter," *Business Week,* May 31, 1976, pp. 50–54.

Loomis, Carol J. "An Accident Report on Geico," *Fortune,* June 1976, pp. 126–131, 192, 194, 196.

Fine, L. H. "Why Do Managers Pay Lip Service to Management Control," *Management Accounting (London),* vol. 45, July-August 1976, pp. 269–270.

Rose, Sanford. "They're Still Pioneering at Wells Fargo Bank," *Fortune,* July 1976, pp. 122–130.

Goldress, Jerry E., and **Roger W. Christian,** "Management in Crisis," *Management Review,* August 1976,pp. 29–37.

Macchiaverna, Paul. "Lessons from the Recession for Financial-Management," *Conference Board Record* 13 (September 1976):32–35.

"The Demand for Lumber Is Finally Booming," *Business Week,* Oct. 18, 1976, pp. 63, 66.

Neuschel, Robert. "Leadership Style and Organizational Achievement," *McKinsey Quarterly Review,* Winter 1976, pp. 14–19.

"Another Chrysler Turnaround: But Is This One for Real?" *Forbes Magazine,* Nov. 15, 1976, pp. 39–42.

"The Sigoloff Surgery That Saved Daylin," *Business Week,* Nov. 15, 1976, p. 44.

"Rockwell's Surprising Winner: Collins Radio," *Business Week,* Nov. 15, 1976, pp. 111–114.

Grisanti, Frank. "10 Ways to Improve the Handling of Problem Loans," *Banking,* vol. 68, December 1976, pp. 38–39, 66.

"Turning a Troubled Company Around," *Nation's Business*, Dec. 1, 1976, p. 28.

Evans, Richard H. "Add Soft Data to Product Elimination Decisions," *Industrial Marketing Management*, vol. 2, 1977, pp. 91–94.

Berry, Dick. "Profit Contribution: Accounting and Marketing Interface," *Industrial Marketing Management*, vol. 6, 1977, pp. 125–128.

Pearson, Barrie. "A Market Oriented Approach for Turnaround Situations," *Industrial Marketing Management*, vol. 6, 1977, pp. 135–140.

DeWelt, Robert L. "Cost Control—Key to Profit Improvement," *AACE Transactions*, 1977, pp. 244–249.

"Here Comes Another Kaiser," *Fortune*, February 1977, pp. 156–160, 162.

Bennett, Chris. "Preventive Maintenance from Some Corporate Doctors," *Los Angeles Magazine*, February 1977, pp. 110, 116, 167.

"Gillette—After the Diversification That Failed," *Business Week*, Feb. 28, 1977, pp. 58–62.

"In the Grip of 'Hands-On' Management," *Fortune*, March 1977, pp. 170–178.

Locander, William B., and **Richard W. Scamell.** "An Evaluative Model to Identify Weak Products for the Elimination Decision," *Journal of Business Administration*, vol. 8, Spring 1977, pp. 1–18.

"Arden-Mayfair's Fifth Turnaround Try," *Business Week*, Mar. 14, 1977, p. 30.

"The Bonus Is a Real Incentive," *Business Week*, Mar. 14, 1977, pp. 54–55.

"Price, Pride, and Profitability," *Fortune*, April 1977, p. 20.

Pearson, Barrie. "Is Corporate Planning a Waste of Time?" *Management Accounting (London)*, vol. 44, April 1977, pp. 156–157.

Pearson, Barrie. "How to Manage Turnarounds," *Management Today*, April 1977, pp. 74–77.

Kinder, William F. "A Look at the Leaders—Managing the Turnaround," *Best's Review*, vol. 78, June 1977, pp. 14–16, 81–84.

"Danger—Cash Needs Ahead," *Forbes Magazine*, June 15, 1977, pp. 53–54.

"American Microsystems Bets on a New Chip," *Business Week*, June 20, 1977, pp. 38, 40.

"Curing the Lethargy Syndrome at Foremost," *Business Week*, June 27, 1977, pp. 98–99.

Clifford, Donald K., Jr. "Thriving in a Recession," *Harvard Business Review*, July-August 1977, pp. 47–59.

Kumar, Parmanana. "Corporate Growth Through Acquisition," *Managerial Planning*, July-August 1977, pp. 9–12, 39.

"A New Levitt Corps Rises from the Dust," *Business Week*, July 11, 1977, p. 27.

"Slide into Bankruptcy," *Fortune*, August 1977, p. 20.

"Where Were You When the Lights Went On?" *Fortune*, August 1977, p. 2.

"A Rancorous Bout with Chapter XI," *Business Week*, Aug. 1, 1977, p. 22.

"Financial Controls Help a Valve Maker Expand," *Business Week*, Aug. 1, 1977, pp. 47–48.

"The Drastic Surgery at Texfli," *Business Week*, Aug. 15, 1977, p. 108.

"The Master Tinkerer at Bunker Ramo," *Business Week*, Aug. 15, 1977, pp. 121–122.

"Canteen's Profitable New Menu," *Business Week*, Aug. 15, 1977, p. 134.

"Motorola's Fast Catch-Up in Microprocesses," *Business Week*, Aug. 29, 1977, p. 66.

"How Boothe Courier Came Bouncing Back," *Business Week*, Aug. 22, 1977, pp. 44–45.

Heinemann, Robert E. "Controlling T&E in a Fast-Moving Firm," *Administrative Management*, vol. 38, September 1977, pp. 63–66, 86, 90.

"Pan-Am: In the Black for Now," *Business Week*, Sept. 5, 1977, pp. 52–56.

"Recognition Equipment Revives Itself," *Business Week*, Sept. 5, 1977, pp. 88, 90.

"A Revived Miller-Wohl Lures a Dutch Bidder," *Business Week*, Sept. 19, 1977, pp. 110–114.

"The Difference at White Consolidated," *Business Week*, Sept. 26, 1977, pp. 135, 138.

Getzler, Abraham E. "When to Throw Good Money After Bad—And When Not To," *Banking*, vol. 69, October 1977, pp. 128–138, 186–188.

Nelson, Robert E., Jr. "The Practice of Business-Liquidity Improvement—A Management Approach," *Business Horizons*, vol. 20, October 1977, pp. 54–60.

"The Turn at IDS," *Business Week*, Oct. 3, 1977, p. 92.

"Avco Gets Its Act Together for Profit," *Business Week*, Oct. 3, 1977, pp. 115–116.

"Corporate Travel Revives Cook's," *Business Week*, Oct. 3, 1977, pp. 118, 120.

"When a Good Try Was Not Enough," *Business Week*, Oct. 10, 1977, p. 36.

"An Apparel Maker Who Bucked the Trend," *Business Week*, Oct. 24, 1977, p. 101.

"Relearning a Mission," *Fortune*, November 1977, p. 58.

Kotler, Philip. "From Sales Obsession to Marketing Effectiveness," *Harvard Business Review*, November-December 1977, p. 70–72.

Suver, James D., and **Ray L. Brown,** "Where Does Zero Base Budgeting Work," *Harvard Business Review,* November-December 1977, pp. 76–84.

Skinner, Wichahun, and **W. E. Sasser,** "Managers with Impact: Versatile and Inconsistent," *Harvard Business Review,* November-December 1977, pp. 142–154.

"Why APECO Preferred Filing Bankruptcy," *Business Week,* Nov. 7, 1977, pp. 25–26.

"After the Beer at Chock Full O'Nuts," *Business Week,* Nov. 7, 1977, p. 81.

Keegan, Warren J. "Strategic Marketing: International Diversification Versus National Concentration," *Columbia Journal of World Business,* Winter 1977, pp. 120–128.

"In Unity There is Strength?" *Fortune,* December 1977, p. 22.

"Japan's Way Thrives in U.S.," *Business Week,* Dec. 12, 1977, pp. 156–157.

"Woolworth: The Last Stand of the Variety Store," *Business Week,* Jan. 9, 1978, pp. 84, 85.

"Ward Foods—Future Is Unsettled Again," *Business Week,* Jan. 16, 1978, pp. 31, 33.

"A New Helicopter Lifts Aerospatiale's Hopes," *Business Week,* Jan. 16, 1978, p. 42.

"Trafalgar House: Acquiring and Reviving the Grand Old Names," *Business Week,* Jan. 16, 1978, pp. 105–106.

"How G.M. Turned Itself Around," *Fortune,* Jan. 16, 1978, pp. 92–102.

"The Chain: A Survival Formula for Hospitals" *Business Week,* Jan. 23, 1978, pp. 64–65.

"Monfort of Colorado: Cutting Costs to Soften Profit Gyrations," *Business Week,* Jan. 23, 1978, pp. 65, 66.

"A Case History of Employee Pride," *Small Business Report,* February 1978, p. 20.

"Victor Palmieri, the Amazing Rent-a-Boss," *Fortune,* Feb. 13, 1978, pp. 78–82.

"Revell: What to Do When Profits Refuse to Grow," *Business Week,* Feb. 13, 1978, pp. 104–105.

"GAF Takes a Writeoff," *Business Week,* Feb. 20, 1978, p. 38.

Kraar, Louis. "Roy Ash Is Having Fun at Addressogrief-Multigrief," *Fortune,* Feb. 27, 1978, pp. 46–52.

"Weyerhaeuser's Layoffs," *Business Week,* Feb. 27, 1978, p. 42.

"Untimely Expansions Hurt Massey-Ferguson," *Business Week,* Mar. 6, 1978, p. 34.

"Something Good Is Happening at Rapid American," *Business Week,* Mar. 6, 1978, pp. 112, 114.

"Rhone-Poulene in the Vise of French Politics," *Fortune*, Mar. 13, 1978, pp. 115-120.

"Cash Management: The New Art of Wringing More Profit from Corporate Funds," *Business Week*, Mar. 13, 1978, pp. 58-74.

"Waste Management: Reaping Profits by Sticking to Garbage Collection," *Business Week*, Mar. 13, 1978, pp. 102-103.

"Amcord: A Cautious Second Try at Diversifying Beyond Cement," *Business Week*, Mar. 13, 1978, pp. 104, 106.

"End Game for Rock Island?" *Business Week*, Mar. 27, 1978, pp. 102-106.

"The Red-Ink Troubles at Sherwin Williams," *Business Week*, Mar. 27, 1978, p. 43.

Searby, Frederick Wright. "Use Your Hidden Cash Resources," *McKinsey Quarterly Review*, Spring 1978, pp. 35-47.

"Why Kaiser Cement Got Out of Gypsum," *Business Week*, Apr. 3, 1978, p. 25.

"Putting Genesco Back on the Track," *Business Week*, Apr. 3, 1978, pp. 70, 74.

"Hercules: Excising the Losers in a Campaign to Consolidate," *Business Week*, Apr. 3, 1978, pp. 94-95.

"Nucor Corporation," *Value Line Selection and Opinion*, Apr. 7, 1978, pp. 784-785.

"Irvine: Taking an Unexpected Route to Reduce Its Huge Debt," *Business Week*, Apr. 10, 1978, pp. 106-107.

"Bangor Punta: Pushing Internal Growth After the Piper Victory," *Business Week*, Apr. 10, 1978, pp. 110-114.

Hamermesh, R. G., M. J. Anderson, Jr., and **J. E. Harris.** "Strategies for Low Market Share Businesses," *Harvard Business Review*, May-June 1978, pp. 95-102.

"Arcata: A Plan to Hang Tough in the Business It Knows Best," *Business Week*, May 1, 1978, pp. 96-97.

"Emhart: Making a Good Fit for USM'S Shoe Machinery," *Business Week*, May 1, 1978, pp. 98, 102.

"Peter Grace's Long Search for Security," *Fortune*, May 8, 1978, pp. 116-130.

"Memorex: Paying the Costs of a Difficult Turnaround," *Business Week*, May 22, 1978, pp. 166, 171.

"Simmons: A Turnaround Proves Hard to Bring Off," *Business Week*, June 5, 1978, pp. 146-147.

"Sanitas: After Resuscitation a Renewed Drive for Growth," *Business Week*, June 5, 1978, pp. 150, 154.

"The Day the Profits Stopped at Citizens & Southern," *Fortune*, June 5, 1978, pp. 194-108, 110, 112, 114, 116.

"How to Digest an Expensive Acquisition," *Business Week,* June 19, 1978, pp. 94, 98.

Schuyten, Peter J. "Chrysler Goes for Broke," *Fortune,* June 19, 1978, pp. 48–56.

"Hesston: Cushioning the Shock of Farm Equipment Cycles," *Business Week,* June 26, 1978, pp. 64, 66.

"International Harvester: Axing the Fat Off a Company Gone Flabby," *Business Week,* June 26, 1978, pp. 66–71.

Adler, Frederick. "Secrets of Improving Corporate Performance," *Boardroom Reports,* June 30, 1978, p. 6.

"Colt Industries: Seeking a Mix of Products That Don't Cycle Together," *Business Week,* July 3, 1978, pp. 102–106.

"Saving Leyland Is a Job for Hercules," *Fortune,* July 3, 1978, pp. 56–64.

"McGraw-Edison: Expanding Again Now That the Pieces Are Together," *Business Week,* July 10, 1978, pp. 96–97.

"Simmons Co. Pushes a Simmons Out," *Business Week,* July 17, 1978, pp. 34–36.

"SAFECO: 'Redlining' Two States to Bolster Insurance Profits," *Business Week,* July 17, 1978, pp. 88–89.

"How Phoenix Steel Finally Put It All Together," *Iron Age,* July 31, 1978, pp. 33–36.

"On the Verge of Bankruptcy," *Credit and Financial Management,* August 1978, p. 32.

"WARNACO: Returning to Profits by Cutting Back New Products," *Business Week,* Aug. 28, 1978, pp. 112, 116.

Dearden, John. "Cost Accounting Comes to the Service Industries," *Harvard Business Review,* September-October 1978, pp. 132–140.

"A Busy Chris-Craft Looks Back to Its Boats," *Business Week,* Sept. 4, 1978, pp. 27–28.

"The Miller Myers Formula for a Turnaround," *Business Week,* Sept. 11, 1978, pp. 108, 110.

"Action: A Switch to Snack Foods Has Made It Profitable," *Business Week,* Sept. 25, 1978, pp. 131, 133.

Sathe, Vijoy. "Who Should Control Division Controllers?" *Harvard Business Review,* September-October 1978, pp. 99–104.

"Overseas National Exits in Style," *Business Week,* Oct. 2, 1978, p. 36.

"Green Giant: The New Course That Makes It Attractive to Pillsbury," *Business Week,* Oct. 2, 1978, p. 71.

"Traumatic Changes at Massey-Ferguson," *Business Week,* Oct. 9, 1978, pp. 60–61.

"Di Giorgio: A Food Processor Pushes Its Name Brands," *Business Week*, Oct. 9, 1978, pp. 70, 75.

"How the Industry Leader Helped Dethrone Itself," *Business Week*, Oct. 9, 1978, p. 104.

"Back to Basics on Auto Supply," *Business Week*, Oct. 9, 1978, pp. 141, 143.

"GEICO: Insuring Its Profit Picture by Spreading Out and Slowing Down," *Business Week*, Oct. 16, 1978, pp. 182, 184.

"Rough Ride for ConRail," *Fortune*, Oct. 23, 1978, pp. 84–90.

Bernstein, Peter W. "Johnathan Scott's Surprising Failure at A&P," *Fortune*, Nov. 6, 1978, pp. 32–40.

"Paramount Pictures: Applying a TV Formula for Success," *Business Week*, Nov. 27, 1978, p. 94.

"Philips Industries: Homebuilders Are the New Target for Its Products," *Business Week*, Nov. 27, 1978, pp. 102, 104.

"Dean Foods: Diversifying to Supplement a Low-Growth Business," *Business Week*, Dec. 18, 1978, pp. 74, 76.

"GAF Corporation: Will It Stumble with Its Fresh Start?" *Business Week*, Jan. 22, 1979, pp. 66–65, 68.

"Saving the Company That Acquired Him," *Business Week*, Feb. 19, 1979, pp. 47–48, 50.

"Boise Cascade: Expansionism That Now Sticks Close to Home," *Business Week*, Feb. 19, 1979, pp. 54–55.

Quint, John. "Ming the Merciless Loses His Prize: Turnaround Specialist Sandy Sigoloff Brought Daylin Out of Bankruptcy but Couldn't Save It from Grace," *Fortune*, May 7, 1979, pp. 140–142, 146, 148.

"Bekins: Banking On a Turnaround Specialist to Save Its Moving Business," *Business Week*, June 4, 1979, pp. 90, 93, 96.

O'Hanlon, Thomas. "A Rejuvenated Litton Is Once Again Off to the Races," *Fortune*, Oct. 8, 1979, pp. 154–164.

"One Hell of a Team," *Fortune*, Oct. 22, 1979, p. 28.

Bohr, Peter. "Chrysler's Pie-in-the-Sky Plan for Survival," *Fortune*, Oct. 22, 1979, pp. 46–48, 50, 52.

Ball, Robert. "A Confident Capitalist Redesigns Olivetti," *Fortune*, Oct. 22, 1979, pp. 78, 79, 82, 86.

Tracy, Elenor Johnson. "She Has Three Years to Turn Olivetti America Around," *Fortune*, Oct. 22, 1979, pp. 87, 88, 90.

O'Hanlon, Thomas. "Behind the Snafu at Singer," *Fortune*, Nov. 5, 1979, pp. 76–80.

"MacMillan Bloedel: A Renewed Emphasis on Forest Products," *Business Week,* Nov. 12, 1979, pp. 124, 128.

Self, Thomas M. "Memorex Corporation's Robert C. Wilson," *Executive,* December 1979, pp. 10–13.

Easten, Elmer. "Surviving Bankruptcy," *Inc.,* December 1979, pp. 43–47.

Moore, Harrison L. "Better Off Dead," *Inc.,* December 1979, pp. 50–54.

"Where Companies Go Wrong," *Inc.,* December 1979, pp. 57, 58.

"Rose-Colored Clouds at AM International," *Business Week,* Dec. 10, 1979, p. 100.

"First Pennsylvania Is Hard to Turn Around," *Business Week,* Feb. 4, 1980, p. 28.

Morrison, Ann M. "A Farm Boy's Miracle at National Student Marketing," *Fortune,* Mar. 24, 1980, pp. 132–134.

Quint, John. "How Greyhound Made a U-Turn," *Fortune,* Mar. 24, 1980, pp. 139, 140.

"Stunning Turnaround at Tarrytown," *Time,* May 5, 1980, p. 87.

"How Far Can Chrysler Stretch Its First Aid?" *Business Week,* May 26, 1980, pp. 55, 56.

Benner, Susan. "Peter Sprague Loves to Make Trouble (For Himself)," *Inc.,* June 1980, pp. 38, 39, 42, 44, 46, 48, 49.

"A Turnaround 'Master' Takes on Kroehler," *Business Week,* June 16, 1980, pp. 82–86.

Tsunami, Yoshi. "How to Handle the Next Chrysler," *Fortune,* June 16, 1980, pp. 87, 88.

Kraar, Louis. "The Brooklyn Boy Who Debugged Loral," *Fortune,* June 16, 1980, pp. 102–104, 107, 111.

OTHER REFERENCE MATERIALS – DISSERTATIONS, SPEECHES, INTERVIEWS, UNPUBLISHED MATERIALS (BY AUTHORS' LAST NAMES):

Anderson, William S. "The Turnaround at NCR Corporation," address at Beta Gamma Sigma dinner, Wright State University, Apr. 19, 1976.

Anderson, William S. "NCR Progress in Perspective," report presented to the financial community, Dayton, Ohio, October 1977.

Andrews, K. R. "The Effectiveness of University Management Development Programs," Division of Research, Harvard Graduate School of Business Administration, Boston, 1966.

Ansley, John, president, Tupperware Manufacturing Co., Los Angeles, Calif., interview, February 1978.

Blonder, Mauritz D. "Organizational Repercussion of Personnel Cutbacks: Import of Layoff on Retained Employees," Ph.D. dissertation, City University of New York, 1976.

Brown, Robert C., president, R. C. Brown & Co., San Francisco, Calif., interview, February 1978.

Byers, John, vice president, Wells Fargo Bank, San Francisco, Calif., interview, May 1978.

Casey, William J. "Investor Relations and Corporate Credibility," paper presented at a meeting of the National Investor Relations Institute, Washington, D.C., October 1972.

Chanin, Jeffrey, former executive vice president, Daylin Corp., Los Angeles, Calif., interview, February 1978.

Comerford, R. A. "Bankruptcy as Business Strategy: A Multivariate Analysis of the Financial Characteristics of Firms Which Have Succeeded in Chapter XI Compared to Those Which Have Failed," Ph.D. dissertation, University of Massachusetts, 1976.

Cook, Ransom, chairman and president (retired), Wells Fargo Bank, San Francisco, Calif., interview, February 1978.

Di Giorgio, Robert, chairman, Di Giorgio Corp., San Francisco, Calif., interview, February 1978.

Federal Trade Commission. *Reports on Corporate Mergers and Acquisitions* (Washington, D.C.: Government Printing Office, 1973).

Friedman, Gary, vice chairman, Itel Corp., San Francisco, Calif., interview, February 1978.

Greiner, Larry E. "Patterns of Organizational Change," report of Division of Research, Harvard Business School, 1971.

Grimm, W. T., & Co. "Merger and Acquisition Statistics," Chicago, 1970–1977.

Grisanti, Frank A., president, Grisanti and Galef, Los Angeles, Calif., interview, February 1978.

Gwinner, Ross, former president, Capitol Film Labs, Washington, D.C., interview, February 1978.

Kappel, Frederick R. "Vitality in Business Enterprise." McKinsey Foundation for Management Research Lecture Series, Graduate School of Business, Columbia University, 1964.

Madden, Richard B., chairman, Potlatch Corp., San Francisco, Calif., interview, February 1978.

Michel, Kenneth D. "A Marketing Appraisal Guide," editorial contribution to National Society of Sales Training Executives, Nov. 22, 1972.

Moscarello, Michael A. "The Anatomy of a Turnaround," address to Western Association of Venture Capitalists, San Francisco, Calif., June 18, 1974.

Penisten, Glenn E., president, American Microsystems, Santa Clara, Calif., interview, February 1978.

Penisten, Glenn E. Address before the corporate planners' association, San Francisco, Calif., Jan. 19, 1978.

"PIMS—Research Findings." Cambridge, Mass.: Strategic Planning Institute, February 1975.

Sackman, Robert, President, Rodal Corp., Palo Alto, Ca. Interview, February 1978.

Schendel, Dan, and **Richard Patton,** "An Empirical Study of Corporate Stagnation and Turnaround." *Proceedings of the Acedemy of Management*, August 1975, pp. 49–51.

Schendel, Dan, Richard Patton, and **James Riggs,** "Corporate Turnaround Strategies." Krannert Graduate School of Industrial Administration, Purdue University. Paper no. 986, March 1975.

Schmidt, Chauncey F., chairman, Bank of California, San Francisco, Ca. Interview, February 1978.

Schmidt, Klaus D. "New Directions in Corporate Governance." D.B.A. dissertation, Golden Gate University, 1978.

Stanley, David T., and **Marjore Groth,** "Bankruptcy: Problem, Process, Reform." Washington, D.C.: Brookings Institute, 1972.

Taube, Thaddeus N., chairman, Koracorp Industries, San Francisco, Ca. Interview, February 1978.

Thompson, John S., senior vice president, Crocker National Bank, San Francisco, Ca. Interview, January 1978.

Wendell, Herbert. "The Marketing Audit." contributed paper, National Society of Sales Training Executives, May 1972. (Typewritten.)

Wilson, Robert C. address before Business School, Arizona State University, 13 March 1975. (Typewritten.)

Wilson, Robert C. address before Peninsula Stock and Bond Club, 3 June 1976. (Typewritten.)

Wilson, Robert C., chairman and president, Memorex Corp., Santa Clara, Ca. Interview, January 1978.

Woodman, Roy. president, International Video Corp., Sunnyvale, Ca. Interview, February 1978.

INDEX